REDISTRIBUTION THROUGH THE FINANCIAL SYSTEM

Kenneth E. Boulding
Thomas Frederick Wilson
Editors

REDISTRIBUTION THROUGH THE FINANCIAL SYSTEM

The Grants Economics of Money and Credit

PRAEGER PUBLISHERS
Praeger Special Studies

New York • London • Sydney • Toronto

Library of Congress Cataloging in Publication Data
Main entry under title:

Redistribution through the financial system.

Includes index.
1. Grants-in-aid--United States. 2. Monetary policy --United States. 3. Credit--United States.
I. Boulding, Kenneth Ewart, 1910-
II. Wilson, Thomas Frederick.
HJ275.R33 1978 336.1'83 78-18017
ISBN 0-03-045341-0

PRAEGER SPECIAL STUDIES
383 Madison Avenue, New York, N.Y. 10017, U.S.A.

Published in the United States of America in 1978
by Praeger Publishers,
A Division of Holt, Rinehart and Winston, CBS, Inc.

89 038 987654321

Printed in the United States of America

PREFACE

The application of the principles of grants economics to the monetary and financial system is by no means a new idea. Most of the essential principles of grants economics indeed can be found in Adam Smith and David Ricardo. They exist in the writings of these authors, however, in scattered passages and in the form of insights rather than of systematic analysis. It has always been my contention indeed that the development of grants economics as a subdiscipline mainly involved bringing together insights that have been developed over two centuries into a more systematic and coherent body of thought.

In both Adam Smith and Ricardo the discussion of the impact of subsidies, "bounties," taxes, and tariffs is a subtle exercise in both the explicit and implicit aspects of one-way transfers that still makes very good sense today. It is amazing indeed how accurate the classical economists manged to be in these rather subtle and complex matters, in spite of the fact that they did not have the apparatus of supply and demand functions, elasticities, and mathematical analysis that are at the command of the modern economist. Furthermore, Adam Smith understood very well the distortions of the system that were produced by government regulations and prohibitions, for instance, in the grain trade, which created what today we would call implicit grants. There is little in modern economics that is not foreshadowed by Adam Smith in The Wealth of Nations. It is certainly not surprising, therefore, to find that grants economics is foreshadowed in many places in classical economics.

In both Adam Smith and Ricardo are interesting discussions of the subject of this volume—the impact of changes in the system of money and finance in regard to what today would be called both explicit and implicit grants. Thus, Adam Smith, in the famous chapter on "Money" (The Wealth of Nations, Book II, Chapter 2), shows that the development of paper money and a banking system, assuming, as he frequently does, no changes in the total volume of trade, liberates gold and silver for export. This export brings back real goods and services, which are, as it were, a free gift from the foreigners who have taken the gold and silver, although they are, fortunately, quite unaware of this. He even sees that it matters what is brought back in exchange for the gold and silver that is exported. If it is the luxuries of the rich that are imported, this is a one-shot operation that benefits none but the rich themselves. If, however, what is brought back is "an additional stock of materials, tools, and provisions in order to maintain and employ an additional number of industrious people, who reproduce, with a profit, the value of their annual consumption" (The Wealth of Nations, Modern Library Edition, p. 278), it represents a net addition to the real capital of the society, which may be regarded as permanent until it is consumed by future profligacies. Here the concept of seigniorage on paper money is very clearly expressed.

It is interesting to note, also, apropos of the Maine law against loan sharks, that Adam Smith was not averse to a maximum legal rate of interest, though he thought this should be safely above the rate at which ordinary, decent people could borrow. Thus, he writes, "If the legal rate of interest in Great Britain, for example, was fixed so high as eight or ten percent, the greater part of the money which was to be lent, would be lent to prodigals and projectors, who alone would be willing to give this high interest. Sober people, who would give for the use of money no more than a part of what they are likely to make by the use of it, would not venture into the competition" (Modern Library Edition, p. 339). Here he seems to violate his own principle of natural liberty in the interest of protecting sober people from the excesses of the prodigals and the projectors, to which he might have added in our day subsidized borrowers from the government.

Ricardo, in Principles of Political Economy and Taxation, has many brilliant discussions of the incidence of taxation and subsidies, in which he is not always right because of the somewhat stark limitations of his "strong cases" system, but which, nevertheless, are as sophisticated in their own limits as the most refined modern analysis. He has a famous passage in which he points out, "When money is taxed, though a large tax might be received, nobody would pay it" (Principles of Political Economy and Taxation, Chapter 13). This strange paradox can be explained only in terms of the essential arbitrariness of the unit of account. Neither Adam Smith nor Ricardo is very sensitive to the dynamic impact of inflation or deflation, and both tend to treat these problems in terms of comparative statics, which makes their analyses somewhat weak in terms of short-run problems.

It is now more than 200 years since the publication of The Wealth of Nations and we have come a long way from the classical economists in terms of sophistication of method, collection of data, complexity of institutions, and refinement of analysis. Nevertheless, we are still clearly building on the foundations that they laid, and it is interesting in this volume to see how much of the work can be interpreted in a sense as elegant and elaborate variations on the classical themes. That the creation of money involves a grant of real goods to its creator as it is spent is an idea that is certainly not unfamiliar to Adam Smith or Ricardo. The idea that government subsidies of loans, for instance, often end up in strange pockets all over the system is, again, something that would not have surprised the classical economists. Nevertheless, we have come somewhere in 200 years and we can now follow these movements in greater detail and with greater accuracy than could the earlier writers.

The present volume is in some sense a monument to 200 years' improvement in data collection and in techniques of analysis. Nevertheless, the ideas behind these essays are still relatively simply. One very broad, general principle indeed guides the theory of implicit grants, which is essentially an extension of the classical theory of incidence. It is that when anybody makes an alteration in the system, those who can adjust will adjust, and those who cannot will not, so that the ultimate impact of the system in terms of distribution ends up with the nonadjustable, those who have inelastic demands or supplies. One possible modification of the principle is that sometimes there are those who could adjust but who do not, out of ignorance, uncertainty, or unawareness of what is going on.

We can modify the principle a little further indeed and say that those who cannot adjust pay the costs and those who can adjust get the benefits of programs of all sorts. This is perhaps the basic explanation for Director's law, as quoted in the chapter by Patric Hendershott and Kevin Vilanni, but nearly all social legislation seems to result in redistributing away from the poor and the rich toward the middle. The poor have few alternatives and are unadaptable, and hence find it hard to escape costs imposed through taxes, changing price structures, or interest rates. The rich are economically adaptable, but politically vulnerable. The middle are economically adaptable and politically secure, so it is much easier for the middle to command a political majority. Conservative parties indeed can only have success when they are alliances of the rich and the poor against the middle. This is a somewhat precarious alliance, and a reasonably solid middle can usually straddle a 51 percent majority of the voters. One is almost tempted to define social democracy as how the government subsidizes the middle in the name of subsidizing the poor. There is a good deal of evidence for this in the present volume.

One aspect of the grants economy that is somewhat neglected in these chapters is the impact of the creation of money and of public regulations, taxes, and subsidies on the overall distribution of resources in the economy, as well as on the distribution of income. Thus, if the gains to the creation of money through the banking system tend to stay within that system—and some of it certainly does, though it is hard to say how much—the impact, especially if the banking system is reasonably competitive, is not to make banking unusually profitable but to expand it as an industry beyond what is really necessary to conduct its social functions. Bank regulation, especially the prohibition of branch banking, may have the opposite effect and perhaps an offsetting one. I would like to see some evidence on the relative profitability of different sectors of the financial industry as compared with other industries. I suspect that its rates of return are not excessive, suggesting that whatever subsidies it receives tend to be passed on. But this still will not preclude an overexpansion of the industry.

Traditionally, banks have created an external impression of plushness in their architecture, furnishings, and services. Part of this, of course, is tradition and is advertising expenditure contrived to give an air of respectability and affluence. However, there is still a suggestion in this also that banks and other financial institutions occupy a certain nodal position of power in the total structure that is not quite possessed even by department stores. Some of this may be the result of the indirect subsidies that arise out of seigniorage. Whether the total financial system is expanding beyond what is really necessary to provide the information to organize the economy is an unanswerable question. It would be fun, however, to do a comparative cost-benefit analysis of, shall we say, the financial system in a highly capitalist country, with the complex planning and management organization in a comparable socialist state. It would be interesting to know whether Wall Street absorbed more real resources than the Gosplan, and if so, whether we could justify this on the basis of increased efficiency in their use. Studies of the grants economy in the socialist countries, though they would be extremely illuminating, seem to be in the future, however.

The field covered in this volume is highly technical. Almost the whole burden of the editing has fallen on Thomas Wilson, who has done an excellent and most useful job in coordinating these chapters. I have learned a great deal from reading them. They can be recommended to anyone who wants to be brought up to date in what is today perhaps one of the liveliest and most interesting fields in economics. It is a field, furthermore, where large changes are taking place, particularly under the impact of legislation, of which most people in this country are unaware. Because of the technical nature of this subject, legislation in the field is dominated by a very few people. It is all the more important that it should be subject to technical criticism of a high order; otherwise, we may easily make quite catastrophic and unintentional mistakes in our economic policy. Financial legislation almost inevitably is the product of a small, informed community. It is to the better informing of that community that this volume is dedicated.

Kenneth E. Boulding

ACKNOWLEDGMENTS

The impetus for this volume was provided by Kenneth Boulding's book, The Economy of Love and Fear: A Preface to Grants Economics. In that work, Boulding expressed the view that the implicit grants structure in the system of credit and finance is a richly endowed research area that had received little attention. I concurred with this observation, and, when Janos Horvath offered me the responsibility of organizing a grants economics session at the Allied Social Sciences Association meetings in Dallas (December 1975), I chose to focus that session on implicit transfers within the financial system.

The session in Dallas was sponsored jointly by the American Economic Association and the Association for the Study of the Grants Economy. The success of that session reflected the distinguished service of its chairman, Andrew Brimmer, who contributed valuable insights and sparked a lively discussion of Regulation Q, under which the Federal Reserve Board sets interest rate ceilings on savings and time deposits. Patric Hendershott and Kevin Villani incorporated Brimmer's comments into their article. My paper and those written by George von Furstenberg and Richard Cohn are also revised versions of the papers presented in Dallas. Joseph Scherer and Thomas Havrilesky served as worthy discussants.

Praeger Publishers invited Kenneth Boulding to expand the literature on grants economics, and he perceived this set of papers as the core around which a volume could be built. Boulding and I asked other economists to examine areas where the prospective return in interest and originality was high. In selecting these persons, emphasis was given to a solid research base from which grants analyses could be developed. This volume represents the culmination of that effort.

We sincerely appreciate the generous contributions of time and energy by the authors, who truly made this a joint venture. We were particularly grateful for their full cooperation, and we are very pleased by the quality of scholarship expressed in their writings. These chapters have not been published previously, except von Furstenberg's article, which appeared in the Journal of Money, Credit and Banking.

A sad note came with the death of Harry Johnson, whose work was a special inspiration to economists. We value highly his contribution to this volume.

I am personally thankful for the guidance of Janos Horvath and for Patric Hendershott's comments on the Introduction. I derived considerable satisfaction from working with Kenneth Boulding, whose wise counsel and devotion to fine craftsmanship are reflected in this volume.

Thomas F. Wilson

CONTENTS

		Page
PREFACE Kenneth E. Boulding		v
ACKNOWLEDGMENTS Thomas F. Wilson		ix
LIST OF TABLES		xiv
LIST OF FIGURES		xviii
LIST OF ABBREVIATIONS		xix
REDISTRIBUTION THROUGH THE FINANCIAL SYSTEM: AN INTRODUCTION Thomas F. Wilson		xx

PART I: THE PROFIT FROM MONEY CREATION

Chapter		
1	MONEY, WEALTH, AND SEIGNIORAGE Benjamin Klein	3
2	SEIGNIORAGE AND THE "INFLATION TAX" IN AN INTERNATIONAL SETTING Harry G. Johnson	20
3	IDENTIFICATION AND MEASUREMENT OF GRANT ELEMENTS IN MONETARY POLICY Thomas F. Wilson	38

PART II: DISTRIBUTIONAL IMPACT OF MONETARY POLICY

4	MOTIVES BEHIND INFLATIONARY MONETARY EXPANSION Charlotte E. Ruebling	59

Chapter | Page

5 THE DISTRIBUTION OF INCOME AND MONETARY POLICY
Thomas Havrilesky 70

PART III: GRANT FLOWS AND GOVERNMENT REGULATION OF FINANCIAL INSTITUTIONS

6 INTEREST RATE CEILINGS AND NET WORTH LOSSES BY SAVERS
David H. Pyle 87

7 IMPLICATIONS FOR MORTGAGE LENDERS OF REMOVING DEPOSIT RATE CEILINGS
Richard A. Cohn 102

8 IMPLICIT GRANTS OF BANK RESERVE REQUIREMENTS AND RESTRICTIONS ON BRANCHING
Marvin Phaup 114

PART IV: IMPLICIT TRANSFERS ASSOCIATED WITH PRIVATE PRACTICES AND GOVERNMENT REGULATIONS

9 IMPLICIT GRANTS IN THE FINANCIAL SYSTEM: THE CASE OF THE EQUAL CREDIT OPPORTUNITY ACT
Joseph Scherer 149

10 THE TRANSFER IMPLICATIONS OF CONSUMER CREDIT REGULATION
William C. Dunkelberg 155

11 IMPLICIT TRANSFERS IN THE EXTENSION OF TRADE CREDIT
Robert A. Schwartz and David K. Whitcomb 191

PART V: SUBSIDIES IN FEDERAL CREDIT PROGRAMS

12 THE USE OF THE GOVERNMENT'S CREDIT POWER
Murray L. Weidenbaum 211

Chapter | Page

13	GRANT ELEMENTS IN THE OPERATION OF FEDERALLY SPONSORED CREDIT AGENCIES IN THE HOME MORTGAGE MARKET Patric H. Hendershott and Kevin E. Villani	227
14	DISTRIBUTION EFFECTS OF GNMA HOME MORTGAGE PURCHASES AND COMMITMENTS UNDER THE TANDEM PLANS George M. von Furstenberg	244
15	GRANT ELEMENTS IMPLIED BY PRESENT AND PROPOSED TAX TREATMENT OF INCOME ON STATE AND LOCAL GOVERNMENT SECURITIES Patric H. Hendershott and Timothy W. Koch	267
	PART VI: CONCLUSION	
16	GRANTS ECONOMICS IN THE FUTURE OF THE FINANCIAL SYSTEM Thomas F. Wilson and Kenneth E. Boulding	289
INDEX		291
ABOUT THE EDITORS AND CONTRIBUTORS		297

LIST OF TABLES

Table		Page
2.A.1	Nominal and Real Foreign Liabilities, Quarterly	33
2.A.2	Real Gains or Losses on Foreign Dollar Holdings	34
2.A.3	Real Gains or Losses on Foreign Dollar Holdings by Comparison with 2 Percent Annual Real Gain	35
2.A.4	Treasury Bill Three-Month Market Rate Minus the Inflation Rate	36
4.1	Wealth Effects of Inflation	65
4.2	Inflation, Earnings, and Unemployment	66
6.1	Annual Average Stock of Thrift Deposits at Savings Institutions	88
6.2	Predicted and Actual Average Deposit Interest Rates at Thrift Institutions	94
6.3	Net Worth Losses Imposed on Savers by the Interest Rate Adjustment Act of 1966	97
8.1	Simplified Balance Sheets of the Central Bank and All Commercial Banks, before and after the Imposition of a 20 Percent Reserve Requirement	117
8.2	Regression Results, Dependent Variable = Cash-Assets, Fourth District Banks, 1971-75	124
8.3	Regression Results, Dependent Variable = Net Income-Assets, Fourth District Banks, 1971-75	126
8.4	Regression Results, Dependent Variable = Net Income-Equity, Fourth District Banks, 1971-75	127
8.5	Regression Results, Dependent Variable = Equity-Assets, Fourth District Banks, 1971-75	129
8.6	Regression Results, Dependent Variable = U.S. Treasury Securities-Earning Assets, Fourth District Banks, 1971-75	131

Table		Page
8.7	Regression Results, Dependent Variable = Securities Issued by State and Political Subdivisions-Earning Assets, Fourth District Banks, 1971-75	132
8.8	Regression Results, Dependent Variable = Loans-Earning Assets, Fourth District Banks, 1971-75	133
8.9	Regression Results, Dependent Variable = Time and Savings Deposits-Total Deposits, Fourth District Banks, 1971-75	135
8.10	Regression Results, Dependent Variable = Interest and Fees on Loans-Loans, Fourth District Banks, 1971-75	137
10.1	Consumer Installment Credit, November 1976	157
10.2	Number of Credit Accounts, 1975	158
10.3	Comparative Card Ownership	167
10.4	Total Number of Cards Owned	168
10.5	Bank Card Statistics, California and Washington, 1973-75	170
10.6	Simulated Rejections of Credit Card Holders by Credit Score Cutoff Points, New York Retail Credit Card Users, 1973	171
10.7	Account Data by Family Income Groups, New York Retail Credit Card Users	172
10.8	Borrowing Activity and Attitudes, 1971	173
10.9	Estimated Transfers from Bad Debt Losses, 1976	176
10.10	Bad Debt Transfers among Credit Card Users	177
10.11	Deficiency of Credit Costs over Credit Revenues, New York and California	179
10.12	Socioeconomic Determinants of Net Revenues for Retail Credit Card Users, New York	180

Table		Page
10.A.1	Distribution of Rate of Return on a Washer and Drier	186
10.A.2	Credit Costs as a Percent of Net Revolving Credit Sales	187
11.1	Trade Credit and Risk Ratios for Corporations, by Size and Type, First Quarter 1976	198
11.2	Illustration of Price Effect of Changes in Trade Credit Terms	202
12.1	Major Federal Credit Programs, Fiscal Year 1975	212
12.2	Impact of Federal Government on Credit Markets	219
12.3	Interest Subsidies in Federal Credit Programs, Fiscal Year 1975	222
13.1	Net Federal Support for the Home Mortgage Market	229
13.2	The Composition of FSCA Holdings	230
13.3	Cumulative Impact of Approximate Freeze in FSCA Mortgage Holdings at End-1965 Level	232
13.4	Annual Net Interest Income Redistribution Effects of FSCA Activities	234
13.5	Gains and Losses Assuming That Higher Thrift Income in the Absence of FSCA Purchases Would Have Been Passed through to Depositors via Higher Deposit Rates and Commercial Banks Would Have Raised Deposit Rates Equally	238
13.6	Percentage Distribution of Household Asset Holdings, Liability Outstandings, and Tax Payments by Ascending Income Quintiles	239
13.7	Gains or Losses Induced by the Increase in FSCA Mortgage Holdings, by Income Quintiles	240
14.1	Interest Savings to Mortgagors under the FHA/VA Extended Tandem Programs, GNMA	248

Table		Page
14.2	Interest Savings to Mortgagors under the Conventional Extended Tandem Programs	252
14.3	Mortgage Interest Rates in Primary and Secondary Markets on Loans Closed, Rates on Advances and Commitments, January 1974 through June 1975	256
15.1	Flow of Funds within the Market for Tax-Exempt Securities	271
15.2	Distribution of Household Tax-Exempt Purchases by Marginal Federal Income Tax Rate	273
15.3	A Possible Distribution of Windfalls Owing to the Interest Exemption	276

LIST OF FIGURES

Figure		Page
2.1	The Rate of Inflation and the Domestic and Foreign Demand for Real Balances	30
11.1	The Kinked Demand Curve Model of Price Enforcement with Adjustable Trade Credit Terms	201
14.1	Mortgage Credit Supply and Demand with Random Selection of Subsidy Recipients	263
15.1	The Market for Tax-Exempt Securities	272
15.2	The Subsidy Components in the Present Treatment of Tax-Exempt Securities	274
15.3	Market for STL Debt with Subsidized Taxable Bonds	280

LIST OF ABBREVIATIONS

AT&T	American Telephone and Telegraph Company
CB	commercial bank
CBCT	customer-bank communications terminal
CD	large ($100,000 or more) negotiable certificate of deposit
CPI	consumer price index
ECO Act	Equal Credit Opportunity Act
EHPA	Emergency Home Purchase Act of 1974
FDIC	Federal Deposit Insurance Corporation
FHA	Federal Housing Administration
FHLB	Federal Home Loan Bank
FHLMC	Federal Home Loan Mortgage Corporation
FNMA	Federal National Mortgage Association
FSCA	federally sponsored credit agency
GM	General Motors
GNMA	Government National Mortgage Association
HUD	Housing and Urban Development
IMF	International Monetary Fund
M-1	money supply, currency plus demand deposits held by the nonbank public
M-2	M-1 plus savings and time deposits with commercial banks, excluding CDs
M-5	M-2 plus savings deposits with thrift institutions and certificates of deposit
MSB	Mutual Savings Bank
NOW	negotiable order of withdrawal
OMB	Office of Management and Budget
PBO	Boeckh construction cost-price index for residences
PINS	property insurance companies
PLAM	price level adjusted mortgage
SDRs	special drawing rights
SLA	savings and loan association
STLs	state and local governments
VA	Veterans Administration

REDISTRIBUTION THROUGH THE FINANCIAL SYSTEM: An Introduction

THOMAS FREDERICK WILSON

The financial system is organized around a set of markets in which transactions are often accompanied by a redistribution of income or wealth. The bulk of the literature on money and credit ignores these redistributive transfers. In contrast, the papers published in this volume focus on such transfers through the financial system. A grants economics theme, therefore, runs through this volume.[1] The emphasis here, then, is on such factors as the distributional effects of government restrictions on markets and private interference with otherwise impersonal and competitive market processes. Given the size and complexity of the financial network, the articles contained in this volume represent a small sample from the pool of potentially meaningful grants economics studies.

Grants economics recognizes the dual nature of the transfer of exchangeables in the economic organization of societies.* Traditional economics emphasizes transactions involving the two-way transfer of economic goods whereby no redistribution of net worth takes place. Grants economics accentuates the redistributive component that exists in many transactions. In the polar case, unilateral transfers, whether motivated by "love" or "fear," alter the distribution of net worth, as an economic good passes one way but no exchangeable passes the other way. Nonexchangeables may, of course, pass between the parties.[2] Conventional economics does consider unilateral transfers, but there remains a persistent and misleading tendency to force grants into the mold of exchange, that is, to define grants in effect as exchange. The presence of nonexchangeables, for example, satisfaction derived by the donor from a charitable contribution, is a source of much confusion. This should not be troubling. If attention focuses on the redistribution of income or wealth that accompanies grants, then the distinction between grants and exchange is readily discernible.†

---

*Grants may be positive or negative, and they may be explicit or implicit. A corresponding description applies to subsidies and taxes, which may also be explicit or implicit. One-way (unilateral) transfers are pure grants, and two-way transfers of equal values are pure exchange—if unequal, there is a grant component in the transaction. The word "transfer" must be interpreted from its context, such that it may imply exchange but usually refers to a grant.

†Charitable contributions clearly are unilateral transfers. A grant element is present if a person, perhaps motivated by patriotism,

Grants are often tightly woven into economic relationships. When unequal market values are involved in a transaction, a grant element is present. The conceptual and measurement problems are more serious when transactions embody such grant elements. This occurs, for example, when borrowing terms in foreign economic assistance programs or concessionary credits to promote exports reflect a subsidy component.[3] Similarly, homeowners, state and local governments, students, and farmers may, as beneficiaries of federal subsidies, borrow at below-market rates. The subsidy component, however, is not often explicit but appears within the implicit grants economy.

The implicit grants economy presents the greatest challenge to researchers. Kenneth Boulding has defined implicit grants and indicated the nature of the problem:

> Implicit grants may be defined as redistributions of income or wealth that take place as a result of structural changes or manipulations in the set of prices and wages, licenses, prohibitions, opportunity or access; they are anything, in fact, that is not a direct and explicit grant yet leads to economic redistributions. . . .
>
> The problem in defining implicit grants is that the concept always implies some norm or reference point in the distribution of income or wealth, divergencies from which constitute the implicit grant structure.[4]

The studies published in this volume venture into this complex realm of the implicit grants economy. The reader is advised to bear in mind the precise source of the grant being scrutinized and the norm from which that grant is assessed or measured.

The distributional ramifications of public policies often remain submerged in the implicit grants economy, even though legislative bodies increasingly and enthusiastically have committed time and energy to income redistribution. State legislators in each session adroitly rearrange the flows of implicit transfers, frequently conferring new privileges through licensing and regulation, besides adjusting the flow of explicit transfers. Congress deliberates at length on the

---

buys a U.S. savings bond when the return is below the rates on comparable uses of his funds. On the other hand, a sense of malevolence may underlie the determination of a person to invest in tax-exempt securities even if his after-tax income, as a consequence, is lower. In these instances, the presence of psychological factors does not dispose of the existence of redistributive transfers.

pattern of grant flows, often creating as well as rechanneling transfers through regulatory reform, tax restructuring, changes in the complexion of expenditure programs, and the establishment of new agencies. Disproportionate attention is given to explicit transfers, however, as implicit taxes and subsidies are often enormous and have far-reaching implications. Moreover, the fruits of these endeavors may be inconsistent with stated objectives. In agreement with Boulding's principle of "implicit irony," legislative "acts that are designed to benefit or injure one group of people often benefit or injure other groups."[5] The study of the grants economy seeks to identify and measure the distributional impact of public policies. Implicit grants arising from the exercise of governmental power in the financial system are analyzed in this volume.

Grants economics also explores the nature and significance of the redistribution of income or wealth within the private sector. Income transfers reflect the expression of benevolence as well as exploitative gains. Governments seek to reinforce certain private practices while eliminating others. The Federal Reserve is sensitive to high interest rates and the accompanying adverse effect on home building, such that it encourages nonprice rationing of business loans and the private allocation of funds to support residential construction. On the other hand, the government has enacted laws proscribing the exercise of monopolistic power and a host of discriminatory practices in the provision of consumer and mortgage credit. Within the intricate pattern of financial transactions in an advanced credit economy, there could be numerous varieties of private transfers, and laws prohibiting such practices may not be effectively administered. Several of these private practices are examined in this volume.

The organization of this book could reasonably take different forms, as most of the articles are interrelated in some way. Parts I and II, "The Profit from Money Creation" and the "Distributional Impact of Monetary Policy," share much common ground, but there is a clear distinction between them. Part I focuses on money as such and the grants that may arise from its issuance in the domestic and international economies. Inflation is a subject covered in both Parts I and II. The two chapters specifically related to monetary policy provide contrasting views of income redistribution as an explanation of the inflationary bias in the management of the nation's money supply.

Part III, "Grant Flows and Government Regulation of Financial Institutions," examines interest rate ceilings, reserve requirements, and restrictions on bank branching. These regulations pertain chiefly to government efforts to remodel or preserve the structure of financial institutions. Chapters in Part IV, "Implicit Transfers Associated with Private Practices and Government Regulations," accent the private practices that generate income redistribution, with the accompanying attempt of government to reduce such transfers. Part V, "Subsidies in Federal Credit Programs," assesses the grant component in government policy designed to channel funds into high national priority sectors.

This introduction emphasizes interrelationships among the chapters and the contrasts in points of view among the authors. Attention is also given to related issues and clarification of technical matters. Brief summaries are offered in the following paragraphs, but a deliberate effort has been made to avoid removing specific quantitative conclusions from their natural environment.

The profit from the issuance of money, a subject largely neglected in mainstream economics for many years, has undergone a revival of interest, largely because of the heightening tempo of inflation. The debasement of money as a means of achieving an "elastic" currency has a lengthy history,[6] and now the inflation tax has assumed a prominent position in the economic literature. Furthermore, Adam Smith, as Boulding describes in the Preface, correctly observed that the substitution of paper money for commodity money yields a resource gain. Thus, there are several issues at stake here. A social saving arises from the substitution of paper money or credit money for commodity money, and this saving involves a grant from society to the issuer of money, who is allowed to capture for himself the resource gain. A government may appropriate seigniorage, as a profit, from issuing money for which the cost falls below its purchasing power on the market. Likewise, commercial banks under a fractional reserve system may extract seigniorage through the multiple expansion of deposits. Competition among banks for deposits and loan customers will tend to pass that return on to the public.*

The government, however, may exercise monopolistic control over the provision of currency and reserve deposits held by the central bank, that is, "high-powered money" or the "monetary base." To the extent that interest is not paid on money, such that the grant is not passed on to those who hold money, the full social saving is not realized. In this sense, reserve requirements above the minimum needed for operations constitute a "tax" on banks. In other words, the search for and the use of substitutes for money, resulting from increased profit potential from cash management, require the employment of resources.

This analysis may be extended into an inflationary economy. The transfers accompanying an "unanticipated" inflation may be enor-

*Boulding takes a firmer position in the Preface. He maintains that banks certainly do retain some of this profit, and that it is probably used to expand the banking industry beyond its optimum size.

mous, but economic units can adjust accordingly, with one exception, to a "correctly anticipated" inflation, as nominal rates of return reflect inflationary expectations. The "inflation tax" will persist. If the return on money remains zero, inflation reduces real cash balances. As the private sector builds its money holdings, the government collects a profit from the issuance of that money—those who hold larger cash balances would be expected to "pay" more of the "tax." There is a clear parallel between seigniorage and the "tax" associated with "correctly anticipated" inflation. Thomas Wilson treats the "inflation tax," as defined, as a form of seigniorage, whereas Harry Johnson draws a sharp distinction between them, by restricting seigniorage to situations when the price level is essentially constant.

Benjamin Klein, Johnson, and Wilson examine such profits from the issuance of money. Klein argues that seigniorage is likely to be small because of certain, usually unmeasured, implicit returns on money, and understatement of the costs of maintaining the acceptability of money, for which the "brand-name capital" outlays are sizable. Klein contends that Wilson and Johnson have ignored some of these, perhaps substantial, costs in evaluating seigniorage. Wilson replies to Klein's comments on his work. Klein further draws seigniorage implications from a broad, liquidity concept of money.

Wilson estimates seigniorage in the domestic economy, suggesting that this explains the several billion dollars of net earnings that the Federal Reserve System turns over each year to the Treasury, and that an even larger sum represents the private gain from money creation. Wilson claims that there is no constitutional basis for the retention of such profit by the federal government, and that it is not wise to permit it to extract such a monopolistic return. Wilson's conclusion is compatible with a proposal advanced by Federal Reserve Board Chairman Arthur Burns. Burns's proposal would allow banks nationwide to offer negotiable-orders-of-withdrawal (NOW) accounts, which are essentially interest-bearing checking accounts, and the Federal Reserve would pay interest to commercial banks on their reserve balances. Charlotte Ruebling also explores the topic of seigniorage, and Marvin Phaup further discusses issues related to reserve requirements.

Johnson devotes much of his chapter to the returns from the use of the dollar as a reserve currency. Klein also extends his analysis into the international sphere. They agree that the seigniorage return specifically to the United States is negligible. The difference between the magnitude on international and domestic seigniorage is attributable to the payment of interest on international dollar holdings. A corresponding result applies domestically for the interest-bearing components of the broader concepts of money, for which reserve requirements are low. Eurodollar deposits, that is, dollar-denominated deposits in European banks and branches of U.S. banks, yield an interest return.* The underlying reserves in the United States are very small, with the multiple creation of deposits subject only to "prudence," a matter often judged ex post.† A shift of funds from a domestic office of a U.S. bank to its European branch by a multinational corporation, for example, creates Eurodollars. A reserve here underlies that original deposit, but, beyond that, further expansion in Eurodollar deposits may take place without additional reserve holdings. Foreign dollar holdings are also placed in Treasury securities. Johnson, in his appendix, calculates the inflation tax associated with these investments, and finds that the return to the United States was only significant under conditions of "unanticipated" inflation.

Ruebling and Thomas Havrilesky find the same symptom, but different causes, in their diagnoses of the distributional impact of monetary policy. There is agreement on the role of money in inflation, and that the lack of fiscal discipline and the distributional objectives of government underlie the actual inflationary monetary policy. Beyond this, the arguments are developed along different lines. Ruebling suggests that the benefits derived by the government from overly expansive policies provide an incentive for their continuation. (Some of these benefits are reviewed by Richard Cohn.) Havrilesky is highly critical of "ultrarational" explanations of inflation, according to which the government sets the economy on the inflationary course most suitable to its purposes. Havrilesky's chapter is tightly reasoned and highly instructive, as it sharpens the focus on several lively issues encountered elsewhere in this volume. His expositions of the costs of inflation and the pursuit of distributional and allocational objectives refer specifically to subjects studied in most of the chapters in this book. He further develops a strong case against the use of credit allocation devices, which divert the monetary authorities from their proper function of promoting economic stability. There are, of course, enthusiastic supporters of strict credit allocation in this country—a practice firmly established in many foreign countries.[7]

The redistribution of income associated with "unanticipated" inflation has not been treated lightly here or in previous works, but the

---

*Eurodollars are part of the Eurocurrency deposits, which are foreign-currency-denominated deposits in Europe (similar deposits exist elsewhere in the world). There are, accordingly, Eurodollar and Eurocurrency markets.

†The borrowings of U.S. banks from their foreign branches (and similar sources of funds) are subject to a special reserve requirement, but such borrowings are very modest relative to the size of Eurodollar deposits, though they grow somewhat larger with domestic monetary stringency.

redistributive impact of inflation cannot be fully appreciated until the magnitude of those transfers has been calculated. Johnson did compute the transfers associated with foreign holdings of Treasury bills; however, this is a small proportion of the total volume of securities outstanding. Individual and institutional investors, for example, have sustained heavy capital losses in their corporate and government bond portfolios. Ruebling illustrates this phenomenon for a five-year Treasury note, whereby the investor received virtually no return on the investment and, of course, the real interest cost to the government was essentially zero. This might be illustrated differently. The 3.875 percent coupon bond of American Telephone and Telegraph Company (AT&T) reaches maturity in 1990. This $1,000 bond was issued in 1956, and now trades around 70 (or $700) in the market. The drop in the price reflects an upward revision in inflationary expectations, so that the yield to maturity at 7.6 percent is aligned with that for other fixed-income obligations of comparable quality. While investors have experienced a loss, AT&T still has use of that $1,000 at an interest cost of 3.875 percent. Moreover, the time period for full adjustment to "unanticipated" inflation may be very long indeed, and the transfers caused by the adjustment to a new inflationary outlook are not temporary but permanent.

A similar phenomenon has affected the housing market.* Homeowners who, prior to the sharp increase in the prices of houses, leveraged their investment with a large mortgage have reaped substantial capital gains, which enable them to make down payments for the purchase of more expensive homes. Many young and poor families have been excluded from participation in these windfall (speculative) gains. Mortgage lenders, on the other hand, have absorbed capital losses, as the market values of their portfolios have fallen. Savings and loan associations, in particular, hold mainly long-term assets while their deposit liabilities are short term. The rising trend in inflation over the past 15 years has forced interest rates to higher levels. Mortgage portfolios consequently shrink in value, and increases in deposit rates, which must be paid to all their depositors, threaten their solvency. Interest rate ceilings on savings deposits have been imposed by the government, therefore, to protect mortgage lenders and, concomitantly, the mortgage market. The longer run upward trend in interest rates, in sympathy with inflation, and the pronounced cyclical amplitude of interest rates contribute periodically to the distress of mortgage lenders.

The imposition of interest rate ceilings probably accentuates disintermediation, such that the cyclical swing in residential construction

---

*This illustration was drawn from an unpublished study by Patric Hendershott.

activity is enhanced. When short-term, open-market interest rates rise above the deposit rate ceilings, financial intermediaries experience withdrawals of funds, which are placed in money market instruments, for example, Treasury bills, commercial paper, and large ($100,000 or more) negotiable certificates of deposit issued by commercial banks, that are not subject to such ceilings. Disintermediation, therefore, is a reversal of the normal intermediation process carried out by financial institutions.*

David Pyle analyzes the distributional consequences of the Interest Rate Adjustment Act of 1966, which established maximum rates payable by savings and loan associations and mutual savings banks (the thrift institutions), coupled with the ceilings on savings and time deposits set by the Federal Reserve Board under Regulation Q. Pyle uses econometric methods to estimate what deposit rates would have been in the absence of ceilings. Transfers among institutions and among individuals are examined. The transfers among institutions benefited commercial banks. Persons with modest savings were the most adversely affected, in part because the minimum size of the investment in money market instruments prevented them from shifting to alternative investments (the advent of money market mutual funds has reduced the minimum necessary investment). Pyle computes the accumulative loss to savers expressed in 1975 dollars. The grants generated by the prohibition of interest payments on demand deposits under the Banking Act of 1933 are not assessed in this study.

Richard Cohn asserts that deposit rate ceilings cannot simply be removed without endangering the thrift institutions and seriously damaging the mortgage market. He gives a rationale for subsidizing thrift institutions and criticizes several proposals designed to eliminate deposit rate ceilings and ensure the stability of these institutions. Cohn offers his own plan for withdrawing gradually the protective umbrella of government regulation. This subject is discussed further by Patric Hendershott and Kevin Villani in their study of the operations of the federally sponsored credit agencies in the home mortgage market.

Commercial banks operate in a strikingly uneven regulatory environment, and this is especially pronounced for reserve requirement ratios and restrictions on branching. Reserve requirements impose a "tax" on commercial banks when the level exceeds that which banks would choose to hold without such requirements. There is a significant differential in this burden between member and nonmem-

---

*Insurance companies are financial intermediaries as well, and they experience an increase in policy loans in response to a rise in interest rates.

ber banks. The Federal Reserve Board sets, within permissible ranges established by the Congress, the reserve ratios for member banks, and the individual state authorities determine the reserve ratios for nonmember banks, which may be so low as to imply a zero "tax." State laws govern branching, and they allow variations from unit banking to statewide branching; interstate branching is prohibited. Unit banking may impede competition and forfeit scale economies, thus imposing on the public an extra cost for banking services.

Marvin Phaup conducted statistical analyses of banks in the fourth (Cleveland) Federal Reserve district to determine the character of the grants. Phaup detected no consistent, systematic relationships between profitability and member-nonmember status or the extent of branching. Other things adjust, however, such as the accessibility of banking services and the composition of the banks' portfolios. Unit-banking states have fewer offices.* Less convenient services translate into higher costs borne by customers. Member banks hold larger reserves, and their operating income relative to total assets tends to be lower (their expenses relative to total assets are lower as well).

One adjustment member banks apparently make is to invest more heavily in the less liquid, tax-exempt securities of state and local governments. If this is a response to the higher "tax" on member banks, then state and local governments are beneficiaries of this regulation. Similarly, the Treasury benefits from Federal Reserve support of the market for its obligations. The "tax" is not now administered uniformly across member banks, because reserve requirements on demand deposits are graduated. The Federal Reserve, nonetheless, has repeatedly requested congressional authority to set "uniform" reserve requirements on nonmember institutions. The Federal Reserve contends that the erosion of membership weakens its capacity to control the money supply, and that this decline stems from its stiffer reserve requirements and pressures to provide services to nonmember banks and thrift institutions. Phaup opposes this further concentration of power in the hands of the Federal Reserve System.

A flurry of federal legislative activity commenced a few years ago to protect individuals and certain groups from "unfair" practices (and therefore transfers) in the private sector of the grants economy. The Truth in Lending Act was aimed, in part, at the alleviation of

---

*Pyle points out that interest rate ceilings may have increased the number of savings and loan offices.

certain deceptive, exploitative practices in quoting finance charges. The Home Mortgage Disclosure Act of 1975 sets forth guidelines for depositary institutions to report on mortgage loans by geographic areas. The purpose of the law is to uncover, and presumably reduce, "redlining," that is, the exclusion of certain areas from consideration for mortgage loans. The Equal Credit Opportunity Act of 1975 forbids discrimination by creditors on the basis of sex or marital status. While the actual results are still pending, its purpose is clearly to ensure that creditworthiness serves its proper function in the extension of credit. Significant resource costs, however, are associated with these regulations. Joseph Scherer carefully explores the new set of implicit grants created by this piece of legislation and other ramifications.

William Dunkelberg identifies several varieties of transfers in his study of consumer credit, and stresses the role of state laws in modifying the pattern of implicit grants. Regulations may reduce the size of some grants, or spawn a new set of transfers. Usury laws, which have long historic roots, and restraints on collection practices favorably affect some borrowers, at the expense of depositors, and adversely affect others who are rationed out of the market. Cash customers subsidize users of credit cards when payments are made before assessment of the full costs of that service. Dunkelberg discusses these free riders, and deadbeats as well. Bad debt losses imply transfers, of course. Dunkelberg presents a number of statistical studies to verify the significance of these varieties of implicit grants. This chapter is suggestive of legal remedies (for example, bankruptcy) for failure of the exchange economy and illegal activities (for example, the services of loan sharks) that emerge to moderate the impact of the grants economy, despite the fact that usury laws subsidize loan sharks. Such linkages between the legal and illegal tiers of the exchange and grants economies generally are not well understood.

Robert Schwartz and David Whitcomb investigate implicit grants in the extension of credit by nonfinancial businesses, that is, trade credit. They survey the literature on nonprice rationing of business loans and observe that trade credit serves in part as an alternative source of funds when bank credit is rationed. Under conditions of monetary stringency, trade credit bulges and large firms extend more credit and small firms extend less credit. Trade credit may serve as a means to circumvent usury laws, and the flexible terms under which trade credit is offered provide an escape route from price controls. The availability and terms for the provision of trade credit therefore are part of the price package. Adjustments in credit terms allow disguised price changes in oligopolistic markets, and price discrimination as well. Variations in the treatment of customers, as Schwartz and Whitcomb point out, may be exploitative or benevolent, as a form of corporate philanthropy. The Dunkelberg and Schwartz-Whitcomb studies reveal intricate grant structures in practically neglected areas, even though they are of considerable importance in the economy.

The last group of chapters delves into a prime growth area of government involvement in the financial system: the market impact of federally sponsored credit agencies. This has not been a neglected area, but some very naive perceptions of the implications for the credit markets of such agencies and of the size and nature of their redistributive impact still persist. Most of these government programs are of recent vintage. An old one is considered as well, and that is the tax-exempt status of state and local government obligations. While this is ordinarily categorized as a "tax expenditure"* rather than an overt federal credit program, the chapter by Patric Hendershott and Timothy Koch is placed in this group because the provision of a tax exemption and the subsidization of borrowers through federal credit programs represent close alternatives. The objectives of government intervention may be laudatory, but the outcome is not always consistent with the objectives.[8] Grants economics seeks to expose the actual distributional implications of these government efforts, not because the market somehow yields an equitable solution but because the redistributive consequences should at least be known, and preferably the subsidies should be made directly to the beneficiaries. It seems that in this area the ingenuity of subterfuge is endless.

Murray Weidenbaum documents the growth and proliferation of government-sponsored credit programs. He identifies the types of grants implicit in these programs and estimates the interest subsidy accruing to federally assisted borrowers. Weidenbaum dispels the commonly held notion that there is a "free good" inherent in these programs and suggests means by which the government might exercise closer control of its credit programs. There are, of course, political advantages, which are cited by Weidenbaum, to these forms of subsidy programs, such that peaks in the trends in the size and number of such agencies are not in sight. Strong pressure continues for the augmentation of selective credit controls.

There is also under way an effort to "repossess" one of the agencies that was spun off from the government under a special charter in 1968. The Federal National Mortgage Association (FNMA) is

---

*Tax expenditures apply to tax-exempt income or outlays subject to a tax credit or tax deduction, such that, it is reasoned, these special provisions in the tax law mean in effect that the private sector is spending some money that would otherwise be tax revenue to the government.

a government-created, quasi-private corporation. It is wholly owned by private stockholders, but the president appoints 5 of the 15 members of the board of directors. On the grounds that FNMA is placing the profit motive ahead of the public interest, as private corporations sometimes do, by shunning a heavy commitment of funds to high-risk mortgages, Senator William Proxmire is leading an effort to increase the number of presidentially appointed directors to 9 in an enlarged board of 19 members. Weidenbaum's comprehensive review and analysis of the government's credit programs cover the mortgage-related agencies, such as FNMA. Hendershott and Villani and George von Furstenberg probe more deeply the impact of the activities of these organizations.

Hendershott and Villani examine the distributional impact of one of the major tools used by government to support home building and promote homeownership.[9] They conduct an analysis to determine the effects of operations in the home mortgage market of federally sponsored credit agencies (FSCAs), which include FNMA, the Federal Home Loan Banks (FHLBs), and the Government National Mortgage Association (GNMA).* They estimate the effects on financial markets of FSCA home mortgage purchases (and security sales) and translate them into changes in net interest income by sector. After weighing the influence of deposit rate ceilings and passing the gains and losses of nonhousehold sectors through to households, the ultimate distributional impact is summarized by income quintiles. This procedure constitutes a useful framework, and it could serve as a model for tracing the paths of other such grant flows. The findings of the Hendershott-Villani study are in agreement with Director's law, as cited by Boulding in the Preface.

George von Furstenberg looks into the narrowly defined area of GNMA operations under the tandem plans. The tandem plans allow GNMA to sell at a discount the mortgages it acquires, thus permitting a recycling of funds back into the mortgage market. Because only the net lending of on-budget government agencies is recorded as an outlay, the budgetary consequences are reduced under these tandem arrangements. GNMA operations under the tandem plans were initially restricted to mortgages insured by the Federal Housing Administration, but in September 1971 this arrangement was extended to mortgages guaranteed by the Veterans Administration. Limited commitments to conventional mortgages commenced in October 1974. The tandem plans from January 1974 to June 1975, according to von

---

*FNMA is known colloquially as Fannie Mae, GNMA as Ginnie Mae, and the FHLBs' subsidiary, the Federal Home Loan Mortgage Corporation (FHLMC), as Freddie Mac.

Furstenberg, conveyed modest benefits to mortgage lenders and significant gains to mortgagors, mostly through reduced mortgage rates, but the impact on housing starts was small.

Hendershott and Koch trace the grant flows arising from the federal income tax exemption of interest received on state and local government securities. They demonstrate that the current subsidy is inefficient, because only part of it is actually captured by state and local governments, and inequitable, because high-tax-bracket investors reap substantial gains. The tax exemption causes economic inefficiency as well. They consider on these grounds various alternative subsidy plans. Hendershott and Koch also examine the appropriateness of the tax exemption of interest on pollution control bonds. The political appeal of outright subsidies is mitigated, of course, by the budgetary implications, which in large measure explain the mechanics of government intervention in financial markets as presented in this set of studies.

NOTES

1. There is a substantial literature in grants economics. The concepts are clearly presented and the range of research is well represented in the following works: Kenneth E. Boulding, Martin Pfaff, and Janos Horvath, "Grants Economics: A Simple Introduction," _American Economist_, Spring 1972, pp. 19-35; Kenneth E. Boulding, _The Economy of Love and Fear: A Preface to Grants Economics_ (Belmont, Calif.: Wadsworth, 1973); Kenneth E. Boulding and Martin Pfaff, eds., _Redistribution to the Rich and the Poor: The Grants Economics of Income Distribution_ (Belmont, Calif.: Wadsworth, 1972); Kenneth E. Boulding, Martin Pfaff, and Anita B. Pfaff, eds., _Transfers in an Urbanized Economy: The Grants Economics of Income Distribution_ (Belmont, Calif.: Wadsworth, 1973); and Martin Pfaff, ed., _Grants and Exchange_ (Amsterdam: North-Holland, 1976).

2. Boulding, _The Economy of Love and Fear_, p. 2.

3. Janos Horvath, "On the Evaluation of International Grants Policy," _Public Finance_, no. 2 (1971), pp. 267-81; and "The Scope of International Grants Economy: The Case of the Eximbank," in Martin Pfaff, ed., _Frontiers in Social Thought: Essays in Honor of Kenneth E. Boulding_ (Amsterdam: North-Holland, 1976), pp. 121-42.

4. Boulding, _The Economy of Love and Fear_, p. 49.

5. Ibid., p. 52.

6. Isaiah 1:22.

7. See, for example, Donald R. Hodgman, _Selective Credit Controls in Western Europe_, Trustees of the Banking Research Fund, Association of Reserve City Bankers, 1976.

8. Ira Kaminow and James M. O'Brien, eds., Studies in Selective Credit Policies (Philadelphia: Federal Reserve Bank of Philadelphia, 1975).

9. For a discussion of other tools, see Henry Aaron, "Implicit Transfers to Homeowners in the Federal Budget," in Boulding and Pfaff, eds., Redistribution to the Rich and the Poor, pp. 204-19.

PART I

The Profit from Money Creation

1

Money, Wealth, and Seigniorage

BENJAMIN KLEIN

INTRODUCTION

This chapter examines the nature and size of seigniorage under alternative monetary systems. Seigniorage is commonly defined as the difference between the exchange value of money and the cost of producing and maintaining it. Historically, seigniorage was identified with the charge, over and above the cost of minting, which was collected by the government or some government franchisee for turning gold or silver into money. It is somewhat misleading to use the term "money" exclusively for minted coins in this context because bullion also circulated in exchange as a substitute for minted coins. In fact, the existence of substitute media of exchange placed a limit on the amount of profit or seigniorage that could be collected by the government. This competitive limitation is also present now in the international money market and, as will be seen, may partially explain the recent inflationary behavior of the United States in its international role as the dominant money supplier.

Seigniorage, therefore, is generally considered as a monopolistic (rather than monopoly) rent on the right to produce a particular form of money. Under present monetary arrangements of fiduciary rather than commodity money, it is said to be essentially costless to produce cash balances, and the seigniorage or profit on money issue is considered as a pure resource gain, or "grant," to the government. This grant is said to be shared with commercial banks if reserve requirements are set below 100 percent. In what follows this standard argument is critically analyzed and important implications for the nature of money and wealth derived.

REALISTIC BENCH MARKS

A mistake that is often made in defining seigniorage is assuming that interest payments on money are zero. Empirical work by the author on the long-term U.S. demand for money [7] clearly indicates that it is reasonable to assume that implicit competitive interest payments are made on commercial bank deposits. In the international context, the evidence is more obvious, as foreign official and private holdings of "dollars" consist primarily of holdings of Treasury securities or of interest-bearing Eurodollar deposits, which are essentially unbacked by high-powered dollar reserves.*

In addition, some high-powered money may bear interest. Although currency is non-interest-bearing, bank reserves may be yielding an implicit return in the form of Federal Reserve and Treasury "subsidies" from the Federal Reserve member bank borrowing privilege, Treasury tax and loan accounts, or Federal Reserve insurance against failure.[1] When calculating "grants," one must also be careful to use a general equilibrium framework. What appears as a unilateral transfer may in fact turn out to be merely an indirect payment for other services rendered. In the international market, for example, Germany may decide "voluntarily" to hold additional dollar reserves earning less than the market rate of interest as payment for the stationing of U.S. troops in Germany. (This political transaction was in fact made quite explicit at times during the 1960s.) The increased foreign holdings of dollars in such a situation should obviously not be considered an official settlements deficit in the balance of payments, but rather merely official payment to the United States for export of protection services.

In addition to the hidden presence across markets and over time of a quid pro quo of the standard market type of exchange, the analysis of grants economics also suffers from the absence of an obvious bench mark from which to measure a subsidy. What is the relevant starting point for income and wealth, or, more generally, how are private property rights initially defined? The alternative bench marks of zero government or of a fully totalitarian government are unrealistic, that is, they are inconsistent with any real-world, positive transaction costs, political equilibrium. For example, does the existence of fractional reserve banking imply government sharing of the money-issuing "privilege" with commercial banks (and hence a subsidy) or merely government taxation of a private firm? Thomas Wilson [13] uses 100 percent reserve requirements as his bench mark for defining a grant. Anything less than 100 percent reserves is a "subsidy" or seigniorage for commercial banks within his framework. Even if

---

*A very low reserve ratio is maintained behind Eurodollar deposits in the form of demand deposits held at domestic commercial banks (primarily a few New York City institutions), which, in turn, possess a required high-powered reserve backing.

bank profit were zero, he asserts, that is, if all returns were competitively passed on to bank depositors in the payment of interest, seigniorage would be present in the system because of the government grant of the "privilege" to engage in fractional reserve banking. Wilson's analysis under this arbitrary assumption is consistent, but not very useful. An analogous assumption applied to the entire economy would imply that all capital, including human capital, "belonged" to the sovereign and any tax less than 100 percent would represent "a grant."

The grants economics calculations presented in this volume should be considered crude in the sense that they generally ignore real-world constraints and thereby assume that institutional change is costless. It is assumed that the government can do whatever it wishes or that government coercion capital is unlimited. Could, for example, the government actually tax banks by imposing 100 percent non-interest-bearing reserve requirements, that is, drastically increase the tax on depositors, and survive? An alternative working assumption is that at any instant of time the government has a given quantity of coercion capital upon which it is earning a normal rate of return and that all marginal institutional changes must be consistent with a more general political equilibrium. This, of course, leaves one much more pessimistic regarding policy changes, but it is probably more realistic (that is, predictive) than talking about essentially designing a new "optimal" system. Similarly, in the international money market it does not make sense to consider the dominant (reserve currency) position of the dollar as exogenous. Historical evidence and recent experience clearly suggest that a country cannot do whatever it wishes without fear of losing such a position.

MONETARY CONFIDENCE

The second major mistake commonly made in defining seigniorage is the assumption that the dominant money, whether domestic or international, does not, under the present fiduciary money arrangement, require "backing." However, as noted in detail elsewhere, consumer confidence regarding future performance of the money supplier (that is, the degree of expected unanticipated inflation) is likely to be an important determinant of demand.[2] Reliable information about anticipated performance is costly to produce, and therefore consumer confidence is not a free good. Commodity money produces consumer confidence by placing a physical constraint on money production and hence on the possible unanticipated depreciation. "Guaranteed" convertibility of a money into a commodity (or into another more predictable money) is another way to obtain consumer confidence, and any stocks of the commodity (or the high confidence money) held as reserves to increase that assurance should also be considered an investment (or what has been called a "brand-name" capital outlay) by the money supplier in building confidence in its brand-name money. Other confidence-producing brand-name capital expenditures may take the form, for example, of advertising, luxurious offices, an impressive vault, employment of responsible individuals, and payments made to a certifying or insurance agency, such as the Federal Reserve, the Federal Deposit Insurance Corporation (FDIC), or a private clearinghouse. Most important, the major way in which monetary confidence is produced is successful past performance.

The important theoretical point is that, even under fiduciary monetary arrangements, confidence-creating costs cannot arbitrarily be considered to be zero. Once it is recognized that one lives in a world of positive information costs, even if the costs of producing cash balances are zero, as assumed in a pure fiduciary money world, the real seigniorage return per unit time cannot be identified with the usual gross profit as defined in Equation (1):

$$\pi = (i - r_M)(M/P) \qquad (1)$$

where i is "the" nominal market rate of interest on bonds (that is, on debt yielding no marginal monetary services),* r_M is the nominal rate of interest paid on money, and (M/P) is the value of real cash balances outstanding. It may be useful to refer to π as the real <u>gross</u> seigniorage return.

The brand-name costs that permit a money supplier to charge a price for its money greater than its marginal cost of production (that is, to set r_M below i) must be explicitly considered. The cost of brand-name capital, which includes the explicit confidence-creating expenditures, can be thought of as the cost of "selling," as opposed to "producing," real cash balances. If a money supplier's brand-name capital is measured properly as a residual element earning a

---

*When the bench mark interest rate, i, is assumed to be on a financial asset yielding no monetary services, then $(i - r_M)$, the pecuniary alternative cost per unit time of holding money, conveniently measures, in equilibrium, the value of the monetary service (or liquidity) stream from a marginal unit of money. Equilibrium implies that every financial asset yields a total return on the margin, that is, a pecuniary (or interest yield) plus a nonpecuniary (or liquidity yield), equal to "the" interest rate, i. The liquidity, or monetary service, return is assumed, with customary vagueness, to consist of increased marketability and future predictability of the asset.

normal real rate of return, then the average brand-name "selling costs" must be such as to make the net real "pure profit" or real <u>net</u> seigniorage zero.

If one assumes for a moment static conditions of a given level of infinitely long-lived brand-name capital and ignores the dynamic problems of investment and disinvestment in brand-name capital by unanticipated superior or inferior performance, the real market value of the brand-name capital (or "backing"), β, of the fiduciary money supplier's output is:

$$\beta = \frac{i - r_M}{\rho} (M/P) \qquad (2)$$

where ρ is the real rate of discount of the money supplier's gross profit stream. The ratio of the real alternative cost of holding the fiduciary money supplier's money to "the" real rate of interest therefore can be thought of as the supplier's brand-name capital (or net wealth) "backing" per real unit of its money.

One may think it useful to divide brand-name capital into monetary confidence capital and coercion capital, with perhaps only the return on the latter considered as pure seigniorage. But there are real costs of creating the ability to coerce effectively (such as maintaining a police force and army), and it is difficult to distinguish analytically between these two related forms of capital. A government creates monetary confidence capital in part by performing its national defense activities well. Confidence is not merely created by government fiat. The government's coercive power to declare its money "legal tender," for example, is neither necessary nor sufficient for the supply of monetary confidence and may not even be important.[3]

Even if there are no direct outlays by the money supplier in creating brand-name capital, the firm still faces these brand-name costs. For example, assume that the firm obtains its brand-name confidence capital solely by "luck," such as choosing the correct name for its money (a highly unrealistic description of the world). In a dynamic context the money supplier has the alternative cost of "selling" this real asset by intentional depreciation, that is, by unanticipated money supply growth, thereby increasing short-run gross profit in exchange for lower long-run or steady state gross profit. And this alternative cost can usefully be considered to be present with regard to both confidence and coercion capital. An obvious and possibly rational example of this type of intentional depreciation was involved in the decision by England after World War II to adopt a policy of devaluation, with a resulting loss of pound brand-name capital, rather than a policy of a reduced rate of growth of money to "repay" the borrowings it made against its monetary brand-name capital during the war when it credited foreign accounts at the Bank of England in exchange for real resources.

The important point to recognize here is that if the price is greater than the marginal cost of production, the money supplier does have something to lose (future seigniorage) if it "messes up." This implies that consumers paying seigniorage are necessarily purchasing some quality assurance. Brand-name capital is a form of collateral and gross seigniorage is equivalent to an insurance premium.

COMMODITY VERSUS FIDUCIARY MONEY

To understand the presence of brand-name costs within the context of a fiduciary money system, it is necessary (as noted above) to think of these costs as the costs of "selling," rather than "producing," real cash balances. The fact that it is costless to "add a zero," that is, the marginal cost of producing nominal money can reasonably be assumed to be zero, implies nothing about the marginal cost of creating real cash balances. Failure to distinguish between these two costs is a general problem present in the optimum quantity of money literature, which mistakenly assumes that $(i - r_M) = 0$ is the optimal solution because money is produced costlessly on the margin.[4] Since (M/P) is not a control variable in a money-producing firm's production function, but rather is determined on the demand side, it is difficult to conceptualize "the marginal cost of real cash balances."

A useful way to think of this theoretically is to start with the public's demand for "monetary services," which implies a derived demand for "monetary confidence" (similar to the derived demand for entrepreneurial services). Given this demand for confidence, the marginal cost of producing confidence (for example, holding gold stocks, maintaining an army and a police force, or expending resources on any other inputs that create confidence capital) implies an equilibrium quantity of confidence and thus a demand for real cash balances function. More generally, given information costs about future performance, monetary confidence, or brand names will have value independent of any explicit confidence-creating expenditures. Consumer demand for collateral or "backing" would necessarily imply a positive $(i - r_M)$ such that a normal rate of return is earned on the residually measured intangible brand-name capital. This "profit" stream, or seigniorage, can also be thought of as a cost to the money supplier of selling the real cash balances at the anticipated price rather than depreciating the monetary brand name.

In a strict sense, therefore, the type of costly information equilibrium outlined here implies that all money is at least partially "commodity" money, as all money is based on costly confidence capital. On the margin, an unanticipated increase in the nominal quantity of a competitive firm's money implies a real marginal cost to that money supplier because of the loss of consumer confidence and resulting fall in its demand. In equilibrium the alternative cost to the supplier of consumer confidence, in the sense of what the brand-name asset could be "sold" to consumers for via depreciation, is equal to the present value of the money supplier's nondeceiving gross profit stream. Common economic use of the term "commodity money" refers to particular types of production costs while failing to recognize that, in an imperfect information world, confidence costs are crucially important. The fact that the marginal cost of producing nominal money is zero is not relevant in this context.*

INTERNATIONAL MONETARY IMPLICATIONS

Failure to consider these confidence costs results in misleading analysis and policy conclusions. This is especially the case in the international monetary area where monetary confidence remains a significant problem. For example, Harry Johnson presents an obvious case of such an intellectual experiment that abstracts from these real-world information costs in his "Note on Seigniorage and the Social Saving from Substituting Credit for Commodity Money,"[5] where he implicitly assumes that confidence capital has a zero cost of creation and maintenance. In Johnson's analysis, therefore, commodity money is merely a deadweight social cost and fiduciary money is merely a costless invention that someone happens to think of. His analysis,

---

*It is interesting to note that even the standard definition of pure commodity money, which equates the narrow marginal cost of production of money with its exchange value, is only present under conditions of perfect competition. Because South Africa, for example, has some monopoly power in the supply of gold, the price or exchange value will be above its marginal production cost and seigniorage will be positive. To concentrate on marginal producers of gold would be analogous to concentrating on marginal competitive counterfeiters of dollar bills, where expected marginal costs of production and sale equal the expected exchange value. Although the outstanding supply of gold is very large relative to current production, South Africa does hold large inventories and attempts at times to stabilize the market price, in addition to advertising its coins and the stability of gold. That is, South Africa does attempt to maintain confidence in gold, as one would expect a monopolistic fiduciary money supplier collecting a seigniorage return to do.

however, should be correctly thought of as providing an estimate of the maximum social saving of moving from a commodity to a fiduciary monetary system. If confidence necessary to sell fiduciary money costs as much to produce as the commodity, the social saving would be zero. If confidence is, as Johnson assumes, costless under a credit money arrangement, the obvious historical question is why credi money did not replace commodity money before it did. A reasonable explanation is not that someone did not happen to think of the credit money idea (which is clearly untrue, as many firms and countries tried unsuccessfully to introduce credit money), but rather that commodity money was, at the time, the cheapest way to produce confidence. A forced movement from commodity to pure fiduciary money, for example, in the nineteenth century, would have implied a negative social saving.

Herbert Grubel, using an analysis very similar to Johnson's in discussing the distribution of seigniorage from the creation of a fiat money "acceptable to all countries in the settlement of debts" by a supranational agency, makes the crucial implicit assumption somewhat more transparent when he asserts that "money is what society wants it to be: precious metals, stones, coins, paper currency, demand deposits, saving accounts, negotiable paper, and the like. Any of these instruments can serve the purposes of money as a medium of exchange and store of wealth *if the proper social and economic institutions and conventions exist*" [2, p. 270, emphasis added]. The last phrase, of course, begs the important question of whether or not monetary confidence costs are positive. It is common for social reformers to make the assumption that institutions can essentially be altered or new ones developed costlessly, but seldom is it as explicitly stated as by Grubel.

The discussions of international monetary reform and the creation of SDRs (special drawing rights) (or "paper gold") have also largely assumed that "money is merely what society wants it to be" or that the International Monetary Fund (IMF) has unlimited brand-name capital. Leland B. Yeager, for example, in a review of Fritz Machlup's book, *Remaking the International Monetary System: The Rio Agreement and Beyond*, states that:

> Machlup welcomes SDRs as an ingenious and workable novelty. They will be created outright and will not appear as liabilities matching assets in the portfolio of any issuing institution. Rio signals progress in puncturing the hoary myth that money is debt and must have backing. [14, p. 1212]

This makes no economic sense. Every economist should recognize that net wealth cannot be created out of nothing, that is, real

SDRs cannot be merely "created outright." The existence of SDRs is predicated on demand or acceptability, which is based on the real value of IMF brand-name capital. That is, given flexible exchange rates, the IMF can make the nominal quantity of SDRs whatever it wishes. However, even if SDRs were a reserve currency, the real quantity outstanding is determined, like all monies, on the demand side. And this real demand is determined by the IMF's brand-name or monetary confidence capital.

From Equation (2), one sees that a stationary equilibrium market measure of the IMF's limited real brand-name capital can be obtained by multiplying the difference between "the" market interest rate and the rate that is paid on SDRs, $(i - r_{SDR})$, by the real value of the SDRs "in circulation."* This finite value of the brand name of SDRs is largely based not on the confidence and coercion capital possessed by the IMF but to a large extent on the brand-name monetary confidence capital of the United States and its willingness to accept SDRs.[†] In any event, it is this real but intangible brand-name asset in the portfolio of the issuing institution that "matches the outstanding liabilities."

The last sentence in the Yeager quote is contradictory. If money is not pure debt, that is, r_{SDR} is less than i (the rate of interest paid on pure debt—an asset yielding no marginal monetary services), then the money is at least partially net wealth, that is, is a source of valuable monetary services on the margin and, as can be seen from Equation (2), the money possesses "backing." It is not nec-

---

*Since SDRs cannot be used in transactions (even official international transactions) like dollars or gold (in fact, the IMF has explicit rules and penalties against excessive use), the quantity of SDRs effectively demanded, or voluntarily held, is difficult to measure. Clearly, aggregate IMF "allocations" are an overestimate of effective money demand. But even some SDRs voluntarily taken by a country after negotiation as payment for a balance-of-payments surplus may only be a new way to supply foreign aid credits and therefore also an upward biased measure of real money demand.

[†]One possible explanation of U.S. policy is that it is based on a failure to understand fully the international position of the dollar. To a large extent, the post-World War II increase in foreign holdings of dollar assets has resulted from the relative rise of the dollar brand name. It represents the export of monetary services and therefore should be thought of as a surplus item in complete balance of trade accounts, rather than accumulating "deficits," and hence does not imply the existence of a "dollar overhang" problem that must be solved by the creation of a new international asset.

essary for the money to have formal backing, for example, gold reserves, but it has backing, or brand-name capital reserves, nonetheless. The backing, which we have called brand-name capital, consists of whatever permits the IMF to set r_{SDR} less than i.

It is this real IMF brand-name asset, made visible by official international transactions, that also places a constraint on the real supply of SDRs outstanding. Given the real value of the brand-name asset in steady state equilibrium and i, the real value of SDRs can only be increased if the IMF increases r_{SDR}, that is, only if it increases real demand. Alternatively, if the real value of SDRs increases in the short run without an increase in r_{SDR}, this implies that the brand-name capital is depreciating. Current real gross profit has increased, but this is not sustainable. Future real gross profit must decrease to keep the present discounted value of real gross profit, or the given initial real brand-name capital, unchanged. This short-run unsustainable increase in real money, which represents the depreciation (or "sale") by a money supplier of some of its monetary brand-name capital in international exchange, is the only theoretically meaningful definition of a balance-of-payments "deficit" under fixed exchange rates.

A reserve currency country such as the United States is limited by these same forces represented by a given finite value of real brand-name capital and the possibility of a short-run "deficit" in the sense of depreciation of this capital. If the depreciation proceeds far enough, the country could, in the long run, lose its valuable reserve currency position. Therefore, concern by the United States for its balance-of-payments position, correctly defined, is legitimate and is analogous to the concern of a business firm for its credit rating.[6]

Although the dollar brand name has depreciated over the last decade owing to unexpectedly poor inflation performance, the dollar does remain as the dominant international currency. However, as has been emphasized, this position is certainly not exogenous. The limited depreciating value of the dollar brand-name capital, evidenced by the recent movement out of dollars as a reserve currency and the implied foregone future profit or gross seigniorage, essentially is the balance-of-payments constraint under which the United States is currently operating. The seigniorage earned on foreign holdings of high-powered dollars should be thought of as payment by foreigners for the use of U.S. monetary confidence and as a normal return on the dollar brand-name capital. As already noted, however, this seigniorage is extremely low because competitive foreign commercial banks and governments can essentially get a free ride on the dollar brand name merely by denominating deposits in dollars without being required to hold dollar reserves* and by tying their currency to the dollar.

This free ride, in fact, may rationally explain why the United States may have intentionally depreciated the international brand-name value of the dollar via an unexpectedly high inflation rate over the last decade. Because the existence of competitive substitutes for the U.S. dollar (for example, Eurodollars and alternative currencies tied to the dollar)† significantly reduced the seigniorage earned by the United States in supplying the dominant money, it also significantly reduced the incentive on the United States to "do a good job" (the fear of the loss of future seigniorage). In fact, existing international institutional arrangements created a profit incentive for the United States to produce an unexpectedly rapid inflation and thereby make a large short-run profit. Wealth maximization would dictate a short-run policy of deception and intentional depreciation of the dollar brand name, as the longer run reduced profit consequences would be minor. If the expected steady state seigniorage return is small, then little is being given up in the future with such a policy. While the United States engages in short-run unexpected inflation, foreign (surplus country) governments accumulate dollar balances in an attempt to maintain the fixed exchange rate. This foreign sterilization in the face of a balance-of-trade surplus implies a trade of foreign consumption and investment goods for dollar balances and an implicit transfer of wealth away from foreigners to U.S. consumers. The purchase of the U.S. dollars by foreign central banks at incorrect (nonmarket) prices is a speculative activity that represents an implicit tax on foreign citizens, collected in part by U.S. citizens.‡ It is not claimed,

---

*The Federal Reserve has eliminated part of this free ride by requiring reserves be held against dollar deposits in foreign branches of U.S. banks, but, of course, are unable to regulate foreign dollar deposits in foreign banks.

†The yen before 1971 is an obvious example. With Japan maintaining a rigidly fixed exchange rate with the dollar for 25 years, the country must have seemed to be just another Federal Reserve district. Since long-term monetary policy was determined essentially by the Federal Reserve Board in Washington, D.C., a blurring of some of the distinction between the dollar and the yen in the minds of international transactors must have been produced.

‡To get some idea of the magnitude of losses involved, during the first quarter of 1973 the Bank of Japan purchased about $10 billion at about 300 yen/dollar in an unsuccessful attempt to keep the yen

of course, that this wealth transfer is conscious U.S. policy, but merely that such a short-run policy is likely to be wealth maximizing under current international seigniorage arrangements. If the insurance premium (seigniorage) is not paid by consumers, then the money producer has nothing to lose if he "messes up" and therefore sells his collateral (brand-name capital) by intentional deception.

Finally, the international role of the dollar clearly indicates that the presence of gross seigniorage does not imply the existence of a monopoly franchise. The United States has its current international monetary position not because of artificially imposed government regulations, but primarily because of its past and prospective performance.* The small international seigniorage collected by the United States is certainly not a return on coercion capital, as no one forces foreigners to use the dollar as an international unit of account, medium of exchange, or store of value.

DOMESTIC IMPLICATIONS: MONEY, DEBT, AND WEALTH

Although the identification of the source of gross seigniorage with coercion or government regulation appears obviously incorrect in the international money market, it is also a false identification for the domestic market. If one assumes that confidence were completely costless to produce, then the value of the money supplier's brand-name capital, β, and the net wealth value of the money would vanish and competitive interest payments on the money would equal "the" market rate of interest. One would then be operating in a world where money supply changes were perfectly and costlessly anticipated and the existence of any positive gross seigniorage could only be attributed to government coercion. In the real world of positive confidence costs, however, such an inference is incorrect.

For example, Johnson [5] has made the useful analytic point, entirely consistent with this author's analysis, that the common distinction between "inside" and "outside" money is really the distinction

---

from appreciating. The market exchange rate rose to about 265 yen per dollar when the Bank of Japan finally gave up, implying a "loss" of about $1.2 billion over a period of a couple of months.

*It should be noted that economists do not have a very good understanding of how and why a particular money becomes a dominant money. Future research on the fundamental unanswered questions regarding the nature of the monetary service stream and the production function for monetary confidence will throw light on this issue.

between competitive interest-bearing and non-interest-bearing (or, in my terms, non-brand-name backed and brand-name backed) money.[7] Unfortunately, Johnson then identifies the equity or net wealth of a commercial bank, which permits it to borrow at a rate of interest less than "the" market rate at which it lends, solely with government regulation in the money industry. This assumes, however, that monetary services and hence monetary confidence can be produced costlessly. If monetary services are costly to produce, repeal of all legal restrictions on the domestic banking industry would still leave some proportion of bank deposits as "outside" money. Competitive interest paid on deposits would remain below "the" market rate of interest on assets yielding no monetary services. The usual T-accounts analysis of money and wealth in the banking industry, therefore, is not economically useful because it generally excludes from consideration one important asset, the brand-name capital that permits a competitive banking firm to pay less interest than it receives, that is, to create monetary services that are valuable on the margin.[8]

This leads to an explicit examination of the question of the particular bench mark interest rate, i, used in defining the gross seigniorage, or profit, of Equation (1). This bench mark rate was defined as the rate of interest on a financial asset yielding no monetary services, that is, the rate of interest on "pure debt." Therefore, $(i - r_M)$ measures, in equilibrium, the value of the monetary service stream from a marginal unit of money. If, in fact, monetary services and hence confidence were costless to produce, r_M would therefore equal i, the nominal return on an asset that yielded no monetary services. In this context most financial assets are only partially pure debt because they do yield on the margin some liquidity services (usually defined in terms of marketability and predictability characteristics). The source of these services, or the present discounted value of the monetary service stream, represents net wealth. It is difficult, in fact, to conceive of a financial asset that yielded absolutely no liquidity services, but it is certainly known that such an asset will pay much more than the 5 or 10 percent interest return observed on highly marketable securities.

Seen in this way even if there were perfect competition in banking and all government regulations, including reserve requirements and all other portfolio restrictions, were eliminated, interest payments on deposits would certainly be less than i, because the average return on voluntarily held commercial bank assets, r_A, would be less than i (and the net wealth of the banking system would not vanish). Commercial banks would not hold perfectly illiquid pure debt, but rather assets that were somewhat liquid (including some working vault cash). This clearly indicates that monetary services are costly to produce. The net receipts, R, to the commercial bank, or the difference between what it receives on its assets and what it pays on its real deposit liabilities, can be represented by

$$R = [(i - r_D) - (i - r_A)](D/P) = (r_A - r_D)(D/P) \tag{3}$$

where $(i - r_D)$ can be considered as the price of the bank deposits (and the value of the marginal monetary services from the deposits) and $(i - r_A)$ considered as the alternative cost to the bank of holding assets that are somewhat liquid. The difference between i and r_A reflects explicit bank operating costs and more implicit confidence costs.

Thomas Wilson's [13, pp. 54-57] measurement of the seigniorage collected by government, which is obtained by multiplying the outstanding high-powered money stock by the average rate of return on Treasury and Federal Reserve securities, is therefore low. Since Treasury securities certainly yield a liquidity return to their holders, the bench-mark interest rate used to make the calculation is arbitrary and biased downward. Alternatively, one could say that because Treasury securities yield some monetary services on the margin they should also be considered partially "money" in this sense and their marginal liquidity return included in the seigniorage calculation.* That is, the government pays a rate of interest less than i when it sells its bonds and this gap represents a "return" to the government based in part upon its coercion capital, that is, its ability to tax, and its monetary confidence capital. The market transaction that takes place when the government sells its bonds merely makes this real capital or wealth visible.

But once again it should be emphasized that this is a gross seigniorage return, as government confidence in the financial markets is costly, in regard to both alternative cost and direct outlay. Even General Motors, for example, when it sells a bond does not have to pay a rate of interest on its bonds, r_B, equal to i. Its bonds yield liquidity services on the margin that must be costly to produce because GM is demanding and receiving a positive price, that is, $(i - r_B) > 0$, in the absence of any coercion or government restrictions. To be consistent, therefore, one would have to include a percentage of GM bonds (in a stationary state $[i - r_B]/\rho$ would be the percentage) as part of the net wealth possessed by GM and included in aggregate social wealth. The GM bond is not "pure debt," but a market indication of the brand-name capital that produces this monetary service stream.

---

*Note that government bonds are considered "money" here solely as a source of monetary services and therefore a form of wealth, without implying anything about their inclusion, for example, in the proper (predictive) definition of money for macroeconomic purposes.

The capital can be considered as the market value of GM's credit rating and is fully reflected in the firm's stock market value. Therefore, a bond market transaction is not necessary to make the intangible wealth visible, as in the case of government bonds, and any explicit inclusion of GM bonds in social wealth calculations that include equity values would entail double counting. Most important to remember, this brand-name asset is costly to produce and maintain. Therefore, although gross seigniorage is in some sense much larger than previously considered, net seigniorage, or a pure monopoly profit, is much smaller or possibly nonexistent. Surely GM does not possess a government "grant" to collect payment for monetary services supplied.

NOTES

1. It is unclear whether there is a systematic differential "grant" among banking institutions. The Federal Reserve, for example, appears to discriminate in favor of small banks by requiring lower reserve ratios. The evidence indicates, however, that large commercial banks are more likely to be members of the Federal Reserve System and therefore must be receiving larger benefits or "subsidies" from Federal Reserve membership. See Klein [10].

2. The real demand for an individual perfectly competitive firm's money output is assumed to be a positive function of the consumer confidence in the money, measured by the degree of future price predictability in terms of the money. See Klein [8]. The empirical time series evidence for the monopolistic domestic U.S. market indicates, however, that price variability enters the demand for money positively (see Klein [9]), while a significant amount of switching between national currencies (and gold) may now exist in the more competitive international money market.

3. The designation "legal tender" means that creditors cannot legally refuse the money as payment for a claim, that is, they cannot use the courts and police to force discharge of a contract in an alternative money. However, there is much evidence that relatively informal legally unenforceable contractual practices predominate in business and that reliance on explicit legal sanctions is extremely rare. See Klein [8 p. 448] for further discussion and references to the historical evidence on the existence of nonlegal tender circulating monies.

4. See, for example, Friedman [1].

5. Johnson [6]; see also Johnson [5].

6. This concern is, of course, contrary to much current economic thinking and is explicitly opposed to the original "benign neglect" policy statement of Haberler and Willet [4].

7. Gurley and Shaw [3] originally made the distinction between demand deposits, or money created "inside" the economic system, and currency, or money created "outside" the economic system. They asserted that, as "inside" money represented matching assets and liabilities, there was no corresponding net wealth, while "outside" money represented an asset of the holders without any liability of the government issuer. Johnson, along with Pesek and Saving [12], recognized that as long as interest on demand deposits was zero, the deposits also represented net wealth of the commercial bank stockholders. Equation (2) similarly indicates that demand deposits would be pure wealth or fully brand name backed if real interest payments on the deposits were zero.

8. See, for example, Pesek and Saving [12] for an important T-account analysis of the banking industry that ignores the brand-name capital asset. Also, much of the T-account analysis of trade credit as money (see, for example, Laffer [11]) makes this fundamental error of ignoring brand-name capital and assuming that lines of credit can be costlessly created out of thin air.

REFERENCES

[1] Milton Friedman. "The Optimum Quantity of Money." In The Optimum Quantity of Money and Other Essays, pp. 1-50. Chicago: Aldine, 1969.

[2] Herbert G. Grubel. "The Distribution of Seigniorage from International Liquidity Creation." In Monetary Problems of the International Economy, edited by R. A. Mundell and A. K. Swoboda, pp. 269-82. Chicago: University of Chicago Press, 1969.

[3] John G. Gurley and Edward S. Shaw. Money in a Theory of Finance. Washington, D.C.: Brookings Institution, 1960.

[4] Gottfried Haberler and Thomas D. Willet. "A Strategy for U.S. Balance of Payments Policy." Washington, D.C.: American Enterprise Institute Special Analysis, 1971.

[5] Harry G. Johnson. "Inside Money, Outside Money, Income, Wealth, and Welfare in Monetary Theory." Journal of Money, Credit and Banking 1 (February 1969):30-45.

[6] _____. "A Note on Seigniorage and the Social Saving from Substituting Credit for Commodity Money." In Monetary Problems of the International Economy, edited by R. A. Mundell and

A. K. Swoboda, pp. 323-29. Chicago: University of Chicago Press, 1969.

[7] Benjamin Klein. "Competitive Interest Payments on Bank Deposits and the Long-Run Demand for Money." American Economic Review 64, no. 5 (December 1974):931-49.

[8] _____. "The Competitive Supply of Money." Journal of Money, Credit and Banking 6, no. 4 (November 1974):423-53.

[9] _____. "The Demand for Quality-Adjusted Cash Balances: Price Uncertainty in the U.S. Demand for Money Function." Journal of Political Economy 85, no. 4 (August 1977): 691-716.

[10] _____. "Determinants of Membership in the Federal Reserve System," unpublished manuscript, 1976.

[11] Arthur B. Laffer. "Trade Credit and the Money Market." Journal of Political Economy 78, no. 2 (April 1970): 239-67.

[12] Boris P. Pesek and Thomas R. Saving. Money, Wealth and Economic Theory. New York: Macmillan, 1967.

[13] Thomas F. Wilson. "Identification and Measurement of Grant Elements in Monetary Policy," Chapter 3, this volume.

[14] Leland B. Yeager. "Review of Remaking the International Monetary System: The Rio Agreement and Beyond by Fritz Machlup." Journal of Economic Literature 7, no. 4 (December 1969): 1211-13.

2

Seigniorage and the "Inflation Tax" in an International Setting

HARRY G. JOHNSON

INTRODUCTION

The role that particular national currencies have played in the system of international monetary organization—specifically, the pound sterling in the heyday of the "classical" gold standard and the U.S. dollar in the period since World War II, at least until the collapse of the International Monetary Fund system and to an important degree since—has given perennial interest to the question of what economic benefits, if any, a country derives from its currency playing a dominant monetary role. The extreme view is represented, of course, by radical writers in the general Marxian tradition, who ascribe the enjoyment of vast but vaguely specified economic advantages to the international reserve currency function, describing it in such terms as "dollar diplomacy" or "dollar imperialism" (and similar terms applied earlier, or historically, to sterling). More scholarly and scientific analysis of the economic role of a reserve currency, which it is the purpose of this chapter to summarize, suggests that there may be some gains for the reserve currency country, but these gains are likely to be quantitatively relatively small and offset by losses in other directions that may yield a net gain or a net loss.

The elements giving rise to losses primarily concern restrictions on a country's freedom of domestic and international economic policy, resulting from its growing dependence on the confidence of foreign private and official holders of its currency. For this reason, it can be argued, with the support of the historical experience of both Britain and the United States, that the balance of gain comes during the initial phases of the establishment of a country's currency as an international reserve currency, and that the balance fairly soon swings toward progressively larger net losses. It would appear, therefore, contrary to the "radical" argument, that in the longer run historical perspective the role of national provider of an international reserve currency is not a source of economic strength and dominance, but a reflection of existing strength that presages the decay of previously established dominance.

Leaving these large issues to one side, this chapter concerns itself with the narrower and more technical issue of the economic gains that a reserve currency role for its currency may confer upon a country. These gains frequently have been described, by natural analogy with long preindustrial society experience with the sovereign prerogative of minting precious metals into coin, as "the gains from seigniorage." The concept of the gains from seigniorage, however, presupposes a stable and near-stationary economic system, and specifically one in which the level of prices is approximately constant (or changes so slowly that the economic implications of its trend are negligible). This assumption was still roughly appropriate to consideration of "the U.S. dollar standard" as it developed until the mid-1960s. But in the past decade, and especially in the early 1970s, the development of "world inflation" has shifted the attention of international monetary officials, experts, and academic economists from the problem of seigniorage (the profit from a type of monopoly in the issue of money) to the problem of the ability of the country issuing the international reserve money to cause or contribute to world inflation by overissuing it, and in so doing to derive economic benefits for itself at the expense of other countries by imposing an "inflation tax" on them as well as on itself.

Subsequent sections of this chapter deal with "seigniorage" and "the inflation tax" in the context of the international monetary system. The analysis, it sould be emphasized, is mainly concerned with the economics of the fixed exchange rate system that existed until February 1973, though some remarks will be made concerning the system of "managed" floating of exchange rates that currently prevails.

THE THEORY OF SEIGNIORAGE AND THE SOCIAL SAVING FROM REPLACING COMMODITY BY CREDIT MONEY[1]

The original meaning of seigniorage, the difference between the circulating value of a coin and the cost of the bullion and minting, involves a once for all gain to the issuer on the issue of money. Owing to the durability of the precious metals, especially gold, one can reasonably assume that this gain is realized only once per unit of money in existence, though, presumably, worn, clipped, or sweated coins would come back eventually for melting down and reissue. If one wished to take account of that, one would regard the money supply as yielding a flow of seigniorage $(v - c)_1$, $(v - c)_2$, . . . , $(v - c)_\infty$, which could in turn be summed into a capital value of the right to issue money:

$$\sum_{t=0}^{\infty} \frac{v - c}{(1 + i)^t} = (v - c)\,\frac{1 + i}{i}$$

where v is circulating value, c cost, and i the interest rate ruling over the period between recoinages. This expression differs from the usual formula for the capitalized value of an income flow because the first yield accrues immediately.

Seigniorage can be levied, presumably, because the public is prepared to pay a premium for the convenience of having coins of uniform size and certified as to weight and fineness of metal, greater than the cost of minting precious metal into such coins, and because the state can impose a monopoly of minting and thereby extract the difference. By taxing the conversion of metal into coins, the state discourages the use of coins in payment as contrasted with the barter of precious metal for goods, and thereby imposes a welfare loss on the community. On the other hand, to the extent that the circulating value of coins is above their real resource cost, the levy of seigniorage reduces the real resources required to be invested in creating any given money supply, and so gives rise to a social saving. A full analysis of the welfare effects of seigniorage in a commodity money system, however, would require an analysis of its effects on the supply of precious metals, which does not seem worthwhile pursuing here, if only because any social saving is likely to be negligible.

Now consider the replacement of a commodity money—the issue of which is assumed for simplicity not to be subject to seigniorage—by a purely paper money, assumed to be non-interest-bearing, and to cost nothing to print. The replacement frees the resources embodied in the stock of commodity money for other more productive uses and yields a social saving equal to the value of these resources. This social saving accrues to the monetary authority, which is able (by assumption) to persuade (or force) the public to surrender the commodity in exchange for paper. The monetary authority can then invest the resources formerly embodied in the money stock in productive assets. The "seigniorage" resulting from the operation can be thought of either as a capital sum—the real value of the money supply —or as a flow of income to the monetary authority equal to the real value of the money supply multiplied by the average rate of return on whatever assets the paper money (more accurately, the fund of resources released by the substitution of paper for commodity money) has been invested in. (These may be government debt, in the case of a central bank, or public goods of some sort, if the government is assumed to appropriate the seigniorage.)

Now, retaining the assumption that money is non-interest-bearing and costless to issue, assume that the economy is growing and that additional money is issued at a rate sufficient to keep the price level stable. The issue of this money entails a social saving by comparison with what would occur under a commodity money system, where real resources would have to be devoted to producing the additional money. If for simplicity the commodity money system is assumed to be able to produce the monetary metal at constant cost, the social saving referred to is equal to the real value of the additional money issued. If, more realistically, the monetary metal is assumed to be a depletable resource, the marginal real cost of extraction of which rises as more is extracted, the price level in the commodity money system would have to fall over time, so that some part of the increase in the money supply would be provided costlessly through appreciation of the existing stock, and the social saving from the issue of additional money instead of the production of additional commodity money would be less than the real value of the increase in the paper money stock. In the extreme case of inability to produce additional commodity money, the additional real balances demanded as a result of economic growth would be provided by a fall in the price level, at zero social cost. This result would also occur in a paper money system in which the money supply was held constant. (Obviously there is no difference between a paper and a commodity money system if the money supply [in nominal terms] is constant.) But social welfare will be higher in a paper money system with a fixed money supply than in one in which the money supply is expanded to keep the price level constant, because in the former system the falling trend of prices provides a yield to the holders of real balances and encourages a greater use of money, which greater use increases welfare at no social cost. (This proposition is subject to the qualification that if prices fall at a percentage rate greater than the rate of return on real assets, the public will want to hold money rather than real assets and the system is likely to break down.)

The issue of additional paper money at a rate sufficient to keep the price level constant yields seigniorage to the monetary authority equal to the real value of the quantity of money multiplied by its rate of growth. It follows from the previous paragraph that this seigniorage will be equal to the social saving implicit in the use of credit money rather than commodity money, if the marginal real cost of production of the monetary commodity is constant, and otherwise will exceed that social saving, which may be zero. Furthermore, by comparison with a paper money system in which the quantity of money is fixed (and subject to the qualification mentioned at the end of the previous paragraph), the levying of seigniorage by a monetary policy of maintaining stable prices involves a social loss, resulting from the restriction of the use of money as a consequence of its zero yield.

In other words, the maintenance of a stable price level imposes an "inflation tax" on holders of money, by comparison with a policy of keeping the money supply constant and allowing prices to fall over time (subject again to the aforementioned qualification).

Putting together the two concepts of seigniorage as the gain from the replacement of commodity by paper money, neither of which bears interest, and the gain to the monetary authority from issuing the additional paper money required to keep the price level stable while growth goes on, total seigniorage at any point of time is the sum of (1) the real growth of the money supply and (2) the yield on the investment of the resources freed by the past substitution of the existing paper money supply for commodity money. That is, seigniorage received by the monetary authority and available for distribution is $(i + g)M$, where i is the interest rate available on assets and g is the growth rate of demand for money at a stable price level, both defined for an appropriate time unit, and M is the existing money supply (indifferently measurable in nominal or real terms).

Now suppose that there are real costs incurred in maintaining the stock of money. In the case of currency, the notes have a production cost that includes the cost of the fine paper and intricate printing necessary to forestall forgery and the cost of maintaining security; in addition, the notes wear out and have to be replaced. In the case of deposit money there are bookkeeping costs. Let these costs be at the rate c per unit of money per period of the previous analysis. Then the seigniorage on the existing stock of money becomes $(i - c)M$. As for the seigniorage on the issue of new money, such issue involves assuming the obligation of the cost stream c, the present value of which will be c/i. Hence the net seigniorage of this kind will be, not gM, but $[(i - c)/i]gM$. The formula for total seigniorage is therefore

$$\left[(i - c) + \frac{(i - c)}{i} g\right]M = (i - c)\frac{(i + g)}{i} M = \frac{(i - c)}{i}(i + g)M.$$

This formula also represents the social gain from the substitution of paper money for commodity money when the paper money is expanded so as to maintain a stable price level and when in the commodity money system the real cost of production of the commodity money is constant so that the price level would be stable in that system also.

The foregoing formula applies at a moment of time and adds together an income flow from the existing money stock and a capital gain for the monetary authority accruing from the expansion of the stock; it therefore assumes implicitly that the capital gain on past increases of the money supply has been invested by the monetary authority at the ruling rate of interest. The flow of income from seigniorage available to the monetary authority for current utilization may be one or the other of these two elements of income, but cannot be the sum of the two. That is, by always investing the capital gain the monetary authority can secure an income stream $(i - c)M_t$, where M_t is the stock of money at time t; alternatively, by always consuming the capital gain the monetary authority can secure an income stream $(i - c)M_0 + \{[(i - c)/i]gM_t\}$, where M_0 is the money stock existent at the time the policy of consuming capital gains commenced and will be zero if that policy has always been followed.

In the preceding formulas, c has been defined as a real cost stream associated with the operation of a unit of the money supply. Alternatively, c may be conceived as an interest charge paid to the holders of money to induce them to hold it. Such a charge represents not a social cost, but a transfer of seigniorage (and of social benefit from a paper money as compared with a constant-cost commodity money system) from the monetary authority to the holders of money. If the provision of money were competitive, as, for example, it would be in an unregulated deposit-banking system, c would be equal to i and there would be no seigniorage and no income flow for the monetary authorities either from earnings on the stock of money or from capital gains. Such a system would obviously require some means of limiting the rate of increase of the money supply to what would be consistent with a stable price level; alternatively, the monetary authority might deliberately forego seigniorage and pay interest on money equal to what it earned on the assets backing the money supply. The payment of interest on money would eliminate the social loss due to the restriction of the use of money by the extraction of seigniorage.

SEIGNIORAGE, THE RESERVE CURRENCY ROLE, AND AN ARTIFICIAL INTERNATIONAL ASSET

The concept of seigniorage, applied superficially to the area of international monetary organization and reform, suggests, first, that a country whose currency functions as an international reserve currency derives very large seigniorage gains as a result; and that in consequence there are large gains to be made by the rest of the world through the substitution of an internationally designed and controlled artificial credit asset for the national currency in its function as an international reserve money. A particular manifestation of this last proposition is the view, which has been to some extent accepted and implemented in international monetary arrangements, that any creation of new international reserve assets should be accompanied by distribution of all, or a large part, of the new assets to the "developing" countries as a form of aid—the aid coming through the "earning back" of the reserve assets by the developed countries through the development of export surpluses with the developing country recipients (that is, through developing country import surpluses paid for by spending their receipts of the newly created international money).

The belief that the reserve currency function yields substantial seigniorage profits is, however, largely an illusion or an error of analysis—a mistake for which, however, considerable blame is attributable to the conventional practice of monetary theory of assuming that money necessarily, or legally effectively, bears no interest. This is the assumption of the pure theory of seigniorage outlined in the previous section. It is true enough that coins bear no interest, nor do paper notes, nor do commercial bank reserves held as deposits at the central bank, so that the central bank (and in the last resort the government, which normally receives any excess profit earned by the central bank) receives seigniorage on these constituents of the domestic money supply (or, in the case of commercial bank reserves, the part of the deposit money used by the public that is backed by reserves of central bank notes and deposits). But when a national currency is held as an international monetary asset, it is only to a negligible extent held in the form of coins, notes, or non-interest-bearing liabilities of the central bank or government of the nation in question.

Foreign holdings of such assets may be divided into official reserve holdings and private commercial holdings. The official holdings are normally invested in the country's public debt, typically Treasury bills and other short-term debt, with a certain amount held as working balances in commercial banks. The seigniorage earned on the first form of official holdings is limited to the amount of any premium for liquidity that lowers the yield on public debt by comparison with private debt in the reserve currency country, or on that country's debt as compared with other countries' public (or possibly marketable private) debt. The seigniorage earned on the second form of official holdings—and also on the part of private commercial holdings that is invested in commercial bank deposits—is measured by the reduction in yield on such assets that is attributable to the nonpayment of interest on commercial bank reserves of notes and deposits at the central bank, together with any other restrictions on commercial banking operations that may be imposed by law and regulation. Both the official and the private foreign holders of assets in the reserve currency have the alternative, if the yields are sufficiently depressed by the collection of seigniorage, of resorting to holding the liabilities of near-banks or of investing directly in market financial assets; and these alternatives limit the amount of seigniorage that the reserve currency country can extract from its reserve currency position (and incidentally make seigniorage gains extremely difficult to quantify).

Nor is this the only limit, or even the most important one. The growth of the Eurodollar and other Eurocurrency markets has meant the provision of close substitutes for dollars, provided competitively and without control being exercised or exercisable by the Federal Reserve as the central bank of the United States and the U.S. government as regulator of the American banking system. (Indeed, the growth of the Eurodollar market was in large part the consequence of efforts by the U.S. monetary authorities to depress the yields on U.S. financial assets—bank deposits, and U.S. public debt—which stimulated both U.S. banking affiliates abroad and European, Canadian, and Japanese banks to provide more attractive assets denominated in U.S. dollars but not issued or regulated by U.S. official institutions.) With substitutes for dollars provided competitively by banks outside the United States, there may, of course, still be some vestiges of seigniorage, to the extent that only a limited number of large banks have the resources and ability to compete; but any such seigniorage profits accrue to the banks in question, and not to the U.S. government.

This being so, it follows that there is not a large pool of seigniorage profit available to be tapped by the creation and growth of a new international monetary asset and redistributable as aid for economic development of the developing countries. Of course, it would be possible by sufficiently determined international agreement to enforce creation and use of a new international money that was non-interest-bearing, or bore interest at a rate below the yield on comparable competitive monetary assets, and to direct the seigniorage profit toward the developing countries, either by giving them first proprietorship of the new assets or by allocating to them the seigniorage profit collected (directly or through the intermediation of the multilateral international aid agencies). But two important qualifications to this proposition must be noted. First, to the extent that the new reserve asset is designed to extract seigniorage, it must be less attractive to hold than the privately, competitively provided substitutes available, the Eurodollar and other Eurocurrencies and the U.S. dollar itself. Second, to the extent that the purpose in instituting the new international reserve money is to redistribute seigniorage away from advanced toward developing countries, its issue involves a tax transfer from the former toward the latter, a feature likely to motivate the former to restrict the amount issued and the rate of growth of the issue.

In this connection, it should be remarked that the special drawing rights (SDRs) at the International Monetary Fund, which are based on the recognition that an international reserve asset does not require "backing" in the form of marketable interest-bearing investment assets, but only acceptance of the reserve money in settlement of international payments balances, subject to an obligation to earn the money back again by reversing the initial payments imbalance, would, providing that countries on balance maintained average holdings of SDRs equal to the amounts they were initially issued, automatically restore to each country the amount of seigniorage it paid. Any social inefficiency that might result would be associated with the ability of some countries to incur, and the obligation of other countries to make, loans at interest rates below competitive market rates. Any agreement requiring that advanced countries initially gave away SDRs that they were obliged later to earn back by export surpluses would, however, involve a tax transfer arrangement in no way required by the provision of international reserve assets in itself.

THE THEORY OF THE INFLATION TAX

As is well known from recent work on the theory of inflation, any economic analysis of the phenomenon involves a preliminary distinction between "unanticipated" and "anticipated" inflation. An "unanticipated" inflation, such as occurs typically during or after a major war (for reasons unnecessary to discuss here), transfers wealth from the owners of wealth whose capital value and interest payments are specified in nominal terms (the interest rates having been set in a preceding period of price stability or of a significantly lower rate of inflation) to debtors whose obligations are fixed in nominal terms (including "the government" or "the taxpayers" as indirect debtors). It also transfers income from income earners whose incomes are fixed in money terms and alterable only with a significant lag to those whose incomes are adjusted quickly to inflation, until inflation becomes well enough anticipated for contracts to be adjusted to the expectation of inflation. In the meantime, there are windfall gains and losses (transfers) of income and wealth. But there are by definition no social losses, in the sense of creation and response to incentives to behave differently in order to avoid the losses, or take advantage of the gains, from expected inflation. (There may, of course, be social losses in a somewhat different and nonoperational sense, to the extent that the observer regards some of the gainers or losers as especially socially meritorious or deserving of punishment.)

Once inflation becomes "anticipated," however (more accurately, "correctly anticipated"), the windfall transfers in principle disappear, as economic contractors revise money contracts so as to compensate for the expected effects of inflation. In particular, money rates of interest will be adjusted upward so that the "real" rate of return (the nominal or "money" rate of interest <u>minus</u> the expected rate of inflation) will be comparable to the real rate of return on nonmonetary assets (alternatively, the money rate of interest must be comparable to the rate of return on real investment in real terms, plus the rate of increase of the price level). The only adjustment that cannot be made by the public through revision of contracts is avoidance of the loss of real value of money itself (assumed to be non-interest-bearing) through inflation. In order to keep the real value of its money balances intact, the money-holding public must add continually to its nominal money balances, in the process foregoing current consumption, the current output foregone being purchased instead with the expansion of the supply of nominal money.

Expected inflation therefore constitutes a tax on the holding of real balances, a tax paid by the holders of money to the issuers of money in the form of surrender of command over real resources. And, like any other tax, this tax will induce the public to economize on the use of the taxed commodity by resorting to substitutes whose cost gross of tax is lower but whose cost net of tax is higher. The resort to higher (social) cost substitutes involves economic inefficiency and a reduction of economic welfare below maximum potential —what is, somewhat misleadingly, described technically as the "collection cost" of the tax. Further, because the higher the inflation tax is, the lower the amount of real balances that can be taxed and the larger the marginal and total waste involved in the "collection cost," there must normally be a maximum yield collectable by means of the inflation tax. (The exception requires that the demand for real balances be of less than unit elasticity with respect to the rate of inflation, regardless of the level of the inflation rate—a condition that is extremely implausible.)

The theory of "the inflation tax" under conditions of expected inflation is usually developed to illustrate the existence of a maximum revenue inflation tax, and the probability of the collection cost being high in relation to the amount of tax collected.[2] Such an exposition simplifies the problem by assuming that the government appears only as a recipient of the tax proceeds, and the public as paying both the tax and the collection cost (the difference constituting the "social cost" of inflation). But, for some purposes, including the present one of application to the international monetary system, it is more useful to assume that the monetary authority responsible for the inflation both pays to itself part of the proceeds of the inflation tax and bears part of the collection cost through adjusting its behavior in order to economize on the use of real balances.[3]

The analysis is illustrated in Figure 2.1, where Π is the expected (and actual) rate of inflation (fixed by an appropriate rate of monetary expansion); B is the quantity of real balances demanded; and $D_hD'_h$ is the domestic, $D_fD'_f$ the foreign, and $D_{f+h}D'_{f+h}$ the total demand for real balances as a function of the inflation rate (for simplicity, growth is ignored and therefore is seigniorage collectable by

FIGURE 2.1

The Rate of Inflation and the Domestic and Foreign Demand for Real Balances

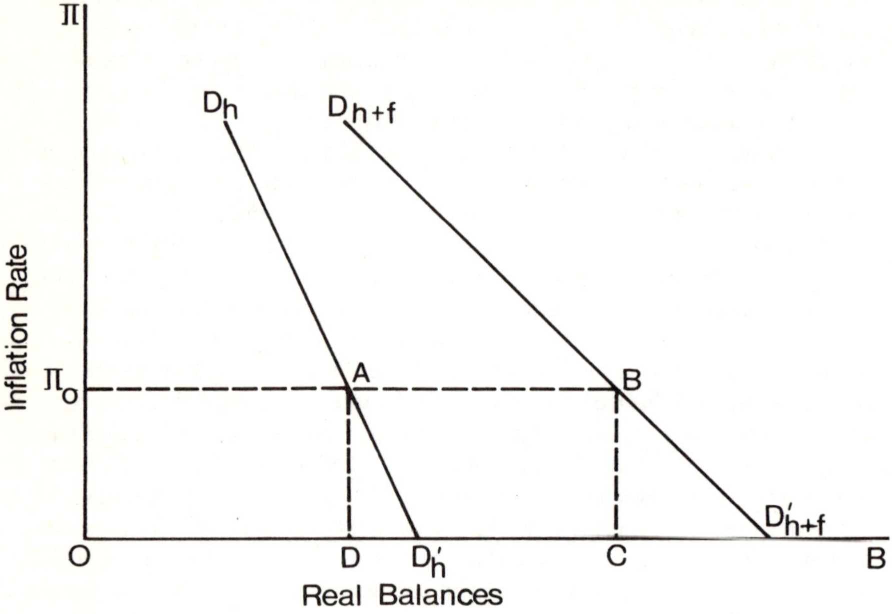

Source: Compiled by the author.

the maintenance of price stability). "Domestic" and "foreign" can be interpreted to mean included in and excluded from the purview of government concern. In the usual analysis, with inflation at the rate Π_0, the proceeds of the inflation tax are $0\Pi_0BC$, and the collection cost BCD'_{f+h}, the government's problem being to maximize the tax collection by choosing Π such that the elasticity of $D_{h+f}D'_{h+f}$ is unity (with a straight-line demand curve, the relevant level of Π corresponds to the point on $D_{h+f}D'_{h+f}$ vertically above the midway point between 0 and D'_{h+f}).

In the present analysis, inflation at the rate Π_0 yields a gross tax revenue from the foreigners of ABCD and a net revenue (after deduction of domestic collection cost) of ABCD'. It is obvious from general considerations that deduction of the domestic collection cost from the tax revenue tends to lower the maximum yield rate of inflation, whereas inclusion of the tax revenue derived from the foreigners only will tend to lower or raise the maximum gain rate of inflation, depending on whether the foreign demand for real balances is less or more elastic than the domestic demand. Algebraically, the domestic revenue from the inflation tax will be maximized when

$$\eta_f = 1 - \frac{b_h}{b_f} \eta_h$$

where η_f and η_h are the inflation rate elasticities of foreign and domestic demand for real balances and b_h and b_f are the domestic and foreign quantities of real balances demanded (at the maximum net yield inflation rate).

THE INFLATION TAX AND THE RESERVE CURRENCY ROLE

The foregoing analysis, applied fairly literally to the analysis of an international monetary system dominated by a national currency that serves as an international reserve asset, suggests strongly that maximization of the net domestic revenue from world inflation initiated by the reserve currency country and transmitted through the fixed exchange rate system, and even the receipt of a positive net revenue, requires a low and possibly negligible rate of inflation, if that inflation is assumed to be of the expected inflation variety. The reasons are that b_f is likely to be very small by comparison with b_h, if both are interpreted as that part of the money balance holding that yields effectively no interest to the holder, and that the elasticity of foreign demand for such real balances with respect to the inflation rate is likely to become high fairly quickly as the inflation tax exceeds the nonnegligible level. The same general conclusion could be reached by accounting explicitly for those elements of the costs of attracting foreign holdings of money and near-money balances, such as interest rates on foreign deposits and domestic market rates of interest generally, that are likely to rise automatically to compensate for expected inflation.

It follows that the gains available to a reserve currency country through inflation are most likely to be of the unexpected inflation windfall gain variety. Further, while such gains may be significant in the short run and in the first experience of inflationary policy following a normally expected policy of maintenance of approximate price stability, they are likely to become dwarfed in time by the manifold uncertainties generated by the experience of unexpected inflation and the costs (including abnormal unemployment rates) of restoring a reasonable degree of confidence in the stability of monetary policy and of macroeconomic policy generally. (Note that restoration of confidence in the stability of policy is not the same thing as the restoration of confidence in the stability of prices, as policy stability could entail agreement on a range or band within which the rate of inflation would be confined.) In short, exploitation of the power of imposing international transfers in favor of the reserve currency country through resort to unexpected inflation is likely in the long run to entail a net loss rather than a net gain to the country concerned.

In actual current historical fact, the resort of the United States during the escalation of the war in Vietnam to inflationary public financing had the effect of precipitating the collapse of the fixed exchange rate system and its replacement by the present regime of "managed" floating of exchange rates. The floating, however, has not been universal; while some major countries have taken advantage of the opportunity to reduce the influence of the dollar and of U.S. monetary policy in their internal monetary affairs, others closely linked to the United States by trade and investment ties (notably Canada and Japan) have kept the international values of their currencies closely in line with the dollar. In these cases, the payment of any transfers to the United States can scarcely be described as "involuntary" or analyzed in terms of "seigniorage" or "the inflation tax"; and in any case, for reasons presented earlier, the amounts of transfer involved are likely to have been of negligible quantitative importance.

APPENDIX

The argument of this chapter has dealt with seigniorage, the inflation tax, and related problems in general qualitative terms. This appendix is a first rough attempt to quantify the "inflation tax" received by the United States through world inflation with the continuing (and expanding) use of the dollar as an international reserve money; the data have been collected and computed by my research collaborator Clark Nardinelli of the University of Chicago.

Table 2.A.1, as a preliminary, presents the growth of U.S. foreign liabilities from the end of 1964 to mid-1976. The most interesting aspect of the table is the fact that, while liabilities in nominal dollars increased by 222 percent over the period, in real terms the liabilities increased by only 76 percent—a distinction frequently neglected in popular discussions of the "problem" of the rapid growth of foreign holdings of U.S. dollars.

Tables 2.A.2 and 2.A.3 estimate the real gains or losses to foreign holders of dollars, on the basis of comparison, first, with maintenance of real purchasing power and, second, with a notional

TABLE 2.A.1

Nominal and Real Foreign Liabilities, Quarterly
(millions of 1967 dollars)

Year	March		June		September		December	
	Nominal	Real	Nominal	Real	Nominal	Real	Nominal	Real
1964	—	—	—	—	—	—	28,873	30,847
1965	28,263	30,067	27,264	29,203	28,763	30,309	29,013	30,412
1966	28,865	29,850	29,170	29,949	30,469	30,932	27,010	27,394
1967	26,303	26,542	26,844	26,790	28,436	28,154	30,290	29,696
1968	29,758	28,863	29,866	28,580	30,784	29,124	29,598	27,739
1969	31,061	28,575	35,119	31,868	38,812	34,778	38,322	33,823
1970	39,470	34,262	39,992	34,269	41,100	34,801	40,173	33,702
1971	41,827	34,798	44,465	36,507	50,765	41,475	53,270	43,239
1972	55,746	44,848	55,631	44,327	56,976	45,005	58,812	46,055
1973	63,917	48,904	64,504	48,608	64,843	47,469	66,470	47,581
1974	70,873	49,252	78,302	52,907	84,852	55,459	90,823	58,183
1975	88,829	56,008	88,075	54,267	87,044	52,882	88,194	52,906
1976	89,709	53,335	93,149	54,441	—	—	—	—

Note: The figures are for the end of the month. The nominal data are from the Federal Reserve Bulletin. The real totals are computed using the consumer price index to convert current dollars into 1967 dollars. Because of continual revisions in the data, the series is not as consistent as it should be. The main difficulty for purposes of this study is that the 1964-66 figures are too high.

Source: Compiled by the author.

TABLE 2.A.2

Real Gains or Losses on Foreign Dollar Holdings
(in millions of 1967 dollars)

	1965	1966	1967	1968	1969	1970	1971	1972	1973	1974	1975	1976
January	69.7	116.1	107.7	22.0	51.5	100.6	96.6	85.8	61.8	-104.3	41.7	86.9
February	100.5	-46.4	78.8	24.0	30.5	21.0	47.6	-95.4	-107.6	-318.7	-140.7	88.2
March	72.7	7.0	47.7	4.0	-96.0	9.5	-17.6	67.7	-204.3	-219.3	42.0	96.4
April	23.3	-19.7	16.4	33.0	-40.2	-22.8	-4.3	29.9	-83.1	66.9	-22.9	-6.2
May	14.5	38.3	11.2	40.3	64.9	46.8	-56.6	-8.0	-37.6	-211.9	-3.3	-89.7
June	-40.9	32.7	-15.0	-11.7	-32.6	13.4	-74.4	36.4	-41.1	-156.0	-206.3	-47.5
July	66.4	12.0	-22.3	-22.2	39.3	67.1	72.7	-30.3	215.1	-63.9	-297.1	-84.8
August	147.6	-9.0	3.6	28.4	42.9	122.9	58.0	78.1	-529.1	-290.9	123.5	—
September	41.9	56.3	53.9	53.7	75.7	-2.3	125.9	-5.3	188.4	-292.7	23.6	—
October	46.0	29.1	10.6	-37.6	78.0	-5.8	85.0	35.3	-98.1	-131.3	-59.1	—
November	47.9	114.4	39.5	13.5	21.6	34.2	78.3	75.8	38.7	-126.4	-79.4	—
December	1.8	106.2	21.9	78.2	9.1	-35.7	-31.2	48.7	-13.9	-68.4	15.4	—
Annual total	591.4	437.0	354.0	225.6	244.7	348.9	380.0	318.7	-610.8	-1,916.9	-562.6	43.3

Note: This is an attempt to compute gains and losses to foreigners holding short-term dollar liabilities. The rate of gain was computed as the market rate on U.S. Treasury three-month bills (*Federal Reserve Bulletin* was the source) minus the rate of inflation (measured as the percentage change in the consumer price index). The rate of gain was applied to real liabilities held at the beginning of the month. The data listed holdings at the end of the month, so the calculations were made using Treasury bill rate minus inflation rate for the month after the figure used for real liabilities. Thus, the entry in the table for March 1970 is the Treasury bill minus the inflation rate for that month multiplied by real foreign dollar holdings for the end of February 1970. Incidentally, all figures were divided by 12 because inflation and Treasury bill rates are given in annual terms and the calculation relates to monthly gains and losses. Algebraically, the entries in Table 2.A.2 are as follows:

$$\frac{(F\$)_{t-1}}{P_t/P_{1967}} \cdot \frac{\left[r_t - \left[\mathring{P}/P\right]_t\right.}{12} = X_t$$

where F\$ = foreign nominal dollar holdings in month t - 1, P_t = consumer price index in month t, $P_{1967} = 100$, r_t = market rate on Treasury bills in month t, $(\mathring{P}/P)_t$ = percentage change in consumer price index in month t, and X_t = gains or losses from holding dollars in month t.

Source: Compiled by the author.

TABLE 2.A.3

Real Gains or Losses on Foreign Dollar Holdings by Comparison with 2 Percent Annual Real Gain
(in millions of 1967 dollars)

	1965	1966	1967	1968	1969	1970	1971	1972	1973	1974	1975	1976
January	18.3	65.4	62.1	-27.5	5.3	44.3	40.4	13.7	-15.0	-183.6	-55.3	-1.3
February	49.3	-96.6	34.5	-25.5	-15.7	-36.5	-8.7	-168.2	-181.8	-394.7	-234.5	-0.9
March	21.3	-42.8	3.5	-45.7	-142.9	-47.9	-74.3	-6.7	-284.3	-297.1	-52.4	4.6
April	-26.8	-69.4	-27.9	-15.2	-87.9	-79.9	-62.3	-44.8	-164.6	-15.2	-116.2	-95.1
May	-34.7	-11.8	-33.5	-8.5	17.4	-10.6	-117.1	-80.9	-117.7	-295.5	-97.2	-184.1
June	-89.1	-17.6	-59.9	-60.5	-83.9	-43.7	-140.3	-35.7	-122.3	-242.6	-298.9	-143.4
July	17.8	-37.9	-67.0	-64.1	-13.8	10.0	11.9	-104.2	134.1	-152.1	-387.6	-175.6
August	98.7	-60.4	-41.6	-19.7	-11.7	65.9	-2.1	4.4	-610.3	-381.3	33.3	—
September	-7.0	4.2	7.4	4.9	19.2	-59.6	57.7	-80.7	108.0	-385.0	-67.2	—
October	-4.5	-22.4	-36.4	-86.2	20.0	-63.8	15.9	-39.8	-177.2	-223.7	-147.2	—
November	-3.1	61.3	-9.3	-35.6	-36.8	-23.7	7.8	-0.8	-41.1	-218.9	-166.7	—
December	-48.9	52.6	-29.0	26.8	-49.5	-93.7	-101.4	-28.0	-93.2	-162.8	-75.0	—
Annual total	-8.7	-175.4	-197.1	-356.8	-308.3	-339.2	-372.5	-571.7	-1,565.4	-2,952.5	-1,664.9	-595.8

Note: Table 2.A.3 is the same as Table 2.A.2, except that the entries are compared to a 2 percent gain on real foreign dollar holdings. Using the notation from the note to Table 2.A.3, the entries in this table (denoted y_t) are:

$$\frac{(F\$)_{t-1}}{P_t/P_{1967}} \cdot \frac{\left[r_t - \left[\mathring{P}/P\right]_t - 0.02\right]}{12} = y_t$$

Source: Compiled by the author.

TABLE 2.A.4

Treasury Bill Three-Month Market Rate Minus the Inflation Rate

Year	Treasury Bill Minus the Inflation Rate
1960	1.27
1961	1.36
1962	1.67
1963	1.96
1964	2.24
1965	2.25
1966	1.40
1967	1.30
1968	0.44
1969	0.72
1970	1.02
1971	1.00
1972	0.70
1973	-1.27
1974	-3.75
1975	-1.03
1976 (seven months)	0.10
Average	
1960–75	0.71
1960–65	1.79
1966–75	0.05

Note: This table was compiled to get an idea of how the rate of gain has changed over the past 16 years. The break in the earlier upward trend occurred in 1966, so that the two subaverages for 1960-65 and 1966-75 are computed. The inflation rate was measured by the percentage change in the consumer price index.

Alternatively, p/P is the percentage change in the consumer price index.

Source: Compiled by the author.

real rate of return of 2 percent taken to be roughly the "normal return" on liquid assets at the start of the inflationary period; these figures are discussed below. Table 2.A.4 gives the real return on liquid assets year by year, from 1960 to 1976 (seven months only).

These figures show the real return on liquidity trending upward from 1960 to 1965—perhaps a symptom of growing distrust of the dollar as a reserve currency—then returning to its early 1960s level until 1972, becoming significantly negative in 1973-75 inclusive and strongly negative in 1974 and then becoming (barely) positive in 1976. These figures may be said to conform to theoretical expectations, especially if the 1962-65 figures are attributed to growing doubts about the dollar requiring payment of a higher return on dollar holdings and a real yield of 1 to 1.5 percent assumed as normal. The positive yield turns into an "inflation tax" in the three years of "exploding world inflation," 1973-75, and turns positive in 1976, when world inflation can be judged to have come visibly under control.

The calculations in Table 2.A.2 show that the foreign holders of U.S. dollar obligations earned a positive return on their assets with the exception of losses of 610.8, 1916.9, and 562.6 million 1967 dollars in 1972, 1973, and 1974. Their losses on their dollar assets in real terms in these years ($3,090.2 million) slightly outweighed their gains on the earlier years, 1965 to 1971 inclusive ($2,900.3 million). The calculations in Table 2.A.3 show a net loss for foreign holders in every year, averaging 300.2 million 1967 dollars per year in 1965-71 inclusive, 2,060.9 million 1967 dollars per year in 1972-75, and 780.4 million 1967 dollars per year overall. Both calculations confirm the general proposition of the text, that the amount of inflation tax collectable is substantial only in the early stages of an unexpected inflation.

NOTES

1. The argument of this section reproduces the technical analysis of Harry G. Johnson, "Appendix: A Note on Seigniorage and the Social Saving from Substituting Credit for Commodity Money," in Monetary Problems of the International Economy, ed. R. A. Mundell and A. K. Swoboda (Chicago: University of Chicago Press, 1969), pp. 323-29. (Quoted with permission of the University of Chicago Press. Monetary Problems of the International Economy: Copyright 1969 by the University of Chicago. All rights reserved. Published 1969. Second Impression 1970. Printed in the United States of America.

2. See Martin J. Bailey, "The Welfare Cost of Inflationary Finance," Journal of Political Economy 64 (April 1956):93-110.

3. The following analysis takes its departure from Robert A. Mundell, "The Optimal Balance of Payments Deficit," in Stabilization Policies in Interdependent Economies, ed. E. Claassen and P. Salin (Amsterdam: North-Holland, 1972), pp. 69-86.

3

Identification and Measurement of Grant Elements in Monetary Policy

THOMAS FREDERICK WILSON

Explicit recognition of the grants economy elevates the vantage point from which one may observe economic phenomena; this is especially true when one assesses the significance of money in the economy. Money serves as a "medium for transactions" involving grants as well as exchange, and money today is essentially a product of the grants economy, providing an economic return in the form of "seigniorage." Seigniorage is a grant, giving the producers (or "creators") of money, or those to whom the grant has been transferred, command over resources in the economy.

The structure of the financial system reflects the forces of economic change and an accumulation of measures designed to constrain its operations and to modify its development. The magnitude and distribution of seigniorage depend upon these trends, but the nature and legitimacy of the distribution of this monetary grant and even its size under such changing conditions have received little more than passing explicit attention, though they implicitly underlie much of the monetary policy debate.

This nation's policy toward money is expressed in the law under the Constitution and in the institutional structure. The participation of the private sector as well as government in the issuance of money is a manifestation of that policy. The Federal Reserve, as the nation's central bank, has been assigned the responsibility for the management of monetary policy in a conventional sense within this institutional arrangement, and its policy alternatives are narrowly limited by the law. This study seeks to identify and measure those grants that arise from the nation's policy toward money and to assess the impact of the Federal Reserve System on the distribution of those grants.

The author appreciates the many constructive comments and suggestions offered by Thomas Havrilesky and Randy Loser.

Thorough treatment of money in terms of equity and efficiency, for example, the social costs and benefits associated with the size and composition of the money supply, is beyond the scope of this study. Likewise, the implications for inflationary or deflationary monetary policy are not fully weighed. Emphasis is placed on grant flows without dwelling on issues related to control of the money supply. Analyses focus on the M-1 definition of money,* but other concepts of money are given attention; the proliferation of money supply definitions burdens the examination of grants just as it obfuscates the appraisal of monetary policy.

SEIGNIORAGE

The issuance of commodity money need not yield a grant; a grant in the form of pure rent, however, may accrue to the producers of a commodity that serves as money. A resource saving is associated with the transition from barter to money, but this need not be accompanied by grants in the issuance of money [11]. A government may issue coins for which the circulating value is equivalent to the bullion plus other costs of production. When persons possessing such commodities present them at the mint for the striking of coins and only a service charge ("brassage") is levied by the mint, a system of "free coinage" may be said to prevail. A government may gain seigniorage in the issuance of coins insofar as it is able to collect a payment in excess of the full production costs. The establishment and enforcement of a monopoly through coercion or respect for its sovereign authority are necessary conditions for the government to extract seigniorage. In a strict, conventional sense, seigniorage constitutes this monopoly profit, that is, the difference between the circulating value of coins and the cost of production. In the contemporary monetary system, the term seigniorage applies to the gains reaped by the U.S. Treasury and the Federal Reserve System arising from the issuance of "high-powered" or "base" money, that is, currency held by the nonbank public and bank reserves.

The participation of commercial banks in seigniorage depends on their role in money creation and on the structure of the banking system. On one extreme, the government could appropriate the seigniorage by requiring banks to hold 100 percent reserves; thus banks would be prohibited from creating money in any traditional sense by lending commodity money, issuing notes, or writing up deposits.

---

*The M-1 concept of money includes currency plus demand deposits held by the nonbank public.

Moreover, a purely competitive banking industry, in the absence of government intervention, would imply ultimately a commodity standard or barter, with no seigniorage. Under monopolistic competition, a banking system could survive indefinitely [20]. In this case, economic profit in the long run would be eliminated, but seigniorage would be transferred to the banks' customers. A private monopoly, on the other extreme, could seize the entire grant. The private or public exercise of monopolistic power implies seigniorage, to the extent that resource costs fall below the circulating value of money. In the contemporary domestic monetary system, the federal government restricts the size of the money supply, thus governing a monopoly over money, but it grants franchises (explicitly or implicitly in the case of state-chartered institutions) to banks to enable them to participate in the issuance of part of the money stock and in the origination of the seigniorage that so results.

Seigniorage, then, is defined here to encompass both the difference between the purchasing power of new money and the resource costs incurred in the issuance of that money and the implicit return on the previously issued, outstanding money stock. The definition of seigniorage in recent literature has yet to be firmly established, so the author's definition ought to be contrasted with other at least equally productive usages. Herbert Grubel and Harry Johnson, among other participants in a Conference on International Monetary Problems, considered the implications for seigniorage of alternative international monetary systems. Their discussion dealt extensively with the nature of seigniorage [26, pp. 269-82, 305-7, 313-17, 323-29]. Grubel defined seigniorage as "the net value of resources accruing to the issuer of money" [26, p. 269]. The question remains, though, whether seigniorage disappears if the wherewithal to purchase such resources is transferred to others. In the case of the monetary authority, Johnson suggests that seigniorage may be transferred by the payment of interest [26, pp. 326-27]. For commercial banking, Grubel contends that competition tends to eliminate seigniorage:

> Even in the United States, where entry [into commercial banking] is not free and interest payments on demand deposits are illegal, seigniorage gets eliminated or at least reduced substantially, by the competitive offering of services and by the development of substitutes for demand deposits, such as savings accounts, which do yield interest. [26, p. 271].

While seigniorage may be eliminated (or substantially reduced) for the issuer of money, the fact yet remains that a dollar may be created for use in the purchase of a dollar's worth of the nation's product at a minimal cost in real resources.

Charlotte Ruebling offers an alternative definition of seigniorage:

> The gains which accrue to issuers of money are derived from the difference between the costs of issuing money and the initial purchasing power of new money in circulation. Such gains are called seigniorage. [29, p. 15]

Ruebling asserts, however, that seigniorage may be distributed to the banks' depositors and/or their loan customers [29, pp. 181-9]. Competition in the sources and/or the uses of funds would tend to diminish the seigniorage gain for banks, deposit rates would accordingly be bid upward, and interest charges would be negotiated downward. In the absence of stiff competition for funds, lower lending rates would reflect the transfer of seigniorage to borrowers under competitive conditions. While these transfers of seigniorage depend on the spirit of competition and the structure of the financial system, they originate with the privilege to engage in fractional reserve banking, the source of which is society's grant under the law, a subject that now will be discussed.

LEGAL FOUNDATIONS OF THE SEIGNIORAGE GRANT

It has been asserted that the monetary authority ought to devolve upon the state as a power expressing its sovereign right. This view, however, is an assumption, unless the society grants that power to the state. For the United States, the Constitution prescribes the extent to which the monetary authority is transferred from the people to the government.* On the other hand, the exercise of this power

---

*In reply to Benjamin Klein's interpretation of this analysis in Chapter 1 [21], several points require emphasis:

1. Commercial banking is viewed as a "privilege" in the United States because of the requirement for a charter.
2. The bench mark for defining a grant is assumed to be a commodity money standard; a 100 percent reserve system is introduced as a convenient basis for measuring that grant.
3. In the United States, the people (society) possess the inherent right to determine the nature of money, and "the Constitution prescribes the extent to which the monetary authority is transferred from the people to the government."
4. The Constitution, as interpreted (perhaps inappropriately) by the courts, has allowed for the extraction of seigniorage by, in ef-

under the law has lagged far behind the evolution of the monetary system. That which has been designated as "lawful money" or "legal tender," for example, has had little in common with economic definitions of money.

The spectacular depreciation of the Continental currency, excessive issuance of "bills of credit" (paper money) by the states, and the vast and confusing array of circulating media formed the backdrop for the monetary provisions of the Constitution. The subsequent course of events notwithstanding, the Constitution was a "hard money" document:

> The Congress shall have Power . . . To Coin Money, regulate the Value thereof, and of foreign Coin. [Article I, Sec. 8]
>
> No State shall . . . coin Money; emit Bills of Credit; make any thing but gold and silver Coin a Tender in Payment of Debts; pass any Bill of Attainder, ex post facto law, or Law impairing the Obligation of Contracts. [Article I, Sec. 10]

Under these provisions, Congress authorized establishment of the mint, set the precious metal content of coins, and granted legal ten-

---

fect, granting a "charter" to the federal government to preside over a monopoly in the issuance of money.

5. The profit from money creation is, therefore, a grant from society to those who issue money rather than a "tax," even though the notion that a higher reserve requirement imposes a larger "tax" on the gain otherwise accruing to commercial banks is not inconsistent with the view that the total profit constitutes a grant.

6. The concept of "brand-name capital" is useful, but there remains some doubt that all the outlays identified by Klein inspire confidence in money rather than the confidence in money being a reflection of the strength of the economy, despite government policies in many instances.

His argument here is elliptical, seemingly suggesting that there is virtually no monopolistic profit from the issuance of money because part of the costs of national defense and other such extraneous expenditures must be deducted from the gross profit. Despite these differences in views, Klein's exploration of the costs of issuing money is highly instructive, and the implications derived from this perspective on seigniorage are insightful, especially as they relate to the broader issues he examines.

der status to the Spanish dollar. There was no confusion between coins and paper money; a proposal to give Congress the authority to emit bills of credit, which it had under the Articles of Confederation, was struck down in the Constitutional Convention. The federal government, however, was given the power to borrow money, which was later used as a guise for issuing notes that circulated as paper money. The Congress was not delegated the authority to interfere with private contracts, and the Tenth Amendment reserved powers not specifically granted the federal government to the states and the people. The states were granted no monetary powers as understood at the time. The contention that the Constitution mandated a federal monopoly of the money supply has a historical basis, but the Constitution prescribes that such a money supply consist of coins. The framers of the Constitution intended to define narrowly the monetary authority of the federal government. Full-valued coins were supposed to serve as the only form of money to their understanding, thus no seigniorage would result [12, pp. 10-22; 18, pp. 91-103].

The federal government's monetary authority has broadened immensely since ratification of the Constitution, and the Constitution has accommodated this exercise of powers. Invoking the "necessary and proper" clause, the Supreme Court upheld in McCullock v. Maryland (1819) the authority of Congress to establish a bank, the second Bank of the United States in this case. The successful assault on the bank by the Jacksonians delayed the extension of federal power, and the right of states to charter and control commercial banks was confirmed in Briscoe v. Bank of Kentucky (1837). This meant that state bank notes were not being issued in violation of the Constitution. The Civil War and later court rulings greatly enhanced the monetary powers of the federal government. The Supreme Court upheld a prohibitive tax on notes issued by state-chartered banks, Veazie Bank v. Fenno (1869), and the Legal Tender Cases (1870) and Juilliard v. Greenman (1884) supported the legal tender status of the greenbacks. This power was fully consolidated in the gold clause cases, for example, Norman v. Baltimore and Ohio (1935), which upheld the Gold Exchange Act of 1934, nullified the original intent of the Constitution pertaining to the legal tender status of gold and silver, and held such private contracts were an attempt to frustrate a dominant power of Congress despite Fifth Amendment guarantees of "due process."

These decisions were based on a broad interpretation of the Constitution rather than on the specific monetary clause [12, pp. 82-90; 18, pp. 107-11]. To conclude, as Paul Meek does [25, p. 7], that the Federal Reserve System derives its power to create bank reserves from the Congress, which in turn is granted this authority on the basis of the monetary clause alone, is at best a gross oversimplification. Meek's position, however, is not totally unfounded [23, pp.

28-31, 41-47]. The exercise of federal monetary authority has been supported specifically by interpretations of the commerce clause. While in Nathan v. Louisiana (1850) the practice of lending money in interstate commerce was judged as not itself interstate commerce, commercial banking was itself considered interstate commerce in Lorenzetti v. American Trust Company (1942) [12, pp. 63-64].

The power to issue currency was eventually brought under federal auspices, along with the concomitant seigniorage, but this virtual monopoly—with traveler's checks one possible exception—did not encompass fully money as ordinarily defined. The tax on state bank notes failed to destroy those institutions, of course, and demand deposits grew in importance as a component of the money supply. Commercial banking, as "banks of issue," commenced in the United States in the 1780s. Several of the participants in the Constitutional Convention were instrumental in founding these banks, so it might not be surprising to find no prohibition of private bank note issues, which yield seigniorage, in that document [18, pp. 104-5]. It is also an interesting historical note that the first commercial bank was chartered by Congress under the Articles of Confederation, the second bank operated several years without a charter according to the common law tradition that private banking was a business, and the third bank was state chartered [27, pp. 44-45]. Despite the generally prevailing laissez-faire disposition, banking was soon treated as a franchise, requiring a charter. Allusions to the common law tradition were made in legal arguments, but that position weakened through time.

In the early years of the Republic, bank notes were not viewed as money, but surrogates, which owed their value to convertibility; this was not true of bills of credit. The Briscoe and Veazie Bank cases, in effect, upheld the power of states to charter banks even if that was a mark of restraint by the Congress, rather than an implied power of the states. Later, the wholesale collection of checks by the Federal Reserve banks was declared unconstitutional in American Bank & Trust Co. v. Federal Reserve Bank of Atlanta (1921), which essentially supports the existence of fractional reserve banking. The Supreme Court ruled that the Federal Reserve could not do that which Congress did not authorize it to do. The power of Congress in monetary matters is thus limited only by the ballot box, even though it has not seen fit, perhaps wisely, to exercise fully those powers [12, pp. 59-63].

The monetary authority in the United States has, through a process of economic change and legal rulings, devolved to the Congress, giving that body essentially unconstrained sovereign power over money. The Congress has not exercised that power completely, thus allowing the privilege of money creation to remain in part in private hands. Nonetheless, the hesitancy so far exhibited by the Congress to extract all the seigniorage arising from the issuance of money, among other areas where it could claim its monetary powers, should not be interpreted to mean, as Irving Fisher so vehemently argues [15, pp. 19, 201-2], that private interests are accordingly acting in violation of the Constitution.

MEASUREMENT OF THE SEIGNIORAGE GAIN OF THE FEDERAL GOVERNMENT

The federal government gains seigniorage both from the issuance of currency and from the creation of member bank deposits with the Federal Reserve banks. The federal government, then, appropriates this return through the issuance of "high-powered" money. High-powered money may be defined either as currency outside the Treasury and the Federal Reserve System ("currency in circulation"), plus member bank deposits with the Federal Reserve banks, or as currency held by the nonbank public, plus bank reserves. Currency held by the nonbank public is a component of M-1, but currency as vault cash serves as bank reserves. Bank reserves may be held against the demand deposit component of M-1, but they also serve other purposes, both as excess reserves and reserves behind other deposit and nondeposit items. Both the Treasury and the Federal Reserve banks issue currency, so both participate directly in the seigniorage return. The monetization of gold provides interest-free funds to the Treasury as well. Let us view first seigniorage in terms of the return to the federal government from the issuance of high-powered money and then turn to the shares accruing directly to the Treasury and the Federal Reserve System.

The seigniorage gain to the government may be calculated either as an accumulative total or as a return for a specific period. Following Grubel [26, p. 273], the total gross accumulated seigniorage is equivalent to currency in circulation plus member bank reserves held with the Federal Reserve. This figure represents the dollars spent for which no interest payments to the public are required. Ignoring costs, the total of such high-powered money in 1974 was $103.6 billion [7, pp. A3, A5, A12, A14]. For any specific year, the gross return may be estimated by inserting the appropriate implicit market rate of return. The relevant interest rate for 1974 reflects a combination of the implicit return to the Treasury (7.27 percent) and the interest rate on Federal Reserve loans and securities (7.30 percent), which give a weighted average return of 7.29 percent [6, p. 281] (these figures are explained more fully below). The seigniorage gain in 1974 was then $7.6 billion. For comparison, Grubel estimated seigniorage for 1965 of $3.3 billion; he also computes a seigniorage return for Treasury bills. This calculation of seigniorage encompasses the "inflation tax"; Johnson, in his contribution to this volume, distinguishes between seigniorage and the "inflation tax."

The Federal Reserve System in 1974 furnished $85.2 billion in high-powered money [7, p. A4]. In the process of issuing this money, the Federal Reserve acquires earning assets: U.S. Treasury securities, federal agency obligations, bankers' acceptances, and loans to member banks. The average rate of return on these loans and securities was 7.30 percent. This translates into a gross seigniorage gain of $6.2 billion and represents the bulk of the earnings of the Federal Reserve System in 1974 [6, pp. 300-1].

The earnings of the Federal Reserve System are largely a manifestation of seigniorage. The Federal Reserve in 1974 turned over to the Treasury, as "interest on Federal Reserve notes," $5,550 million. Interest is not paid, of course, to those who hold Federal Reserve notes or to member banks on their reserves held with the Federal Reserve banks. Total current earnings amounted to $6,280 million, from which $548 million for net expenses was deducted to give current net earnings of $5,733 million. After adjustments, net earnings before the payment to the Treasury were $5,654 million. Statutory dividends of $53 million were paid to member banks, and $51 million was added to surplus. Dividends constitute a transfer of seigniorage to the member banks; moreover, they benefit from services provided at no cost by the Federal Reserve System. The addition to surplus and the $5,550 million paid to the Treasury might be considered a rough estimate of the net seigniorage gain accruing directly to the Federal Reserve. Not all those expenses are necessarily incurred in producing money, of course. Thus, the net seigniorage estimate of $5.6 billion overstates the true gain [6, pp. 300-1].

The Treasury gains seigniorage directly from the implicit interest on Treasury currency outstanding less Treasury cash holdings and Treasury deposits with the Federal Reserve, and on monetized gold and special drawing rights (SDRs); this total was $18.4 billion in 1974 [7, pp. A2-A5]. Conceptually, the Treasury's monetary functions could be transferred to the Federal Reserve System. In that event, the Treasury might have borrowed the funds raised through the issuance of currency and certificates. Assume that such interest costs would reflect the composition of Treasury obligations held by the Federal Reserve. Applying this interest rate on U.S. government securities (7.27 percent), the gross seigniorage return to the Treasury in 1974 was $1.3 billion. To arrive at a net figure, the associated costs of operating the mint, transportation charges, the costs of enforcing the laws against counterfeiting, and so forth ought to be deducted. A crude estimate would place them at roughly $100 million, thus yielding a net return of $1.2 billion [30, pp. 736-39].

The gross seigniorage gain extracted by the federal government in 1974 was $7.6 billion. The Federal Reserve System accounted for $6.2 billion of that return, and the Treasury's direct return was $1.3 billion (these figures do not equal the total because of rounding). On a net basis, the Federal Reserve System gained $5.6 billion, most of which was paid to the Treasury. The Treasury received a net return, excluding the payment by the Federal Reserve, of $1.2 billion.

THE SEIGNIORAGE GAIN OF COMMERCIAL BANKS

Commercial banks in 1974 issued $175.1 billion of M-1, that is, the money supply less currency held by the nonbank public and bank reserves; all reserves are included here [7, pp. A3, A5, A12, A14]. The seigniorage gain may be assessed by contrasting the fractional reserve banking system with 100 percent reserve banking. A 100 percent reserve requirement would clearly transform banks into very different institutions, so long as other constraints remain intact [1, pp. 437-56; 4; 15; 16, pp. 65-76]. Such a system might be established by Federal Reserve purchases of assets in sufficient volume to allow the banks to meet the 100 percent reserve requirement (it is assumed for analytic purposes that other reserve requirements would be abolished). The return on such assets, then, represents an estimate of the gross return attributable to fractional reserve banking.

The procedure by which the Federal Reserve might institute 100 percent reserve banking provides a basis for assessing the gain traceable to private money creation. This might be accomplished by purchasing a representative proportion of bank assets. A restriction of purchases to Treasury securities and high-grade bonds, as usually recommended, would strip the banks of their highest quality assets, thus potentially disturbing the financial markets as the banks correct for imbalances in their portfolios. While this analysis need not consider the practicality or advisability of a 100 percent money plan, there must be recognition of the effect of fractional reserve banking on the structure of assets held by those institutions. It is on this basis that the argument is made for a central bank purchase that covers the full quality spectrum, not simply that there exists an insufficient volume of government securities in the banks' portfolios or that a high marginal cost of funds is reflected in lower quality, higher yielding assets. In effect, the Federal Reserve would be assuming a proportionate share of the risk by purchasing such a representative proportion of assets.*

---

*The 100 percent reserve plans advanced by Milton Friedman and Fisher are briefly reviewed below.

The income generated by commercial banks in 1974, with allowance for the special tax treatment of interest on state and local government obligations, suggests an average rate of return on loans and investments of 9.4 percent. Federal funds sold and securities purchased under resale agreement were excluded, but that adjustment had no effect on the rate of return when rounded [8; 7, pp. A16, A18]. A purchase by the Federal Reserve of $175.1 billion of the commercial banks' loans and investments would provide a gross seigniorage return of $16.5 billion. Interest rates were, of course, extraordinarily high in 1974 by historical standards, and the rate of return does not fully incorporate capital losses.

The cost to the Federal Reserve System associated with the administration, supervision, and control of 100 percent reserve banking was estimated with a statistical cost function in order to appraise the net monetary grant to commercial banks. Current expenses represented costs in the regression equation, and these figures were expressed in constant 1974 dollars by deflating them with an index of unit labor costs for the private economy; output was measured in terms of current-dollar, high-powered money. Using data covering the period 1959-74, a linear cost equation performed the best on statistical grounds. The marginal cost of issuing money was an estimated 0.524 cents per dollar [6, pp. 303, 318; 30, pp. 80, 111]. With a projected incremental cost of $918 million, the net seigniorage gain from fractional reserve banking in 1974 amounted to $15.6 billion.

The monetary grant to commercial banks in 1974 exceeded their earnings. Presumably, depositors benefited from seigniorage by receiving free services or interest, and loan customers enjoyed reduced interest charges. The division of this grant among depositors, loan customers, and banks is a matter worthy of thorough examination; however, because of its complexity, attention is given below only to the role of the Federal Reserve System in the distribution of that grant. It might also be noted that the procedures used above to estimate seigniorage could be applied to broader concepts of money, but that exercise would not be very productive in the light of arguments presented later in this study.

DISTRIBUTION OF THE GRANT THROUGH MONETARY POLICY

Seigniorage is a grant appropriated in part by the federal government. Fractional reserve banking provides private institutions a share of that grant, which in turn is largely transferred to their customers. In 1974, the gross return from the issuance of money was

$24.1 billion, with $7.6 billion captured by the government and $16.5 billion retained by the private sector. On a net basis those shares were $6.8 billion and $15.6 billion, respectively. The structure of the financial system determines in large measure this public-private split, but monetary policy influences those shares as well. Let us now look more closely at the distribution of that monetary grant.

The level of reserve requirement ratios and the rate of return on reserves largely explain the breakdown of seigniorage between the public and private sectors. In the absence of interest paid on reserves, higher reserve ratios shift the gain to the government. The payment of interest on reserves held with the Federal Reserve banks would, of course, divert earnings from the government into the commercial banks. In the conduct of monetary policy, variations in reserve ratios alter the distribution of this grant and, consequently, the profitability of the banking system. An increase in a reserve requirement ratio reduces the share of seigniorage accruing to commercial banks. While in one sense this may be described as a higher implicit tax on banks, because the government's return on money is now larger, the logic of this analysis suggests alternatively that an increase in a reserve ratio simply alters the division of the profit from the issuance of money between the private sector and the public sector. (For differing views, refer to the arguments developed by Neil Jacoby [13, p. 174] and Sherman Maisel [22, p. 157]; the latter viewpoint is consistent with the author's position.)

The downward trend in legal reserve ratios for demand deposits since World War II shifted seigniorage from the government to the private sector. Permission to count vault cash as reserves also effectively cut reserve requirements as well, and reduced Federal Reserve earnings. These steps apparently reflect concern for bank earnings and the disincentive for membership in the System presented by more costly reserve requirements than those established for nonmember banks [13, p. 183]. While reserve ratios for time deposits have also been reduced, special marginal reserve requirements have been imposed on certain deposit and nondeposit items. This practice translates into a larger proportionate reserve liability for bigger banks.

A new basis for determining a bank's reserve liability for demand deposits was instituted in 1972. Graduated reserve ratios replaced a system patterned on geographic location, though exceptions were allowed. This modification of reserve requirements, net of a cut in float, released about $1.5 billion in reserves [9, p. 626]. The logic behind this policy change, according to the Federal Reserve, was "to equalize competitive conditions among member banks" [9, pp. 626, 628]. While the assignment of reserve requirements by location is recognized as no longer equitable, no arguments are offered in support of the graduated basis. A set of graduated reserve requirements provides a lower implicit cost of funds for marginal member banks. This larger grant to smaller banks, along with branching restrictions, helps to perpetuate the existence of below-optimum-sized organizations, while retaining fringe members of the Federal Reserve System. Compulsory membership and elimination of graduated reserve ratios would thus partly correct for imbalances in the distribution of the monetary grant among institutions and perhaps increase the share seized by the government.

The use of tax and loan accounts and the treatment of Federal Reserve float enlarge the grant received by commercial banks. Float provides a credit to the reserve accounts of commercial banks that may be used to support outstanding deposit liabilities. Since positive Federal Reserve float usually exceeds substantially negative Federal Reserve float, it represents a sizable grant to the commercial banks. The greater the magnitude of float, then, the larger the share of seigniorage gained by commercial banks [19]. The Treasury's tax and loan accounts at commercial banks, on which no interest is paid, yield a return to those institutions, though that return is at least offset in part by the provision of services at no charge. When deposits are transferred to the Federal Reserve banks, the seigniorage gains are altered accordingly. The prohibition of interest payments on demand deposits prevents a direct return to the Treasury on its tax and loan accounts [10, pp. 16-17].

The absence of interest payments on currency and the legal prohibition of such payments on demand deposits block any explicit interest return to those who hold money. An interest return on deposit money would encourage its use; a substitution of deposits for currency would reduce the seigniorage return of the government. Regulation Q ceilings limit the return on deposits that serve as close substitutes for M-1. As a result, the monetary grant accruing to the banking system is largely divided among the financial institutions and debtors. To the extent that Regulation Q functions as a policy instrument, changes in the ceiling rates may alter the flow of seigniorage. David Pyle's study suggests a $25 billion loss of interest income by savers because of such government regulations [28]. These ceilings, of course, discriminate particularly against the saver with modest means.

Open-market operations also affect the distribution of seigniorage. Open-market operations were conducted initially to bolster the earnings of the Federal Reserve banks [2, p. 8; 14, p. 12]. Through such purchases of securities, the Federal Reserve has accumulated a substantial proportion of the public debt. The Treasury in effect recoups the bulk of the interest paid on its obligations held by the Federal Reserve banks. In fact, back in 1947, Treasury officials sought assurances that higher Federal Reserve earnings resulting from higher bill rates would be turned over to the Treasury. The

Federal Reserve obliged by agreeing to turn over to the Treasury approximately 90 percent of the net earnings after payment of dividends as an interest charge on Federal Reserve notes (a franchise tax had been in effect before passage of the Banking Act of 1933) [2, pp. 102, 149].

The bulk of Federal Reserve net open-market purchases involves Treasury obligations, most of which are short-term instruments. The Federal Reserve also holds federal agency issues and bankers' acceptances. This policy does support those markets, thus influencing interest rate differentials and concomitantly the cost to the Treasury of financing the public debt. From 1934 to 1959, the Federal Reserve had the authority to make loans and purchase obligations of commercial and industrial businesses [14, pp. 10-17]. The purchase of higher yielding securities can, of course, increase the earnings of the Federal Reserve System. Though the risk exposure would be greater, the Federal Reserve could gain a larger share of the seigniorage by so altering the mix of its portfolio.

The conduct of open-market operations in New York with 20 or so primary dealers in government securities would seem to be a source of special treatment, but the Federal Reserve is not of this opinion [25, pp. 8, 18]. The conformity of movements in interest rates across the nation supports this contention. On the other hand, the unevenness of the sectoral impact of monetary policy would appear along geographic lines; however, such distributional implications extend beyond the scope of this study.

Use of the discount facility is viewed as a privilege by the Federal Reserve System. Banks apparently are motivated by the prospect of profits when they borrow at the discount window, but the tradition of reluctance to borrow prevails and it is encouraged by the Federal Reserve. The Federal Reserve banks can and do turn away would-be borrowers. In contrast with other policy instruments, a grant is provided to those banks willing and able to use the discount facility, otherwise they would not be borrowing from the Federal Reserve banks. In the case of Franklin National Bank, the subsidy was exceptionally large, though the point may be lost that the Federal Reserve did preside over the liquidation of that institution [17, p. 70]. The Federal Reserve, however, has instituted a special discount rate for troubled banks. The overall distribution of seigniorage depends upon the differential between the discount rates and the yield on securities purchased by the Federal Reserve.

THE APPROPRIATE DISTRIBUTION OF THE MONETARY GRANT

The willingness of society to accept money for which the resource cost falls below its purchasing power yields a grant to the issuers of that money. Society's claim on those resources may be respected by the payment of interest on money. On the other hand, the federal government might use its responsibility to control the money supply and its authority to "coin" money to extract a monopoly gain in the form of seigniorage. There is, then, a similarity here to an unregulated public utility. The government might also explicitly or implicitly delegate power to private institutions to enable them to participate in the issuance of money, and thereby allow them to secure a share of the seigniorage gain. Control of the money supply does not imply the power for government to extract seigniorage, and a strict interpretation of the Constitution does not suggest that society has, in fact, granted this power to the government. While it is impractical to pay interest on currency, no such constraint applies to reserves held by the Federal Reserve banks or to demand deposits. The payment of interest on those reserves would remove one incentive for laxity in the conduct of the nation's financial affairs [24]. The elimination of other ceilings and controls on interest rates, along with energetic efforts to promote competition among financial institutions, would be consistent with efficiency in the use of resources and equity in the distribution of the monetary grant [3; 5].

Milton Friedman [16, pp. 71-78] has urged the adoption of a 100 percent reserve plan chiefly as a means to ensure closer control of the money supply, and he also argues in favor of a shift in seigniorage to the private sector on efficiency grounds. These two proposals are mutually exclusive. Although Friedman includes savings and time deposits at commercial banks in his 100 percent money plan, other viable substitutes (for M-2)* exist and others would probably be spawned. The accompanying allocation of real resources to manage cash balances would reduce society's gain from the issuance of low-cost money. In response, Friedman proposes the payment of interest on reserves, thus permitting interest payments to those holding deposit money; no interest would be paid on currency holdings. This constitutes a rechanneling of seigniorage back through the banking system.† He further contends that the Treasury should be re-

---

*M-2 equals M-1 plus savings and time deposits held with commercial banks.

†The 100 percent money plans share common ground on the matter of monetary control, but the seigniorage implications differ markedly. In contrast to Friedman, Fisher advocates appropriation by government of the private gain from the multiple expansion of deposits. Under Fisher's plan, a new government agency would purchase bank assets in a volume sufficient to establish a 100 percent cash reserve behind demand deposits. While no interest would be paid on reserves,

quired to borrow funds at open-market rates, thus curtailing its power to finance some government spending at essentially no cost. Should the Federal Reserve System absorb the Treasury's monetary functions and pay interest to the full amount of net earnings to member banks on their reserves under a fractional reserve regime, all the monetary grant would pass into the private sector.

The essentially arbitrary nature of the definition of money leaves any seigniorage calculation somewhat less than satisfactory, and it also places in doubt the appropriateness of the federal government's seizure of part (or all) of that grant. The closeness of substitutability among types of deposits and between deposits and money market instruments explains the tenuous nature of any specific, working definition of money. The extension of the concepts of money by the Federal Reserve to M-5 emphasizes this fact. Moreover, the inclusion of large negotiable certificates of deposit (CDs) in the money supply suggests that money should logically encompass commercial paper. Then the door is open for a host of debt instruments as candidates for the distinction as money. Society's grant of the right to issue debt instruments is thus reflected in these transactions, and this is a grant that banks share with many others. The only meaningful difference is that banks, and other financial institutions to a lesser extent, face strict laws and regulations that prohibit or restrict the transference of part of the return to those willing to hold money. These measures are, of course, designed to protect depositors and certain institutions from competition, and, as a consequence, they are costly. Thus, it is well worth establishing the size and assessing the distribution of seigniorage arising from the issuance of M-1, because in that instance, the monetary grant is most clearly diverted from its appropriate course.

CONCLUSION

The nation's monetary authority rests in the hands of the Congress, largely because the courts have interpreted the Constitution

---

Fisher did support reimbursement of banks for their loss of earning assets, but he supposed that this compensation would amount to a modest sum. Fisher computed the seigniorage still accruing to banks in 1926 at less than $119 million, which amounted to less than half of earnings or 1.2 percent of demand deposits. He advised service charges on checking accounts, and argued that according to his proposal the banks' profits would largely arise from interest on loans and investments of their capital and funds placed in savings and time deposits [15, pp. 89-92, 152-58].

in a manner to accommodate the exercise of federal power. The government presides over a monopoly of the money supply (M-1), for which the market value far exceeds the resource costs of production. This seigniorage gain is divided in the first instance between the government and the commercial banks, which retain the privilege to issue money as an implicit expression of congressional restraint, which means that private money creation does not violate the Constitution. The gross seigniorage return in 1974 was an estimated $24.1 billion, with the federal government extracting $7.6 billion and the commercial banks generating $16.5 billion through the deposit-creation process; the latter sum was no doubt diffused widely in the economy. Net of costs, this monetary grant amounted to an estimated $22.4 billion.

Monetary policy and the laws governing the operation of financial institutions determine the distribution of this grant. In terms of efficiency in resource allocation and equity in the distribution of seigniorage (and strict constitutional limitations as well), it is argued that the grant should flow to those persons and organizations who hold money. This objective would best be served with the payment of interest on commercial bank reserves held with the Federal Reserve banks, the removal of restrictions on interest payments to depositors, and the promotion of spirited competition among financial institutions. Seizure of the grant by the government is not a requisite for monetary control, and society should recover in the form of interest the return from the government's exercise of its monetary powers.

REFERENCES

[1] American Economic Association, ed. Readings in Monetary Theory. New York: Blakiston, 1951.

[2] Anderson, Clay J. A Half-Century of Federal Reserve Policy-making, 1914-1964. Federal Reserve Bank of Philadelphia, 1965.

[3] Auernheimer, Leonardo. "The Honest Government's Guide to the Revenue from the Creation of Money." Journal of Political Economy 82, no. 3 (May/June 1974):598-606.

[4] Barber, G. Russell, Jr. "The One Hundred Percent Reserve System." American Economist 17, no. 1 (Spring 1973):115-27.

[5] Benston, George J. "An Analysis and Evaluation of Alternative Reserve Requirement Plans." Journal of Finance 24, no. 5 (December 1969):849-70.

[6] Board of Governors of the Federal Reserve System. Annual Report. 1974.

[7] _____. Federal Reserve Bulletin 61, nos. 2-8 (February-August 1975):A2-5, A12, A14, A16, A18.

[8] _____. "Member Bank Income in 1974." Federal Reserve Bulletin 61, no. 6 (June 1975):349-55.

[9] _____. "Recent Regulatory Changes in Reserve Requirements and Check Collection." Federal Reserve Bulletin 58, no. 7 (July 1972):626-30.

[10] Brockschmidt, Peggy. "Treasury Cash Balances." Monthly Review (Federal Reserve Bank of Kansas City), July-August 1975, pp. 12-20.

[11] Brunner, Karl, and Allen H. Meltzer. "The Uses of Money: Money in the Theory of an Exchange Economy." American Economic Review 61, no. 5 (December 1971):784-805.

[12] Dunne, Gerald. Monetary Decisions of the Supreme Court. New Brunswick, N.J.: Rutgers University Press, 1960.

[13] Entine, Alan D., ed. Monetary Economics: Readings. Belmont, Calif.: Wadsworth, 1968.

[14] Federal Reserve Bank of Philadelphia. 50 Years of the Federal Reserve Act. 1964.

[15] Fisher, Irving. 100% Money, 3rd ed. New Haven, Conn.: City Printing, 1945.

[16] Friedman, Milton. A Program for Monetary Stability. New York: Fordham University Press, 1960.

[17] _____. "Subsidizing Banks." Newsweek, July 15, 1974, p. 70.

[18] Hammond, Bray. Banks and Politics in America. Princeton, N.J.: Princeton University Press, 1957.

[19] Hoel, Arline. "A Primer on Federal Reserve Float." _Monthly Review_ (Federal Reserve Bank of New York), October 1975, pp. 245-53.

[20] Klein, Benjamin. "The Competitive Supply of Money." _Journal of Money, Credit and Banking_, November 1974, pp. 423-53.

[21] _____. "Money, Wealth, and Seigniorage," Chapter 1, this volume.

[22] Maisel, Sherman J. _Managing the Dollar_. New York: Norton, 1973.

[23] Manne, Henry G., and Roger LeRoy Miller, eds. _Gold, Money and the Law_. Chicago: Aldine, 1975.

[24] Marty, Alvin L. "Growth, Satiety, and the Tax Revenue from Money Creation." _Journal of Political Economy_ 81, no. 5 (September/October 1973):1136-52.

[25] Meek, Paul. _Open-Market Operations_. Federal Reserve Bank of New York. 1973.

[26] Mundell, Robert A., and Alexander K. Swoboda, eds. _Monetary Problems of the International Economy_. Chicago: University of Chicago Press, 1969.

[27] Nussbaum, Arthur. _A History of the Dollar_. New York: Columbia University Press, 1957.

[28] Pyle, David H. "Interest Rate Ceilings and Net Worth Losses by Savers," Chapter 6, this volume.

[29] Ruebling, Charlotte E. "Financing Government through Monetary Expansion and Inflation." _Review_ (Federal Reserve Bank of St. Louis) 57, no. 2 (February 1975):15-23.

[30] U.S., Department of Commerce. _Business Conditions Digest_. August 1975.

[31] U.S., Executive Office of the President, Office of Management and Budget. _The Budget of the United States Government, Fiscal Year 1976—Appendix_. Washington, D.C.: U.S. Government Printing Office, 1975.

PART II

Distributional Impact of Monetary Policy

4

Motives Behind Inflationary Monetary Expansion

CHARLOTTE E. RUEBLING

INTRODUCTION

Looking back from the beginning of 1977, one sees that yearly price increases in the U.S. economy have averaged over 5 percent for the past ten years. The prevalence of inflation is well known, but one frequently wonders why it is that this pattern has come to be, where the costs fall, and whether there are any good things to be said for inflation. A good deal has been written in attempting to answer these questions.[1] The scope of this chapter is limited to describing the incentives for government policies that contribute to inflation and to pointing out the considerations necessary to analyze the distributional effects of inflation.

Two incentives behind policy actions that produce inflation are (1) monetary expansion is, in the short run, a relatively painless way to finance federal government programs and (2) monetary and fiscal stimuli are believed to enhance the achievement of employment and distributional objectives. Monetary expansion contributes to government finance in several related, but nevertheless different, ways. First, there is seigniorage, which is the gain that accrues to the source of new money in the economy. Second, to the extent that accelerated monetary expansion produces inflation, tax revenues rise more than proportionately. Third, if the inflation is unanticipated by the public, the government benefits from its status as a net monetary debtor. The real value of past debt is diminished by the occurrence of unanticipated inflation.

Much of this chapter was written while the author was employed as an economist at the Federal Reserve Bank of St. Louis. Use of the bank's research facilities and helpful comments from the bank's staff are gratefully acknowledged. The author, of course, remains solely responsible for the contents of the chapter.

SEIGNIORAGE AND EXPEDIENCY

Gains that accrue as the result of new money entering circulation are referred to as seigniorage. The rate of seigniorage, the amount per unit of new money, is equal to the difference between the costs of issuing a unit of money and its purchasing power in circulation. If it costs 25 cents to produce a unit of money that circulates at a face value of one dollar, the seigniorage is 75 cents.[2]

Seigniorage typically is presumed to go to the issuer of new money, and in practice this generally means the government or the central bank and commercial banks. However, this need not be the case. Under certain arrangements, it will accrue to money users. In general, the distribution of seigniorage between issuers of money and users of money depends on the institutional arrangements through which monetary expansion is accomplished. These arrangements pertain to the proportions of government fiat money relative to bank deposit money in the system, the level of reserve requirements on deposits, and whether or not competitive interest payments can be paid on deposits.

If the government were the sole issuer of money, all the seigniorage would go to the government. Members of the private sector who acquired additional money balances would give up real goods and services in exchange for the services of money. To them, the cost for the services of money would equal the value of the goods and services exchanged, while to the government, the cost would be only the outlay for paper, printing, and bookkeeping.

In the United States today, however, demand deposits issued by commercial banks comprise about three-fourths of what is regarded as the money stock, while currency and coin make up the remainder. Bank deposits are issued on the basis of reserves and reserves represent Federal Reserve liabilities. Increases in Federal Reserve liabilities, primarily Federal Reserve notes and deposits of member banks, can result from a number of actions, but for the most part they result from increases in Federal Reserve holdings of government securities at the initiative of the Federal Open Market Committee.

If banks were required to hold reserves equal to 100 percent of deposits while there were no interest payments on money or reserves, the result would be the same as if the government were the sole issuer of money. (This assumes that central bank earnings are returned to the Treasury.) Bank reserves of member banks, however, are far less than 100 percent. Consequently, commercial banks have an opportunity to earn seigniorage on deposits issued. Banks gain from issuing money if the stream of income from loans and investments, undertaken with reserves in excess of requirements, exceeds bookkeeping expenses and other costs of issuing deposits.

It is difficult to determine just how much banks obtain in the way of seigniorage. To the extent that banks charge an interest rate on loans that is less than an appropriate market rate, some of banks' seigniorage would be distributed to loan customers. Moreover, if interest were not prohibited on demand deposits, competition for deposit holders through interest payments would result in seigniorage being distributed to deposit holders through interest payments.* As it is, banks compete through offering other services.[3]

The inducement to excessive monetary growth resulting from seigniorage in the present institutional setting is not insignificant. While reserve requirements serve as an effective brake on commercial bank issuance of deposits, given a limited amount of bank reserves, there is no legal limitation on the expansion of bank reserves through Federal Reserve actions. By purchasing government securities over the years, the Federal Reserve not only has increased the growth of bank reserves but also has increased its earnings, which are returned to the Treasury. In 1976, for example, the Federal Reserve turned over to the U.S. Treasury about $6 billion as "interest on Federal Reserve notes."

Behind this lies the expediency of financing government spending through sales of securities. This is important to government flexibility and ability to respond to problems, but it also allows Congress to increase spending initiatives while postponing politically difficult tax decisions. If the Federal Reserve through open-market purchases, at the same time, attempts to relieve interest rate pressures that would otherwise result from increased debts incurred by the Treasury, there is, by and large, little perceived effect of this means of finance in the short run. Soon, however, monetary growth increases, and the longer term effects are inflation and higher interest rates. Seigniorage, then, encourages inflationary financial policies, and inflation itself generates a set of incentives for its continuation, which is a subject explored below.

INFLATION AND THE DISTRIBUTION OF WEALTH

The distributional effects of policy actions and inflation can be described in terms of changes in relative prices, incomes, or wealth. Of these, relative price changes are the easiest to see objectively but are less easily related to the distribution of total well-being. Numerous factors determine the significance of a given price change to the

---

*Since 1933, commercial banks in the United States have been prohibited by law from making explicit interest payments on deposits.

distribution of income and wealth. Import restrictions on shoes, for example, raise their relative prices and, in turn, the incomes of workers and owners in the domestic shoe industry relative to other members of society. The size of resulting relative changes in income is more difficult to determine, however.

Wealth and income are definitionally related, but also bear different connotations in discussions of welfare distribution. Income represents the flow of earnings from a stock of wealth, and wealth can be defined as the present value of future income flows. In principle, distributional effects couched in terms of income can be translated into changes in wealth and vice versa. In practice, however, discussions of distributional effects judged according to income differ from those judged according to wealth. One reason is that wealth is measured at a point in time (which reflects the market's evaluation of future income from the assets comprising wealth), while income is measured over a finite period (which is shorter than the period implicitly reflected in market evaluation of assets).

Another reason that studies of income may lead to different distributional implications than studies of wealth is that certain ingredients in the U.S. standard of living are most readily measured in terms of income flows, while others are most readily evaluated by asset prices at a point of time. For example, the wealth embodied in human productive abilities typically is measured in terms of earnings during some period of time rather than by the capitalized value of those earnings over a lifetime. An obvious reason is the uncertainty about the duration of life and the pattern of future earnings. On the other hand, the wealth embodied in a house or other physical property is typically measured by its price rather than by the value of the annual flow services.

In addition, models of inflation used to describe implications for income distribution tend to differ from those that describe implications for wealth distribution. The theories underlying the former tend to be Keynesian, while the theories underlying the latter tend to be monetarist.[4]

Whether the effects of inflation are measured in terms of changes in relative prices, incomes, or wealth, or all three, anticipations and institutional arrangements regarding contracts, price flexibility, indexation, and tax structure affect distributional consequences of inflation. Consider the wealth effects of unanticipated inflation. On a balance sheet, net wealth can be classified as follows:

Assets	Liabilities and Net Wealth
Monetary assets	Monetary liabilities
Real assets	Real liabilities
	Net wealth

Monetary assets are claims to a fixed amount of dollars, money, bonds, or contracts to receive a certain amount of money in exchange for goods or services in the future. Real assets, on the other hand, are claims to things whose dollar value can vary. Monetary liabilities are obligations to deliver a fixed amount of dollars, while real liabilities are obligations to deliver goods or services whose price may change between the time of the agreement and the time of delivery. Net monetary creditors are those whose monetary assets exceed their monetary liabilities. Net monetary debtors are those whose monetary liabilities exceed their monetary assets.

When inflation is unanticipated, that is, when it is expected that the price level will rise at a slower rate than it actually does, monetary creditors lose relative to monetary debtors. This is illustrated in the balance sheets in Table 4.1. Shown are the before-and-after-inflation wealth positions of a net monetary debtor, a net monetary creditor, and a wealth holder with a neutral monetary position. It is assumed that prices double and that real assets and liabilities adjust precisely to this change.

It is important to regard the change in inflation as unanticipated. Expectations that prices would rise at an accelerated rate would motivate actions to prevent loss from the inflation. For example, demands for credit and supplies would shift to result in a higher equilibrium nominal interest rate. An interest payment on monetary assets and liabilities to offset the change in the real value of the face amount owing to inflation would reduce or eliminate the wealth transfer from net monetary creditors to net monetary debtors.

The U.S. federal government is the largest monetary debtor in our economy. In September 1976, the outstanding debt of the federal government was about $635 billion, with about 60 percent of this held by private investors. Federal agencies and trust funds had an additional $145 billion in debt outstanding. Inflation, to the extent that it has been underanticipated, has reduced the amount of purchasing power that the government has had to pay to holders of maturing securities. A five-year $1,000 government note bought in 1967, for example, could be redeemed in 1972 at only $805 in real purchasing power. Meanwhile, interest receipts from the note issued at about 5 percent yielded $50 per year. Ignoring possible reinvestment of these funds, the real purchasing power embodied in interest receipts over the five years amounted to only $219. With a $195 loss in the real purchasing power of the principal, offset by only a $219 payment in real purchasing power for interest, the security holder received virtually nothing for allowing the government use of his funds for the five years.

An unanticipated deflation has just the opposite effect on distribution—monetary debtors lose relative to monetary creditors. The same is true if the rate of inflation falls from that anticipated. An unanticipated deceleration in the rate of inflation would increase the real cost of debt already incurred. The government (taxpayers) would lose relative to bondholders and private debtors would also incur an unexpected real cost. Debtors are often believed to be least capable of bearing such a distributional shock. Hence, some fear economic disruption from an unexpected reduction in inflation.

INFLATION AND TAXATION

Inflation provides another windfall to the government in the form of increased tax revenues, in real terms as well as nominal. Growth in nominal income paralleling the rate of inflation moves income recipients into higher tax brackets, given the progressive tax structure. Inflation creates illusory capital gains, which are taxed, and with conventional tax-accounting procedures, corporate income tax liabilities are inflated as well.

The fact that taxes increase as a result of inflation is sometimes regarded as a built-in stabilizer in the economy. A fiscal restraint is automatically enacted in the presence of inflation. An additional result, however, is that command over real resources is transferred from the private sector to the public sector.[5]

INFLATION AND THE LABOR MARKET

Perhaps the strongest incentive for inflationary policies stems from the belief that stimulative policies will reduce unemployment, tightening the labor market and thereby benefiting the poor members of society.[6] Experience suggests that the salutary effects of inflationary stimuli on labor market conditions are relatively short-lived. Table 4.2 shows that wage rates kept pace with the consumer price index fairly well. However, in a comparison of unemployment rates it is also apparent that inflationary pressures do not necessarily generate a tight labor market, unless possibly there is accelerating inflation.

As the pace of inflation rose during the 1960s, the rate of unemployment decreased from more than 6 percent to less than 4 percent. Further increases in inflation, however, were accompanied by higher rates of unemployment. Some of the price increases and some of the unemployment experienced in the 1970s have been due to special supply constraints, such as the oil embargo. Still, the underlying rate of inflation is 5 to 6 percent and unemployment has been over 6 percent.

TABLE 4.1

Wealth Effects of Inflation
(dollars)

Before Inflation				After Inflation: In Money Terms				After Inflation: In Real Terms			
Assets		Liabilities		Assets		Liabilities		Assets		Liabilities	
Net Monetary Debtor											
MA	100	ML	200	MA	100	ML	200	MA	50	ML	100
RA	200	RL	0	RA	400	RL	0	RA	200	RL	0
		NW	100			NW	300			NW	150
Net Monetary Creditor											
MA	100	ML	0	MA	100	ML	0	MA	50	MA	0
RA	200	RL	200	RA	400	RL	400	RA	200	RL	200
		NW	100			NW	100			NW	50
Neither Net Monetary Debtor nor Creditor											
MA	200	ML	200	MA	200	ML	200	MA	100	ML	100
RA	100	RL	0	RA	200	RL	0	RA	100	RL	0
		NW	100			NW	200			NW	100

MA = monetary asset, RA = real asset, ML = monetary liability, RL = real liability, NW = net wealth.

Source: Compiled by the author.

TABLE 4.2

Inflation, Earnings, and Unemployment

	Yearly Percentage Change			Unemployment Rate
	Consumer Prices	Average Gross Earnings[a] Nominal	Average Gross Earnings[a] Real[b]	
1961	1.0	2.4	1.4	6.7
1962	1.1	4.0	2.9	5.5
1963	1.2	3.0	1.7	5.7
1964	1.3	3.2	1.9	5.2
1965	1.7	4.1	2.3	4.5
1966	2.9	4.0	1.1	3.8
1967	2.9	3.1	0.1	3.8
1968	4.2	5.8	1.5	3.6
1969	5.4	6.4	1.0	3.5
1970	5.9	4.2	-1.5	4.9
1971	4.3	6.5	2.2	5.9
1972	3.3	7.0	3.6	5.6
1973	6.2	6.8	1.0	4.9
1974	11.0	6.2	-4.3	5.6
1975	9.1	6.1	-2.8	8.5
1976	5.8	7.6	1.7	7.7
1977	6.5	7.3	0.8	7.0

[a]Average gross weekly earnings of total private nonagricultural production or nonsupervisory workers.

[b]Nominal earnings deflated by the consumer price index.

Source: Economic Report of the President, January 1978, pp. 294, 299, 313.

There are various explanations for this development. One explanation pertains to the longer run adjustments to inflationary pressures in labor markets. One adjustment that comes from a tight labor market and a relative rise in wages is a shift to labor-saving devices with a subsequent rise in structural unemployment for the unskilled. It might be argued that the tight labor market can thereby be given credit for stimulating technical advance as well as for upgrading incomes. For such a situation to be sustained, however, technological advance would have to proceed at a faster pace than inflation. This is possible only at low rates of inflation, not at the successively higher that would be required to retighten the labor market following each wave toward increased unemployment prompted by the change in relative wages.

The experience of rising unemployment accompanying inflation can also result from shifts in the supply curve of labor as unemployment compensation and other transfer payments increase for unemployed individuals. Increased transfer payments can be used to increase the incomes of the poor and unemployed. To the extent that transfer payments reduce the supply of labor at a given wage, and thereby output for a given level of demand, however, the transfer payments feed inflationary pressures.

DEBASEMENT OF THE MONETARY SYSTEM

Inflation means a decline in the value of a unit of money. Over time, continuing inflation reduces the efficiency of the monetary system for transacting exchanges of goods and services. Anticipated inflation, for example, leads to attempts by the public to economize on cash balances and hence minimize losses from holding this monetary asset.[7] Uncertainties about inflation have the same effect and also reduce the willingness of financial intermediaries to lend funds for longer time periods.

The reduced efficiency of the monetary system has some distributional consequences. It is injurious to those whose enterprises depend on a well-functioning system for making transactions. Then, too, it reduces opportunities for entering business if long-term debt financing is required. Uncertainties about inflation raise the real cost of this debt.

While inflation causes relative gains for some and losses to others in accordance with the composition of net wealth, it imposes a cost on the society as a whole to the extent that the efficiency of the monetary system declines. This is referred to as the "welfare cost" of inflation.[8]

SUMMARY AND CONCLUSIONS

Inflationary policies feed on the illusion that resources and goods and services are not scarce, that more can be had one place in the economy without there being less somewhere else. At times, of course, it is true that resources are not being utilized because of low levels of demand and that raising demand is a first step to raising output. When demand pressures produce inflation, however, it is a signal that bottlenecks are impinging on the ability of the economy to achieve supply consistent with demand.

Opportunities for expediency in financing government programs and the belief that improvements in distributional equity can be obtained through stimulative policies appear to have brought on the policies that increased the rate of inflation from the early 1960s to the early 1970s.

The distributional effects of inflation depend on institutional factors, such as laws regarding contracts, taxes, prices, and interest rates, and on whether or not the rate of inflation is correctly anticipated. Because distribution can be measured in different ways (wealth and income) and because distribution depends on a multitude of factors, it is difficult to conduct a thorough empirical analysis and draw solid conclusions about the role of inflation in the distributional changes experienced in the economy.

One result in practice as well as in principle is that inflation increases the public sector's command over resources relative to the private sector. Beyond this, the distributional consequences of inflation are far from clear-cut. Monetary debtors gain at the expense of monetary creditors only if the inflation is unanticipated. Gains to unskilled workers and recipients of transfer payments occur only in the short run. Attempts to keep their incomes ahead of inflation would require an accelerating inflation. This, in turn, would impose a welfare cost on the society as a whole.

NOTES

1. This literature includes the following: G. L. Bach and Albert Ando, "The Redistributional Effects of Inflation," Review of Economics and Statistics, February 1957, pp. 1-13; G. L. Bach and James B. Stephenson, "Inflation and the Redistribution of Wealth," Review of Economics and Statistics, February 1974, pp. 1-13; Albert E. Burger, "The Effects of Inflation (1960-68)," Review (Federal Bank of St. Louis), November 1969, pp. 25-36; Robinson G. Hollister and John L. Palmer, "The Impact of Inflation on the Poor," in Redistribution to the Rich and the Poor—The Grants Economics of Income Distribution, ed. Kenneth E. Boulding and Martin Pfaff (Belmont, Calif.: Wadsworth, 1972), pp. 240-70; W. Lee Hoskins, "Inflation: Gainers and Losers," Business Review (Federal Reserve Bank of Philadelphia), February 1970, pp. 23-30; and Reuben A. Kessell and Armen A. Alchian, "Effects of Inflation," Journal of Political Economy, December 1962, pp. 521-37.

2. For other descriptions of seigniorage, see the chapters by Benjamin Klein, Harry Johnson, and Thomas Wilson in this volume. See also the discussions by Herbert G. Grubel, Harry G. Johnson, and Wilson E. Schmidt in Monetary Problems of the International

Economy, ed. Robert A. Mundell and Alexander K. Swoboda (Chicago: University of Chicago Press, 1969). See also Martin J. Bailey, "The Welfare Cost of Inflationary Finance," Journal of Political Economy, April 1956, pp. 103-4; Phillip Cagan, "The Monetary Dynamics of Hyperinflation," in Studies in the Quantity Theory of Money, ed. Milton Friedman (Chicago: University of Chicago Press, 1956), p. 79.

3. For further discussion and estimates of seigniorage, see Thomas Wilson, "Identification and Measurement of Grant Elements in Monetary Policy," Chapter 3, this volume.

4. See Harry G. Johnson, "A Survey of Theories of Inflation," in Essays in Monetary Economics, 2d ed. (Cambridge, Mass.: Harvard University Press, 1969), pp. 104-42.

5. For a more detailed discussion of the impact of tax structure, see Nancy Jianakopolos, "Paying More Taxes and Affording It Less," Review (Federal Reserve Bank of St. Louis), July 1975, pp. 9-13.

6. For an analysis that leads to this conclusion, see Hollister and Palmer, "The Impact of Inflation on the Poor."

7. Inflation is frequently described as a tax on money. References regarding this tax and the mechanics of computing it are provided by the author in "Financing Government through Monetary Expansion and Inflation," Review (Federal Reserve Bank of St. Louis), February 1975, pp. 21-22.

8. A considerable amount has been written on this subject. See, for example, Bailey, "The Welfare Cost of Inflationary Finance." For a more recent survey and analysis, see John A. Tatum, "The Welfare Cost of Inflation," Review (Federal Reserve Bank of St. Louis), November 1976, pp. 9-22.

5

The Distribution of Income and Monetary Policy

THOMAS HAVRILESKY

INFLATION

If asked to select the single most persistent and pernicious economic problem of recent times many would choose inflation. After over a decade of high and highly variable rates of inflation, fewer and fewer economists would agree with the once conventional adage that "a little inflation is an O.K. thing."

There are a number of compelling reasons why high and highly variable rates of inflation should not be lightly regarded. One reason is that when the rate of inflation is highly variable, its movements tend not to be completely anticipated. Unanticipated variations in prices, nominal wages, and interest rates will cause a misallocation of resources. Therefore, changing rates of inflation tend to create inefficiencies and to redistribute income.

Another reason why erratic rates of inflation are bothersome is that pervasive uncertainty about future prices, wages, and interest rates generates those inelastic expectations that "Keynesianize" the structure of an economy. Inelastic expectations impede the facile adjustment of prices, wages, and interest rates to economic perturbations. In the face of an excess demand, decision makers will not know the "correct" market-clearing prices for goods, services, and productive factors. Consequently, they will adjust the quantities they exchange rather than the prices at which equilibrium quantities are exchanged. Thereby, an economy will become more prone to quantity adjustments (of production and employment) to exogenous shocks.[1] The same crippling uncertainty may help to explain the volatility of

This study has benefited from discussion with Michael Fratianni, Pieter Korteweg, and Ed Tower. Much of the material was inspired by an inflation seminar led by me at Erasmus University, Rotterdam, in 1977.

those "animal spirits" of businessmen that permeate the world view of unreconstructed Cambridge Keynesians.

This analysis of the link between variable rates of inflation and a Keynesian economic structure may also serve as a bridge between Keynesian and neoclassical theory. If uncertainty is the philosopher's stone of the Keynesian theory, then an unstable monetary environment is the crucible in which it is refined.

There is yet another link between the variability of inflation and the behavior of economic agents. Unexpected shifts in policymaker behavior, resulting in surprise variations in money supply growth, can generate unanticipated changes in inflation and temporarily alter perceived real wage and interest rates. This, in turn, changes the responses of labor suppliers, labor demanders, and asset holders to observed inflation and consequently has temporary effects on output and employment.

In contrast to highly variable rates of inflation, high levels of inflation are a problem for a modern economy for a number of reasons. Chief among these is that high money rates of interest are associated with high levels of inflation. Increases in market rates of interest are a means by which some individuals are given an incentive to postpone their spending plans. Thus, during periods of rapid inflation, the flow of credit to some sectors of the economy may be curtailed. Later in this chapter problems of inefficiency and income distribution related to high rates of interest will be examined.

THE SOURCE OF MONETARY INSTABILITY

If inflation is so noxious, why is it tolerated? Surely, there is sufficient knowledge of the problem. In fact, economists have had an unfalsified theory of inflation for hundreds of years. They generally are aware of the fact that there has never been in the history of the Western world a period of sustained price inflation that has not been associated with a rapid increase in the rate of growth of the money supply. Yet, the problem continues to plague modern economies. Why has man been unable to control his money? The supply of money is an important economic quantity, yet its control almost always lies with central government. An answer to this question, therefore, involves political as well as economic considerations. The political economy refers to the union of political and economic, government and market, subsystems of the social system. The study of political economy refers to analyses of the intersection of these two (among several) ways in which man organizes his social life. An examination of the phenomenon of inflation, therefore, is a problem in political economy.

Central banks, usually acting as agents of central government, are supposed to be able to control the supply of money. Economists have estimated reactions of the money supply and other variables controlled by the monetary authority to the state of the economy as measured by the actual and predicted rates of price inflation, levels of unemployment, and other indexes of economic well-being.[2] The sign and direction of these monetary policy reactions roughly correspond to the implicit countercyclical mandate imposed on the central bank by government. Nevertheless, there is evidence that these reaction patterns are quite variable over time.[3] For instance, between the early years of the Johnson administration, when William McChesney Martin was chairman of the Board of Governors of the Federal Reserve System, and the later years of the Nixon administration, when Arthur Burns was chairman of the Board of Governors, there was a marked decline in the antiinflationary policy reactions of the Federal Reserve.[4]

What might account for this variability? Casual observation[5] and empirical studies[6] suggest that, in addition to the conventional problems of inflation, unemployment, and the balance of payments, such factors as the funding and refunding of the government debt, union contract negotiations, oligopolistic price increases, and the behavior of natural resource price makers have had a systematic impact on monetary policy. For example, during the early 1970s, Federal Reserve officials claimed that the formation of the oil cartel made traditional antiinflationary militancy untenable. As other examples, during the late 1960s, they said that the size of the federal deficit, a crisis in the housing sector, and excessive wage increases made necessary less monetary stringency.[7]

One is drawn to the conjecture that the apparent erratic element in the behavior of the money supply, and hence the instability that bedevils the economy, arises from the effect of these exceptionable forces on the behavior of the monetary authority. Moreover, it appears that these "special" circumstances have a common thread running through them. They reflect the growing importance of distributional and allocational considerations in monetary policy deliberations. Whenever the monetary authority has allowed that it must alter its preferences, and therefore revise its reactions to the state of economy,* it seems to have done so because of perceived problems in the distribution of income and allocation of resources.

---

*The reaction function is a reduced form relation derived from the optimization of the preference function of the monetary authority subject to a given hypothetical structure of the economy. Therefore, estimated reaction coefficients can change also because of changes in the structure of the economy.

HOW DISTRIBUTIONAL CONSIDERATIONS AFFECT MONETARY POLICY

The best example of how distributional considerations impinge on monetary policy involves the interface between the government budgetary process and monetary policy actions. Many economists model the budgetary process as the outcome of deliberate cost-benefit calculations. This perspective does little to illuminate the actual relationship between the government budgetary process and monetary policy. The manifestly destabilizing and hence extremely costly monetary policies of many Western economies in recent decades could hardly have been grounded in ultrarational government budgetary deliberations. A better perspective on recent monetary policy can be gained if, instead, both government expenditure and taxation processes are viewed as the outcome of a complex array of pressures, wherein the costs and benefits are perceived only after long lags.

Let us first outline the roles played by elected officials, voters, and bureaucrats in the determination of the size of government expenditures. The evasiveness of elected officials on the issue of the allocation of national income between public and private expenditures is legend. Politicians win office generally on the basis of their promises to deliver government largesse, not on pledges regarding how these services will be financed. Opinion leaders in the press and electronic media find it in their self-interest to applaud, somewhat ingenuously, activism in government, often with little regard to future outcomes. The ambiance of domestic and international ideological struggle heightens government's tendency to overreact to real or imagined crises. Voters typically will adamantly support particular spending programs from which they benefit and be only vaguely opposed to "excessive government." The archetypical bureaucrat often seems to have precious little incentive to do anything other than promote the growth of his domain.

As a result of these incentives facing elected officials, voters, and bureaucrats, information regarding the costs and benefits of government programs is likely to be unreliable and/or inefficiently utilized until after a lengthy lag. In such an environment it is naive to regard the allocation of income between public and private uses as the upshot of stolid, ultrarational cost-benefit deliberations. Moreover, this viewpoint provides little insight into the related problem of monetary instability.

The ultrarational view of the government budgetary process seems even less credible when it is extended to the financing of government expenditures. Given the size of government expenditures, it is often contended that consideration of marginal administrative and tax avoidance costs of various modes of taxation determines how the expenditures will be financed. Once again, this disposition cannot easily explain the interrelation between the budgetary process and monetary instability.

Consider a world in which there are two kinds of taxation: conventional (income) taxation and taxation from fully anticipated inflation. Each type of taxation will have a marginal cost relation, and a cost-minimizing mix between the two types of financing may ideally be attainable. Now assume that there occurs a "temporary" increase in the desired size of government. It is commonly argued that massive boosts in conventional taxation are costlier to collect and generate a greater private investment in tax avoidance capital than increases in taxation from inflation.[8] Even when the inordinate welfare burden of the inflation tax is considered,[9] it is often said that this form of taxation is less costly. From the perspective of monetary theory, this ultrarational explanation of the rate of inflation is not particularly appealing. Too many of the costs associated with inflation are ignored. For example, recent experience shows there will be sizable private expenditures in avoiding the tax from anticipated inflation by finding substitutes for cash. Some examples of capital expenditures in this area are investments in credit-card technology, point-of-sale terminals, and electronic funds transfer systems. Some examples of current expenditures are outlays for more closely managing a cash position, as well as outlays to search for and provide more credit, including trade credit. Other costs include that of gathering information in order to be able to anticipate inflation better, that is, to avoid the tax from unanticipated inflation, as well as that of changing money prices.

Another important class of costs associated with anticipated inflation stems from the observation that high rates of inflation distort relative prices and increase the instability of money prices about their trend.[10] This, together with the uncertainty created by inflation, reduces the information content of any price and may generate considerable costs of searching for additional price information. In short, the more rapid the inflation, the greater the rate of depreciation of price information. Thus, inflation reallocates resources away from individuals who make frequent price searches.

Elsewhere in this chapter other sources of inefficiency and redistribution associated with high and highly variable rates of inflation are adduced. Many of these arguments suggest that persistent inflation damages the market-exchange subsystem of the social system. As the market diminishes as a social organizer, the domain of government coercion in the social system increases. Therefore, the persistence of inflation (monetary instability) must be of elemental concern to those who would preserve the market-exchange system.

The conclusion is that the true costs of inflation are quite sizable. Therefore, it seems unlikely that high inflation rates, similar to those experienced in Western economies in recent years, could be the outcome of careful, well-informed policy deliberations. Moreover, the ultrarational approach to inflation cannot easily explain the variability of inflation rates and abrupt intermittent attempts at deflation. In contrast, it is believed that the inflation associated with government spending stems, first, from the multiplicity of forces that influence the growth rate of government expenditures. Next, because there seems to be a lag in perception of its true costs, the deficit financing of these expenditures grows rather persistently. As these costs become more fully perceived, the monetary authority will slow the inflation and thereby induce recession. Thus, a learning dynamic underlies the inflation-recession process associated with the growth in government spending.

To be more specific: One consequence of growth in government spending in a fully employed economy is upward pressure on market rates of interest and a crowding out of private expenditures by public expenditures. Even for an underemployed (inflexible nominal wage) economy, it has been shown that a bond-financed government deficit can sustain far greater pressure on market rates than standard textbooks usually allow.* For fully employed (flexible wage) economies, of course, crowding out will generally be complete, regardless of how government spending is financed. A squeeze on credit is a direct consequence of an increased government deficit. Thus, it is hardly surprising that monetary policy makers will often find themselves under pressure to mask the effect of government deficits on interest rates by increasing the money supply. Increased liquidity will reduce market rates of interest as individuals use newly created money balances to acquire financial assets. However, the decline in interest rates will only be temporary because lower rates of interest will be inconsistent with the full employment equilibrium level of output. The lower market rates will stimulate private expenditures and, in a fully employed economy, will cause an increase in the general price level. The higher price level will reduce the real value of nominal financial wealth and cause market rates to rise to their initial level.

If monetary policy makers continue to find themselves under pressure to do something about "tight money," the money supply will continue to increase in the above manner, period after period, and

---

*Standard textbooks usually omit financing constraints and wealth constraints from their macroeconomic models. As a result, deficits (flows) are not shown to have an effect on wealth (stocks) and hence on financial asset demand functions.

any resulting liquidity effect of money on interest will, period after period, be wiped out by consequent increases in the price level. It is in this willy-nilly fashion, rather than through ultrarational deliberations, that government opts for inflationary financing.

As mentioned at the outset of this chapter, a number of grants arise because of unanticipated inflation. For example, there will be the well-known unilateral transfer from creditors to debtors as the purchasing power of nominal debt claims unexpectedly declines. This grant process is arrested when the new inflation becomes fully anticipated and creditors insist on higher nominal yields to compensate them for the expected loss in the purchasing power of the debt they hold. This "price expectations effect" will drive interest rates even higher and further aggravate the credit squeeze on certain sectors of the economy.*

Another familiar grant arising from accelerating inflation is the unilateral transfer of time from labor suppliers to labor employers and away from leisure activity. Assuming substitution effects outweigh income effects, this occurs as labor suppliers overestimate the real value of their nominal wage because of the unanticipated acceleration of inflation. It, too, ceases when the rate of inflation becomes fully anticipated. This grant process is analyzed in a wealth of literature on the expectations-augmented Phillips curve.[11]

Upon discovering the true costs of inflation, the monetary authority may curtail the money supply growth rate, whereupon the reduction in liquidity will temporarily drive interest rates even higher. The credit crunch will reduce aggregate expenditures and temporarily generate underemployment. Such unemployment, of course, can be described as an involuntary transfer of resources from production to idleness. In addition, as money supply growth rate decelerates, there will follow patterns of redistribution that are roughly symmetical to those that occur during acceleration—there will be unilateral transfers of resources from debtors to creditors and from employment to leisure.

The preceding analysis suggests that the cyclical pattern of costs, inefficiency, and redistribution that follows from unstable behavior of the money supply is, in turn, closely linked to the government budgetary process. In essence, it arises from the inability of elected officials and voters to resolve openly and critically the desired allocation of resources between public and private use.

Other distributional problems also impinge on monetary policy actions. Consider, for example, either the effect of a wage settle-

---

*The price expectations effect, of course, cannot be sustained unless money continues to grow at the new higher rate.

ment wherein nominal wage increases exceed productivity gains or the effect of an international conflict whereby the price of an imported raw material rises. Either of these factors will increase costs to domestic business firms. Assume that these firms raise their prices corresponding to the increase in costs. There then ensues a general upward movement in many nominal wages and prices as individuals try to circumvent the loss in real income. The resulting increase in the general price level (the acceleration in inflation) would, ceteris paribus, reduce the real value of financial wealth in the economy and thereby drive interest rates upward. A decrease in aggregate demand persists until some prices and wages fall.

In this situation the monetary authority has a choice. It can wait for a corrective reduction in the price level (a deceleration in inflation) to its full employment equilibrium level (rate of change). As an alternative, the monetary authority can validate the new price level (the new rate of inflation), prevent a decline in any wages or prices, and "cover up" the redistribution that is taking place by increasing the money supply (the money supply growth rate). The latter alternative forestalls the necessity of an immediate corrective adjustment in aggregate demand, but results in an acceleration of inflation and ultimately the cyclical processes described above.

In the case of the growing government deficit, the monetary authority has a similar choice: It could allow interest rates to rise, consistent with a new equilibrium or, in order to cover up the reallocation of credit that is taking place, it could try to sustain lower interest rates in the short run at the cost of further inflation and higher interest rates in the long run. The monetary authority often resolves these choices on the side of inflation and monetary instability, but sometimes it does not. One of the most undeveloped areas in economics, which is briefly examined in the conclusion to this chapter, is the theory of monetary instability.

INFLATION AND INTEREST RATES: A DIGRESSION

The true relationship between the rate of inflation and the equilibrium nominal rate of interest is probably not a proportional one. The demand for funds by debtors may not increase by the full amount of the anticipated inflation. While the demand for funds by private firms may increase in anticipation of inflation, some government entities, as well as regulated utilities, may have statutory limitations on their borrowing capacity. Therefore, the overall demand for funds may not rise proportionally.

In contrast, the supply of funds may increase more than proportionally as individuals unhoard money balances because of the tax on them associated with anticipated inflation. In addition, to the extent that a high level of inflation enhances uncertainty, consumers may save more as a hedge against the future. Finally, as interest rates rise and financial asset prices fall, private portfolios shrink in value. To the degree that portfolio holders do not view their wealth positions as being enhanced by the declining real debt burdens of business and government entities, total wealth is perceived to decline. This will also stimulate saving.

Overall, with a greater than proportional increase in supply and a less than proportional increase in demand, the nominal market rate of interest will not rise proportionately with the fully anticipated rate of inflation. The real rate of interest, the observed nominal rate less the anticipated rate of inflation, will therefore decline. In recent years many inflationary economies have experienced very low and even negative real rates of interest.

One problem with the preceding analysis is that it does not explain the low rate of private capital formation that is commonly observed in inflationary economies. A low real rate of interest and a low rate of private capital formation would arise from a sharper decline in the demand for funds relative to the aforementioned increase in supply. To the extent that a high rate of inflation is positively correlated with a highly variable rate of inflation, the decrease in demand may be explained by the subsequent uncertainty associated with future returns. Businessmen are inclined to shorten their investment horizons when confronted by increased uncertainty of future returns that is in this case associated with variable rates of inflation.

So far this analysis of the effect of money-financed government deficits has been concerned only with the level of interest rates. There will also be effects on the term structure of interest rates. To the extent that future inflation is expected, it will be reflected in higher, expected future rates of interest. Therefore, the yield curve will assume a steeper slope. To the extent that the rate of inflation is highly variable, it can be expected to bolster the risk premium associated with long-term yields. Thereby, the yield curve will further assume a steeper slope.

When it comes to the variability of the yield curve, the effects are not so easy to predict. Once again, assuming that inflation is highly variable, the effect of variations in money supply growth on the yield curve depends on the degree to which they generate an anticipation of inflation. Liquidity effects can be expected to show up more strongly on the short-term end of the yield curve where monetary policy actions have their initial impact. However, an increase in the anticipated rate of inflation will also have stronger effects on short-term rates than long-term rates. The two effects therefore have impacts on interest rates that are opposite in sign. Without further assumptions concerning the way expectations are formed, the effect of inflation on the variability of the yield curve is ambiguous.

In a world of adaptive expectations, the period of past inflation, which is used to anticipate future inflation, varies positively with the term to maturity. Therefore, for shorter maturities liquidity effects may be so quickly overshadowed by price expectations effects that they may not be evident from available data. On balance, however, the short end of the yield curve will probably show more volatility than the long end. In a world of rational expectations, liquidity effects will be nil. Moreover, price expectations effects will have a more facile impact on the longer maturities and the yield curve will fluctuate less than in a world of adaptive expectations.

THE SCARCITY OF CREDIT

If the monetary authority continually increases money supply growth in the face of the sort of disturbances described above, the rate of inflation will increase. As also discussed previously, this will tend to increase market rates of interest, which in turn will choke off the supply of credit to certain sectors of the economy.[12] These are generally sectors where financial intermediaries can engage in nonprice rationing of funds and where there is considerable interest sensitivity. It is often claimed that not only is this pattern distributionally unjust but that it leads to inefficiencies as resources flow into and out of these sectors with the business cycle. These contentions elicit arguments for government credit allocation.[13] Thus, there seems to be a remarkable complementarity between the unstable <u>macro</u> policy environment that generates a Keynesian structure and the concomitant <u>micro</u> policy actions that follow from and help to perpetuate that structure.

Where the variation of credit flows is the result of elasticities of consumer demand, it can be cogently maintained that it simply reflects an efficiently functioning economy and that production in certain sectors should be curtailed when interest rates rise. On the other hand, where the variation in credit flows is the product of institutional constraints, such as regulations and licensing, there may reasonably be latitude for intervention in the form of removing the regulatory obstacles to a freer flow of credit. For example, when the yield curve reflecting the term structure of interest rates is upward sloping, savings institutions can profitably channel funds to the housing industry. When the yield curve is downward sloping (short-term rates exceeding long-term rates), as it often becomes near cyclical turning points (when liquidity effects outweigh price expectations effects), savings institutions may find intermediation less profitable. As a consequence, the cyclical amplitude of credit flows to the housing sector is exaggerated. The problem, however, as recognized by a number of studies,[14] seems to be excessive regulation of financial markets, as exemplified by ceilings on deposit and mortgage rates of interest, usury laws, and limitations on the permissible range of investments available to financial intermediaries.

It has also been contended that mortgage rate ceilings have adverse distributional implications, as they result in nonprice rationing of mortgage funds, which tends to favor the wealthier and politically more powerful borrowers whenever market rates exceed ceiling rates. Even more devastating is the distributional impact of ceilings on deposit rates of interest. Deposit ceilings have been shown to shortchange normally less sophisticated low-income savers.[15]

Because commercial banks have an exclusive license to issue demand deposit claims, they are prone to tie in the extension of a line of credit and other financial services to the size of one's depositary wealth. This tendency is amplified by the absence of price competition for deposits. Bank customers are, of course, willing to forego interest by holding excessive deposits because in so doing they hedge against future shortages of credit. This phenomenon of tie-in selling by commercial banks has received scant attention in the literature and yet it appears to be an important source of the distribution of income in favor of the wealthy as well as a misallocation of resources, away from the creditworthy to the rich.

Removal of interest rate ceilings, usury laws, investment restrictions, and entry restrictions for financial intermediaries not only will moderate the cyclical fluctuation of credit to housing and improve the efficiency of credit markets but they will also make more equitable the distribution of income.

CONCLUSION

In view of so many adverse long-run consequences, it seems, on the surface, perfectly unreasonable to allow conventional monetary stabilization policy to be fettered by distributional and allocational constraints. Monetary officials often indicate that distributional and allocational constraints on their proper stabilization activity stem from the failure of elected officials, union leaders, and businessmen to resolve distributional conflicts effectively and realistically. On the other hand, individuals and organizations have learned from experience that the central bank will insure the economy from adverse short-run impact of their actions on production and employment. They are generally willing to "bet" on more inflation in their decisions.

It would be fanciful to suppose that the monetary authority could refuse to monetize a whopping deficit or validate a sizable and significant wage-price hike without strong congressional or presidential support. The monetary authority simply lacks a broad supportive constituency.[16] Moreover, the monetary authority as a bureaucracy, can be expected to be notably eclectic in its reflexive willingness to appear to be able to "do something" about distributional problems. For example, the central bank is not a novice at the game of credit allocation. The maintenance of differential reserve requirements and eligibility requirements for member bank borrowing and the administration of selective controls and deposit ceilings represent indefatigable attempts by the central bank to channel credit. The weight of historical evidence suggests not only that these activities have distracted the monetary authority from its main task of stabilization policy but it also reveals how easily private individuals can circumvent these controls through market substitution and other means.[17]

It would be equally fanciful to suppose that elected officials, union leaders, and businessmen can regularly reach "noninflationary" decisions. Their bargaining is often the focal point of ideological and social antagonisms that make "fair" and "realistic" resolution difficult. Consequently, the monetary authority can often serve as a convenient scapegoat for their failures.[18]

Still, to drag the monetary authority further into the distributional morass ultimately can only widen the distributional conflict, impede the economy, damage the market system, and tarnish the legitimacy of the central bank as an institution. The monetary authority can reduce the degree to which it hedges the risk of parties to distributional conflicts, but it cannot avoid being drawn into the problem. This is the real source of monetary instability.

Progress in the theory of economic policy requires an analysis of the circumstances whereby redistributive pressures generate monetary instability. The degree to which the monetary authorities will accommodate distributional pressures varies greatly at any point in time between nations and over time within the same nation. Historically, attempts at redistribution generate political discordance from groups who are harmed by the change. This "discordance cost" of redistribution should be quite sensitive to the influence that harmed groups have over the existing government. In situations where governments come into power partly because of pledges made to improve the economic circumstances of certain groups, and yet cannot afford to redistribute income away from other groups, there should be a pronounced tendency toward monetary instability. Monetary instability should be viewed as a consequence of attempts to cover up the attempts at redistribution that are taking place.[19]

NOTES

1. See, for instance, A. G. Hines, On the Reappraisal of Keynesian Economics (London: Martin Robertson, 1971), pp. 7-22. Reprinted in part in Thomas Havrilesky and John Boorman, Current Issues in Monetary Theory and Policy (Arlington Heights, Ill.: AHM, 1976).

2. For example, see James W. Christian, "A Further Analysis of the Objectives of American Monetary Policy," Journal of Finance 23 (June 1968):465-77; Ann F. Friedlaender, "Macro Policy Goals and Revealed Preference," Quarterly Journal of Economics 87 (February 1973): 24-43; Richard T. Froyen, "A Test of the Endogeneity of Monetary Policy," Journal of Econometrics 2 (July 1974):175-88; Thomas Havrilesky, "A Test of Monetary Policy Action," Journal of Political Economy 75 (June 1967):299-304; and John A. Wood, "A Model of Federal Reserve Behavior," in Monetary Process and Policy: A Symposium, ed. George Horwich (Homewood, Ill.: Irwin, 1967), pp. 135-66.

3. Thomas Havrilesky, Robert Sapp, and Robert Schweitzer, "Tests of the Federal Reserve's Reaction to the State of the Economy: 1964-74," Social Science Quarterly 55, no. 4 (March 1975):835-52. Reprinted in Havrilesky and Boorman, Current Issues.

4. Sherman J. Maisel, Managing the Dollar (New York: Norton, 1973), pp. 113-23.

5. See ibid.; or Sanford Rose, "The Agony of the Federal Reserve," Fortune, July 1974, pp. 91-93. Any reading of the minutes of the Federal Open Market Committee of the Federal Reserve System will also give this impression. These minutes are published regularly in the Federal Reserve Bulletin.

6. Froyen, "A Test of the Endogeneity of Monetary Policy"; Raymond E. Lombra and Raymond G. Torto, "Federal Reserve Defensive Behavior and the Reserve Causation Argument," Staff Economic Study, Board of Governors of the Federal Reserve System, November 1972.

7. See Maisel, Managing the Dollar; Leonard Silk, Nixonomics (New York: Praeger, 1973); and Arthur Burns, "The Role of the Money Supply in the Conduct of Monetary Policy," Monthly Review (Federal Reserve Bank of Richmond), December 1973, pp. 2-8. Reprinted in Havrilesky and Boorman, Current Issues.

8. Robert Gordon, "The Demand for and Supply of Inflation," Journal of Law and Economics, December 1975, pp. 807-36.

9. John A. Tatom, "The Welfare Cost of Inflation," Review (Federal Reserve Bank of St. Louis), November 1976, pp. 5-10.

10. See Benjamin Klein, "The Social Costs of the Recent Inflation: The Mirage of Steady, 'Anticipated' Inflation," in Institutional

Arrangements and the Inflation Problem, ed. Karl Brunner and Allan H. Meltzer, vol. 3, Carnegie-Rochester Conference Series on Public Policy (Amsterdam: North-Holland, 1974); John Felming, *Inflation* (Oxford University Press, 1976).

11. For example, see Thomas M. Humphrey, "Changing Views of the Phillips Curve," *Monthly Review* (Federal Reserve Bank of Richmond), July 1973, pp. 2-13. Reprinted in Havrilesky and Boorman, *Current Issues*.

12. There are several studies of the interest sensitivity of credit flows. For example, Jacob Cohen, "Direct versus Indirect Controls as Instruments of Monetary Policy," *Quarterly Review of Economics and Business* 10 (1970):25-34.

13. See, for example, Lester C. Thurow, "Proposals for Re-channeling Funds to Meet Social Priorities," in *Policies for a More Competitive Financial Sector* (Boston: Federal Reserve Bank of Boston, 1972), pp. 179-89. Reprinted in Thomas Havrilesky and John Boorman, *Current Perspectives in Banking* (Arlington Heights, Ill.: AHM, 1976).

14. See *The Report of the President's Commission on Financial Structure and Regulation*, December 1971; and U.S., Congress, House Committee on Banking, Currency and Housing, *Financial Institutions and the Nation's Economy*, 94 Cong., 1st sess., November 1975.

15. See Edward J. Kane, "Short-Changing the Small Saver," *Journal of Money, Credit and Banking* 2 (1970):513-22; David H. Pyle, "The Losses on Savings Deposits from Interest Rate Regulation," *Bell Journal of Economics and Management Science* 5 (1974):614-22; and David H. Pyle, "Interest Rate Ceilings and Net Worth Losses by Savers," Chapter 6, this volume.

16. For detailed discussion, see Edward J. Kane, "All for the Best: The Federal Reserve Board's 60th Annual Report," *American Economic Review* 64, no. 6 (December 1974):842-50. Reprinted in Havrilesky and Boorman, *Current Perspectives*.

17. Thomas Havrilesky, William Yohe, and David Schirm, "The Economic Affiliations of Directors of Federal Reserve District Banks," *Social Science Quarterly*, December 1973, pp. 608-22.

18. A most interesting view of this proposition is Edward J. Kane, "How Much Do New Congressional Restraints Lessen Federal Reserve Independence?" *Challenge*, November/December 1975, pp. 37-44. Reprinted in Havrilesky and Boorman, *Current Issues*.

19. The causes and concomitants of monetary instability are discussed more fully in Thomas Havrilesky, "Sources and Symptoms of Monetary Instability," in *Institutional Economics*, ed. John Q. Adams (Leiden: Martinus Neihoff, forthcoming). A theory of monetary instability is developed and tested in Thomas Havrilesky, "A Theory of Monetary Instability," in *The Political Economy of Policy-making*, ed. Raymond Lombra and Herbert Kaufman (New York: Sage, forthcoming).

PART III

Grant Flows and Government Regulation of Financial Institutions

6

Interest Rate Ceilings and Net Worth Losses by Savers

DAVID H. PYLE

INTRODUCTION

In the literature on grants economics (see, for example, Boulding [27]) an essential characteristic of a grant is the redistribution of net worth from one person or group to another. In the Interest Rate Adjustment Act of 1966, Congress established maximum deposit interest rate regulations for all the major savings institutions in the United States. The act also established a positive spread between the maximum rates payable by savings and loan associations (and savings banks) and the maximum rates payable by commercial banks.[1] This interest rate regulation resulted from concern regarding the solvency of savings and loan associations and savings banks in a period of rapidly rising short-term interest rates and concern that weakness in these savings institutions might adversely affect the supply of funds to housing finance.[2]

As a result of the regulation of the maximum interest rates payable by such institutions, savers who held interest-bearing accounts at all three types of savings institutions received less interest income than they would otherwise have received. This study, as did an earlier study on the same theme [11], considers the implicit grant resulting from the joint regulation of maximum deposit interest rates payable by commercial banks, mutual savings banks, and savings and loan associations.[3] The implicit grant estimated here is an estimate of the net worth loss imposed by the Interest Rate Adjustment Act of 1966 on savers who did not find suitable alternative ways of saving during the period 1968–75.

As shown in Table 6.1, thrift deposits at the major savings institutions grew in every year of the period under study.* Why did

*Thrift deposits is the generic term used for savings and time deposits (other than large CDs) at commercial banks, regular and

TABLE 6.1

Annual Average Stock of Thrift Deposits at Savings Institutions (billions of dollars)

	Thrift Deposits at Commercial Banks	Thrift Deposits at Savings and Loan Associations	Thrift Deposits at Savings Banks
1968	171.2	128.1	62.5
1969	183.4	133.6	66.0
1970	191.5	141.0	68.9
1971	224.5	160.4	76.5
1972	255.9	190.5	86.5
1973	285.8	216.9	94.1
1974	317.7	235.0	97.6
1975	351.3	264.5	104.3

Source: Board of Governors of the Federal Reserve System, "Revision of Money Stock Measures," Federal Reserve Bulletin, December 1974, p. 822; February 1976, p. 86; and U.S. Savings and Loan League, Savings and Loan Fact Book, 1976, p. 14.

thrift deposit savers not find suitable alternatives when other savers did find alternatives to deposits subject to rate ceilings, for example, the holders of large certificates of deposit (CDs) at commercial banks whose balances in this instrument fell by 53 percent in 1969? Presumably, this was because many thrift deposit savers did not know of or could not avail themselves of alternatives offering higher rates. Transaction costs, minimum transaction quantities, information costs, and inconvenience prevented many savers from buying short-term market securities.* Most important, in terms of the net worth losses reported here, interest rate ceilings precluded interest rate

---

special savings accounts at savings banks, and all types of savings at savings and loan associations.

*On February 25, 1970, the minimum noncompetitive bid for Treasury bills was increased from a bid for $1,000 in bills to a bid for $10,000 in bills. See Mullineaux [9] for evidence regarding the resulting reduction in disintermediation. (Disintermediation refers to the withdrawal of funds from financial intermediaries and their placement directly into the financial instruments of the ultimate borrower.)

competition among savings institutions that had previously provided low transaction cost, low minimum balance, well-known, convenient alternatives for thrift deposit savers.

PREDICTING DEPOSIT INTEREST RATES IN THE ABSENCE OF CEILINGS

To estimate the size of the net worth losses to savers as a result of the Interest Rate Adjustment Act of 1966, an estimate is needed of the interest rates that would have been paid on thrift deposits in the absence of this law. Note that the emphasis here is not on the effects of maximum deposit rates, per se, as commercial banks were subject to ceiling rates under Regulation Q prior to the passage of the Interest Rate Adjustment Act. Rather, the emphasis is on the particular effects of the joint regulation of maximum rates at all major savings institutions.

The evidence from the growth rate of thrift deposits and from simple regressions of the average interest rates paid on deposits on market interest rates suggests that the rates paid by savings institutions in 1967 were not significantly affected by the 1966 legislation. Consequently, this observation was used in obtaining the prediction equations.*

To obtain a set of prediction equations for the annual average rates paid by the three major types of savings institutions, the following simultaneous rate-adjustment model was estimated for the period 1952-67, using two-stage least squares:[4]

$$i_{SL}(t) = i_{SL}(t-1) + a_1[i_G(t) - i_{SL}(t-1) + k_{SL}] + a_2[i_{CB}(t) - i_{SL}(t-1) + \ell_{SL}] + u_{SL}(t) \qquad (1)$$

$$i_{CB}(t) = i_{CB}(t-1) + b_1[i_G(t) - i_{CB}(t-1) + k_{CB}] + b_2[i_{SL}(t) - i_{CB}(t-1) + \ell_{CB}] + b_3 d(t) + u_{CB}(t) \qquad (2)$$

$$i_{MS}(t) = i_{MS}(t-1) + c_1[i_G(t) - i_{MS}(t-1) + k_{MS}] + c_2[i_{CB}(t) - i_{MS}(t-1) + \ell_{MS}] + u_{MS}(t) \qquad (3)$$

*The predictions are not significantly altered if this observation is dropped.

where i_{SL}, i_{CB}, and i_{MS} are annual average rates of interest paid on thrift deposits by savings and loan associations, commercial banks, and mutual savings banks, respectively; i_G is the annual average yield to maturity on five-year U.S. government bonds; d is a dummy variable, which is 0 before 1962 and 1 thereafter; k and ℓ are constants in the various rate adjustment functions; and u is the error term.

The logic of this adjustment model is that the current average rate paid by a savings institution is its most recent average rate adjusted by the difference between the most recent rate and the current rate on a primary security and by the difference between the most recent rate and the current rate on a competitive secondary security. The constants in these adjustment functions may be interpreted as normal or steady state spreads between the various rates. The dummy variable in the commercial bank equation is intended to capture the effect of changing competitive attitudes by commercial banks with respect to savings and time deposits. The introduction of negotiable CDs in 1961 is an objective indicator of this shift in bank behavior.

The results of the experiment with this model suggested that the average rate paid on the competitive secondary security (i_{CB}) was not a significant determinant of the average rate paid by savings and loan associations ($\hat{a}_2 = 0.034$, with a t-statistic of 0.169), and that the average yield on the primary security (i_G) was not a significant determinant of the average rate paid by mutual savings banks ($\hat{c}_1 = 0.0089$, with a t-statistic of 0.166).* Elimination of these variables reduced the rate-adjustment equations to a recursive system, which was then reestimated using ordinary least squares.

In the earlier study [11], this recursive system was estimated by unconstrained ordinary least squares. Over the five-year forecast period considered there, the resulting predictions appeared reasonable. In particular, it was shown that the forecasts for 1971 and 1972 (when the behavior of savings and loan associations and mutual savings banks was presumably unconstrained by interest rate ceilings) were close to the actual rates paid by those institutions (on average).† However, experiments with the unconstrained least squares

---

*In the two-stage regressions, Equations (1) to (3) were estimated without the coefficient constraints implied by the rate-adjustment specification. As indicated later, these coefficient constraints appear to be an acceptable specification for Equations (1) and (2). If imposed here, they would improve the efficiency of the coefficient estimation. However, given the reported t-statistics for the dropped variables, it seems unlikely that this would change the decision to treat the equation system as recursive.

†The forecasts for 1971 and 1972 were based on actual (rather than forecast) values of the independent variables. As noted later,

forecasts for the longer period of this study suggested that forecast errors that appeared to be reasonable in shorter term forecasts accumulate and lead to unreasonable forecasts in later years.* As a result of this concern over the longer run properties of the prediction equations, the original specification was subjected to two tests.

First, the three unconstrained equations were tested to see if the sum of the coefficients of the independent variables in each equation is significantly different from 1, the constraint implied by the rate-adjustment model. The results of the t-test for each equation are:[5]

Savings and loan rate equation	t(13) = -0.69
Commercial bank rate equation	t(11) = 2.10
Mutual savings bank rate equation	t(13) = -2.69

It appears that one can reject the exact rate-adjustment specification for the mutual savings bank rate equation and that many investigators would not reject the exact rate-adjustment specification for the savings and loan rate equation. The commercial bank equation does not fall so clearly into either of these categories. It is conservative with respect to the net worth losses by savers to accept the hypothesis that the exact rate-adjustment specification holds for the rates paid by commercial banks. Therefore, the predicting equations for savings and loan rates and for commercial bank rates were estimated by constrained least squares, while the mutual savings bank rate equation was estimated by unconstrained least squares.

The second question about model specification concerns the potential autocorrelation of the disturbances in each of the equations. Because there are lagged dependent variables in the equations, a test discussed in J. Durbin [4] was used to check for autocorrelation. Durbin's test is asymptotically valid for large samples, and its properties for small samples are not known. The test statistic, h, is a standard normal deviate (in large samples). The results obtained in this application of the test are:

---

there were still net worth losses to savers in these years associated with the dynamic consequences of the earlier suppression of the interest rates paid by the savings institutions.

*In particular, the predicting equations used in the 1974 study lead to a forecast that the average rate paid by commercial banks on thrift deposits should exceed the average rate paid by savings and loan associations in 1975.

Constrained savings and loan rate equation	h = -1.23
Constrained commercial bank rate equation	h = 0.53
Unconstrained mutual savings bank rate equation	h = 0.09

To the extent that the test has validity for n = 16, only the savings and loan equation appears to show significant autocorrelation in the residuals. The probability of getting a value of h less than -1.23 for zero autocorrelation and h normal is about 10 percent.* The conservative specification here is to accept the hypothesis of negatively autocorrelated residuals for the constrained savings and loan rate equation but not for the other two equations. Therefore, the savings and loan rate predictions are based on a constrained generalized least squares estimate using the Cochrane-Orcutt method [3].

Given these considerations regarding equation specification, the prediction equations for the recursive system of rate equations are (coefficient t-statistics are reported in parentheses below each coefficient):

$$i_{SL}(t) - i_{SL}(t-1) = \underset{(8.77)}{0.12} - \underset{(-1.27)}{0.30}\,(i_{SL}(t-1) - i_{SL}(t-2)) + \underset{(3.82)}{0.12}\left[(i_G(t) - i_{SL}(t-1) + \underset{(1.27)}{0.3}\,(i_G(t-1) - i_{SL}(t-2))\right] \tag{1'}$$

Standard error of regression = 0.072; Durbin-Watson statistic = 2.17

$$i_{CB}(t) - i_{CB}(t-1) = \underset{(-2.38)}{-0.57} + \underset{(3.35)}{0.35}\,d(t) + \underset{(2.84)}{0.18}\,(i_G(t) - i_{CB}(t-1)) + \underset{(2.20)}{0.31}\,(i_{SL}(t) - i_{CB}(t-1)) \tag{2'}$$

*The test is for first-order autocorrelation. Another test can be obtained by estimating equations of the form:

$$y(t) = X(t)\beta + \rho u(t-1) + e(t)$$

where u is the first-order autocorrelated error and e is an uncorrelated error. From such regressions, one obtains an estimate of ρ, the autocorrelation coefficient, as the coefficient of the lagged value of y. For the three equations considered here, only for the savings and loan rate equation does ρ have a t-statistic with an absolute value greater than 1 (-1.89). This may lend some credence to the results obtained using the large sample statistic, h.

Standard error of regression = 0.10; Durbin-Watson statistic = 1.74

$$i_{MS}(t) = \underset{(3.79)}{0.94} + \underset{(2.22)}{0.39}\, i_{MS}(t-1) + \underset{(3.56)}{0.47}\, i_{CB}(t) \qquad (3')$$

Standard error of regression = 0.074; Durbin-Watson statistic = 1.97

The coefficients of these regressions have the expected signs, including the constant terms, that are consistent in all cases with the logic of the model and historical rate spreads. The negative autocorrelation in the savings and loan rate equation suggests an error adjustment by savings and loan associations that is not captured in the basic rate-adjustment model, but that is a reasonable adjustment process.

Using Equations (1'), (2'), and (3'), one can use two methods to predict deposit rates for subsequent years. First, predictions of each interest rate in a given year can be made on the basis of the actual values of the independent variables in that and previous years. This provides a measure of the reduction in the deposit interest rate resulting from the interest rate ceilings in that year alone. Alternatively, predictions of each deposit rate in a given year can be based on the predicted values of the independent variables in that and previous years. This provides a measure of the dynamic as well as the static consequences of the ceilings and is the basis for the calculation of the net worth losses to savers reported in the next section of this chapter.

The interest rate predictions using both of these methods are given in Table 6.2. A comparison of the predicted rates with the actual rates paid reveals some striking differences among the three types of savings institutions in their behavior under deposit rate ceilings. In 1971 and 1972, the fall in market interest rates allowed savings and loan associations and mutual savings banks more freedom in setting deposit interest rates. If one compares the predictions based on actual values of the independent variables ($\bar{i}_j$) with the actual interest rates paid (i_j) in those two years, the difference in rates ($\bar{i}_j - i_j$) for savings and loan associations is found to be -2 basis points (that is, -.02 percentage points) in 1971 and +8 basis points in 1972 (the forecast standard error was 8 basis points for each year). A similar comparison for mutual savings banks gives a difference of -2 basis points in 1971 and -6 basis points in 1972 (forecast standard errors of 10 and 11 basis points, respectively).

In contrast, commercial banks were less free to determine their own deposit interest rates because of the lower ceilings imposed on commercial bank interest rates by the Interest Rate Adjustment

TABLE 6.2

Predicted and Actual Average Deposit Interest Rates at Thrift Institutions
(percent)

Year	$\hat{i}_{SL}$	$\bar{i}_{SL}$	i_{SL}	$\hat{i}_{CB}$	$\bar{i}_{CB}$	i_{CB}	$\hat{i}_{MS}$	$\bar{i}_{MS}$	i_{MS}
1968	4.85	4.85	4.68	4.41	4.35	4.25	4.86	4.79	4.76
1969	5.18	5.08	4.80	4.85	4.65	4.34	5.11	4.85	4.89
1970	5.54	5.28	5.06	5.31	4.90	4.72	5.43	5.07	5.01
1971	5.69	5.31	5.33	5.32	4.91	4.74	5.56	5.12	5.14
1972	5.80	5.47	5.39	5.35	4.93	4.74	5.62	5.17	5.23
1973	6.01	5.68	5.55	5.59	5.13	5.02	5.76	5.34	5.45
1974	6.31	5.94	5.98	5.98	5.59	5.39	6.00	5.60	5.76
1975	6.58	6.26	6.22	6.25	5.85	5.50	6.22	5.77	5.89

$\hat{i}_j$ = Predicted rate using predicted values of independent variables for thrift institution j.

$\bar{i}_j$ = Predicted rate using actual values of independent variables for thrift institution j.

i_j = Actual rate paid by thrift institution j.

Source: Compiled by the author.

Act of 1966. In fact, it can be demonstrated that the average rate payable by commercial banks under the act was lower than the predicted interest rates for commercial banks in both 1971 and 1972. The result was that the commercial bank shortfall from predicted interest rates was 17 basis points in 1971 and 19 basis points in 1972 (with a forecast standard error of 12 basis points in both years).

The implied behavior after 1972 is also worth noting. The differences between the predicted interest rate based on actual values of independent variables and the actual rate paid for savings and loan associations in 1973-75 are

$$\bar{i}_{SL}(73) - i_{SL}(73) = 0.13\ (0.09)$$
$$\bar{i}_{SL}(74) - i_{SL}(74) = 0.04\ (0.11)$$
$$\bar{i}_{SL}(75) - i_{SL}(75) = 0.04\ (0.10)$$

where the numbers in parentheses are forecast standard errors for $\bar{i}_{SL}$. These results suggest that, since 1970, savings and loan associations have not been paying rates significantly lower than one might have predicted based on actual market interest rates and actual interest rates paid by the savings and loan associations in previous years. There are net worth losses to savers at savings and loan associations in these five years because the average rate paid in 1970 was significantly below the rate that would have been paid had the Interest Rate Adjustment Act not been in effect during 1968-70.*

For mutual savings banks, the differences between $\bar{i}_{MS}$ and i_{MS} are:

$$\bar{i}_{MS}(73) - i_{MS}(73) = -0.11\ (0.11)$$
$$\bar{i}_{MS}(74) - i_{MS}(74) = -0.16\ (0.11)$$
$$\bar{i}_{MS}(75) - i_{MS}(75) = -0.12\ (0.12)$$

These results suggest that mutual savings banks may have become more aggressive in interest rate competition since 1972. Special accounts at mutual savings banks provide a mechanism for this to occur, as such accounts can pay higher interest rates to longer term deposits and to deposits above certain minimum sizes. However, it is also possible that the conservative assumptions used in the model specification have biased the mutual savings bank interest rate predictions downward. The fact that all of the differences between the predicted interest rate and the actual rate paid by mutual savings banks have been negative since 1970 lends some credence to this suggestion of a bias. Whether or not there is a downward bias, it appears that net worth losses at mutual savings banks during 1971-75 are also chiefly attributable to the dynamic consequences of the 1968-70 losses.

For commercial banks, a picture quite different from that implied by the predictions for the other two savings institutions emerges. The differences between $\bar{i}_{CB}$ and i_{CB} are:

$$\bar{i}_{CB}(73) - i_{CB}(73) = 0.11\ (0.13)$$
$$\bar{i}_{CB}(74) - i_{CB}(74) = 0.20\ (0.16)$$

---

*The ability of savings and loan associations in 1973-75 to behave in a manner similar to their behavior prior to 1968, despite a sharp rise in market interest rates, is undoubtedly associated with the increased reliance of these institutions on certificate accounts. Substantially higher ceiling rates on longer term certificates (one year or more) were permitted beginning in 1973. The percentage of deposits in passbook savings at savings and loan associations fell from 54.6 percent in 1972 to 42.7 percent in 1975.

$$\bar{i}_{CB}(75) - i_{CB}(75) = 0.35\ (0.14)$$

These results suggest that commercial banks consistently have paid less in the period 1973–75 than would have been anticipated, even when the dynamic consequences of prior suppression of the interest rates paid because of the rate ceilings are not considered. The shortfall in 1975 is particularly striking.* Given the interest rate ceilings, then, commercial banks felt less compelled to bid aggressively for savings deposits, thus benefiting from the existence of those ceilings.

THE NEGATIVE GRANTS IMPOSED ON SAVERS

From the viewpoint of this study, the negative grants imposed on savers by the Interest Rate Adjustment Act of 1966 include the consequences of shortfalls from predicted rates on rates paid in subsequent years. Therefore, the estimate of net worth losses to those who held thrift deposits will be measured by the product of the difference between the predicted rates (using predicted values of those independent variables that are thrift deposit interest rates and actual values of the market interest rate variable) and actual rates paid times the appropriate average stock of thrift deposits (taken from Table 6.1). These net worth losses for each year and in total are given in Table 6.3. Table 6.3 also provides estimates of net worth losses in which the interest loss for savers at each institution for each year has been compounded at the predicted deposit interest rate for that institution in subsequent years. The latter estimates put each year's loss into 1975 values on a basis that places a value on the time between the date of loss and the terminal date of this study.

Based on the annual losses in 1975 values, the estimate of the total net worth loss to savers as a result of the ceilings in interest rates is about $22 billion. This estimated loss is an important frac-

---

*As one might expect, the losses were felt most heavily by savers who used passbook accounts. This is illustrated by the following comparisons taken from the Federal Reserve surveys of time and savings deposits:

Date	Percent Savings Deposits at Maximum Rate Allowed	Percent Time Deposits at Maximum Rate Allowed
1/31/73	69.0	95.2
1/31/74	67.6	90.4
1/31/75	73.4	93.3

TABLE 6.3

Net Worth Losses Imposed on Savers by the Interest Rate Adjustment Act of 1966
(billions of dollars)

	On All Savings at Savings and Loan Associations		On Time and Savings Deposits (Other than Large CDs) at Commercial Banks		On Savings and Special Accounts at Mutual Savings Banks	
	Nominal Values[a]	1975 Values[b]	Nominal Values	1975 Values	Nominal Values	1975 Values
1968	0.22	0.33	0.27	0.40	0.06	0.09
1969	0.51	0.72	0.94	1.30	0.15	0.20
1970	0.68	0.91	1.13	1.49	0.29	0.38
1971	0.58	0.73	1.30	1.63	0.32	0.40
1972	0.78	0.94	1.56	1.86	0.34	0.41
1973	1.00	1.13	1.63	1.83	0.29	0.33
1974	0.78	0.83	1.87	1.99	0.23	0.25
1975	0.95	0.95	2.64	2.64	0.34	0.34
Total	5.50	6.54	11.34	13.14	2.02	2.40

[a]Nominal values for year t are $(\hat{i}_j(t) - i_j(t))$ times average thrift deposits at institution j during time t.

[b]1975 values for year t are nominal values times

$$\prod_{\tau = t+1}^{1975} (1 + \hat{i}_j(\tau))$$

Source: Compiled by the author.

tion of the total interest income reported on individual tax returns. On a year-by-year basis, the net worth losses reported here average approximately 10 percent of the total interest income reported in each year and approximately 20 percent of total interest income reported by those taxpayers with adjusted gross incomes of less than $15,000.

A relevant question at this point is whether there are tangible gains accruing to the savers that might offset some of the estimated losses. As suggested earlier, the evidence regarding the costs of housing finance or other loans at the savings institutions does not support the existence of a significant, offsetting grant to borrowers.

Even if such a positive grant exists as a result of the interest rate ceilings, it does not follow that it accrues to the savers who incurred the net worth losses on their thrift deposits. The effect of the ceilings in preventing insolvency from being realized at some institutions is also of dubious value to thrift savers who are likely to be fully protected by deposit insurance. This benefit accrues to the owners of the institutions and perhaps to the general taxpayer through its effect in limiting the liability of the federal agencies that provide deposit insurance.

Another less tangible source of benefits to savers could result from an increase in services received in lieu of interest. In the case of savings and loans, where the information is most readily available, advertising expenses (which include premiums and gifts) have increased as a percentage of total operating expenses over the period under study, particularly in years when market interest rates were high. However, even if the entire excess over trend is taken as an added benefit to savers, the effect is to offset less than $0.1 billion of the estimated $6.5 billion in net worth losses at savings and loan institutions.

Perhaps a more important source of intangible benefit has resulted from increases in transaction services provided to savers and from increases in convenience for savers. The data on savings and loan associations suggest that there may be some intangible yields of this sort. For example, the average number of employees per 1,000 accounts has increased from 2.17 in 1966 to 2.44 in 1974 (the last year for which data are currently available). Since deposit growth over the period has involved a shift to less labor-intensive certificate accounts, the resulting increase in transaction services may be even greater than is implied by the approximately 1.5 percent annual average growth rate in the number of employees per account. Also, there is evidence of an increase in the number of savings and loan offices. The population per savings and loan office (main and branch) for the United States fell from 21,200 in 1966 to 13,900 in 1975. It is not clear what value savers place on these increases in services and convenience.[6]

CONCLUSION

The evidence presented here suggests that a conservative estimate of the net worth losses incurred by savers who used thrift deposits in the period 1968-75 is $22 billion (1975 values). At least in the case of commercial bank depositors where evidence is available, these losses are felt most heavily by the savers who use passbook accounts. The major justification of this negative grant imposed by the Interest Rate Adjustment Act of 1966 has been the need to protect the solvency of savings and loan associations and savings banks, which might have been accomplished, but the major beneficiaries of the legislation in terms of grant flows have been the owners of commercial banks or the users of bank services or both. This is true not only because of the large share of total thrift deposits that are held by commercial banks but also because the rates paid by commercial banks after passage of the act have shown a greater shortfall from what they would have been expected to pay without the ceilings. As further evidence of the latter point, it can be noted that the spread between the average rate paid by savings and loan associations and the average rate paid by commercial banks was 51 basis points in 1967 and 72 basis points in 1975.

Although there is substantial evidence to the contrary, one still might conclude that the positive grants resulting from the Interest Rate Adjustment Act of 1966 are justified. Based on the results of this study, the question still remains as to whether the negative grant should be imposed on the savers who use thrift deposits instead of on the general taxpayer.

NOTES

1. Ceilings on the deposit interest rates payable by commercial banks under Regulation Q existed before 1966. However, there is reason to believe that those ceilings were not particularly effective in constraining the rates paid prior to 1966. For example, between 1960 and 1966, the spread between the average rate paid by savings and loan associations and the average rate paid by commercial banks narrowed from 130 basis points to 51 basis points. See Pye and Young [10] for a discussion of the macroeconomic effects of interest ceilings and Kane [7] for a discussion of the policy implications of these ceilings. (A basis point equals 0.01 percentage points.)

2. There appears to be little doubt that some savings institutions with large portfolios of mortgages would have been forced to recognize their economic insolvency in the absence of deposit rate ceilings. However, it is not clear that the savers at such institutions should incur negative grants to ensure the solvency (or rather the continued operation—solvent or not) of such institutions. Furthermore, there is considerable doubt that interest rate ceilings provide an effective means of subsidizing home builders and buyers. See Jaffee [5] and Meltzer [8].

3. The effects of large negotiable certificates of deposit at commercial banks have not been included in the loss estimates. Basically, this is a judgment that these larger deposits could have been

transferred to market securities, had the owners so wished. See Pyle [11, pp. 614-15] for further discussion of the reasons for this exclusion.

4. The data on average savings deposit rates are from the 1973 Savings and Loan Fact Book (Chicago: United States Savings and Loan League), p. 17, except for the commercial bank rates after 1964. Due to insignificant interest payments on negotiable CDs after 1964, the data in the Fact Book are unsatisfactory for the purpose of this research. In 1965 and 1966, the rate on savings deposits at commercial banks was calculated by deducting interest payments on business deposits from total interest and dividing by non-CD average deposits. From 1967 on, a weighted average of the most common interest rates paid on savings deposits and time deposits of less than $100,000 taken for Federal Reserve surveys was used.

The data on the average amounts of thrift deposits outstanding are taken from "Revisions of Money Stock Series," Federal Reserve Bulletin (various issues) for commercial bank thrift deposits, and from the Savings and Loan Fact Book (1976) for savings and loan association and mutual savings bank thrift deposits.

5. See Johnston [6, p. 155] for a description of this test.

6. In a recent study, Baxter, Cootner, and Scott [1, p. 32] suggest that with deposit ceilings" . . . the impact of varying market rates of interest over time should show up primarily in the number of bank offices per capita and in the degree by which services are underpriced." They suggest that the increase in bank offices per capita will have benefits that accrue chiefly to depositors with large balances.

REFERENCES

[1] Baxter, W. F., P. H. Cootner, and K. E. Scott. Retail Banking in the Electronic Age: The Law and Economics of Electronic Funds Transfer. Montclair, N.J.: Alanheld, Osmun & Co., 1977.

[2] Boulding, K. E. The Economy of Love and Fear: A Preface to Grants Economics. Belmont, Calif.: Wadsworth, 1973.

[3] Cochrane, D., and G. H. Orcutt. "Application of Least-Squares Regressions to Relationships Containing Autocorrelated Error Terms." Journal of the American Statistical Association 44 (1949):32-61.

[4] Durbin, J. "Treating for Serial Correlation in Least-Squares Regression When Some of the Regressors Are Lagged Dependent Variables." Econometrica 38 (1970):410-21.

[5] Jaffee, D. M. Credit Rationing and the Commercial Loan Market. New York: Wiley, 1971.

[6] Johnston, J. Econometric Methods, 2d ed. New York: McGraw-Hill, 1972.

[7] Kane, E. "Short-Changing the Small Saver: Federal Discrimination against the Small Saver during the Vietnam War." Journal of Money, Credit and Banking 2 (1970):513-22.

[8] Meltzer, A. H. "Credit Availability and Economic Decisions: Some Evidence from Mortgage and Housing Markets." Journal of Finance 29 (1974):763-77.

[9] Mullineaux, D. J. "Deposit Rate Ceilings and Noncompetitive Bidding for U.S. Treasury Bills." Journal of Money, Credit and Banking 5 (1973):201-12.

[10] Pye, G., and I. Young. "The Effects of Deposit Rate Ceilings on Aggregate Income." Journal of Finance 27 (1972):1023-31.

[11] Pyle, D. H. "The Losses on Savings Deposits from Interest Rate Regulation." Bell Journal of Economics and Management Science 5 (1974):614-22.

7

Implications for Mortgage Lenders of Removing Deposit Rate Ceilings

RICHARD A. COHN

Interest rate ceilings on thrift institution deposits are such an established fact of life in the United States that it is perhaps difficult to recall that they have been in effect for less than ten years. They were instituted in 1966, during a period of rising interest rates, through the passage of the Interest Rate Adjustment Act, a result of fears concerning the supply of mortgage funds and the continuing viability of thrift institutions.

This chapter seeks to explore some of the distributional implications of an outright removal or a phasing out of deposit interest rate ceilings. It has two principal emphases. First, the need for government subsidies during the transition from a fixed to a free environment is investigated. Second, the implications of a removal of deposit rate ceilings on lender asset-liability portfolio management and resulting distributional effects are pursued.

The plan of the chapter is as follows. The first section deals with the dual social role of thrift institutions as mortgage lenders and deposit issuers. The next section outlines the manner in which the standard mortgage contract led to the development of a perceived need for deposit rate ceilings. The following section highlights the equity and efficiency gains that would accrue from a removal of these ceilings by discussing the impact that they have had on savers, house buyers, and the construction industry. This section presents arguments favoring government subsidies to thrift institutions to allow them to survive and to hasten their ability to compete in a ceiling-free environment. It also indicates the type of subsidy that is needed.

A final section argues that the postceiling need of thrift institutions to match asset and liability maturities will give rise to a demand

---

*The author expresses his appreciation to Susan R. Borghaus for research assistance.

for new types of mortgages. It discusses the potential attractiveness of these new mortgage designs for institutional investors other than thrift institutions and also indicates the likely distributional effects of these new designs on household borrowers. Some concluding remarks summarize the principal arguments.

DUAL SOCIAL ROLE OF THRIFT INSTITUTIONS

Thrift institutions are the major residential mortgage lenders in the United States. This term usually includes both savings and loan associations and mutual savings banks. The savings and loan associations are larger than the mutual savings banks in terms of assets and also devote a larger proportion of their assets to residential mortgages.

The provision of mortgage financing for owner-occupied housing is one of the two major social roles of thrift institutions. The instrument through which these loans are made is the standard mortgage, a contract that prescribes a fixed maturity, a fixed nominal rate of interest, and a fixed monthly payment in nominal dollars. These contracts are long-term instruments. Original maturities of 25 or 30 years are not uncommon. The effective maturity is somewhat shorter as a result of prepayments and refinancings occasioned by house sales and declines in interest rates, but the average maturity of a mortgage is nevertheless on the order of 12 years [12, p. 49]. Standard mortgages constitute the bulk of savings and loan association asset portfolios.

The other major social role served by thrift institutions is that of a repository for savings in a safe and liquid form. Their liabilities, which take the form of deposits, are important assets in household portfolios for a variety of reasons.

There is no asset available in the financial markets that combines safety, liquidity, divisibility, and return in a way superior to thrift institution savings deposits. The safety aspect is provided by government deposit insurance.* Although mutual funds can provide in principle the same divisibility feature as savings accounts, they

*Deposit insurance has grants features that are seldom recognized. While the risk of insolvency for an insured institution is a direct function of the risk of the asset portfolio, the insurance premium is not. Deposit insurance provides a subsidy for bearing asset risk, for to some extent the risk is not borne by the depositor or even by the equity holder but by the insurance fund.

lack government insurance.* The essentially infinite divisibility of savings deposits, coupled with safety, especially recommends them as asset holdings for lower income households. There is essentially no minimum balance requirement for a passbook savings account, while the standard minimum denomination for corporate bonds is $1,000 and that for commercial paper is even higher.[1] Furthermore, the current structure of deposit rate ceilings allows thrift institutions to offer higher deposit yields than commercial banks.

Not all thrift institution deposits are of the immediate-term "passbook" variety. There has been a tendency in recent years toward a lengthening of the maturity of the liability portfolio as a result of the issuance of "term" deposits. For the typical thrift institution, however, the weighted-average maturity of its liabilities tends to be significantly shorter than that of its asset portfolio.

It is this dual nature of thrift institutions as investors in mortgages and as issuers of deposits that produces the distributional implications of removing deposit rate ceilings, which are discussed below. The next section analyzes the role played by the standard mortgage.

THE STANDARD MORTGAGE

The standard, fully amortized, level-payment mortgage has its roots in the Great Depression of the 1930s. Prior to that time, residential mortgages were generally "interest only" and had original maturities shorter than is now customary. At maturity, mortgages were renegotiated or otherwise refinanced or, less often, extinguished by repayment.

The multidimensional contraction of the 1930s adversely affected the ability and willingness of mortgage lenders to refinance maturing mortgages, and foreclosures rose to alarming levels. Government responded by supporting the development of thrift institutions that specialized in acquiring fully amortized, level-payment mortgages, which eliminated by design the need for refinancing at maturity.

To this day federally chartered savings and loan associations are limited to mortgages of the standard variety. With the relatively

---

*One of the results of the historically high nominal interest rates of 1974 was the rapid growth of "money market" mutual funds, which invest in short-term paper, such as large commercial bank certificates of deposit. When it was determined that such funds that were organized as trusts could perhaps be entitled to the benefits of deposit insurance, the government quickly moved to ensure that such was not the case.

minor exceptions of cash and government securities held for liquidity purposes and of passbook loans, these intermediaries are essentially restricted to investment in standard mortgages.

In the absence of deposit rate ceilings, thrift institution deposits must compete with other short-term investments. If the general level of interest rates were to increase, then deposit yields would also have to rise. Owing to the longer average maturity of the mortgage portfolio, which consists largely of standard mortgages, however, the average asset yield would rise more slowly. This mismatching of maturities in the thrift institution asset-liability portfolio results in the intermediary's yield spread being squeezed when interest rates increase.

From the 1930s until the early 1960s, prices and interest rates were relatively stable, and thrift institutions, particularly savings and loan associations, prospered. But when interest rates rose in 1966 as a result of rapid increases in expectations of inflation, it was feared that many thrift institutions, which were unhedged in the maturity dimension, might not be able to survive. The government reacted to these fears by establishing deposit rate ceilings. These ceilings can be viewed as a direct result of the concentration of thrift institution assets in standard mortgages, a concentration encouraged by government policy.

Deposit rate ceilings have served to increase sharply the level of disintermediation resulting from increases in market rates of interest by limiting the ability of thrift institutions to bid for funds when the ceilings are binding. The skill with which savers have engaged in disintermediation seems to have increased over time. Ceilings have resulted in net deposits and withdrawals, and hence in the supply of mortgage funds, becoming sensitive to the level of nominal interest rates. Consequently, inflation, as a result of its impact on nominal interest rates, has, in conjunction with deposit rate ceilings, a negative effect on the supply of mortgage credit.

The effect of inflation on the standard mortgage produces a negative impact on the demand for mortgage credit as well [7]. The basic difficulty results from the fact that, because the standard mortgage specifies a payment that is level in nominal terms, the stream of real payments will depend on the pattern of inflation over the life of the mortgage. An increase in the mortgage interest rate in response to an increase in the anticipated rate of inflation over the life of the mortgage results in an increase in the initial payment. A rise in the initial payment tends to serve as a device for rationing mortgage credit.

As interest rates rise as a result of increasing expectations of inflation, more and more households, particularly those at earlier stages of the life cycle, find themselves unable to afford to purchase the housing that they could afford to finance in the absence of inflationary anticipations. This tendency is exacerbated by the use of rules of thumb on the part of mortgage lenders that limit the initial payment to a particular proportion of household income. These rules of thumb, like the standard mortgage, were developed in a period of relatively stable prices.

The difficulties caused by the standard mortgage have been augmented by an asymmetry related to interest rates induced by the repayment clauses that typically form part of the contract. When interest rates fall, the borrower, subject perhaps to a penalty, can often profitably refinance his mortgage debt at the new market rate. When interest rates rise, on the other hand, the lender is unable to call in the mortgage. The mortgage lender, in granting a repayment privilege to the borrower, is in effect selling the borrower a valuable option, the price of which is presumably reflected in the mortgage interest rate.

While the price of this option may be an equilibrium one, the lender is unable to hedge effectively against the asymmetry even if his mortgage portfolio were to be financed with long-term deposits. While the lender may be earning a positive yield spread at the time the mortgage contract is negotiated, this spread may vanish if interest rates fall and the borrower chooses to refinance his mortgage while the lender must continue to pay interest on the deposits that served to finance the original mortgage.

Refinancing privileges in household mortgages are sometimes required by state law. It might be in the interest of public policy to eliminate legal requirements that thrift institutions grant repayment privileges other than in the case of the sale of the house.

Thus, it can be seen that the standard mortgage entails severe drawbacks in a period of inflation and has produced difficulties as a result for both mortgage lenders and borrowers. Any proposal for eliminating deposit rate ceilings must take these problems into account.

IMPACT OF DEPOSIT RATE CEILINGS AND THEIR REMOVAL

Deposit rate ceilings have produced equity and efficiency losses that would presumably be eliminated by their removal. Numerous groups have been affected by deposit rate ceilings in addition to mortgage lenders themselves. Included among them are savers, house buyers, and factors in the construction industry.

Savers in commercial banks and thrift institutions have suffered from a loss of interest income in periods in which rate ceilings have been binding [5]. David Pyle [9] estimates the cumulative (1975 dollars) pretax loss to savers in commercial banks, mutual savings banks, and savings and loan associations through 1975 at $22 billion. These opportunity losses have not been distributed evenly over the population of savers. In particular, it is the small saver who has differentially experienced losses as a result of deposit rate ceilings.

While savers have lost, those households that have been successful in obtaining mortgages in those periods in which ceilings were binding have gained. Deposit rate ceilings are a subsidy to mortgage lenders that lowers their financing costs in relation to what they would be otherwise. Competition among mortgage lenders has caused some of this subsidy to be passed on to house buyers in the form of lower mortgage interest rates. Thus, deposit rate ceilings can be viewed as transferring income from lower income savers to middle-income house buyers. Those households that have found themselves unable to obtain mortgage funds as a result of the impact of ceilings on the supply of mortgage funds have, of course, suffered.

Deposit rate ceilings also have increased the cyclical instability of housing construction as a result of their effects on the supply of mortgage credit. Indeed, ceilings can be viewed as a vehicle for increasing the effectiveness with which monetary policy affects the construction sector.

Thus, a removal of deposit rate ceilings would increase returns to savers and also lower the cyclical instability of the construction industry by reducing the threat of disintermediation. The principal drawback to removing these ceilings continues to be fears concerning the viability of the thrift institutions, the same fears that gave rise to the institution of ceilings in the first place.

The potential gains from removing rate ceilings would seem to justify the government subsidy that would be needed to maintain the integrity of the thrift institutions. This argument is reinforced by consideration of the fact that ceilings are in themselves a subsidy [6].

While it seems unreasonable to single out one group of net monetary creditors for ex post compensation for losses sustained as a result of unanticipated inflation, the thrift institutions are a special case. The basic problem that they face is not that of a net monetary creditor position but one of maturity mismatching. This unhedged position is largely a result of government regulation and policy that have fostered the simultaneous acquisition of standard mortgages and issuance of short-term deposits. A subsidy would represent one way for the government to undo the negative effects of regulation.

A further argument for having the federal taxpayer subsidize the thrift institutions would apply to compensating for any loss suffered from unanticipated inflation. This argument is based on the notion that it is the federal government that stands to gain the most as a result of inflation. These potential gains stem from four major sources. First, the government is the largest net monetary debtor in the economy. Second, because the federal income tax is progressive and tax brackets are specified in nominal terms, tax revenues increase ceteris paribus as a result of inflation. Even if tax brackets are periodically adjusted, this essentially short-run result has real effects in the long run. Third, increases in nominal asset values produced by inflation give rise to capital gains taxes when realized. Fourth, if the price level is expected to increase, part of nominal interest represents principal in the sense that it is expected to compensate reductions in the real value of principal caused by inflation. But it is nominal interest, not real interest, that is taxed as interest income. While the thrust of this particular argument does not apply only to thrift institutions, it would seem to indicate that the government could "afford" to subsidize these mortgage lenders.

One proposal for eliminating ceilings that is designed in part to reduce the needed subsidy is that the removal become effective at some specified date in the intermediate or long-term future. In this manner the thrift institutions would have time to prepare for the introduction of the new rate-setting environment. But it does not necessarily follow that a deferred elimination of deposit rate ceilings would reduce the need for a subsidy. If thrift institutions are not granted increased asset management flexibility and continue to invest in standard mortgages, the need for subsidies will depend on the extent to which market rates of interest are in excess of ceilings at the time the ceilings are eliminated. The potential gains from an elimination of ceilings would therefore seem to warrant their removal in the immediate-term future, especially when it is realized that most of the necessary subsidies would be passed on to savers in the form of higher deposit rates. The remainder of this section is devoted to proposing a design for this subsidy.

Most proposals for government subsidies to thrift institutions as quid pro quo for the removal of deposit rate ceilings are prospective in nature. E. J. Kane [5], for example, proposes payments to originators of new mortgages. G. G. Kaufman [6] suggests that thrift institutions be allowed to borrow funds needed for the payment of interest until such borrowings are no longer required. Another proposal calls for a limited tax exemption for deposit interest. The adverse equity and efficiency implications of this latter proposal are obvious.

What is needed is a subsidy that would make up for losses that the thrift institutions have implicitly already suffered on their mortgage portfolios. This subsidy, coupled with greater asset management flexibility, would allow these mortgage lenders to pay competitive rates on deposits.

An appropriately designed subsidy would be limited to some proportion of the shortfall between the interest earnings on the mortgage portfolio, taken at book value, at the time that ceilings are removed and the interest that must be paid on a like amount of deposits. Only a fraction, rather than all, of the shortfall should be subsidized so as to offset profits that the thrift institutions have earned in the past as a result of ceilings. While most of the losses experienced by savers as a result of deposit rate ceilings represent gains to mortgage borrowers, thrift institutions also have shared in the gain. The fractional subsidy should be set with the viability of thrift institutions in mind.

Prior to the removal of ceilings, thrift institutions would specify the set of mortgages for which they wish to receive the subsidy. This designation should not be subject to a later reversal; otherwise, the lenders could stand to gain from a decline in the level of interest rates. The dollar amount of eligible mortgages would be reduced by amortizations of nominal principal, prepayments, and by the amount of default in the payment of principal. This last provision would ensure that default risk is borne by the lender's reserve funds.

The appropriate interest rate for the deposit base would be determined quarterly by the regional Federal Home Loan Bank as the average yield on passbook savings accounts for the region for the immediately preceding quarter. Thrift institutions could choose to issue other types of deposits, however.

One advantage of this subsidy design is that it is self-liquidating. As mortgages are repaid, they are removed from the set eligible for the subsidy. Another attractive feature is that the expenses of servicing the mortgage portfolio are, in principle, not subsidized.[2] At the time that ceilings are eliminated, holders of notice accounts and term deposits should be allowed to withdraw their funds without notice or penalty. They could then take advantage of potentially higher yields on their savings.

IMPLICATIONS OF POSTCEILING HEDGING BEHAVIOR

The maturity mismatching that now exists in thrift institution asset-liability portfolios is unusual for financial intermediaries. Intermediaries typically tend to hedge the maturity structure of their liabilities by investing in assets with a similar structure. Hedging is a process that allows the financial intermediary to reduce its risk exposure without necessarily lowering its expected return. Hedging behavior is consistent with models of financial intermediation that posit an institutional utility function as the normative criterion [2; 10].

Another model of financial intermediation that produces hedging behavior is one based on a normative criterion of equity value maximization. While the relevance of such a model to thrift institutions is perhaps questionable because the industry is characterized mainly by mutual firms,* a number of the largest savings and loan associations are shareholder-owned. If a financial intermediary faces perfectly competitive asset and liability markets but real costs in the event of insolvency, it will maximize the value of its equity by seeking to minimize the probability of insolvency. It will behave as though it were attempting to minimize the variance of the real rate of return on equity.

The extent of maturity mismatching exhibited by thrift institutions is not a freely competitive result. It is a result rather of government regulation. Once deposit rate ceilings are removed, thrift institutions presumably will engage in hedging behavior to a greater extent. Legislation designed to eliminate ceilings consequently should allow the thrift institutions greater asset management flexibility if they are to retain their role as issuers of short-term deposits.

If thrift institutions continue to be forced to invest in standard mortgages, they will need to finance these assets with long-term deposits in order to hedge. In order for these deposits to provide an effective hedge, refinancing clauses will have to be eliminated for the reasons indicated above.

Increased asset management flexibility need not take the form of the ability to diversify out of mortgages. Thrift institutions could continue to issue short-term deposits and still invest in mortgages if they were allowed to acquire mortgages whose nominal rate of return varies with the level of short-term interest rates.

Such a variable rate mortgage need not take the form that exists today and that has met significant borrower resistance, a design that specifies a nominal payment that moves with changes in some reference interest rate over the life of the mortgage. One proposed new design, for example, incorporates an initial payment that is independent of the expected rate of inflation together with a variable return to the lender.[3] The payments specified by this design tend to be fairly stable in real terms. Because payments consequently tend to rise in nominal terms if there is inflation, the initial payment is significantly lower than that specified by the standard mortgage under inflationary conditions. This "low-start" feature would increase the ability of households with stable or rising real incomes to borrow mortgage funds.

---

*Virtually all savings banks are mutual in form, as are most savings and loan associations.

Another "low-start" design that thrift institutions might find to be an attractive investment is the price level adjusted mortgage (PLAM). The PLAM mimics the standard mortgage under conditions of no inflation in the sense that the real periodic payment is constant over the life of the mortgage, as is the real rate of interest earned by the lender and paid by the borrower. Because the real rate of interest on short-term securities is fairly stable over time, thrift institutions might find that a portfolio of PLAMs could be financed by ordinary short-term deposits in a postceiling environment. But they might choose to use the PLAM as the basis for issuing price level adjusted deposits. Such deposits would appeal to savers desiring protection against unanticipated inflation.

Unfortunately, from the standpoint of the thrift institutions, the PLAM is likely to attract additional institutional lenders to the mortgage market. Corporate pension funds and life insurance companies are, in particular, likely candidates. Corporate pension funds have been seeking, apparently without much success, inflation-hedged assets to help offset the effects of inflation on their wage-related liabilities. The PLAM, which provides in principle a guaranteed real rate of return, might constitute just the sort of asset for which they have been searching. Life insurance companies wishing to issue price level adjusted life insurance policies should prove to be interested in the PLAM as an asset in which to invest the reserves underlying such policies.

The introduction of PLAMs and other "low-start" mortgages would presumably benefit one group of borrowers while proving to be relatively disadvantageous to another. The group that would benefit would be the borrowers that have been forced out of the purchased housing market into the market for rental housing or into less expensive housing as a result of the effect of inflationary anticipations on the standard mortgage payment stream. The group that would suffer differentially would be borrowers who could have financed housing with standard mortgages because interest rates would rise to reflect the increased demand for mortgage funds.

CONCLUSION

Deposit rate ceilings have created difficulties not only for mortgage lenders but also for savers, potential mortgage borrowers, and for factors in the construction industry. But if these ceilings are removed at a time when the ceilings are binding, then thrift institutions will suffer a loss of net income unless it is offset by government subsidy. Because the prospective net income loss can be traced directly to the effects of government regulation, it is appropriate for the government partially to subsidize this loss.

Once rate ceilings are removed, new mortgage designs will have to be introduced if thrift institutions are to continue to issue short-term deposits. These new designs will attract additional institutional lenders to the mortgage market and will also have distributional implications for potential mortgage borrowers.

NOTES

1. In 1970, the government raised the minimum Treasury bill denomination from $1,000 to $10,000 in order to increase the attractiveness of thrift institution deposits, for deposit interest rate ceilings were producing disintermediation. That is, funds were being withdrawn from depository financial intermediaries, including the thrift institutions, and invested directly in Treasury bills. This action clearly cut off one option for the small saver [5; 8].

2. The formulation of this subsidy design has benefited from discussion with D. Lessard, F. Modigliani, and other members of the Sloan School Mortgage Study, the results of which study are reported in [7]. The views expressed here, however, are solely those of the author.

3. See [7] for an analysis of this design, the "constant payment factor" variable rate mortgage, and of the price level adjusted mortgage.

REFERENCES

[1] Friend, I. Study of the Savings and Loan Industry. Washington, D.C.: Federal Home Loan Bank Board, 1969.

[2] Hart, O. D., and D. M. Jaffee. "On the Application of Portfolio Theory to Depository Financial Intermediaries." Review of Economic Studies 41 (January 1974):129-47.

[3] Haywood, C. F., and C. M. Linke. The Regulation of Deposit Interest Rates. Chicago: Trustees of the Banking Research Fund, Association of Reserve City Bankers, 1968.

[4] Jaffee, D. M. "Eliminating Deposit Rate Ceilings." Federal Home Loan Bank Board Journal 6 (August 1973):4-12.

[5] Kane, E. J. "Short-Changing the Small Saver: Federal Government Discrimination against Small Savers during the Vietnam War." Journal of Money, Credit and Banking 2 (November 1970):513-22.

[6] Kaufman, G. G. "A Proposal for Eliminating Interest-Rate Ceilings on Thrift Institutions." Journal of Money, Credit and Banking 4 (August 1972):735-43.

[7] Modigliani, F., and D. R. Lessard, eds. New Mortgage Designs for Stable Housing in an Inflationary Environment. Boston: Federal Reserve Bank of Boston, 1975.

[8] Mullineaux, D. J. "Deposit-Rate Ceilings and Noncompetitive Bidding for U.S. Treasury Bills." Journal of Money, Credit and Banking 5 (February 1973):201-12.

[9] Pyle, D. H. "Interest Rate Ceilings and Net Losses by Savers," Chapter 6, this volume.

[10] _____. "On the Theory of Financial Intermediation." Journal of Finance 26 (June 1971):737-47.

[11] Report of the President's Commission on Financial Structure and Regulation. Washington, D.C.: U.S. Government Printing Office, 1971.

[12] Rosen, K. T. "The Role of Pension Funds in Housing Finance." Working Paper no. 35. Joint Center for Urban Studies of the Massachusetts Institute of Technology and Harvard University, June 1975.

[13] Samuelson, P. A. "An Analytical Evaluation of Interest Rate Ceilings." In Friend, Study of the Savings and Loan Industry, pp. 1563-590.

8

Implicit Grants of Bank Reserve Requirements and Restrictions on Branching

MARVIN PHAUP, JR.

> Almost anything a government does in the way of regulations, prohibitions, quotas, quantitative restrictions, licensing, and so on, will alter the relative price structure, which will in turn lead to either temporary or permanent shifts in the distribution of income and assets. [p. 9]
>
> In the long run, the distribution of . . . implicit grants may . . . change.
>
> A good deal of the theory of incidence . . . can . . . be summed up in the proposition that what adjusts is the adjustable and that what is not adjustable has to bear the burdens of adjustment. [p. 52]
>
> Kenneth E. Boulding
> The Economy of Love and Fear

INTRODUCTION

U.S. experience with government regulation of commercial banking is consistent with the view that regulation does affect the dis-

I am indebted to the Federal Reserve Bank of Cleveland for data processing support, to Steve Ruetschi for research assistance, and to John T. Rose for several valuable suggestions. I also wish to thank Darrel Cohen, W. C. Edwards, Donald Fraser, Roger Hinderliter, William Melton, Dwight Phaup, Robert Richard, Edward Stevens, Gordon Tullock, Roger White, Dorothy Kornegay, Janet Meany, Bill Oyster, and Barbara Saragovitz.

The views expressed are the author's and are not necessarily shared by the Congressional Budget Office, the Federal Reserve Bank of Cleveland, or others who contributed to this chapter.

tribution of income and wealth, but that over time, usually as a result of created incentives, these redistributive effects change markedly. Two cases in point are cash reserve requirements and restrictions on branching. Although a major change in reserve requirements or branching law can have significant short-run effects, the earnings performance (defined in terms of return on assets or return on equity) of the vast majority of banks is unaffected by present reserve requirements or branch restrictions. "Other things"—rather than bank profits—bear the burden of adjustment if there is a burden to bear.

Though asserted as true, these statements are not self-evident. In developing the case that long-term bank profitability is independent of reserve requirements or branching restrictions, this chapter describes the institutional structure within which individual optimizing behavior is expected to lead to this result and provides evidence on the nature and incidence of a part of the bank regulatory burden.

CASH RESERVE REQUIREMENTS: A FIRST LOOK

A cash reserve requirement specifies the minimum amount of cash, as a proportion of deposit liabilities, that a bank must hold. As a simple example, banks might be required to hold vault cash and deposits with other banks of, say, 20 percent of their deposits. In practice, the percentage requirements vary with the type of deposit (higher for demand than time deposits) and Federal Reserve regulations specify that only vault cash and deposits with Federal Reserve banks qualify as cash reserves (thereby excluding deposits with other banks).*

Imagine a Federal Reserve regulation suddenly and effectively imposed on a commercial banking system that had previously been unregulated with respect to cash reserves. Because it is almost impossible, and very costly, to operate a bank without some inventories of cash, the banks would have held cash prior to regulation [3; 23; 26; 33]. For simplicity, though, suppose the new regulation causes all banks to increase their holdings of currency and deposit balances with the Federal Reserve.

Redistributive effects emanate from the rise in the ratio of cash to deposits, which implies a decline in the ratio of earning assets to

---

*Deposits and reserves are recorded at one prespecified time per day, for example, the opening of business. The reserve requirement is usually considered to be met if the average of the daily measured reserve positions is equal to the required ratio over a reserve settlement period, for example, for the Federal Reserve, the seven days, Thursday through Wednesday.

deposits for all banks. Bank revenues (and, to a lesser extent, bank costs) and earnings fall. The market value of all banks is reduced and present bank shareholders suffer a loss of income and wealth. The shareholders' loss is the government's gain. The transfer occurs because, as commercial banks hold more currency and central bank deposits (both are non-interest-bearing liabilities of the government), the central bank is able to hold larger quantities of interest-bearing assets and thereby increase its income.*

As shown in Table 8.1, the effect of reserve requirements is to increase the central bank's investments by the amount of decline in commercial bank interest-bearing assets. In effect, the commercial banks are forced by the cash reserve requirement to trade some of their security holdings to the central bank in return for non-interest-bearing reserves issued by the central bank. Cash reserve requirements, therefore, constitute a tax on banks.† Hence, the first redistributional effect of cash reserve requirements is a transfer from bank shareholders to other taxpayers (if the government uses its additional income to reduce taxes) or to the beneficiaries of new government spending financed by the bank tax.

All taxes create avoidance incentives. Although it is difficult to know how bankers will seek to minimize the cost of reserve requirements, it is certain that they will attempt to do so. One possibility is that the forced increase in holdings of cash and the acquired privilege of borrowing from the central bank, a common quid pro quo of reserve requirements, may have increased the liquidity or decreased the risk associated with the bank enterprise.[1] If so, banks may be able to offset the reserve requirement tax by assuming portfolio and capital positions that previously would have been considered undesirably risky. Another possibility is that if reserve requirements are

---

*More precisely, higher reserve requirements enable the central bank to increase its earnings without increasing the privately held money supply. Open-market purchases of assets increase central bank earnings, but also increase the money supply unless reserve requirements are increased. Earnings of the central bank revert to the government. The Federal Reserve pays most of its income (after deducting expenses incurred principally in providing services to member banks, a 6 percent stock dividend for member banks, and provision for capital reserves) to the U.S. Treasury as payment of interest on Federal Reserve notes.

†This tax is effective even if the securities sold by the commercial banks to the central bank are government securities. In this case, the tax does not increase the government's revenue but reduces the interest the Treasury must pay on the debt.

TABLE 8.1

Simplified Balance Sheets of the Central Bank and All Commercial Banks, before and after the Imposition of a 20 Percent Reserve Requirement

Central Bank		All Commercial Banks	
Before			
Investments—$15	Central bank notes outstanding*—$10	Vault cash—$5	Deposits—$100
		Deposits with central bank—$5	
	Deposits of commercial banks—$5	Loans and investments—$90	
After			
Investments—$25	Central bank notes outstanding*—$15	Vault cash—$10	Deposits—$100
		Deposits with central bank—$10	
	Deposits of commercial banks—$10	Loans and investments—$80	

*$5 is held by the nonbank public.

Source: Hypothetical table was compiled by the author.

levied on "deposits," banks may invent "nondeposit" liabilities. If the reserve requirement tax applies uniformly to all suppliers of banking services, the industry may pass the tax on to its customers in higher prices and/or lower interest paid on deposits.

If all efforts to avoid the tax fail, then present bank owners incur a permanent wealth loss. In addition, the flow of capital into the banking industry will be slowed by the reduced relative attractiveness of the industry to investors. The long-run supply of banking services will decline and the relative prices of bank services will rise.* In

*The reduced supply of bank services, the attendant higher prices, and the reduced quantity bought and sold also imply a net deadweight

the meantime, the growth of nonbank, reserve-requirement-exempt financial institutions will accelerate.

CASH RESERVE REQUIREMENTS AND THE U.S. REGULATORY STRUCTURE

The impact of reserve requirements on banks in the United States is very different from the hypothetical case just described. The principal reason for the difference is that U.S. commercial banks have a choice between state and federal authorities that compete for regulatory jurisdiction over the banks.

Two types of regulatory bodies issue charters or licenses to open and operate banks in the United States: the Office of the Comptroller of the Currency (a part of the U.S. Department of Treasury) and the 50 individual state banking departments.* Banks chartered by the comptroller are national banks. Of the 14,600 U.S. commercial banks, about 4,700 are national banks and the rest operate under state charter. (Exact numbers are published in the Federal Reserve Bulletin.) All national banks must be members of the Federal Reserve System. State banks may choose, but are not required, to be members In 1976, there were more than 1,000 state-chartered member banks. Much of the significance of membership is that cash reserve requirements are set for member banks by the Federal Reserve, while nonmember reserve requirements are determined by the state banking authorities. Optional Federal Reserve affiliation for state banks means that these banks have a continuing interest in the relative costs and benefits of Federal Reserve membership and nonmembership. Because withdrawal from membership for a state bank involves only the formality of notifying the Federal Reserve and a six-month waiting period, the cost is negligible. National banks can acquire the option of leaving the Federal Reserve by giving up their national charter for a state charter. Although state charters are usually available to established national banks, the cost of changing from a national to a state nonmember bank is greater than the cost of changing membership status for a state bank.†

---

loss from reserve requirements unless there is some offsetting gain, such as increased economic stability.

*All District of Columbia banks are supervised by the comptroller. Nonmember banks (there is presently one) must maintain cash reserves equal to those required by the Federal Reserve.

†Charter application must be made, filing and legal fees paid, and the name of the bank changed, that is, national banks have the word

Given optional membership, and the assumption that regulators prefer more to fewer banks within their jurisdiction, required reserves would tend to be set by the authorities at the level banks would choose to hold without regulation.* This tendency is weakened, however, by the Federal Reserve's package of free and subsidized services to member banks. These services include discount window loans—usually at a below-market rate—check clearing, wire transfer of funds, securities, and a cost accounting system called functional cost analysis.

State banking regulators do not make loans or provide other services equivalent to those offered by the Federal Reserve; they do permit cash reserve requirements to be met with deposits in other commercial banks. The recipients of these balances, called correspondent banks, offer services to nonmembers similar to those offered by the Federal Reserve. In addition, many correspondent banks are member banks and therefore are able to provide an indirect, "pass-through" access to some Federal Reserve services.

Banks that value direct access to Federal Reserve services will be willing to "pay" for these services by holding additional cash reserves.† The value of these services must be at least equal to any earnings foregone from meeting the higher reserve requirements of the system. Otherwise, the member bank will opt out. Over time, the cost-benefit ratio of Federal Reserve membership for individual banks will vary with interest rates, the level and composition of services provided, the availability of Federal Reserve services to non-

---

"national" in their names or the letters N.A. (for national association) following the name, as in Crews National Bank or Willow Bank, N.A.

*Some regulators are permitted to change reserve requirements at their discretion. For example, the Board of Governors of the Federal Reserve System may vary reserve requirements on demand deposits between 22 and 7 percent and on time deposits between 10 and 3 percent.

†The reserve requirement-services package is not a complete description of factors affecting the membership decision. In some states, national banks are partially exempt from state usury laws. Bankers also have a preference for an accessible regulator that can provide prompt, authoritative, and consistent regulatory interpretations and rulings. These considerations aside, the Federal Reserve has an extra competitive tool: Like the state regulators, it can reduce reserve requirements but it can also increase the flow of services. In fact, services are an inefficient means of refunding the reserve requirement tax. Hence, the proposal is often made that the Federal Reserve should charge for services and pay interest on reserves.

members, and the level of reserve requirements. For example, a rise in interest rates or easier nonmember access to Federal Reserve services would lead to a reduction in the number of member banks [17].

Federal Reserve requirements are, at best, a temporary tax—effective only for as long as it takes a member to become a nonmember. State reserve requirements are expected to be set, effectively, below those of the Federal Reserve system and to approach zero.[2] Thus, neither the long-run market value of member banks nor the long-run supply of bank services is appreciably reduced by reserve requirements in the U.S. regulatory setting.

Some observers abhor the prospect of a competitive regulatory structure, dubbing it "competition in laxity" and asserting that the inevitable result is "unsound banking." Although discussion of optimal regulatory structure is beyond the scope of this chapter, it can be noted that such phrases as "competition in laxity" do not constitute a complete, logical case for regulatory monopoly. At a minimum, such a case ought to contain an explicit statement of the objectives of regulation and a demonstration that the least-cost means of achieving these objectives is through the grant of a monopoly to a single regulatory agency. Then the cost of such a scheme can be weighed against the expected benefits.

Others have speculated that the present structure undermines Federal Reserve monetary control. Most studies, though, have found that state reserve requirements are not a significant barrier to effective monetary control.[3]

RESTRICTIONS ON BANK BRANCHING

State restrictions on branching by banks are often suspected of being a thinly disguised grant from the banking public to the owners of banks.[4] Yet very little evidence exists of a strong and simple relationship between branching law and bank profitability (for example, [1; 2; 5; 8; 10; 15; 16; 24; 31; 32]). Grants, perhaps complex in nature, do seem to be at stake, though, in the choice of a branching law, as witnessed by the intense political struggle surrounding legislative consideration of the issue.

Spokesmen for large urban banks usually favor unrestricted branching, arguing that it is in the public interest to make banks more conveniently accessible and to increase competition in local markets through branching. Many markets, it is asserted, that cannot support an additional bank could accommodate and benefit from the competitive effects of branch entry by existing banks. In fact, branch entry is less costly in terms of capital requirements and in terms of the ease with which regulatory approval may be obtained than the alternative of a new bank charter. Expanded branching is often opposed, though, by small-town bankers on the grounds that city bankers intend to drive the independent banks out of business. However, small unit banks often prosper in direct competition with large branch systems. Therefore, the opposition of these banks to branching is likely owing to their knowledge that maintaining earnings in the face of branch competition may require the bank to behave in an otherwise undesirable way. For example, there is evidence that less restrictive branching leads to higher loan-deposit ratios [7; 24 and references therein], which presumably involve more (undesired) risk.[5] Large banks' support for branching may reflect the tendency of large corporate organizations to give some weight to the preferences of management (rather than shareholders) for corporate growth. The development of a branching network is one means of achieving management growth objectives that apparently does not involve a sacrifice of shareholders' profits.[6]

A highly perceptible consequence of unit banking to the public is the smaller number of banking offices (per capita or per square mile), for example, [14; 19; 30]. In addition, borrowers are confronted with a smaller supply of loan funds by local banks. However, the losses and grants implied by branching restrictions are partially offset by such substitutes as extended banking hours, postage-paid service by mail, drive-in windows, remote facilities, automatic teller machines, and customer-bank communications terminals (CBCTs) (where the latter do not conflict with the branching laws). The adverse impact on consumers from branch prohibition is further mitigated by the induced growth and development of nonbank financial institutions, such as savings and loan associations, credit unions, small loan companies, and currency exchanges. Indeed, it is not certain that the total supply of credit is reduced by restrictions on branching. However, in those states where branching is not prohibited, branch systems do develop and prosper, indicating that at least some customers prefer branch banking to its substitutes.

MEMBERSHIP, BRANCHING, AND PERFORMANCE, 1971-75

The Federal Reserve Bank of Cleveland's 1971-75 data base of balance sheets (end of year) and annual income statements for district banks was used to measure the effect of membership and branch restrictions on current bank earnings and to attempt to identify how banks adjust to these types of regulations. The Cleveland District consists of Ohio, the western third of Pennsylvania, the Ohio River panhandle of West Virginia, and eastern Kentucky. Branching laws vary in these states from unit banking in West Virginia* to countrywide branching with home office protection, that is, branching prohibited in the home office municipality of another bank (Kentucky) to countywide branching (Ohio) to contiguous county branching (Pennsylvania).†

Less variation occurs in state reserve requirements. With negligible exception, present requirements are 7 percent for demand deposits and 3 percent for time and savings deposits in Kentucky, Ohio, and West Virginia (see Appendix for details). Pennsylvania's requirement of 12 percent on demand deposits seems high, but Pennsylvania permits 50 percent of reserves to be held in U.S., Pennsylvania, or local government securities. Kentucky and Ohio also permit some portion of reserves to be invested in interest-bearing securities.

Quite plausibly, nonmember cash reserve requirements are below effective levels in all Fourth District states such that actual cash reserves are at the levels banks would choose to hold without regulation. For example, consider West Virginia, which, because it does not permit reserves to be held in interest-bearing form, appears to have the highest cash reserve requirements in the district. Suppose a West Virginia nonmember bank had 65 percent (the average for such West Virginia banks) of its deposits in time and savings deposits and the remainder in demand deposits. Required reserves, then, would be 4.4 percent of total deposits. By comparison, the ratio of collected cash items to deposits for all nonmember banks in West Virginia on December 31, 1975, averaged 7.6 percent.[7] Pennsylvania had the lowest nonmember cash-deposit ratio in the district, 6.7 percent; and Kentucky had the highest, 11.7 percent. Even with some allowance for "window dressing" of balance sheets, desired reserves appear to be well above required levels for Fourth District nonmember banks. Nominal differences in cash requirements be-

---

*West Virginia banks are permitted "one-limited off-premises facility," such as a drive-in or walk-up teller window within 2,000 feet of the bank.

†With a few "grandfather" exceptions, only Ohio permits multibank holding companies in the Fourth District. Contiguous county branching permits branching in the same county in which the principal office is located and into counties bordering on that county. Cases have occurred with contiguous county branching in which a bank moved its principal office to a contiguous county branch in order to gain access to a more desirable market in a county adjacent to the new principal office.

tween states, therefore, are unlikely to be significant for bank operations.

If it is true that the Federal Reserve imposes a reserve requirement "tax" and provides compensating services to members, then member banks will hold more cash than nonmember banks, but bank profitability will not be adversely affected by much or for long. The actual mix of Federal Reserve services and member bank portfolio adjustments that transforms a lower ratio of earning assets-total assets at member banks into no difference in net earnings must be identified empirically rather than a priori. Additionally, if it is true that the financial structure adjusts over time to eliminate monopoly profits that may arise in the short run from branching restrictions, then no differences will be observed in bank earnings between unit and branching states in the Fourth District where the branching laws have been essentially unchanged for years. Prior observation, however, suggests that unit banking results in lower loan-asset ratios.

Cash Reserves, Profitability, and Capital

In interbank comparisons of cash holdings or other characteristics, it is desirable to take into account and hold constant those factors affecting performance that are not themselves the result of membership or state regulation. The control variables in the cash holdings comparison consist of the ratio of time and savings deposits to total deposits (less cash is held per dollar of savings balances than demand balances) and total assets (to allow for possible economies of scale). State location is represented by three "dummy" variables for Kentucky, Ohio, and Pennsylvania. West Virginia banks are the standard against which the other states are compared. Membership is represented by two dummy variables. The first, a 0, 1 variable (= 1 for members) permits a measure of the effects of membership independent of bank size. Its coefficient is referred to as the membership intercept. The second, the product of the 0, 1 membership variable and total assets, enables size-dependent effects of membership to be detected. Its coefficient is referred to as the membership slope.

The regression comparison of cash (vault cash and interbank and Federal Reserve deposits, excluding items in process of collection) to asset ratios is shown in Table 8.2. The essential message is that member banks in the Fourth District do hold more cash than comparable nonmember banks as evidenced by the positive signs and asterisks in the membership intercept column.

TABLE 8.2

Regression Results, Dependent Variable = Cash-Assets, Fourth District Banks, 1971-75

Year	Independent Variables											
	Constant	Membership Intercept[a]	Kentucky	Ohio	Pennsylvania	Total Time and Savings Deposits	Assets[b]	Membership Slope[c]	R^2	SEE	F	n
1971	0.1667*	0.0157*	0.0133	0.0025	-0.0050	-0.1335*	-0.0153*	0.0109	0.28	0.0345	42.94	768
	(18.78)	(5.06)	(1.83)	(0.36)	(-0.65)	(-13.07)	(-2.04)	(1.39)				
1972	0.1570*	0.0101*	0.0171*	-0.0018	-0.0058	-0.1128*	-0.0117	0.0054	0.22	0.0364	32.18	758
	(16.49)	(3.01)	(2.23)	(-0.25)	(-0.71)	(-10.41)	(-1.69)	(0.73)				
1973	0.1605*	0.0153*	0.0197*	0.0002	-0.0008	-0.1314*	-0.0067	0.0017	0.28	0.0329	42.42	748
	(17.16)	(5.01)	(2.83)	(-0.03)	(-0.11)	(-11.99)	(-1.19)	(0.27)				
1974	0.1628*	0.0139*	0.0214*	-0.0038	-0.0033	-0.1315*	-0.0134*	0.0090	0.33	0.0330	52.52	747
	(17.11)	(4.50)	(3.03)	(-0.58)	(-0.46)	(-12.17)	(-2.73)	(1.67)				
1975	0.1639*	0.0152*	0.0123	0.0006	-0.0012	-0.1418*	-0.0073	-0.0003	0.29	0.0305	44.41	744
	(17.98)	(5.28)	(1.92)	(0.10)	(-0.18)	(-13.72)	(-1.79)	(-0.06)				

[a]Membership intercept is the coefficient for a 0,1 variable, = 1 for member banks.
[b]Unit of measurement for assets is hundreds of millions of dollars.
[c]Membership slope is the coefficient for an interactive dummy variable = product of membership times assets.

* = significant at 0.05; t-values in parentheses.

Note: Some Fourth District banks were omitted, including the 18 banks with deposits in excess of $500 million (all are members) and as many as 15 other banks omitted because of missing or faulty data or because the banks were failing. In December 1975, the distribution of members and nonmembers by size group was:

Total Deposits (millions of dollars)	Member	Nonmember	Total Deposits	Member	Nonmember
0-5	21	47	25-50	95	52
5-10	59	67	50-100	64	15
10-25	160	115	100-500	42	12

The December 1975 distribution of Fourth District banks by state was:

State	Member	Nonmember	State	Member	Nonmember
Kentucky	51	100	Pennsylvania	62	32
Ohio	331	165	West Virginia	15	13

Source: Compiled by the author.

Though all five estimates of the membership slope parameter are positive, none is significantly different from zero. Thus, if there is a different impact of membership on cash holdings per dollar of assets for large and small banks, the difference is not great enough to be statistically significant in this test despite the Federal Reserve's size-graduated reserve requirement schedule (see appendix). The positive signed coefficients and asterisks in the Kentucky column indicate that banks in that state hold significantly larger ratios of cash than banks in West Virginia.* Neither branch law nor state reserve requirements—nominally the lowest in the district—explain the anomalous Kentucky cash holdings. One possible explanation is the very rapid growth of demand deposits, perhaps coal related, at eastern Kentucky banks. During 1971-75, demand deposit funds at these banks increased 55 percent, easily double the rate of increase observed in other Fourth District states. A large share of "new" funds may be held in cash if these deposits are considered to be transitory.

The relative profitability of Fourth District bank groupings is shown in Tables 8.3 and 8.4. The first of these measures profitability in terms of net income after taxes and extraordinary items as a ratio of total assets. The membership coefficients are more frequently positive than negative (8 to 2) but none is significantly different from zero. However, Table 8.4, where net income is related to the book value of equity capital rather than assets, indicates that in some years, members, especially those under $100 million in size,† are more profitable than nonmembers. There is no evidence that nonmembers had an earnings advantage.‡

---

*If the predisposition to hold a lot of cash dominated the membership decision, a high proportion of Kentucky banks would be expected to be members. In fact, Kentucky has the smallest ratio of members to insured commercial banks of any Fourth District state: 29 percent compared to the next smallest value of 60 percent for West Virginia (figures are for December 1975).

†This size proviso is added in recognition of the membership slope estimate for 1971 of -0.0095 (t-value = -1.07). If that estimate is the true value, membership reduces the earnings rate by 0.95 percentage points for each $100 million in assets. For a member bank with assets of $113 million, the positive membership intercept of 0.0107 would be completely offset by the negative membership slope. However, there are only 12 nonmember banks in the Fourth District over $100 million in size.

‡From December 31, 1970, to December 31, 1975, the proportion of Fourth District bank assets held by member banks declined from 87.1 to 85.6 percent. Over the same period, member banks as a pro-

TABLE 8.3

Regression Results, Dependent Variable = Net Income-Assets, Fourth District Banks, 1971-75

Year	Independent Variables										
	Constant	Membership Intercept[a]	Kentucky	Ohio	Pennsylvania	Assets[b]	Membership Slope[c]	$\bar{R}^2$	SEE	F	n
1971	0.0105* (13.94)	0.0003 (1.00)	-0.0011 (-1.40)	-0.0018* (-2.36)	-0.0008 (-0.99)	-0.0007 (-0.76)	0.0008 (0.91)	0.01	0.0038	2.31	763
1972	0.0110* (14.88)	-0.0005 (-1.35)	-0.0016* (-2.07)	-0.0022* (-2.96)	-0.0009 (-1.12)	-0.0009 (-1.31)	0.0010 (1.26)	0.02	0.0037	3.27	754
1973	0.0115* (14.93)	-0.0001 (-0.25)	-0.0005 (-0.67)	-0.0015* (-1.97)	-0.0002 (-0.29)	-0.0017* (-2.63)	0.0009 (1.31)	0.03	0.0039	5.01	745
1974	0.0108* (10.89)	0.0002 (0.37)	0.0006 (0.58)	-0.0005 (-0.55)	0.0004 (0.35)	-0.0016* (-2.24)	0.0008 (0.95)	0.02	0.0049	3.14	744
1975	0.0092* (10.54)	0.0007 (1.58)	0.0015 (1.60)	-0.0006 (-0.66)	0.0008 (0.86)	-0.0007 (-1.18)	0.0003 (0.51)	0.03	0.0044	4.94	742

[a]Membership intercept is the coefficient for a 0,1 variable, = 1 for member banks.
[b]Unit of measurement for assets is hundreds of millions of dollars.
[c]Membership slope is the coefficient for an interactive dummy variable = product of membership times assets.

* = significant at 0.05; t-values in parentheses.

Note: See note on page 124.

Source: Compiled by the author.

TABLE 8.4

Regression Results, Dependent Variable = Net Income-Equity, Fourth District Banks, 1971-75

	Independent Variables										
Year	Constant	Membership Intercept[a]	Kentucky	Ohio	Pennsylvania	Assets[b]	Membership Slope[c]	$\bar{R}^2$	SEE	F	n
1971	0.0936* (12.73)	0.0107* (3.19)	0.0094 (1.21)	-0.0024 (-0.33)	0.0032 (0.39)	0.0137 (1.61)	-0.0095 (-1.07)	0.02	0.0370	4.00	763
1972	0.1039* (14.21)	0.0019 (0.57)	0.0003 (0.04)	-0.0096 (-1.32)	-0.0006 (-0.07)	0.0042 (0.59)	0.0004 (0.05)	0.01	0.0369	2.33	754
1973	0.1092* (15.05)	0.0056 (1.64)	0.0152* (1.99)	-0.0019 (-0.27)	0.0067 (0.82)	-0.0028 (-0.45)	-0.0012 (-0.19)	0.03	0.0364	4.77	745
1974	0.1017* (9.53)	0.0080 (1.60)	0.0346* (3.10)	-0.0051 (0.48)	0.0119 (1.01)	-0.0037 (-0.47)	-0.0008 (-0.09)	0.04	0.0531	6.11	744
1975	0.0895* (10.02)	0.0122* (2.87)	0.0316* (3.37)	0.0011 (0.12)	0.0154 (1.54)	0.0002 (0.04)	0.0011 (0.17)	0.06	0.0454	9.33	742

[a]Membership intercept is the coefficient for a 0,1 variable, = 1 for member banks.
[b]Unit of measurement for assets is hundreds of millions of dollars.
[c]Membership slope is the coefficient for an interactive dummy variable = product of membership times assets.

* = significant at 0.05; t-values in parentheses.

Note: Equity includes all capital and reserves. See note on page 124.

Source: Compiled by the author.

Nor is there evidence that restrictive branching increases profitability. No significant earnings differences exist between unit banking West Virginia and contiguous county branching Pennsylvania. On occasion, West Virginia banks had higher earnings-asset ratios than did Kentucky and Ohio banks; but earnings to equity rates were highest in Kentucky. No differences were found in the ratios of net income-equity for Ohio, Pennsylvania, and West Virginia.

The differences in relative profitability between Tables 8.3 and 8.4 (members appear to be more profitable, West Virginia banks less profitable, in the latter table) imply systematic differences in equity capital. Indeed, as shown in Table 8.5, for banks up to the $50 to $75 million range, members had significantly smaller ratios of capital to assets; and West Virginia unit banks were the most heavily capitalized in the District. Note that if membership in the Federal Reserve reduces risk for smaller banks while unit banking increases the risk against which a capital buffer is held, then these differences in capital do not imply uneven or "unfair" treatment of banks by regulators. However, it does appear that the reserve requirement tax of the Federal Reserve may be overrefunded (if members have a higher return on equity) through lower capital requirements.

Earning Assets

Given that member (and Kentucky) banks hold more cash than comparable banks, then they must hold less in noncash or earning assets. As shown in Tables 8.6 to 8.8, member-nonmember and interstate differences also exist in the <u>composition</u> of earning assets.

U.S. Treasury Securities

While small members and nonmembers hold about the same proportion of earning assets in Treasury paper, the larger member banks tend to hold more earning assets in Treasury securities than large nonmembers, in the early part of the period. An interesting aspect of this result is that none of the members seems to have adjusted to higher cash holdings by decreasing the share of earning assets in relatively liquid, but low-yield Treasury securities. No significant differences were found in Treasury-earning asset ratios between states.

---

portion of the total number of district banks increased slightly from 59.1 to 59.7 percent.

TABLE 8.5

Regression Results, Dependent Variable = Equity-Assets, Fourth District Banks, 1971-75

Year	Independent Variables										
	Constant	Membership Intercept[a]	Kentucky	Ohio	Pennsylvania	Assets[b]	Membership Slope[c]	$\bar{R}^2$	SEE	F	n
1971	0.1191* (25.78)	-0.0092* (-4.43)	-0.0235* (-4.81)	-0.0205* (-4.43)	-0.0150* (-2.92)	-0.0207* (-4.08)	0.0188* (3.54)	0.06	0.0233	9.19	768
1972	0.1143* (17.80)	-0.0103* (-3.47)	-0.0172* (-2.54)	-0.0178* (-2.77)	-0.0117 (-1.63)	-0.0194* (-3.16)	0.0160* (2.42)	0.03	0.0324	5.32	758
1973	0.1118* (21.58)	-0.0094* (-3.92)	-0.0170* (-3.12)	-0.0147* (-2.86)	-0.0099 (-1.73)	-0.0180* (4.05)	0.0141* (2.94)	0.05	0.0260	7.10	748
1974	0.1111* (22.08)	-0.0080* (-3.43)	-0.0214* (-4.07)	-0.0119* (-2.40)	-0.0094 (-1.70)	-0.0161* (-4.33)	0.0117* (2.87)	0.06	0.0251	8.37	747
1975	0.1113* (16.97)	-0.0060 (-1.93)	-0.0194* (-2.81)	-0.0136* (-2.09)	-0.0033 (-0.46)	0.0133* (-3.01)	0.0069 (1.37)	0.03	0.0333	5.29	744

[a]Membership intercept is the coefficient for a 0, 1 variable, = 1 for member banks.
[b]Unit of measurement for assets is hundreds of millions of dollars.
[c]Membership slope is the coefficient for an interactive dummy variable = product of membership times assets.

* = significant at 0.05; t-values in parentheses.

Note: See note on page 124.

Source: Compiled by the author.

State and Local Government Securities

Member banks, especially those under $100 million in assets, allocate a significantly larger share of earning assets to these investments whose income is exempt from federal taxation than do nonmembers. In fact, though not shown here, on average, members hold a larger share of total assets in tax exempts than do nonmembers. Tax-exempt securities are less liquid than taxable issues, but the most profitable banks usually hold relatively large quantities of these securities [27] .* West Virginia banks, followed by those in Pennsylvania, are the district's heaviest investors in tax exempts.

Loans

The ratio of loans to earning assets is not significantly different for members and nonmembers.[8] West Virginia banks, however, do have significantly lower loan-earning asset ratios than those in the other states in the district. This expected result is the only significant difference found in the composition of earning assets between banks in Pennsylvania where branching is most widely permitted and those in unit banking West Virginia.†

In summary, member bank earning asset portfolios, though smaller than those of nonmembers, contain the same proportion of loans and Treasury securities and significantly larger proportions of tax-exempt securities. The additional tax-exempt paper, by an adding-up constraint, must have been substituted for portfolio components not examined here, such as agency securities, federal funds sales, and commercial paper. West Virginia banks appear to have substituted tax exempts for loans.

---

*No significant support could be found for the suggestion that members hold more state and local issues because they also have larger deposits of state and local governments to which the securities are pledged. That is, a regression of state and local government demand deposits as a ratio of total deposits on the independent variables in Table 8.7 failed to produce any significant coefficients for the membership dummies.

†In terms of loan composition, the West Virginia consumer does not seem to be slighted. Regression results (not shown here) indicate that West Virginia banks have higher ratios of both consumer and real estate loans to total loans than banks in Kentucky and Ohio. Somewhat surprisingly, the membership slope was significant and negative in the commercial and industrial loan regressions.

TABLE 8.6

Regression Results, Dependent Variable = U.S. Treasury Securities-Earning Assets, Fourth District Banks, 1971-75

Year	Independent Variables											
	Constant	Membership Intercept[a]	Kentucky	Ohio	Pennsylvania	Assets[b]	Membership Slope[c]	Total Time and Savings Deposits	$\bar{R}^2$	SEE	F	n
1971	0.3462* (12.99)	-0.0170 (-1.83)	0.0354 (1.62)	0.0107 (0.52)	-0.0049 (-0.22)	-0.0968* (-4.29)	0.0593* (2.51)	-0.2066* (-6.74)	0.15	0.1035	21.00	768
1972	0.3142* (11.54)	-0.0066 (-0.69)	0.0324 (1.48)	0.0112 (0.54)	-0.0092 (-0.40)	-0.0740* (-3.74)	0.0376 (1.76)	-0.1914* (-6.18)	0.13	0.1042	16.44	758
1973	0.2557* (9.57)	-0.0117 (-1.34)	0.0110 (0.55)	0.0048 (0.26)	-0.0057 (-0.27)	-0.0701* (-4.36)	0.0371* (2.13)	-0.1263* (-4.13)	0.09	0.0941	11.19	748
1974	0.2210* (8.20)	-0.0056 (-0.70)	0.0011 (0.06)	-0.0003 (-0.02)	-0.0027 (-0.14)	-0.0418* (-3.28)	0.0147 (1.04)	-0.1190* (-4.23)	0.07	0.0860	8.62	747
1975	0.2583* (8.77)	-0.0033 (-0.36)	0.0043 (0.21)	0.0128 (0.66)	0.0015 (0.07)	-0.0350* (-2.67)	0.0078 (0.53)	-0.1437* (-4.30)	0.05	0.0987	6.65	744

[a]Membership intercept is the coefficient for a 0,1 variable, = 1 for member banks.
[b]Unit of measurement for assets is hundreds of millions of dollars.
[c]Membership slope is the coefficient for an interactive dummy variable = product of membership times assets.

* = significant at 0.05; t-values in parentheses.

Note: See note on page 124.

Source: Compiled by the author.

TABLE 8.7

Regression Results, Dependent Variable = Securities Issued by States and Political Subdivisions-Earning Assets, Fourth District Banks, 1971-75

	Independent Variables											
Year	Constant	Membership Intercept[a]	Kentucky	Ohio	Pennsylvania	Assets[b]	Membership Slope[c]	Total Time and Savings Deposits	$\bar{R}^2$	SEE	F	n
1971	0.1135*	0.0228*	-0.0472*	-0.0299*	0.0020	0.0427*	-0.0263	0.0426*	0.10	0.0708	13.59	768
	(6.22)	(3.58)	(-3.16)	(-2.12)	(0.13)	(2.77)	(-1.62)	(2.03)				
1972	0.1185*	0.0206*	-0.0536*	-0.0440*	-0.0125	0.0356*	-0.0220	0.0552*	0.09	0.0693	12.09	758
	(6.54)	(3.23)	(-3.67)	(-3.19)	(-0.81)	(2.71)	(-1.55)	(2.68)				
1973	0.1440*	0.0295*	-0.0618*	-0.0471*	-0.0270	0.0321*	-0.0244	0.0243	0.09	0.0770	10.96	748
	(7.29)	(4.58)	(-4.20)	(-3.40)	(-1.75)	(2.71)	(-1.90)	(1.05)				
1974	0.1440*	0.0226*	-0.0545*	-0.0317*	-0.0219	0.0222*	-0.0173	0.0217	0.06	0.0707	7.99	747
	(7.07)	(3.42)	(-3.62)	(-2.26)	(-1.40)	(2.13)	(-1.50)	(0.94)				
1975	0.1567*	0.0201*	-0.0354*	-0.0208	-0.0145	0.0155	-0.0118	-0.0109	0.03	0.0713	3.85	744
	(7.37)	(3.01)	(-2.37)	(-1.50)	(-0.93)	(1.64)	(-1.10)	(-0.45)				

[a]Membership intercept is the coefficient for a 0,1 variable, = 1 for member banks.
[b]Unit of measurement for assets is hundreds of millions of dollars.
[c]Membership slope is the coefficient for an interactive dummy variable = product of membership times assets.

* = significant at 0.05; t-values in parentheses.

Note: See note on page 124.

Source: Compiled by the author.

TABLE 8.8

Regression Results, Dependent Variable = Loans-Earning Assets, Fourth District Banks, 1971-75

	Independent Variables											
Year	Constant	Membership Intercept[a]	Kentucky	Ohio	Pennsylvania	Assets[b]	Membership Slope[c]	Total Time and Savings Deposits	$\bar{R}^2$	SEE	F	n
1971	0.3348* (11.69)	-0.0113 (-1.13)	0.0755* (3.22)	0.0807* (3.64)	0.0783* (3.18)	0.0223 (0.92)	-0.0058 (-0.23)	0.2200* (6.68)	0.09	0.1112	11.23	768
1972	0.3205* (10.77)	-0.0097 (-0.92)	0.0755* (3.14)	0.0806* (3.56)	0.0798* (3.15)	0.0271 (1.26)	-0.0045 (-0.19)	0.2359* (6.96)	0.09	0.1139	11.95	758
1973	0.3459* (10.60)	0.0003 (0.03)	0.0937* (3.85)	0.0866* (3.79)	0.0706* (2.76)	0.0464* (2.37)	-0.0222 (-1.04)	0.1957* (5.11)	0.07	0.1150	8.52	748
1974	0.3137* (9.32)	-0.0104 (-0.95)	0.0912* (3.66)	0.0901* (3.89)	0.0792* (3.06)	0.0222 (1.28)	0.0039 (0.21)	0.2541* (6.65)	0.09	0.1169	11.64	747
1975	0.3371* (9.98)	-0.0151 (-1.42)	0.0915* (3.85)	0.0713* (3.23)	0.0602* (2.42)	0.0021 (0.14)	0.0106 (0.62)	0.2330* (6.08)	0.06	0.1133	7.26	744

[a]Membership intercept is the coefficient for a 0,1 variable, = 1 for member banks.
[b]Unit of measurement for assets is hundreds of millions of dollars.
[c]Membership slope is the coefficient for an interactive dummy variable = product of membership times assets.

* = significant at 0.05; t-values in parentheses.

<u>Note</u>: See note on page 124.

<u>Source</u>: Compiled by the author.

Deposit Composition

As may be seen in Table 8.9, significant differences in liability composition between members and nonmembers were found only infrequently.* The state differences, though, are often significant and exhibit an interesting pattern. In 1971, West Virginia banks had significantly lower ratios of time and savings to total deposits than did banks in Ohio and Pennsylvania. If unit banking markets, per se, are less competitive than branch markets, then the West Virginia ratio might be due to lower interest rates paid on time and savings deposits.† However, it is noteworthy that, by 1974, the Ohio-Pennsylvania/West Virginia difference had declined to insignificance. Even if the cause of the low time and savings ratio was unit banking, restrictive branching seems able only to delay, not block, the spread of financial innovations. The continuing lag in the ratio of time deposits at Kentucky banks may be due to the earlier noted rapid growth in demand deposits in eastern Kentucky.

Revenues, Expenses, and Loan Rates

Total operating income and expenses as ratios of total assets are very frequently lower, and significantly so, for members than nonmembers. However, this may be due simply to members' lower ratios of earning to total assets. The more pertinent question, therefore, is, are rates earned and costs incurred on earning assets significantly different for members and nonmembers?

Using earning assets as the deflator and controlling for the composition and size of earning assets, liabilities, and equity, an indecisive result emerges (these regression results are not shown here). For total operating income, seven of ten membership coefficients had negative signs, but the only significant coefficient was positive (the intercept in 1975, t-value = 2.09). For total operating expenses, eight of ten membership estimates were negative, but all were insignificant (largest t-value = -1.56). The claim that membership either increases income or decreases cost (per dollar of earning assets) receives little support from these data. The state dummies were all

---

*No evidence was found that membership increases a bank's correspondent deposit liabilities. See [18].

†A direct test of the hypothesis that West Virginia banks pay lower interest rates is not feasible with the data reported on the income statement. However, no significant differences were found between West Virginia and other banks in the ratio of savings deposits (which usually earn the lowest interest rates) to other time deposits.

TABLE 8.9

Regression Results, Dependent Variable = Time and Savings Deposits-Total Deposits, Fourth District Banks, 1971-75

Year	Independent Variables										
	Constant	Membership Intercept[a]	Kentucky	Ohio	Pennsylvania	Assets[b]	Membership Slope[c]	$\bar{R}^2$	SEE	F	n
1971	0.5547*	0.0245*	-0.0746*	0.0703*	0.0772*	0.0393	-0.0688*	0.19	0.1224	31.75	768
	(22.86)	(2.24)	(-2.91)	(2.90)	(2.87)	(1.48)	(-2.47)				
1972	0.5718*	0.0179	-0.0793*	0.0496*	0.0716*	0.0216	-0.0408	0.16	0.1227	25.48	758
	(23.49)	(1.59)	(-3.09)	(2.03)	(2.64)	(0.93)	(-1.62)				
1973	0.6072*	0.0174	-0.0875*	0.0364	0.0526*	0.0184	-0.0337	0.18	0.1104	28.21	748
	(27.60)	(1.70)	(-3.78)	(1.66)	(2.15)	(0.98)	(-1.65)				
1974	0.6317*	0.0153	-0.1128*	0.0252	0.0311	0.0120	-0.0203	0.20	0.1124	32.18	747
	(28.00)	(1.45)	(-4.78)	(1.13)	(1.25)	(0.72)	(-1.11)				
1975	0.6629*	0.0166	-0.1039*	0.0084	0.0163	0.0113	-0.0193	0.15	0.1088	23.51	744
	(30.96)	(1.63)	(-4.62)	(0.40)	(0.68)	(0.78)	(-1.18)				

[a]Membership intercept is the coefficient for a 0,1 variable, = 1 for member banks.
[b]Unit of measurement for assets is hundreds of millions of dollars.
[c]Membership slope is the coefficient for an interactive dummy variable = product of membership times assets.

* = significant at 0.05; t-values in parentheses.

Note: See note on page 124.

Source: Compiled by the author.

insignificant in the revenue-earning assets and expense-earning assets regressions.

As shown in Table 8.10, the evidence is that neither member banks nor West Virginia unit banks charge higher loan rates when loan composition and risk (as proxied by loan losses) is taken into account.

Appraisal of Regression Results

The propositions that member banks hold more cash but have earnings rates equal to those of nonmembers and that banks in states without branching are not more profitable than those in states with branching are consistent with these data. Yet, aside from the results pertaining to equity capital and tax-exempt security holdings, the numbers provide few indications as to the adjustments by which these "bottom-line" equalizations occur. A more sensitive statistical methodology may identify additional details of the process, but it is possible that individual banks and markets adjust to regulatory intervention in such a variety of ways that none appears unique.

SUMMARY

Even though Federal Reserve cash requirements and state branching laws do not significantly affect bank profitability—after allowing time for adjustment—this does not mean that the choice of reserve regulation and branch structure is unimportant from a grants viewpoint. If, as is frequently suggested, the Federal Reserve were to be given authority to apply its reserve requirements to nonmembers, the distributional consequences would be substantial and similar to those described above. Losses would be imposed on shareholders of nonmember banks.* Moreover, freed from competitive restraint, the Federal Reserve might feel compelled to raise reserve requirements in the interest of a "sounder" banking system or increased monetary control. Substantially higher universal reserve requirements would reduce bank earnings in the short run, lower the long-

*It is sometimes said that universal Federal Reserve requirements would be more equitable than the present system, which provides a choice. If nonmembers are to be forced to join the Federal Reserve on grounds of equity, should the present members be forced out of the system on the same grounds? An alternative to universal reserve requirements would be to remove all such requirements and permit the system to price and sell its services explicitly.

TABLE 8.10

Regression Results, Dependent Variable = Interest and Fees on Loans-Loans, Fourth District Banks, 1971-75

	Independent Variables														
Year	Constant	Membership Intercept[a]	Kentucky	Ohio	Pennsylvania	Consumer Loans	Real Estate Loans	Agricultural Loans	Provision for or Actual Loan Losses	Assets[b]	Membership Slope[c]	$\bar{R}^2$	SEE	F	n
1971	0.0662*	0.0006	0.0008	0.0021	-0.0007	0.0087*	-0.0035	-0.0013	0.4101*	0.0019	-0.0014	0.08	0.0072	7.56	763
	(32.99)	(0.88)	(0.53)	(1.48)	(-0.47)	(3.46)	(-1.46)	(-0.39)	(4.13)	(1.11)	(-0.82)				
1972	0.0676*	-0.0001	0.0000	0.0024	0.0006	0.0089*	-0.0039	-0.0020	0.2431*	-0.0001	-0.0008	0.05	0.0077	5.12	754
	(30.54)	(-0.20)	(0.01)	(1.55)	(0.37)	(3.21)	(-1.48)	(-0.55)	(2.24)	(-0.08)	(-0.51)				
1973	0.0666*	-0.0006	0.0011	0.0045*	0.0016	0.0091*	-0.0014	-0.0086*	0.1891	0.0015	0.0001	0.07	0.0091	6.76	745
	(25.62)	(-0.66)	(0.57)	(2.47)	(0.80)	(2.80)	(-0.44)	(-1.98)	(1.79)	(0.94)	(0.05)				
1974	0.0755*	0.0015	0.0009	0.0046*	-0.0003	0.0111*	-0.0153*	-0.0149*	0.2430*	0.0030*	-0.0009	0.20	0.0096	19.32	744
	(28.31)	(1.70)	(0.41)	(2.41)	(-0.12)	(3.28)	(-5.00)	(-3.19)	(5.75)	(2.09)	(-0.59)				
1975	0.0724*	0.0010	0.0034	0.0055*	0.0001	0.0105*	-0.0063	-0.0155*	0.7095*	0.0014	0.0011	0.22	0.0097	21.40	742
	(25.95)	(1.09)	(1.60)	(2.84)	(0.04)	(3.07)	(-1.95)	(-3.20)	(7.82)	(1.05)	(0.71)				

[a]Membership intercept is the coefficient for a 0,1 variable, = 1 for member banks.
[b]Unit of measurement for assets is hundreds of millions of dollars.
[c]Membership slope is the coefficient for an interactive dummy variable = product of membership times assets.

* = significant at 0.05; t-values in parentheses.

Note: See note on page 124.

Source: Compiled by the author.

term supply of bank services, and accelerate the growth of nonbank financial institutions exempt from requirements. Moreover, portfolio composition does differ for member and nonmember banks. The possibility cannot be dismissed that these portfolio differences imply a rechanneling of funds and implicit grants among bank customers.

Unit banking is associated with lower average loan-asset ratios than those observed in branching states. Although the significance of this is unknown without measures of the degree to which this is offset by nonbank financial institutions and growth-oriented banks,* unit banking does reduce the number of banking offices.† Restrictions on branching will continue to have some real effects until a different communications technology displaces the demand for branch services.

POSTSCRIPT

The circulation of this chapter for comment evoked a number of criticisms, some of which have been incorporated here. Three of the unaccommodated criticisms may be of interest to the reader and (possibly) suggestive of further research.

The first is that the Fourth Federal Reserve District from which the data were taken is a special case where membership is not costly. For the rest of the country, this conclusion may not be valid. Support for the "special-case" argument is found in the disparate proportion of banks that are members in the Fourth District: 59.7 percent with 85.6 percent of total bank assets versus 39.6 percent with 76 percent of total assets in the entire United States at year-end, 1975. If the special-case charge is true, reserve requirement differentials are an unlikely explanation, because state reserve requirements seem to be at ineffective levels in the Fourth District.

An alternative explanation might be constructed along the following lines: The Federal Reserve must compete with 50 different state banking regulators in 50 different "markets." The system is constrained in this competition from seeming to discriminate across markets. This constraint forces it to declare uniform national policies that restrict its ability to react to local market competition. The Re-

---

*The loan-asset ratios examined here are not weighted by bank size. Thus, total bank lending per dollar of bank assets in two states may be the same even though unweighted averages of individual ratios are different.

†The ratios of population to banking offices in the Fourth District by state are West Virginia, 7,200; Ohio, 4,900; Pennsylvania, 4,550; and Kentucky, 4,375.

serve banks, however, can and do adjust announced national policies to meet "local conditions." These adjustments consist of variations in access to the discount window, quality of services provided, and the prices of services provided, for example, the charge for wrapped coins. For reasons to be determined, some district banks are better at this competition than others.

The second criticism is that the regression model is ad hoc and not well specified. As a result, the model is not sufficiently discriminating to detect the effects on earnings of Federal Reserve membership or branching. The very low $\bar{R}^2$s, especially in Tables 8.3 and 8.4, are cited as evidence of the model's crudeness. Moreover, the tests should have been carried out with market values for equity and loans rather than book values. However, market data are not generally available. In addition, the low $\bar{R}^2$s can be interpreted as meaning that among the things that do matter for bank performance, membership and branching do not matter very much. The $\bar{R}^2$s in Tables 8.3 and 8.4 can be increased by adding explanatory variables, such as operating expenses-assets, loan losses, and equity-assets. The danger in doing so is that these variables may be affected by membership. By including them in the regression, the "true" effect of membership will be attributed to other causes. Except for Table 8.10, the reported results are regressions in which the explanatory variables are restricted to, at most, total assets, deposit composition, and the dummy variables. Nonetheless, a regression model based on more than parsimony would be welcome.

The third criticism argues that testing for the negative impact of Federal Reserve membership is about as fruitful as measuring the ability of cows to fly: Everything known about firms and regulatory agencies indicates that the supposition of negative impact could not possibly be true. Imagine that a study of U.S. banks found member banks to be significantly less profitable than nonmembers over a period as long as, say, five years. If the transfer costs are as low as indicated, the implications for the theory of the firm would be considerable. If the Federal Reserve has latitude to change the reserve cost-services benefit package, the theory of regulation would have to be revised. In short, few could believe such a result. No difference in earnings between member and nonmember populations is also consistent with the evidence that individual banks that change their membership status either experience an earnings improvement or no change [9; 11]. Those banks for whom it pays to change membership status do so.

APPENDIX: FEDERAL RESERVE AND FOURTH DISTRICT STATE RESERVE REQUIREMENTS, PERCENT OF DEPOSITS

Federal Reserve

Reserve requirements were changed six times by the system during the period 1971-75. To conserve space, only requirements effective at the midpoint of the period (June 1973) are shown. Reserve requirement changes are published in the Federal Reserve Bulletin.

	Net Demand Deposits* (deposit intervals in millions of dollars)						Time Deposits	
	0-2	2-10	10-100	100-400	Over 400	Savings Deposits	0-5	Over 5
Percentage required	8	10	12	13	17.5	3	3	5

*Demand deposits subject to reserve requirements are gross demand deposits minus cash items in process of collection and demand balances due from domestic banks.

Required reserves must be held in deposits with Federal Reserve banks or vault cash.

Kentucky

Requirements were not changed during 1971-75.

Demand Deposits*		
Reserve† City Banks	Country Banks	Time Deposits
10	7	3

*Deposits payable within 30 days.
†None in the Fourth District portion of the state.

Up to 25 percent of the reserve against demand deposits may be in U.S. Treasury or agency securities with a maturity of one year or less or certificates of deposits issued by banks located in Kentucky. The rest of the demand deposit reserve must be held in demand deposits with commercial banks or vault cash. All (100 percent) of the reserve against time deposits may be invested in securities issued by the U.S. Treasury, the Commonwealth of Kentucky, or CDs issued by Kentucky banks.

Ohio

As shown, requirements were changed once during 1971-75.

	Demand Deposits*	Time Deposits
In effect January 1, 1971	12	6
Effective June 1, 1972	7	3

*Deposits payable within 30 days exclusive of U.S. deposits.

Up to 60 percent of the reserve against time deposits may be held in obligations issued or guaranteed by the United States. The rest must be held in demand deposits with commercial banks or vault cash.

Pennsylvania

On March 8, 1974, the share of reserves that may be invested in obligations of the U.S. Treasury, the Commonwealth of Pennsylvania, or any Pennsylvania political subdivision was raised from 40 to 50 percent.

		Time Deposits	
Demand Deposits*	Savings Deposits	$0-$5 Million	Over $5 Million
12	3	3	5

*Deposits payable within 30 days.

Up to 50 percent of reserves may be invested as noted above. The remainder must be held in demand deposits with commercial banks or vault cash.

West Virginia

Requirements were not changed during 1971-75.

Demand Deposits*	Time Deposits
7	3

*Deposits payable within 30 days.

Required reserves must be held in demand deposits with commercial banks or vault cash.

NOTES

1. Required reserves, because they are required, do not afford the same degree of liquidity as unrequired or excess cash reserves [4; 21]. Thus, the example in Table 8.1 incorrectly assumes that banks consider excess reserves and required reserves to be close substitutes, that is, they held $10 of cash in excess of "requirements" before and zero after. Adding excess reserves to the postreserve requirement case increases the reserve requirement tax but does not affect the direction of grant flows.

2. Cash reserve requirements may be lowered in many ways other than by reducing percentage requirements: permitting reserves to be invested in interest-bearing securities, counting uncollected balances as reserves, exempting some types of deposits from requirements, and omitting provision for the monitoring of reserve positions. Nonetheless, it has been argued that some state reserve requirements are not equal to zero. See Goldberg and Rose [12; 13] and Prestopino [28].

3. See, for example, Robertson and Phillips [29].

4. Both state and national banks are subject to the state branching laws. Nonbank financial institutions have become increasingly exempt from these restrictions in recent years. See, for example, Lyons Savings and Loan Association v. FHLBB (377 F. Supp. 11).

5. A theory relating the utility-maximizing combination of risk and return to market structure is given in Edwards and Heggestad [6]. See also [22].

6. Where branching is restricted, management growth objectives can be achieved through the multibank holding company [20; 25; 34]. Smaller banks usually find holding companies less objectionable than branching because holding companies tend to expand by acquiring existing banks rather than by opening new ones.

7. Federal Deposit Insurance Corporation, Assets and Liabilities, Commercial and Mutual Savings Bank, December 31, 1975. Similarly, the ratio of cash to deposits for Illinois nonmember banks (zero cash reserve requirements, branching prohibited) was 7.9 percent.

8. Earlier studies [11; 9] have found member banks to have lower loan-total asset ratios than nonmembers. The same relationship can be observed in the Cleveland District data. For the Fourth District, these results are simply the consequence of lower earning asset-total asset ratios, that is, the mirror image of higher cash-total asset ratios. The author is indebted to John T. Rose for suggesting earning assets as a more useful denominator.

REFERENCES

[1] Bell, Frederick W., and Neil B. Murphy. Costs in Commercial Banking: A Quantitative Analysis of Bank Behavior and Its Relation to Bank Regulation. Research Report no. 41. Boston: Federal Reserve Bank of Boston, 1968.

[2] Benston, George J. "The Optimal Banking Structure: Theory and Evidence." Journal of Bank Research 4 (Winter 1973):220-37.

[3] Carson, Deane. "Is the Federal Reserve System Really Necessary?" Journal of Finance 19, no. 4 (December 1964):652-61.

[4] _____. "Is the Federal Reserve System Really Necessary?: Reply." Journal of Finance 20, no. 3 (September 1965):486-89.

[5] Edwards, Franklin R. "The Banking Competition Controversy." National Banking Review 3 (September 1965):1-34.

[6] Edwards, Franklin R., and Arnold A. Heggestad. "Uncertainty, Market Structure, and Performance in Banking." Quarterly Journal of Economics 87, no. 3 (August 1973):455-73.

[7] Fischer, Gerald C., and Raymond N. Davis. "The Impact of Multi-Office Banking on the Availability of Credit in Smaller Communities." Compendium of Issues Relating to Branching by Financial Institutions. U.S., Congress, Senate, Subcommittee on Financial Institutions of the Committee on Banking, Housing and Urban Affairs, October 1976, pp. 155-89.

[8] Fraser, Donald R., Wallace Phillips, Jr., and Peter S. Rose. "A Canonical Analysis of Bank Performance." Journal of Financial and Quantitative Analysis 9 (March 1974):287-95.

[9] Fraser, Donald R., Peter S. Rose, and Gary L. Schugart. "Federal Reserve Membership and Bank Performance: The Evidence from Texas." Journal of Finance 30, no. 2 (May 1975):641-58.

[10] Gilbert, Gary G., and William A. Longbrake. "The Effects of Branching by Financial Institutions on Competition, Productive Efficiency, and Stability—An Examination of the Evidence." Journal of Bank Research 4 (Autumn 1973):154-67; and (Winter 1974):298-307.

[11] Gilbert, Gary G., and Manferd O. Peterson. "The Impact of Changes in Federal Reserve Membership on Commercial Bank Performance." Journal of Finance 30, no. 3 (June 1975):713-19.

[12] Goldberg, Lawrence G., and John T. Rose. "Do State Reserve Requirements Matter?" Journal of Bank Research 8 (Spring 1977):31-39.

[13] _____. "The Effect on Nonmember Banks of the Imposition of Member Bank Reserve Requirements—with and without Federal Reserve Services." Journal of Finance 31, no. 5 (December 1976):1457-69.

[14] Guttentag, Jack M. "Branch Banking: A Summary of the Issues and the Evidence." Compendium of Issues Relating to Branching by Financial Institutions. U.S., Congress, Senate, Subcommittee on Financial Institutions of the Committee on Banking, Housing, and Urban Affairs, October 1976, pp. 99-112.

[15] Horvitz, Paul M., and Bernard Schull. "The Impact of Branch Banking on Bank Performance." National Banking Review 2 (December 1964):143-88.

[16] Jacobs, Donald. "The Framework of Commercial Bank Regulation: An Appraisal." National Banking Review, vol. 2 (March 1964). Reprinted in Studies in Banking Competition and the Banking Structure. Washington, D.C.: Office of the Comptroller of the Currency, 1966, pp. 337-51.

[17] Klein, Benjamin. "The Determinants of Membership in the Federal Reserve System." Mimeographed. January 1977.

[18] Kreider, Lawrence E. Optional Affiliation with the Federal Reserve System for Reserve Purposes Is Consistent with Equitable Treatment between Banks. Washington, D.C.: Conference of State Bank Supervisors, 1976.

[19] Lanzillotti, Robert E., and Thomas R. Saving. "State Branching Restrictions and the Availability of Banking Services." Journal of Money, Credit and Banking 1 (November 1969):778-88.

[20] Lawrence, Robert J., and Samuel H. Talley. "An Assessment of Bank Holding Companies." Federal Reserve Bulletin 62, no. 1 (January 1976):15-21.

[21] Leonard, James W. "Federal Reserve Membership and Discrimination—A Comment." Journal of Finance 20, no. 3 (September 1965):483-84.

[22] McCall, Alan S., and Manferd O. Peterson. "The Impact of De Novo Commercial Bank Entry." Compendium of Issues Relating to Branching by Financial Institutions. U.S., Congress, Senate, Subcommittee on Financial Institutions of the Committee on Banking, Housing, and Urban Affairs, October 1976, pp. 499-521.

[23] Mayne, Lucille Stringer. The Effect of Federal Reserve System Membership on the Profitability of Illinois Banks, 1961-1963. University Park, Pa.: Center for Research of the College of Business Administration, Pennsylvania State University, 1967.

[24] Mote, Larry R. "The Perennial Issues: Branch Banking." Business Conditions (Federal Reserve Bank of Chicago), February 1974, pp. 3-23.

[25] Moyer, R. Charles, and Edward Sussna. "Registered Bank Holding Company Acquisitions: A Cross-Section Analysis." Journal of Financial and Quantitative Analysis 8 (September 1973):647-61.

[26] Phaup, Marvin. "The Effect of Federal Reserve Membership on Earnings of Fourth District Banks, 1963-1970." Economic Review (Federal Reserve Bank of Cleveland), January/February 1973, pp. 3-18.

[27] _____. "Characteristics of High Performance Banks: 1969-1975." Economic Review (Federal Reserve Bank of Cleveland), Fall 1976, pp. 12-22.

[28] Prestopino, Chris Joseph. "Do Higher Reserve Requirements Discourage Federal Reserve Membership?" Journal of Finance 31, no. 5 (December 1976):1471-80.

[29] Robertson, Ross M., and Almarin Phillips. Optional Affiliation with the Federal Reserve System for Reserve Purposes Is Consistent with Effective Monetary Policies. Washington, D.C.: Conference of State Bank Supervisors, 1974.

[30] Seaver, William L., and Donald R. Fraser. "Branch Banking and the Availability of Banking Services: A Cluster Analysis." Bank Structure and Competition. Conference Proceedings, Federal Reserve Bank of Chicago, September 1976, pp. 120-33.

[31] Shull, Bernard. "Multiple Office Banking and Competition: A Review of the Literature." Compendium of Issues Relating to Branching by Financial Institutions. U.S., Congress, Senate, Subcommittee on Financial Institutions of the Committee on Banking, Housing and Urban Affairs, October 1976, pp. 113-53.

[32] Shull, Bernard, and Paul M. Horvitz. "Branch Banking and the Structure of Competition." National Banking Review 2 (March 1964):301-41.

[33] Smith, Warren L. "Reserve Requirements in the American Monetary System." In Monetary Management. Edited by U.S. Commission on Money and Credit, pp. 175-316. Englewood Cliffs, N.J.: Prentice-Hall, 1963.

[34] Ware, Robert F. "Performance of Banks Acquired by Multi-Bank Holding Companies in Ohio." Economic Review (Federal Reserve Bank of Cleveland), March/April 1973, pp. 19-28.

PART IV

Implicit Transfers Associated with Private Practices and Government Regulations

9

Implicit Grants in the Financial System: The Case of the Equal Credit Opportunity Act

JOSEPH SCHERER

Implicit grants in an economics framework modify the distribution of income or wealth from that which otherwise would prevail under a free market outcome. The implicit grants, therefore, may be simultaneously positive and negative, since redistribution usually involves gains to some economic agents at the expense of others.* Implicit grants often are associated with various programs established by government—federal, state, or local—although implicit grants also may arise from actions instituted by the private sector (businesses or individuals), profit making and nonprofit making. There are a host of implicit grants embedded in the existing institutional arrangements. In the government sector, the more obvious ones are the various subsidy programs and welfare; less obvious are the implicit grants embedded in virtually all of the regulatory activities of all levels of government, including the equal credit regulation, to be explored more fully in this chapter. In the private sector, implicit grants can be detected not only in the operations of foundations and private educational institutions but also in the activities of profit-making firms. New grants, or modifications of existing grants, frequently are introduced whenever changes are made in government laws or regulations, sometimes as a by-product of contractual relationships between two or more parties and sometimes through unilateral actions by private organizations or individuals.

---

*In welfare economies, there is usually an effort to compensate persons or organizations so that no one is made worse off at the same time that some economic units are made better off.

The views expressed do not necessarily reflect those of the Federal Reserve Bank of New York.

While implicit grants cover a wide range of activities, economists usually concentrate on those that affect market prices and/or market functioning. Furthermore, there is a tendency to focus attention on the economic units directly affected; however, the consequences might ramify much more widely, so that third parties might also be affected even without realizing that they have been affected, as illustrated below.

Study of the implicit grants in the government sector, especially at the federal level, has been most heavily directed toward price controls, subsidy-type programs embedded in the tax structure (and now often identified as tax expenditures), cash payments or payments in kind, or credit subsidies. Implicit grants directly or indirectly created by regulatory agencies have been examined less frequently. Nevertheless, new regulations or modified regulations, whether based on new legislation or promulgated by the exercise of a broad grant of authority to one of the regulatory agencies, such as the Interstate Commerce Commission, Federal Trade Commission, or the Federal Reserve System, also can alter the economic structure and market relationships, thereby conferring new benefits to some and/or reducing the welfare of others. As noted earlier, some of those affected might not be aware that their economic circumstances have been altered.

The Equal Credit Opportunity (ECO) Act that went into effect October 28, 1975, is an interesting illustration of the establishment of new implicit grants that, in turn, modify the structure of implicit grants long held by men. This act of Congress forbids discrimination on the basis of sex or marital status by all organizations that regularly extend credit, including banks, finance companies, department stores, and credit card issuers. In implementing the act, the Federal Reserve System issued a new regulation, Regulation B, which states "that sex or marital status of the applicant shall not be used, as such, in evaluating the applicant's creditworthiness" and still not interfere "with the need to preserve the creditor's ability to distinguish, in the creditor's own judgment, between applicants that are, or are not, creditworthy." The regulation identifies certain types of acceptable and unacceptable practices, including the following:

1. The Regulation forbids the use of sex or marital status in credit scoring systems.
2. Creditors may not inquire into birth control practices or into childbearing capabilities or intentions, or assume from her age that an applicant or applicant's spouse may drop out of the labor force due to childbearing and thus have an interruption of income.

3. The creditor may not discount part-time income but may examine the probable continuity of the applicant's job.
4. A creditor may ask to what extent the applicant is relying on alimony or child support or maintenance payments to repay the debt being incurred.

While the above is only a partial list of the practices specifically identified in the regulation, they are sufficient for indicating the general thrust of the Equal Credit Opportunity Act. In the 1976 session of Congress, the act was extended to make it unlawful to discriminate on the basis of age, race, color, religion, national origin, or political affiliation.

The ECO Act is an interesting example of government regulation that is not specifically directed toward affecting market prices; but, nevertheless, by introducing elements that are supposed to modify existing market structures and market behavior, the regulation inevitably brings about shifts in the rates of exchange between and among prices directly in the market being regulated and possibly indirectly in other markets, including the labor market. The extent of impact will be a function of the magnitude of change introduced and the nature of the structural relationships connecting the sector directly affected and those sectors indirectly affected. Comprehensive quantitative data to assess the impact of the ECO Act are lacking, but fragmentary evidence suggests that an appreciable impact will be noticed in at least a few credit markets. For example, the National Commission on Consumer Credit, in its December 1972 report, concluded that there was widespread discrimination against women "in obtaining consumer as well as mortgage credit."[1] At the same time, there is some evidence that women are better credit risks than men.[2]

If the regulation is successful in eliminating sex discrimination in the granting of credit, and if discrimination had been practiced, as suggested in congressional hearings and in the report on consumer credit, then some important consequences can be expected to take place. In the short run, all other things being equal, the supply of funds in particular credit sectors is relatively fixed, but in the sectors where discrimination has been practiced, the ECO Act in effect shifts the demand curve for funds to the right. In the absence of other nonprice factors, including nonprice rationing arrangements (some of which are illegal now under the ECO Act), some men who previously would have obtained credit are no longer able to obtain funds. In the case of the housing sector, the type of housing space and its location that unmarried females or even female heads of families are likely to demand are different at least in part from those of married men with families; for example, there might be a shift to more urban housing, perhaps cooperative or condominium apartments, relative to single-family homes in suburban developments. This shifts the location and type of residential construction, affects land prices in urban relative to suburban areas, and would affect firms catering to these different demand requirements. A whole host of differential impacts can be traced as the ramifications are carried out through successive steps.

The range of impacts can be sketched in broad summary terms. A regulatory change that modifies the distribution of implicit grants has both macro- and microconsequences and these vary depending upon whether the analysis is short run or long run. On the aggregative side, in the short run, as previously noted, there is little change in the aggregate supply of credit in the affected areas, but the quality of loans outstanding would be higher. On the microlevel, there is a change in the distribution of borrowers—more women relative to men than had previously prevailed. There is an implication that the credit markets so affected by the regulation are less than perfectly competitive markets because discrimination based on considerations of sex rather than creditworthiness alone meant that loan losses were higher than they need have been. In that sense the ECO Act serves somewhat like government regulations standardizing weights and measure—a government activity sanction by Adam Smith and all his successors.

Again, as noted earlier, to the extent that the ECO Act redistributes the availability of loanable funds to a somewhat different set of borrowers, there is probably a change in the basket of goods and services to be purchased and, further, a shift in the firms from whom the goods are purchased, compared to the situation that had prevailed previously. This might be particularly true if there is a substantial shift in the male-female ratio of borrowers in the consumer credit sector. In the short run, therefore, the most important changes are probably confined to shifts in the distributional mix of male-female borrowers, industry mix for purchases, and mix of firms within industries making sales. Then, if the behavior of these groups, as reflected in such things as the marginal cost curves of firms and the marginal propensity to consume of the borrowers, differs from what would have prevailed previous to the ECO Act, there begins a set of adjustments that modify the long-run equilibrium to which the system is moving.

If it truly makes a significant difference in the long run, the ECO Act, presumably would shift the relative profitability of different sectors of the credit market. It has been held that the existing discrimination in credit practices is "the result of erroneous or outmoded notions of women's role in society," so that legislation ("a legal remedy") is needed,[3] presumably on the grounds that regulation would ensure that outmoded notions would be corrected. But, as noted earlier, a fully competitive and efficient credit market should have brought about the necessary corrections without legislation.

The foregoing analysis, however, has abstracted from one important factor. The ECO Act, as any regulation, involves record keeping, an enforcement mechanism, and other resource-using factors of production. Some or all segments of the credit markets now will have added costs that will increase either the cost of credit or reduce profits, or some combination of the two, with further ramifications affecting the real economy.[4] At the September 1976 annual meeting of the American Finance Association, James F. Smith, senior economist at the Board of Governors of the Federal Reserve System, provided some cost-benefit estimates of the ECO Act.[5] According to Smith, the various credit-granting organizations (commercial banks, finance companies, and others) in 1975 incurred additional costs of \$293.3 million in complying with Regulation B of the ECO Act—\$174.8 million of nonrecurring costs involving such changes as conversion of records and procedures and \$118.5 million of recurring costs arising from higher data processing costs, longer reports, and other increases in expenses.

Ironically, Smith cites a study that is based on a sample drawn from only one large urban commercial bank that reports "the number of women now getting credit is ten percentage points lower than previously was the case."[6] The inference to be drawn apparently is that there had been discrimination in favor of women previously when their creditworthiness was rated superior to that of men with similar characteristics other than the male-female distinction. Now that discrimination solely on the basis of sex is unlawful, the "favoritism" toward women as women no longer can be used as a criterion to discriminate in their favor. This finding, of course, if it were an accurate generalization for the entire universe of women, would make for a perverse impact of the ECO Act. Unfortunately, the extent of discrimination against women prior to the ECO Act has not been documented in any statistically satisfactory form. Rather, the evidence has tended to be of a qualitative nature, mainly narrative illustrations of discriminatory practices. In the absence of more comprehensive documentation, including evidence of the extent to which women simply never were given the privilege of filling out credit forms, it is not clear just how this "perverse" evidence should be interpreted. In the meantime, reports continue to appear charging that women still believe that they are discriminated against in the granting of credit even after more than a year since the passage of the ECO Act.[7] Nevertheless, the possibility that the ECO Act might prove to be a mixed blessing cannot be dismissed.

In the short run, there is no question that the ECO Act has involved substantial start-up costs for the credit-granting agencies, that it requires continuing costs, and to these costs must be added the government regulatory expenses, as well as the judicial expenses for all participants as legal challenges develop for individual cases. Over the longer run, as compliance with the provisions of the ECO Act becomes more routinized, the recurrent costs might prove less expensive than is the case now. Furthermore, to the extent that there is an expansion of the credit data base providing more uniform details in response to the requirements imposed by the act, it might be possible to determine with more precision the relative creditworthiness of various identifiable classes of borrowers. Presumably, the act should confer certain social benefits, involving human dignity and greater social equity, which must be factored into the evaluation of the ECO Act. The bane of cost-benefit analysis in this area, as in so many other areas of government regulation, increasingly turns on the thorny issue of putting a dollar value on imponderables.

NOTES

1. Report of the National Commission on Consumer Credit, December 1972, pp. 152, 160.

2. Margaret J. Gates, "Credit Discrimination against Women: Causes and Solutions," Vanderbilt Law Review, April 1974, p. 360.

3. Ibid., p. 384.

4. A critical review of a wide range of government regulatory activities can be found in Murray C. Weidenbaum, Business, Government and the Public (Englewood Cliffs, N.J.: Prentice-Hall, 1977).

5. James F. Smith, "The Equal Credit Opportunity Act of 1974: A Cost/Benefit Analysis." Paper delivered September 17, 1976, in Atlantic City, N.J. at the Annual Meeting of the American Finance Association, published in the Proceedings issue of the Journal of Finance, May 1977, pp. 609-22.

6. The study cited is by Gary G. Chandler and David C. Ewert, "Discrimination on the Basis of Sex under the Equal Credit Opportunity Act," Working Paper no. 8, Krannert Graduate School of Management, Purdue University, 1976.

7. "Women Complain That New Equal Credit Law Is Applied Unevenly, Enforced Haphazardly," Wall Street Journal, January 21, 1977, p. 32.

10

The Transfer Implications of Consumer Credit Regulation

WILLIAM C. DUNKELBERG

The purpose of this chapter is to examine the regulation of the consumer credit industry from a somewhat different perspective, viewing the regulations as devices for making transfers between individuals. In some instances, it will be argued, the transfers made are those that were intended by legislators. In others, the transfers are unintended and contrary to the intent of the legislation. Still others, though unintended, may be desirable from the point of view of many consumers and their representatives. Essentially all of the regulations applied to the consumer credit industry result in transfers of income or wealth. Thus, no regulation is all good or all bad. The usefulness or value of the regulation depends on which consumer subgroup point of view is taken.

The following discussion tries to avoid any particular point of view. The objective is to identify the effects on credit markets of several important types of regulations and to provide rough estimates of the transfers that result. When sufficient data are available, recipients or payors are identified. Without a well-developed theory of consumer credit markets that includes enforcement and information costs, it is difficult to identify the variety of responses made by firms and consumers to regulation and thus to identify all subsidies or transfers that arise. But enough is known about the response of market participants to hazard some educated guesses about the distribution of grants generated by the regulatory system. At a minimum, the total amount distributed as a result of certain specific regulations might be reasonably well estimated.

This research was partially supported by a grant from the National Science Foundation Research Applied to National Needs, NSF no. 7618472.

THE CONSUMER CREDIT ENVIRONMENT

In analyzing grants or exchanges in the public sector, the key to the functioning of the market is control (power) rather than ownership, one of the more important factors that distinguishes an exchange from a grant. What legislators and regulators do often has little or no direct financial impact on them personally. The monies and resources they command do not represent their personal incomes or wealth. Nonetheless, they determine the amount of taxes to be collected and the distribution of those funds, and they pass laws and establish regulations that alter the flow of resources in the private sector.

Consumer credit is a commodity produced by the private sector and sold to consumers. Regulations regarding its sale and production are numerous. Most frequently observed are those determining price (interest rates). Information and disclosure regulations are also pervasive (Truth in Lending, for example), and legislation regarding the collection of debts seems to be of increasing importance to regulators and legislators. This chapter focuses on interest rate ceilings and restrictions on the collection of debts. These restrictions result in prices and recoveries of debts that are lower than would likely prevail in a less regulated or unregulated market.[1] The transfer implications of these regulations are complex, involving changes in credit availability, search costs, enforcement costs, and interest charges. Where credit is extended with the sale of merchandise, the cost of goods and services also can be affected.

At the end of 1976, there was about $175 billion of consumer installment credit outstanding (excluding mortgages), including $60 billion tied to the financing of automobiles (see Table 10.1). Commercial banks held the largest amount of installment debt ($84 billion), followed by finance companies and credit unions. Retail and bank revolving credit totaled $30 billion, a fivefold increase from levels in the late 1960s, but composing only about 15 percent of outstanding consumer credit.

Revolving credit is an important means of making transactions in the economy. Substantially more than half of all consumers have some type of credit card. In 1975, revolving credit accounts (with about 1.5 cards per account) numbered about 330 million, compared to about 135 million of the more conventional closed-end accounts (see Table 10.2).* Revolving accounts generated an estimated 5 billion charge slips in 1975, financing an estimated $80 billion in sales.

---

*A revolving account has no fixed obligation or monthly payment. These may be changed each month at the discretion of the consumer

TABLE 10.1

Consumer Installment Credit, November 1976
(millions of dollars)

By type	
Automobile	60,002
Mobile home	11,549
Home improvement	8,790
Bank revolving	13,264
Retailers*	17,726
Personal, other	64,002
Total	175,333
By lender	
Commercial banks	84,278
Finance companies	39,129
Credit unions	30,053
Retailers*	17,726
Other	4,147
Total	175,333

*Excludes $2.214 million of "30-day credit."

Source: Board of Governors, Federal Reserve System, Statistical Release G.19, November 1976.

Over half of all U.S. families owe some type of debt at any given time (excluding mortgage credit), committing between 14 and 16 percent of aggregate disposable income to debt repayment. Nearly two-thirds of all new cars and about half of all used cars are purchased with credit. About 40 percent of all durables are also purchased on credit. In addition, consumers borrow substantial sums from finance companies, credit unions, and other institutions in the form of direct personal loans. In 1970, the median amount of consumer installment debt owed was about $1,000 for debtors.[2] It is clear that consumer credit is an important aspect of consumer finances, especially for young families. With so many consumers involved, it is not surprising that consumer credit is a major political concern.

---

as more purchases are made or more is paid off. Closed-end accounts are for fixed sums of money for fixed periods of time and with constant monthly payments.

TABLE 10.2

Number of Credit Accounts, 1975
(millions of accounts)

Revolving credit	
Bank credit cards	40
Retail credit cards	170
Check credit	3
T&E,[a] airline, rent-a-car, other	20
Oil company	97
Total	330
Nonrevolving credit	
Banks (excluding mortgages)	37
Banks (single payment)	7
Retail	26
Credit unions[b]	24
Finance companies[b]	41
Total	135

[a]Travel and entertainment cards like American Express.
[b]Contains some revolving obligations.

Source: Credit Research Center, Purdue University.

LEGISLATIVE INTERVENTION

Legislative involvement in consumer credit is not new. Promises to abolish debt were common among Roman politicians, and interest rate ceilings as low as 0 percent were set by Roman legislators. There are several basic reasons given for intervention in the credit market on behalf of consumers. First, concern is expressed that there is an imbalance in market power and that the consumer is relatively ignorant of the legal and economic nature of the market.* Thus, it is argued that the consumer will be forced to pay a higher rate of

*This is, no doubt, owing in part to the tremendous complexity of the legal framework imposed on this market. Aside from this, it is not clear that the consumer would be in any better negotiating position when buying a television set or a car or any of the many services typically acquired in the marketplace.

interest than is necessary. A rate ceiling will ensure that the needy borrower is not excessively charged. Other arguments assert that those who are required by a reasonably well functioning market to pay high rates really should not have credit at all. Such consumers will, it is argued, be protected from themselves by the imposition of a rate ceiling that forces firms to ration them out of the market. Senator William Proxmire observed:

> High interest rates are a burden on the budget of the average family, and tend to redistribute income from the poor and middle classes to the wealthy. The ready availability of credit also causes some families to overextend themselves by borrowing more than they can really afford. . . . It would be much cheaper for a family to save the money for a major appliance rather than buying it on time.[3]
>
> One also wonders how seriously the staff [of the National Commission on Consumer Finance] considered alternative methods for channeling credit to needy borrowers unable to obtain credit in today's market. A government loan or a loan guarantee program might achieve the objective without costing anywhere near the estimated 3.5 billion [Senator Proxmire's estimate] which consumers will pay if the higher interest rate ceilings recommended by the Commission staff are adopted.[4]

Finally, there is what might be characterized as the "no one should have to pay that high a rate" view, which argues that rates above some specified level are unconscionable and should not be permitted, even if "economically" justified.

The impact of rate ceilings on the credit industry is well characterized by the literature on price ceilings. Output (extensions of credit) is restricted, and there is excess demand at the regulated price. Extralegal markets expand and devices are found for circumventing the restriction on price. The restriction in loan production does not, however, appear as a simple shortage of goods.* Rather, the "shortage" is selective, restricting credit availability among the riskiest of all applicants (demanders). Typically, these consumers have lower, less stable incomes and are less well educated. Those who still get credit at the lower rate could benefit.†

---

*In the case of goods, the creation of a shortage can result in a distribution in favor of those who can "afford" to queue, those consumers with the lowest opportunity cost of time. This will not occur in the case of credit.

†Credit cards assess only one rate, likely owing to the cost of accurately assessing risk and the variability of risk over the life cy-

Regulatory effects may differ depending on whether the credit is sales credit (provided in conjunction with the sale of goods or services) or cash credit. Some merchants provide "free" credit, but recover credit costs in the price of the merchandise. Thus, the effects of rate ceilings or collection restrictions can, in part, be evaded, and the process of evasion creates new sets of subsidies and transfers. Providers of cash credit are less able to engage in such activities, as their only business is cash lending.

These views are augmented by similar positions regarding the ability of lenders to collect debts. As one regulatory official recently noted: "In ancient Rome, the creditor had the right to kill the defaulting debtor, sell him into slavery or retain him as a personal servant for life. No doubt this decreased the default rate. Some contemporary remedies do the same thing in a slightly more genteel fashion." Such views have been, and continue to be, implemented in laws and regulations that proscribe the collection activities of lenders.*

The consumer who defaults on an obligation generally does so because he cannot meet payment commitments given current income and the need to make other necessary expenditures. Although not exclusively, these consumers tend to be lower income individuals, particularly those with relatively high income variability. There have been no studies of the characteristics of "deadbeats," but one might presume that such individuals would be those who could expect to gain more from a successful default than they would lose from the resulting poor credit rating. Restrictions on the amount of time that "adverse" information can be kept in an individual's credit record lower the cost of bankruptcies and defaults to the consumer involved, whether a deadbeat or not. As these regulations lower the cost of such behavior, one might, ceteris paribus, expect an increase in the frequency of defaults and bankruptcies owing to such regulations.

IDENTIFYING THE SUBSIDIES

By controlling prices in credit markets, legislators hope to effect certain benefits, namely, lower credit costs or protection from the potential costs of overextension. For the most part, the intended

---

cle. Similarly, banks typically charge only a few rates. In general, the rate restriction will make more funds available to "good" customers, lowering rates on loans to those individuals.

*In a study of collection activities at a major retailer in California, repossession was used as a collection device only nine times in a one-in-five sample of 427 delinquent accounts.

recipients are lower income consumers.* The actual outcome, however, is a much more complex set of transfers. To see this, it is instructive to construct a simple model of the lending process. Credit unions provide a good operational example. Some consumers deposit savings at an intermediary. The intermediary makes loans to other consumers. In principle, the intermediary returns the capital (savings) to the depositing consumers, plus all interest earned less the expenses of the intermediary operation.

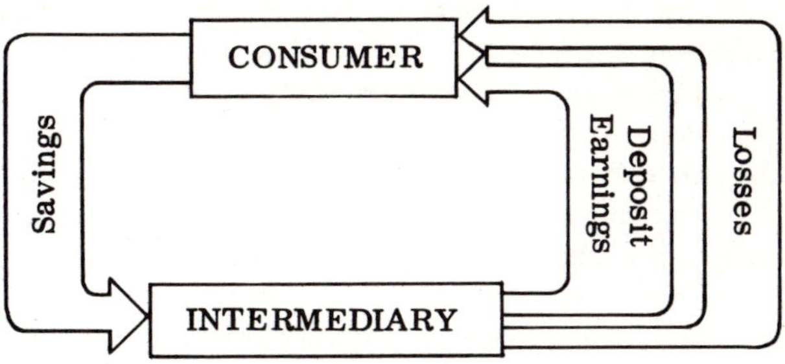

The effect of rate ceilings and limitations on the intermediary's ability to collect delinquent loans is clear. The depositors get a lower return on their savings because of depressed earnings and higher losses of capital. If each depositor were making a single loan, acting as his or her own intermediary, situations in which some savers might lose all their savings when a loan was not collectable would surely arise. Under the current system, all depositors share this cost, but the amount of capital lost is the same (assuming that the same volume of loans is made).[5] Thus, three grants result from laws that limit interest rates or the ability of an intermediary to collect loans:

1. Those who can still borrow are permitted to get credit at a lower rate.
2. Savers get a lower return.
3. When a default occurs, the owed balance is transferred from the saver to the debtor when collection cannot be made.

This, however, is not the end of the story. Other responses occur in a market with alternative investments. Savers, when con-

---

*A general inference based on statements made by legislators in defense of limitations measures and by articles written advocating such restrictions.

fronted with lower yields and higher risk, may put their funds elsewhere. Because loans are made based on assessed risk, the riskier borrower will be rationed out by the intermediary with less funds to loan out. The intermediary can also shift depositors' funds away from consumer loans into alternative investments, resulting in the same rationing.* This will result in two more identifiable transfers:

4. Consumers rationed out by this intermediary may find credit elsewhere, but at a higher price. The loss to this group is approximately $[R_a - R_i] \cdot L$ (assuming that they borrow the same amount), where R_a is the alternative borrowing rate, R_i is the rate charged by the intermediary, and L is the size of the loan.
5. Consumers rationed out who cannot find alternative financing lose the difference between the value of the intended use of the funds net of financing costs and the next best alternative use for the funds that would have been committed to monthly payments.

For some credit markets, the effects are even more complex. Retailers of goods and services and banks provide credit services, but also market many other products and services as well. For such institutions, adjustment in the supply of credit to rate and collection controls may be relatively smaller, or nonexistent, compared to pure lenders, as revenue and capital losses can be recovered from other aspects of the business. The extent to which the loss is apportioned to each type of product depends on the price and credit-availability elasticities of sales.

For example, consider a retail firm that has extended credit in a regulatory framework that permits an 18 percent annual percentage rate. Then the rate is lowered by law to 12 percent. In principle, the firm would now accept only applicants who were 12 percent risks or better, refusing credit to many who qualified at 18 percent.† However,

---

*In some instances, this is prohibited by law, resulting in such phenomena as "disintermediation."

†The situation is more complex, as most credit extensions are made in the form of credit card arrangements. These are not one-time extensions but provide the consumer with a line of credit that is difficult to cancel unless misused. Thus, the firm cannot adjust its expected losses by canceling accounts for consumers who fall in the unacceptable credit risk category at a 12 percent rate. No model of credit-granting behavior is specified here. Thus, it is not clear at what risk level the firm should begin to refuse applicants to preserve a normal rate of return to capital. For the purposes of this chapter, only the direction of the change is of interest.

ever, if sales are more sensitive to credit availability than to an equivalent price change for merchandise or services, then it may be more profitable (less business lost) to raise prices than to curtail credit availability.* Such a change would involve a third group in the transfer process—the cash buyers who receive lower total services for the same price than their credit card using counterparts. Thus, the users of credit are subsidized by the consumers who pay cash. In general, consumers who qualify for credit are relatively better off financially than those who do not. The lower the maximum allowable rate, the higher the economic status of the users of credit will be compared to that of those who do not qualify.† Thus, for sales credit, one additional subsidy is present:

6. Purchasers of goods and services using cash may subsidize the use of credit by credit card users if the costs of providing credit card services are not covered by the credit revenue generated.

One further subsidy is present that is unique to the credit card environment. The credit card provides a line of credit that can be exercised at the discretion of the holder. If a credit card user pays his or her obligation within a specified period, no finance charge is assessed. Thus, the benefits of card use accrue at no cost to the user. The services, however, are produced at a cost, which must be covered either by credit users who pay finance charges, or by cash customers, or both. Currently, between one-quarter and one-third of retail and bank credit card holders use their cards for a year and pay no finance charges on their accounts.[6] This, however, is not due to any particular regulation, but rather to practices based on the use of the now nearly extinct 30-day open accounts run by many stores years ago. In the bank card market, it appears that this subsidy is already being reduced through the imposition of annual fees or monthly handling charges imposed when no finance charge is

---

*The price increase required to recoup the one-third reduction in credit revenues would not be large and would affect the condition of all firms simultaneously.

†Unfortunately, the issue is clouded by the fact that most, if not all, credit card carrying consumers also pay for some goods and services with cash. Some retailers have estimated that for every charge dollar, the average credit card customer makes cash sales of 60 cents. Thus, cash and credit customers are not uniquely identifiable groups for the purposes of estimating subsidies, although those consumers without credit cards must, by definition, always be cash customers.

paid.* Thus, this subsidy is based on the decision of the businessman and is presumably enforced by competition. In some sense, it is a transfer imposed by the threat of the customer to take his business elsewhere (to a firm that will offer a free period). Any one firm providing sales credit that withdrew the free period would run the risk of losing a substantial number of good customers.

More recently, some firms providing sales credit have tried to eliminate the subsidy between free riders and those who pay finance charges by assessing finance charges on the average daily balance. A truly average-daily-balance method would assess the user from the day of the purchase when credit is first extended to the day of payment. This is the basis on which all cash credit is provided.

At the time of writing, legislators in several states have introduced bills that would prevent firms from eliminating the free period or using average-daily-balance methods, thus formalizing by law the transfers from those who pay finance charges to those who do not. These have been accompanied by the usual flood of bills aimed at reducing the maximum allowable rate of finance or interest charge that can be assessed. It is abundantly clear that the basic trend in legislation is to formalize or expand many of the grants identified here.

7. Consumers who pay their revolving credit accounts within the grace period allowed use the services of the credit card but pay no fees. The cost of these services is paid by other customers of the intermediary, including other credit users or cash customers or users of other services.

The transfers and subsidies induced by the regulations are numerous and complex. The discussion presented here is probably not exhaustive, as, without a well-specified theory of firm behavior and regulation, some responses may not be anticipated and identified. However, those identified here are known to exist, and an examination of their nature should be instructive. Overall, the attempt to secure low rates of interest and finance charges and to eliminate certain procedures used to collect obligations have:

---

*These fees have been imposed under two conditions. Most frequently they are found in states with very low rate ceilings (Arkansas with 10 percent, Minnesota with 12 percent). In one other instance, a 50-cent-per-month fee was imposed when no finance charge was assessed on the bill. This is equivalent to a $6 annual charge for "free" use of the card. The position of the bank is that free riders are not profitable (a charge is earned from the merchant discount charged) and that if other banks want those customers, they are welcome to them.

1. Secured lower rates for some consumers.
2. Resulted in lower returns to consumers who supply funds to the credit market.
3. Increased the cost of enforcing contracts, resulting in potentially larger volumes of bad debts, a transfer from the consumer with loanable funds to the consumer who borrows those funds.
4. Caused a reduction in the availability of credit, at least to certain groups of consumers.
5. Caused consumers to incur higher search costs for credit and, in some cases, to use more expensive sources of credit.
6. Produced a subsidization of users of sales credit (revolving credit) by other customers of the firm.
7. Produced a subsidy to users of credit cards who never pay finance charges or any other fees for the use of credit card services.

In the following sections of this chapter, an attempt is made to quantify the subsidies and transfers identified here and to provide some insight into the characteristics of consumers who are party to the grants that are observed.

MEASURING GRANTS: THE CASE OF REVOLVING CREDIT

Although consumer revolving credit makes up only about 10 percent of total consumer installment credit outstanding, it is an important and growing financial service. Many large firms estimate that over 50 percent of their business volume is transacted through the credit card medium, although much of it is paid within the grace periods allowed. The credit card provides other services, including record keeping, easier cash management, less risk than carrying cash, and flexibility in the amount of debt held in the portfolio.[7] Rates that can be charged for credit extended through this medium are established in almost every state, ranging from 10 to 20 percent. The collection of credit card obligations is generally subject to the same restrictions as most other consumer debt.

Studies of the effects of the imposition of (lower) rate ceilings provide more explicit evidence about the nature and incidence of associated grants. In states with border cities, credit-sensitive business has tended to relocate in the state with less restriction, redistributing jobs, incomes, and tax revenues and imposing a different distribution of search and transactions costs on consumers [18].

Subsidies from Changed Credit Availability

The imposition of rate ceilings and restricted creditor remedies results in lower credit costs for consumers who qualify at the restricted rates (less any subsidy paid through higher prices for goods and services). Those who do not qualify for credit from the affected source may find credit elsewhere, possibly at a higher price, or may not get credit at all. A comparison of credit card ownership in Washington, a state that lowered the legal maximum from 18 to 12 percent, to California, New York, and Texas (states where comparable studies have been done) indicated that use of credit cards is less extensive in Washington than in the other three states, and, although other plausible theories could be constructed to explain the differences, the findings are consistent with the predicted effects of a lowering of the rate ceiling. Furthermore, a study made immediately after the rate was lowered indicated that firms tightened their lending standards [12]. The imposition of a 12 percent rate in Minnesota led banks to suspend credit card operations. Subsequently, they were resumed, but with the imposition of an annual charge of $10 for the use of a bank card. The Arkansas courts have held that such a charge does not violate state usury statutes (10 percent on all credit).

Some inferences about the incidence of credit rationing in Washington can be drawn from the data in Tables 10.3 and 10.4. The tables show credit card ownership data for families in Washington, California, Texas, and New York. The families were selected in each state from among those with at least one retail credit card.* By type of card, ownership of a few or no cards is substantially more frequent in Washington than in the other three states (see Table 10.3). The least difference is observed for travel and entertainment cards. This, however, would be expected, as these cards do not offer regular revolving credit options and charge an annual fee. Amounts owed are to be paid upon receipt of the bill, lessening the importance of the low rate ceiling. For oil company cards, New York consumers are the least frequent users, owing to the low rate of car ownership in New York City. Excluding oil company cards from the comparison

---

*In Washington, the basic sample was a representative household sample. Those with at least one retail credit card were selected for analysis. In the other three states, samples were drawn from the files of retailers offering their own credit programs. Because families typically have more than one credit card, the theoretical probability of being selected rises with the number of cards owned. This may result in an upward bias in the observed frequency of multiple-card ownership in California, New York, and Texas.

TABLE 10.3

Comparative Card Ownership
(percent)

	Washington	California	New York	Texas
Retail cards				
None	—	—	—	—
1–2	46	25	26	27
3–4	33	36	34	30
5 or more	21	39	40	43
Bank cards				
None*	43	32	33	32
1	41	48	41	37
2 or more	16	20	26	31
Travel and entertainment				
None*	86	83	77	81
1	12	13	19	16
2 or more	2	4	4	3
Gas cards				
None*	27	16	45	11
1	18	19	16	12
2	23	21	15	18
3 or more	32	44	24	59

*Includes those who did not answer the question. It is assumed that they had no cards of the type specified: 6 percent for bank cards, 21 percent for travel and entertainment cards, and 3 percent for gas cards in the Washington study.

Note: For Washington: All holders of at least one department store credit card selected from a representative sample of Washington households selected by Reuben Donnelley. The survey was conducted in 1974. For California: Based on a sample of retail credit accounts selected from the files of California retailers by Touche Ross & Company. The survey was conducted in 1970. For New York: Based on a sample of retail credit accounts selected from the files of New York retail stores. The survey was conducted in 1973. For Texas: Based on a sample of 550 account holders at Sears Roebuck & Company in Texas. The survey was conducted in 1971.

Source: Compiled by the author.

TABLE 10.4

Total Number of Cards Owned
(percent)

Family Income (dollars)	Number of Cards											
	1-4 Cards			5-9 Cards			10-14 Cards			15 Cards or More		
	Washington	California	New York	Washington	California	New York	Washington	California	New York	Washington	California	New York
Under 7,500	53	52	45	41	24	54	6	22	[b]	[b]	2	[b]
7,501-10,000	49	16	70[a]	43	53	22[a]	6	31	8[a]	2	[b]	[a]
10,001-15,000	41	15	38	47	59	46	10	24	11	2	2	5
15,001-20,000	25	16	24	56	60	51	18	20	21	1	4	4
20,001 or more	12	9	10	47	41	45	32	38	35	9	12	10
All	36	18	30	47	49	45	14	28	20	3	5	5

[a]This jump appears to be caused primarily by lower gasoline card ownership for this income group. Ownership of larger numbers of cards is therefore lower.

[b]Less than 0.5 percent.

Source: Compiled by the author.

leaves Washington consumers using substantially fewer cards than consumers in the other two states.

These results tend to hold for various levels of income.* Table 10.4 indicates that fewer cards are owned more often by all income groups in Washington, once the effect of low oil company card ownership in New York is accounted for. A more recent study of bank credit cards in Washington and California provides further support, indicating delinquency rates in Washington only one-fourth of those in California (1 percent versus 4 percent) and relatively lower delinquent account expenses for Washington banks (Table 10.5). The lower delinquency rates and expense indicate that better average risk customers are served in Washington than in California.

More direct evidence is available from several other studies of the likely impact of a tightening of credit standards [7; 12; 23]. Consumers in each study were scored based on their characteristics, as if they were applying for a retail or bank credit card.† Table 10.6 indicates the distribution of income for various ranges of scores in a study of New York retail credit card users. When a firm tightens its lending standards by raising the minimum acceptable score, the incidence of refusals is disproportionately found among consumers with relatively lower incomes. For example, if the minimum retail score in New York were raised to 80, it would, based on the scoring model used, eliminate 4.9 percent of the current card users in 1973 (Table 10.6). Thirty-five percent of those losing access to this type of credit would have incomes of $7,500 or less, although this group makes up only 9 percent of the retail card-using population.

Use of credit cards is concentrated in the higher income groups, and actual use of the revolving option is also concentrated among the middle- to upper-income groups (Table 10.7). Thus, in terms of access, frequency of actual use, and amount financed, the group that would benefit the most (be damaged least) from the lowering of the ceiling is probably the middle- to upper-income consumer.

There is very little evidence indicating what happens to consumers who are rationed out of one segment of the market. The basic

---

*Inflation and regional differences in incomes compromise the comparisons somewhat, but probably not seriously because of the large intervals in the brackets and the fact that the data were gathered before the major inflationary surge.

†Several different actual scoring models were used, along with an "average" scheme based on the relative importance of variables in each model. In some cases, information on a few characteristics was not available. However, based on the weights used in the models, this probably had little effect on relative scores.

TABLE 10.5

Bank Card Statistics, California and Washington, 1973-75 (averages)

	California	Washington
Percent of total credit revenues earned as		
Customer finance charges	71	55
Merchant discounts	14	28
Late charges	1	2
Percent of active accounts that were delinquent	4	1
Delinquent account costs as a percent of total credit card costs*	36	18

*Includes bad debt losses.

Source: "The Bank Credit Card Market in California," unpublished report, Credit Research Center, Purdue University, 1977.

rationale for a specialized rate structure for finance companies was the pervasiveness of the illegitimate, high-rate lenders in operation. A 1971 study of former customers of closed loan companies in Maine, where recent legislation had driven most of the finance companies out of business, indicated that about 27 percent were able to get some type of bank loan, while 20 percent borrowed from other finance companies and 3 percent from friends or relatives (Table 10.8). Fifty percent did not borrow additional funds [1].* Currently, all finance companies have left the state. When the more restrictive law was passed in 1967, finance company outstandings were $31 million.

Since those losing access to revolving credit when a lower ceiling is imposed are known to be of relatively higher risk, it would seem safe to presume that many (though not all) would get credit only at higher rates. Clearly, such was not the intent of the rate restriction, and the failure to anticipate such a response may be one of the potential information feedback problems that lead to "pathological states of the grants economy" to which Kenneth Boulding refers [2, p. 24].

---

*Some of these consumers bought more goods on credit, clearly a substitute for direct finance company borrowing. Respondents did not consider this to be "borrowing."

TABLE 10.6

Simulated Rejections of Credit Card Holders by Credit Score Cutoff Points, New York Retail Credit Card Users, 1973

	Cumulative Percent of Account Holders Affected[a]	Percent with Income under			
		$7,500	$10,000	$15,000	$20,000
Retail score					
Raise to 70 (70 to 80)	3.9	29	32	48	84
	(1.0)	(53)	(53)	(76)	(99)
Raise to 80 (80 to 90)	4.9	35	37	55	89
	(3.7)	(17)	(31)	(64)	(70)
Raise to 90 (90 to 100)	8.6	27	34	59	81
	(3.5)	(36)	(44)	(53)	(69)
Raise to 100 (100 to 110)	12.1	29	37	57	78
	(5.9)	(7)	(32)	(74)	(85)
Raise to 110 (110 to 120)	18.0	22	36	62	80
	(6.3)	(7)	(28)	(46)	(71)
Raise to 120	24.3	18	34	58	78
Bank score					
Raise to 24 (24 to 29)	1.6	89	89	100	b
	(5.0)	(36)	(48)	(75)	(85)
Raise to 29 (29 to 34)	6.6	50	58	82	89
	(11.8)	(19)	(53)	(74)	(92)
Raise to 34 (34 to 39)	18.4	30	55	77	91
	(17.9)	(8)	(29)	(58)	(84)
Raise to 39	36.3	19	42	68	87
Sample income distribution	—	8.9	17.3	42.0	68.4

[a]Figures in parentheses show the incremental proportions of the population affected and the income distribution for that group alone.
[b]Less than 0.5 percent.

Source: Robert Shay and William Dunkelberg, Retail Store Credit Card Use in New York (New York: Columbia University Press, 1975).

TABLE 10.7

Account Data by Family Income Groups, New York Retail Credit Card Users

	Total Household Income (dollars)							
	5,000 or Under	5,001-7,500	7,501-10,000	10,001-15,000	15,001-20,000	20,001-25,000	25,001 or More	Total
Number of accounts	39	115	153	454	449	212	294	1,716
	(50)	(70)	(90)	252	(212)	(103)	(120)	(897)
Percentage distribution[b]	2.3	6.7	8.9	26.5	26.2	12.4	17.1	100.0
Account average (12-month period)[a]								
Total sales (dollars)	101	172	263	246	253	269	239	243
Net sales[c] (dollars)	92	169	250	219	232	205	224	218
Net revolving sales (dollars)	72	107	172	138	136	85	115	126
Finance charges (dollars)	10.27	5.18	21.26	18.95	14.95	6.74	17.36	15.21
Number of revolving months[d]	4.3	4.1	6.6	5.9	5.2	4.0	4.8	5.2
Percent of net sales revolved	78.2	63.2	68.7	63.1	58.5	41.4	51.6	58.0
Percent of share of net sales[b]	1.0	5.2	10.3	26.6	27.8	11.6	17.6	100.0
Percent of share of finance charges[b]	1.5	2.3	12.5	33.0	25.7	5.5	19.6	100.0
Ratio of finance charge revenues to								
Net sales (percent)	11.2	3.1	8.5	8.7	6.4	3.3	7.8	7.0
Revolving sales (percent)	14.3	4.9	12.4	13.7	11.0	7.9	15.1	12.0

[a]Data weighted according to each store's relative share of credit sales for the 17 stores in the New York study.
[b]Percentages may not add to 100 percent because of rounding.
[c]Net sales = total sales less returns and credits.
[d]Months in which the balance due is not fully paid.

Source: Robert Shay and William Dunkelberg, Retail Store Credit Card Use in New York (New York: Columbia University Press, 1975).

TABLE 10.8

Borrowing Activity and Attitudes, 1971
(n = 460)

Feelings about Loss of Finance Company Lender	Alternative Borrowing Activity (percent)	
	Obtained Other Funds	No Borrowing
Felt better off	74.0	36.3
Rid of "burden"	13.0	29.8
Got better credit	59.4	—
Finance companies a necessary evil	—	6.1
No reason given	1.7	0.4
Felt worse off	7.0	36.3
Too easy to borrow, still under "burden"	6.1	—
No other alternative	—	11.4
Burden of high rates leads to repayment difficulty	—	24.9
No reason given	0.9	*
Felt about same	19.0	27.6
Still with finance company	7.8	
Still borrowing elsewhere	9.5	
Does not matter where you borrow	—	19.7
No reason given	1.7	7.9

*Less than 0.5 percent.

Source: George J. Benston, "An Analysis of Maine's '36 Month Limitation' on Finance Company Small Loans," National Commission on Consumer Finance, Technical Studies, vol. 2 (Washington, D.C.: U.S. Government Printing Office, 1974), p. 41.

To the extent that the lower ceiling prevents some higher risk consumers from getting credit, it might be said that an intended "grant" had been made, and that these consumers would be protected from themselves and the irresistible urge to overextend on credit.*

*It is interesting to note that we might be viewed as being more tolerant of 25,000 auto deaths annually, plus many more injuries and

Because rarely can consumers be expected to borrow just for the fun of it, it is clear that denial of credit also implies the loss of the value that would have been derived from the expenditure of the borrowed sum (less the consumption value of what would have otherwise been monthly payments). At any point in time, between two and four of every hundred accounts might be delinquent (behind one or more payments). Of these, only a few will actually end up written off, in bankruptcy, and so on. If it were possible, the system would have initially discovered these few accounts per hundred and denied them credit. Instead, consumers must be treated ex ante in groups having roughly the same credit-related characteristics. If economic factors require the elimination of those that most frequently have problems and generate high costs, the entire group would have to be rationed out of the market. Thus, to save a few families from the difficulties of overextension, many more may be denied access to at least some credit and its benefits.

When credit is refused, the consumer can search for other sources of credit or simply not borrow. Successful searchers incur additional search costs, as their options are reduced, and most will likely pay a higher rate for the alternative source of credit. Unsuccessful searchers incur the cost of search and must do without the credit, as must those who did not search farther originally.

The cost to the consumer of such outcomes is most difficult to measure. To illustrate the complexity and the approach, a somewhat artificial example is presented. William Dunkelberg and J. Stephenson [11] estimated the rate of return to ownership of a washer and drier when compared to the alternative of using a laundromat. A typical pattern of returns (depending on the number of loads of wash done weekly) is shown in Appendix Table 10.A.1. The distribution of the rate of return (a function of loads per week washed, or family characteristics) was computed by family income class [11, Table 10, p. 57]. Assume rationing occurs in the form of an increase in the minimum required score for retail credit from 10 to 30 points. This would eliminate 6 percent of the population from eligibility.[8] Assuming that the total price ($450) is borrowed for the life of the machine (10 years), an example of the cost can be calculated on the presumption that, for all families in this group, this purchase was the best marginal expenditure available.* Computations are shown for initial

---

the family crises this creates, than we are of the difficulties that arise from the use of credit.

*The assumption of continual financing made for the calculation may not be as unreasonable as it seems at first glance. As consumers are likely to be in debt continually over such a period of time,

credit availability at an 18 percent annual percentage rate. Two measures are computed, one assuming that all affected consumers find alternative credit at 20 percent and another assuming that none gets credit and that the purchase is not made. Search costs are ignored. Both figures are present values:

Loss of value at 20 percent*	\$58.2 million
Gross loss if credit not available†	\$224.4 million

The Transfer Owing to Bad Debt Losses

In viewing bad debt losses as a wealth transfer, there is an additional cost to rationed consumers—the value of bad debt losses that would otherwise accrue to this group. The aggregate amount of such transfers is substantial, and even though the transfer requires a great deal of resources, those receiving it are probably made better off.

In 1976, transfers owing to bad debts came to about \$2 billion (Table 10.9). This figure was derived by applying rather conservative estimates of the loss rates for various types of lenders to outstanding balances at the end of 1976. In addition, considerable expense is incurred in the attempt to collect a debt prior to writing it off. The "cost" of making (or preventing) these transfers is substantial and perhaps counterproductive if the transfer is viewed as desirable.‡

---

and the levels are not likely to vary much in terms of total comitment, it is not too artificial to view the consumer as continually refinancing \$450, always choosing the cheapest method available. It was assumed that this is always at 18 percent for the ten-year period. Other more complex patterns of the marginal cost of funds could be utilized.

*Assumes all members of the group with a rate of return above 20 percent (see Table 10.A.2) would make the purchase. The present value is computed at 20 percent and subtracted from the present value at 18 percent. Seventy-five million families is assumed. It is also assumed that the purchase price is financed for the ten-year period. Thus, \$58.2 million = $75 \times 0.06 \times p \times PV_{18} - PV_{20}$, where p is taken from Table 10.A.2 for groups with a rate of return above 20 percent and PV_{18} is the present value of the purchase at 18 percent.

†Assumes no one can make the purchase because of unavailability of credit. The loss is then equal to the net value (in excess of the 18 percent cost of funds) of ownership. It is assumed that the purchase price would have been financed for the ten-year period. The underlying data are in Table 10.A.2.

‡If the intent of limitations on creditor remedies is to reduce the undesirable aspects (to the debtor) associated with the collection of

TABLE 10.9

Estimated Transfers from Bad Debt Losses, 1976

Credit Outstanding by Type of Lender	Amount (millions)[a]	Estimated Loss Rate (percent)	Estimated Net Bad Debt Losses (millions)
Commercial banks			
Revolving	13,264	1.0	132.6
Other	71,014	0.5	355.1
Retailers	17,726	1.5	265.9
Finance companies	39,129	2.5	978.2
Credit unions	30,053[b]	0.5	150.3
Other	4,147	2.0	82.9
Total			1,965.0

[a]Board of Governors of the Federal Reserve System, Statistical Release G19, November 1976.

[b]Credit unions typically keep delinquent loans on the books for very long periods of time, artificially lowering their loss rate.

Source: Compiled by the author.

In the New York retail credit card study [23], bad debt losses amounted to $11 million. This works out to $2.12 per active account in the 17 stores studied. In California, the losses amounted to nearly $20 million [26]. The nature of the subsidy is complex. Table 10.10 shows the income distribution of delinquent accounts from a study of California retail store credit card users [10]. The average cost of collection per account was $28, only somewhat less than the average loss of $31. The average loss declines with rising income and the frequency with which consumers become delinquent declines. Thus, losses are relatively more frequent and larger among the lower in-

---

debts, then resources devoted to the collection process may be viewed as counterproductive by the legislators or regulators limiting remedies. Furthermore, if the intent of legislation restricting remedies has been to eliminate the harassment or personal tragedy associated with delinquency but not to prevent the repayment of legal debts, then the growing use of credit insurance would seem to be a more sensible alternative.

TABLE 10.10

Bad Debt Transfers among Credit Card Users

Income Group (dollars)	Distribution of Credit Card Users (percent)	Probability of Default	Delinquent Accounts: Distribution of Delinquent Accounts (percent)*	Delinquent Accounts: Average Cost of Collection Activities (dollars)	Delinquent Accounts: Average Debt Written Off (dollars)	Delinquent Accounts: Share of Bad Debt Losses (percent)
Under 5,000	5.8	0.044	6.3	32	45	9.3
5,001-7,500	5.5	0.175	24.1	43	33	26.1
7,501-10,000	14.3	0.070	25.1	23	29	23.8
10,001-15,000	24.5	0.051	31.0	24	23	23.3
15,001-20,000	21.2	0.012	7.6	20	52	12.9
20,000 or more	28.7	0.008	5.9	16	24	4.6
All	100.0	0.040	100.0	28	31	100.0

*Income was not known for 29 percent of the problem accounts. They are excluded from the distributional percentages. Their collection statistics were virtually identical to the lowest income group, but that assumption cannot be strongly supported by the available data.

Source: William Dunkelberg and Robert Smiley, "Subsidies in the Use of Revolving Credit," Journal of Money, Credit and Banking, September 1975.

come groups. Viewing these losses as transfers, it appears that lower income groups are more likely to receive them. Sixty percent of the losses were found among families with incomes below $10,000, about 26 percent of the card-using population.

Free Riders and the Cash Customer Subsidy

There are no "depositors" who will receive lower returns on their deposits in the case of consumer revolving credit, except possibly where bank cards are concerned. Instead, deficiencies from credit card operations will be paid from general revenues, that is, by all customers of the firm, whether or not they use credit cards. An early study of the 12 percent rate in Washington reported that "the majority of retailers responded that they had raised prices on all merchandise to make up for their losses" [12, p. 96]. Several studies of the Arkansas 10 percent rate found that cash prices within the state were higher by approximately enough to cover credit losses. Thus, "credit prices" (the total outlay for an item bought on credit) were the same across state lines, but cash prices were higher in Arkansas [18]. Interestingly, the catalogs of major retailers, which are prepared on a regional basis, make it difficult for merchants to raise prices as high as they would like in order to provide more credit, forcing them to remain relatively more restrictive on credit qualifications.

Based on a study of New York retail credit card users [23], a reduction in the maximum rate to 12 from 18 percent could "save" credit card users $14 million (assuming that the same amount of credit is extended). However, this would increase the deficit in the credit operation by an equal amount, from about $29 million to $43 million (Table 10.11). To continue to earn a competitive return on capital invested, firms would have to raise prices to recover the loss in revenue. The deficiency at 18 percent amounted to 1.3 percent of all sales (3.7 percent of credit sales). At 12 percent, the shortfall would increase to 1.9 percent. Thus, average prices would have to be increased by 0.6 percent, inducing a subsidy of considerable complexity as noted earlier. On a per-account basis, the deficiency would be increased from $5.60 to $8.40. Thus, lowering the ceiling rates applicable to credit cards may provide credit at lower rates for most users. This is done, however, at the expense of higher prices (or adjustments in quality, service, and so on) and the rationing of marginal consumers from this market.

If total revenues produced by credit card use are less than costs for some users, a subsidy exists. About one-quarter of retail credit card users never pay finance charges. Another 50 percent of

TABLE 10.11

Deficiency of Credit Costs over Credit Revenues, New York and California

	California	New York
Credit sales (dollars)	1,413,741,000	776,453,500
Total sales (dollars)	n.a.[f]	2,223,734,000
Current deficiency[a] (dollars)	34,867,361[a]	28,841,000[b]
Deficiency at 12 percent	52,057,300[c]	43,059,900[d]
Deficiency percent of sales		
18	0.9[e]	1.3
12	1.3[e]	1.9

[a]From Touche Ross & Company, "Cost Analysis of Retail Store Revolving Credit: State of California" (Sacramento, Calif.: California Retailers Association, 1971), Exhibit I.

[b]From Robert Shay and William Dunkelberg, Retail Store Credit Card Use in New York (New York: Columbia University Press, 1975), p. 88. Includes 15 stores that use several methods for computing finance charges.

[c]Assumes the same proportionate increase as found in New York.

[d]Robert Shay and William Dunkelberg, Retail Store Credit Card Use in New York, p. 88. Assumes that account holders use their accounts in the same way as when an 18 percent charge was imposed.

[e]Assumes the same ratio of credit sales to total sales as found in New York.

[f]n.a. = not available.

Source: Compiled by the author.

the users ride free at least once in a one-year period. The free riders most frequently occur among the highest and the lowest income users (Table 10.7). The marginal cost of producing credit entails the incurrence of the numerous costs detailed in Table 10.A.2. After the account is open, costs will depend on the number of charges made, the average size of the balance owed, the number of returns and credits, and average collection and capital costs. Revenues result from gross margins on merchandise and finance charges.

To examine the size and distribution of these subsidies, a measure of cost was determined based on use patterns over the period of

TABLE 10.12

Socioeconomic Determinants of Net Revenues for Retail Credit Card Users, New York

	Number of Accounts[a]	Group Mean Less Grand Mean[b] (dollars)	Adjusted Regression Coefficient[c] (dollars)	F[d]
Income (dollars)				
5,000 and under	8	16.6	-5.4	0.5
5,001-7,500	78	-23.2	-24.5	77.8
7,501-10,000	131	-0.9	-1.9	1.3
10,001-15,000	380	1.8	0.8	—
15,001-20,000	407	2.5	4.7	5.1
20,000 and over	460	0.0	0.0	0.2
Age				
Under 25	83	-6.1	0.5	0.7
25-34 years	375	-4.2	-4.7	2.2
35-44 years	371	-1.5	-2.1	—
45-54 years	371	1.2	0.0	1.6
55-64 years	235	5.9	7.7	26.7
65 and over	29	27.1	25.5	33.4
Years with present employer				
Under 1 year	119	-4.1	1.4	2.0
1-2 years	124	-10.0	-8.2	7.0
3-5 years	290	1.1	2.6	7.5
6-10 years	293	3.0	4.9	17.6
11 or more years	638	0.8	-2.0	—
Marital status				
Married	1,135	1.4	0.2	—
Single	208	-14.4	-9.7	23.6

Separated	19	7.3	13.2	6.5
Divorced	36	16.4	17.0	18.9
Widowed	66	9.4	14.7	23.0
Housing status				
Own home	935	1.8	-0.5	—
Rent, other	529	-3.1	0.9	0.8
Sex of respondent				
Male	946	2.2	0.3	—
Female	518	-4.0	-0.5	0.3
Occupation				
Professional	267	-0.9	-0.2	—
Technical, scientific	100	-6.4	-6.3	5.6
Supervisors, self-employed	344	3.9	2.6	2.1
Clerical and sales	308	-4.7	-5.1	5.7
Craftsmen, foremen	141	4.5	4.5	3.5
Service workers	117	1.0	3.3	1.9
Operatives, unskilled	126	8.5	7.6	8.6
Students, housewives, retired	62	-13.4	-10.0	8.1
Constant			15.5	

[a] 1,464 weighted accounts, 722 unweighted. An equal number of accounts were selected from each of 17 stores, regardless of size. Accounts were then weighted to reflect the total volume of receivables they represented. Cases with missing data were omitted.

[b] The deviation of the average net contribution for each group from the overall sample mean of $15 for net contribution.

[c] Adjusted to yield the overall mean of $15.50 as the constant term in the regression equation. Thus, each adjusted coefficient represents a deviation from the sample mean of the dependent variable [5]. The actual regression coefficients for each group can be constructed by subtracting the coefficient for the excluded group from the remaining coefficients in the group.

[d] Excluded category represented by a dash. F statistics are based on differences between the included categories and the category excluded in dummy variable estimation.

Note: $R^2 = 0.20$, standard error of estimate = 21.3, regression F = 15.2.

Source: Compiled by the author.

a year.* As no measure of cash sales was available, only credit card sales were included in the revenue computation. A measure of net revenues, S, was constructed by netting estimated costs against revenues, the variance of which depended on the number of transactions, the volume of sales, the amount of credit actually used, and the expected (average) collection costs based on the users' income. This measure was regressed on the characteristics of the users in an attempt to discover the direction of subsidies (if any) particularly with respect to income. The results for New York are shown in Table 10.12.†

The regression coefficients in Table 10.12 are estimated so that their weighted sum (the sum of the coefficients multiplied by the number of cases in the group) totals zero. All coefficients, then, are deviations from the average measure of S for the sample. Negative coefficients indicate that the average difference between costs and revenues for the group was below the mean for all retail credit card users. Because the cost measure only included variable costs, no absolute statement can be made about user profitability. But it is clear that for some population subgroups, the difference between revenues and variable costs is likely to be negative. For example, the group of users who are young, single, new on the job, and earning a relatively low income could generate an average deficiency between revenues and variable costs of $30 or more.‡ Thus, as a group, they

---

*It was assumed (based on some empirical observation) that the cost of processing one additional charge slip was about five cents, that the cost of capital was 8 percent, and that the margin on goods was 6 percent, both after taxes. Problem account costs were imputed based on the income of the user and the data presented in Table 10.12. No fixed costs were included. Thus, S = finance charge revenues + 0.06 × sales - 0.05 × number of slips - 0.08 × average account balance - expected problem account costs.

†Because bad debt expense was assigned based only on income, the regressions were rerun excluding this from the computation of S. The results were substantially the same.

‡Users with the following characteristics would generate an average deficiency of about $37:

Characteristic	Value (dollars)
Income: $5,001-$7,500	24.50
Age: 25-34	4.70
Years with employer: 1-2	8.20
Single	9.70
Rent	0.90
Occupation: technical trades	6.30
Sample mean	15.50
Deficiency of costs over revenue	37.00

are receiving a substantial subsidy in the use of their credit cards, a subsidy paid for by groups generating excesses of revenues over costs and by all purchasers of goods and services to the extent that deficiencies in the credit card operation are recovered in the price of merchandise.

CONCLUSION

There are an estimated 500 million credit accounts in the United States today (excluding mortgages) used by more than half of all families. There is considerable turnover among credit users, with about 25 percent of the families with installment debt (excluding credit cards) paying off their obligations each year. These are replaced by an approximately equal number of new debtors. In all, these families are using about $175 billion of credit, with an average maturity of about two years.

The use of this credit is controlled by a large body of regulations, some of the more important being rate ceilings, the Equal Credit Opportunity Act, Truth in Lending, the Uniform Commercial Code, various restrictions on creditor remedies, and the Fair Credit Billing Act. This list is far from exhaustive. These laws were instituted with particular objectives in mind, and each could be evaluated on the basis of just how well the objectives were met. This chapter took a slightly different approach. Focusing on rate ceilings and limitations on the ability of creditors to collect debts, an attempt was made to identify the effects, intended or unintended, that these regulations have had. The inventory of effects was not exhaustive, but included many interesting and important ones.

Lower rate ceilings were found to provide credit at lower rates to consumers, but only to those who qualified for credit at the lower rates. For example, credit card ownership was found to be substantially lower in Washington, a state with a 12 percent ceiling, than in other states with 18 percent ceiling rates. Washington consumers also used finance companies more frequently than their counterparts in other states. Finance companies in Washington are not subject to the 12 percent ceiling rate and can loan at rates in excess of 25 percent. Thus, lower rate ceilings in Washington secured lower rates on revolving credit, but for fewer consumers. More consumers turned to finance companies for their credit, paying higher rates and incurring additional search and transactions costs.

It was estimated that a 12 percent rate in New York could save retail credit card users at 17 major stores about $14 million in finance charges, assuming that the same amount of credit remained available. Of course, if credit was not contracted to lower costs, the revenue loss would have to be made up elsewhere, as the retail industry is very competitive, yielding relatively low rates of return on invested capital. If firms recouped the loss through higher prices for merchandise, prices would have to rise about 0.6 percent (over 7 percent at an annual rate). Even so, credit users would benefit on balance, with cash customers paying the balance of the credit card operation deficit. Consumers who could find no alternative source of credit would experience even larger opportunity losses, and would join the ranks of the cash buyers, subsidizing credit card users.

Bad debt losses are usually viewed as part of the cost of lending, one of the determinants of the lending rate. Here, they were considered as transfer payments, from consumers with savings to those who borrow. In 1976, such transfers amounted to about $2 billion. In addition, large sums of money were spent preventing these transfers (by trying to collect debts). Interestingly, in many cases these transfers go to those people who are often the targets of welfare programs: poorer people with unstable employment or people struck by misfortune. But this is not always the case, and many consumers "deserving" of welfare support choose to repay their obligations, even at great personal expense. When the debts of higher income families go bad, the amounts are often larger (though less frequent), so that the transfer payments may be in some sense "regressive." All in all, it is probably not a very efficient transfer payment system (although perhaps as good as the official programs). Unfortunately, the "taxes" used to support the program come only from savers and from borrowers who do repay their loans.

The total amount of transfers identified here is not caused entirely by regulation. Pure economics dictates an optimal level of bad debts—those that are expensive to collect, involve a small sum, or have a low probability of collection. There are better uses for resources. But the regulations can have a substantial effect on the magnitudes of these flows.

Overall, credit rationing that resulted from lower rate ceilings on revolving credit had a disproportionately large effect on lower income retail credit card users. Thus, these consumers will least frequently get the benefits of the lower rates, and will be forced to use more expensive credit or become cash customers, subsidizing the credit use of more affluent consumers. A simulation based on a sample of New York retail credit card users indicated that about 30 percent of the consumers disqualified by higher credit standards among current users of credit cards would have incomes of $7,500 or less, even though they made up about 9 percent of the card-using population. An attempt to measure the value of access to credit indicated substantial sums were involved, because of the high rate of return attached to durable goods used in the analyses.

The grants intended by credit legislation are substantial and it is not surprising that various consituent groups are very concerned about related legislative developments. But the response to regulation sets in motion additional transfers that must be accounted for in the process of identifying and measuring regulatory effects. The successful completion of such analyses as those attempted here would seem to be a prerequisite to meaningful evaluation of the social value of such regulation.

TABLE 10.A.1

Distribution of Rate of Return on a Washer and Drier
(families with retail scores between 10 and 30)

Income Class (dollars)	Percent of Rationed Families[a]	Rate of Return (percent)[b]										
		2.1	6.7	10.9	14.8	22.0	29.0	35.8	42.9	50.1	57.4	All
1,000	7.0	0.67	0.17	0.08	0.03	0.0	0.03	0.02	0.0	0.0	0.02	1.0
1,000-1,999	17.1	0.55	0.35	0.03	0.03	0.01	0.02	0.0	0.01	0.0	0.0	1.0
2,000-2,999	11.0	0.33	0.48	0.06	0.04	0.01	0.02	0.02	0.04	0.0	0.0	1.0
3,000-3,999	13.6	0.27	0.46	0.02	0.09	0.06	0.03	0.01	0.02	0.03	0.02	1.0
4,000-4,999	8.3	0.10	0.57	0.13	0.08	0.03	0.01	0.03	0.01	0.0	0.03	1.0
5,000-5,999	11.4	0.08	0.40	0.13	0.16	0.05	0.07	0.05	0.03	0.01	0.01	1.0
6,000-7,499	11.0	0.09	0.30	0.10	0.18	0.09	0.12	0.03	0.06	0.02	0.01	1.0
7,500-9,999	9.2	0.04	0.27	0.16	0.15	0.13	0.10	0.08	0.05	0.02	0.01	1.0
10,000-14,999	7.9	0.01	0.26	0.16	0.22	0.13	0.10	0.05	0.04	0.02	0.01	1.0
15,000 or more	3.5	0.02	0.27	0.16	0.23	0.14	0.10	0.03	0.02	0.01	0.02	1.0
Total	100.0											

[a]Raising the minimum score from +10 to +30 disqualifies 6 percent of the population based on the 1967 Survey of Consumer Finances. See William Dunkelberg, "A Lower Rate Maximum for Retail Credit: The Impact on Consumers," National Commission on Consumer Finance, Technical Studies, vol. 6 (Washington, D.C.: U.S. Government Printing Office, 1974), Table 10, p. 22.

[b]See William Dunkelberg and J. Stephenson, "Durable Goods Ownership and the Rate of Return," National Commission on Consumer Finance, Technical Studies, vol. 6 (Washington, D.C.: U.S. Government Printing Office, 1974), Table 10.

Source: Compiled by the author.

TABLE 10.A.2

Credit Costs as a Percent of Net Revolving Credit Sales

	New York (1972)[a]	California[b]
Net revolving credit sales (dollars)	776,453,500	1,413,741,084
Total percent	100.0	100.0
Finance charge revenue	7.60	7.8
Credit costs		
Personnel costs		
New accounts	0.50	0.31
Account servicing	1.04	1.35
Account collection	0.42	0.51
Additional sales personnel	0.13	0.10
Supporting services	0.11	0.07
Management	0.05	0.07
Data processing	0.25	0.20
Total personnel costs	2.50	2.61
Data processing equipment	0.16	0.15
Credit investigation	0.14	0.15
Bad debt losses	1.40	1.40
Collection agency fees	0.17	0.15
Credit space and equipment	0.20	0.14
Postage	0.40	—
Communication	0.15	0.91
Supplies and other	0.46	—
Cost of capital	5.73	4.76
Total credit costs	11.31	10.27

[a]From Robert Shay and William Dunkelberg, Retail Store Credit Card Use in New York (New York: Columbia University Press, 1975) p. 76.

[b]From Touche Ross & Company, "Cost Analysis of Retail Store Revolving Credit: State of California" (Sacramento, Calif.: California Retailers Association, 1971), Exhibit 2, p. 11.

Source: Compiled by the author.

NOTES

1. In the case of recoveries, levels of delinquent debts recovered may remain the same, but the cost of recovery will increase. A more precise statement would require a model of the credit-granting process that explicitly modeled the collection process. See Ying [28] and Umbeck and Dunkelberg [27].

2. George Katona, et al., The 1970 Survey of Consumer Finances (Ann Arbor, Mich.: Survey Research Center, University of Michigan, 1971), p. 21.

3. William Proxmire, commentary on Consumer Credit in the United States: The Report of the National Commission on Consumer Finance (Washington, D.C.: U.S. Government Printing Office, 1972), p. 229.

4. Ibid., p. 224.

5. It is quite likely that in such a market, fewer loans would be made, as consumers could not diversify risk and information costs would be too high; see [27].

6. See Dunkelberg [7], Shay and Dunkelberg [21], and Touche Ross & Company [26]. Actually, this is the proportion of active accounts at a representative sample of stores and banks that generate no finance charges. Since consumers typically have numerous cards, if they have any at all, the proportion of consumers (not accounts) who never pay a finance charge could be lower.

7. See Dunkelberg [7] for a more detailed discussion of these other services.

8. See Table 10 [11], p. 22.

REFERENCES

[1] Benston, George J. "An Analysis of Maine's '36 Month Limitation' on Finance Company Small Loans." National Commission on Consumer Finance, Technical Studies, vol. 2. Washington, D.C.: U.S. Government Printing Office, 1974.

[2] Boulding, Kenneth E. The Economy of Love and Fear. Belmont, Calif.: Wadsworth, 1973.

[3] Bowsher, Norman N. "Usury Laws: Harmful When Effective." Review (Federal Reserve Bank of St. Louis) August 1974, pp. 16-23.

[4] Chapman, John M., and Robert P. Shay. The Consumer Finance Industry. New York: Columbia University Press, 1967.

[5] Dunkelberg, William. "Dummy Variables: Their Use and Interpretation." Unpublished manuscript, Purdue University, 1972.

[6] _____. "On Assessing the Impact of Rate Regulation in the Consumer Credit Industry." Unpublished manuscript, Graduate School of Business, Stanford University, 1972.

[7] _____. "A Lower Rate Maximum for Retail Credit: The Impact on Consumers." National Commission on Consumer Finance, Technical Studies, vol. 6. Washington, D.C.: U.S. Government Printing Office, 1974.

[8] _____. "A Fair Charge for Revolving Credit." Unpublished manuscript, Credit Research Center, Purdue University, 1975.

[9] _____. "Credit Card Use in Washington." Unpublished manuscript, Credit Research Center, Purdue University, 1975.

[10] Dunkelberg, William, and Robert Smiley. "Subsidies in the Use of Revolving Credit." Journal of Money, Credit and Banking 7, no. 4 (September 1975):469-90.

[11] Dunkelberg, William, and J. Stephenson. "The Rate of Return on Consumer Durables." National Commission on Consumer Finance, Technical Studies, vol. 6. Washington, D.C.: U.S. Government Printing Office, 1974.

[12] Gordon, Guy, et al. "The Impact of a Consumer Credit Interest Limitation Law: Washington State-Initiative 245." Seattle: Graduate School of Business Administration, University of Washington, 1970.

[13] Havinghurst, Clark C., ed. Consumer Credit Reform. New York: Oceana Publications, 1970.

[14] Johnson, Robert W. "Economic Analysis of Credit Revenues and Costs in Department Stores." In Economic Characteristics of Department Store Credit. New York: National Retail Merchants Association, 1969.

[15] _____. "Regulation of Finance Charges on Consumer Installment Credit." Michigan Law Review 66 (1967):81-114.

[16] Katona, George, et al. The 1967 Survey of Consumer Finances. Ann Arbor, Mich.: Survey Research Center, University of Michigan, 1967. See also later volumes.

[17] Lindsay, Robert. "The Economics of Interest Rate Ceilings." The Bulletin (New York University, Graduate School of Business Administration) December 1970.

[18] Lynch, Gene C. "Consumer Credit at Ten Per Cent Simple: The Arkansas Case." Fayetteville, Ark.: College of Business, University of Arkansas, 1969.

[19] McAlister, E. Ray. "An Empirical Analysis of Retail Revolving Credit." Monograph no. 1. Credit Research Center, Purdue University, 1975.

[20] Miller, Roger L. Economics Today. San Francisco: Canfield Press, 1973, pp. 255-60.

[21] Peterson, Richard, and William Dunkelberg. Short Run Variations in the Aggregate Savings Rate. Graduate School of Business, Research Paper no. 61, 1971, Stanford University.

[22] Russell, Thomas. The Economics of Bank Credit Cards. New York: Praeger, 1975.

[23] Shay, Robert, and William Dunkelberg. Retail Store Credit Card Use in New York. New York: Columbia University Press, 1975.

[24] Stafford, Frank, and William Dunkelberg. "The Cost of Financing Automobile Purchases." Review of Economics and Statistics 51, no. 4 (November 1969):459-64.

[25] Stucki, Roland. "Utah Consumer Credit Report." Provo: University of Utah, 1970.

[26] Touche Ross & Company. "Cost Analysis of Retail Store Revolving Credit: State of California." Sacramento, Calif.: California Retailers Association, 1971.

[27] Umbeck, John, and William Dunkelberg. "Electronic Funds Transfers and the Consumer Credit Market." Unpublished manuscript, Credit Research Center, Purdue University, 1977.

[28] Ying, Louis. "A Theory of Consumer Credit." Unpublished manuscript, Credit Research Center, Purdue University, 1977.

11

Implicit Transfers in the Extension of Trade Credit

ROBERT A. SCHWARTZ
DAVID K. WHITCOMB

Trade credit is short-term funding extended by nonfinancial institutions. It arises from a "buy now, pay later" pricing arrangement, and is thus linked to the purchase of goods and services. Commonly, trade credit is extended by sellers to buyers, although prepayment terms (which imply a credit extension by buyers to sellers) are observed in a few industries.

In the first quarter of 1976, \$106.9 billion of trade debt was outstanding on the books of manufacturing, mining, and wholesale trade corporations. This sum, which was 38.6 percent of total current liabilities, was the largest single source of short-term credit received by corporations. By contrast, also in the first quarter of 1976, outstanding short-term bank credit (including long-term debt maturing within one year) to corporations totaled \$47.9 billion, and total short- and long-term liabilities to banks totaled \$91.4 billion. On the asset side of the balance sheet, corporate receivables from other than the U.S. government were \$186.8 billion—an amount 1.75 times as great as aggregate trade debt for these corporations, which means that corporations were net extenders of trade credit to retailers and unincorporated business.[1]

Its sheer size makes trade credit an important object of analysis. But, beyond that, the transfers implicit in trade credit flows are particularly interesting because trade credit bypasses the financial sector. Several questions are to be asked about the trade credit flows. One might presume that specialized knowledge and economies of scale in lending would give the financial sector a competitive advantage. Why, then, is it that nonfinancial firms make numerous, relatively small loans to other firms rather than simply letting the funding be handled by the financial sector? What sort of firms are net extenders and net receivers of trade credit? Does trade credit tend to mitigate or to perpetuate the forms of credit discrimination that exist in the financial sector? How do trade credit flows respond to cyclical changes in interest rates and to the availability of credit from the financial sector?

As far as is known, the literature contains no comprehensive study of the grants economics of trade credit.[2] Since it seems clear that the motives for trade credit are inextricably linked with the transfers they generate, first an attempt will be made to categorize and model the motives and then the nature and direction of the implicit transfers will be deduced from these models.

A MODEL OF TRADE CREDIT EXTENSION

The terms of seller-to-buyer trade credit usually constitute a two-part credit offer: a discount for payment within a relatively short discount period and a longer net period at the end of which full payment is required. The offer, expressed in conventional shorthand, is

$$d/D, \text{ net } N$$

where d = percent discount for payment within discount period, D = length of discount period in days, and N = length of net period in days. Typical terms are 2/10, net 30 and 2/15, net 60. Occasionally, a discount is not offered, and the terms are simply "net N."

When there is a two-part trade credit offer, the buyer's opportunity cost of foregoing the discount (and hence borrowing (1 - d) times the list price of the purchase) is d/(1 - d) as a rate per N - D days.* The annual implied interest cost to the buyer for so extending trade debt past the discount period is thus

$$\frac{d}{1-d}\,\frac{365}{N-D}$$

For terms of 2/10, net 30, the implied interest cost is 37.2 percent per year; for 2/15, net 60, it is 16.6 percent. These high interest rates are often reduced in practice; M. Seiden [16] cites evidence that sellers frequently allow buyers to extend the credit period beyond the stated terms.† In the ensuing analysis, N shall be taken to be the actual, rather than simply the stated, net period.

---

*This can easily be seen by letting P be the list price of the goods, and recognizing that, if a discount of d percent is given, interest of d · P would have to be paid for the right to delay paying (1 - d)P from the end of the discount period to the end of the net period.

†One of the authors worked his way through college as a bookkeeper for a firm (now defunct) that employed a variety of ingenious

R. Schwartz [15] identified two reasons for trade credit sales: a transactions motive and a financing motive. To these will be added a pricing motive. The transactions motive explains very short-term trade credit (such as that contained in the discount period); it reflects the fact that buyers' transaction costs are reduced if bills are allowed to accumulate for periodic payment. A financing motive exists if some firms can profitably act as retailers of credit owing to operational efficiencies or capital market imperfections. Further, a pricing motive is distinguished, because delayed payment also reduces the effective price of goods or services, and may thus be used to disguise (partially) overall price reductions and discriminatory pricing.

We can incorporate the terms of trade credit into an expression of effective price in a way that will enable examination of both the financing and the pricing motives. The effective price to a buyer is the lesser of the present value of the list price to be paid in N days or the present value of the discount price to be paid in D days. Hence,

$$P^E = \min \left\{ \frac{P^L}{(1 + r_i^B)^N}, \frac{(1 - d)P^L}{(1 + r_i^B)^D} \right\} \tag{1}$$

where r_i^B is the risk-adjusted opportunity cost of credit* for the ith buyer or class of buyers expressed as a rate per day.

The daily interest rate that would make the buyer indifferent between the discount period and the net period may be found by solving for that value of r that equates the two terms in brackets in Equation (1). It is given by

$$1 - d = \frac{1}{(1 + r)}^{N - D} \tag{2}$$

Clearly, buyer i will choose to pay at the end of the net period if $r_i^B > r$; he will take the discount if $r_i^B < r$.

---

devices to extend its average trade debt period to one year (and, finally, to infinity).

*Note that the relevant opportunity cost of funds to be used in taking present values here is the cost of borrowed funds rather than the firm's overall cost of capital. The reason is that the buyer has, presumably, already made the decision to purchase the goods, and is simply choosing between including trade debt or other forms of debt in its capital structure. The issue here is analogous to the lease versus buy decision where the firm uses the cost of debt to assess the cash flows associated with leasing.

It can now be shown why a financing motive may exist. Assume that the buyer pays at day N because of $r_i^B > r$. Letting r_i^S be the risk-adjusted marginal cost to the seller of funds he lends to the ith buyer, the seller will profit from this incremental credit extension (from day D to day N) if $r_i^S < R$, as one would then have

$$\frac{P^L}{(1 + r_i^S)^N} > \frac{(1 - d)P^L}{(1 + r_i^S)^D} \quad (r_i^S < r)$$

That is, for the seller, the present value of P^L to be received on day N exceeds the present value of $(1 - d)P^L$ to be received on day D. It is thus clear that, for the financing motive to be operative, one must have $r_i^S < r_i^B$. Further, when interest rates are so unbalanced, the credit terms can be arranged so as to obtain $r_i^S < r < r_i^B$.[3] As shall be shown, it is possible to have $r_i^S < r_i^B$ if there are credit market imperfections.

Alternatively, in perfect credit markets, with risk-adjusted interest rates, one would expect $r_i^S = r_i^B$. In this case, the financial motive for trade credit would not be operative, but here the existence of the pricing motive can be considered. It is possible for the seller to reduce the effective price to any net period buyer by offering credit terms such that $r < r_i^B (= r_i^S)$. Or he can lower the effective price to any discount period buyer by raising d or D. The benefits of such a price reduction may exceed the costs if it offers an effective means of disguising price competition or price discrimination in imperfectly competitive markets.

In the next two sections, the nature and direction of the transfers implicit in trade credit extension owing to imperfection in credit markets and goods markets will be examined.

GRANTS EFFECTS OF TRADE CREDIT OWING TO FINANCIAL MARKET IMPERFECTIONS

To begin the discussion of the effects of credit market imperfections, perfect credit markets will be considered. One of the central propositions of modern capital markets theory is that if an investment is a component of a well-diversified portfolio and can be bought and sold on an efficient market, the required return on that investment is a function only of the correlation between that investment's return and the return on a market portfolio.[4] This proposition has two implications for trade credit. First, abstracting from differences in transaction costs, it is immaterial whether a loan to buyer i is made directly by a bank (or other financial sector firm) or indirectly by a bank to the seller and then to buyer i; the marginal cost of funds loaned to i is the same to the seller as it is to the bank, so one must necessarily have $r_i^S = r_i^B$.* Second, the riskier the buyer is, the higher r_i^B is.[5] Hence, under perfect credit markets, sellers, even if they are large and financially sound and thus able to borrow at low rates, would have no advantage over financial institutions in the retailing of credit to buyers. In fact, if there are economies of scale and specialization in credit retailing, sellers would be at a relative disadvantage. However, one now relaxes the assumption of perfect capital markets, and in what follows, shall consider three categories of credit market imperfection, any of which may generate the financial motive for extending trade credit.

Credit Rationing

The credit market imperfection that has received the most sophisticated theoretical attention is credit rationing—the practice of limiting loans to very risky customers rather than charging a higher interest rate to compensate for the greater risk. D. Jaffee and F. Modigliani [6] show that while a discriminating monopolistic lender will not credit ration, a monopolistic lender will ration credit if he is forced (or chooses for reasons of cost or goodwill) to charge the same rate to all customers (or all in a given risk category). V. Smith [18] and Arzac, Schwartz, and Whitcomb [1] show, under differing scenarios, that operating risk-constant, competitive lenders will ration loans such that all loan offers bear the same ratio to the borrower's equity when a uniform borrowing rate is required.[6]

Jaffee and Modigliani offer convincing empirical evidence that extensive credit rationing does take place, and any banker will tell you the same (if he will admit it). The firms whose loan demands are not completely satisfied by banks and other financial institutions may then turn to trade credit as a source for further funds.[7] This may explain the relatively high interest rates implied by trade credit terms, and, as shall be developed below, may also partly explain the direction of trade credit flows from the larger, more liquid firms to the smaller firms that are the primary target of credit rationing by the financial sector.

---

*This is not to say that a seller might not borrow funds at 10 percent and lend part to a risky buyer at 15 percent, but the difference would represent credit investigation costs, a normal return on investment, and a risk premium. The marginal cost of an extra dollar lent to i would include the increase in the seller's borrowing rate occasioned by a riskier investment portfolio.

Usury Laws

Where usury laws effectively limit the interest rate and so make loans to risky businesses unprofitable, trade credit extension to these firms may circumvent the credit-limiting effect the law has on the economy. As far as is known, courts have not considered the traditional terms of trade credit to be among the "shifts and devices of usurers to evade the statute." However, about half the states, including many of the largest, do not limit the rate of interest that may be charged corporations, and some also extend the exemption to unincorporated business. Thus, while usury laws may explain some of the flows to individual proprietorships and partnerships, they do not appear to account for the bulk of the flows among corporations.

Imperfect "Unbundling" of Selling Activity and Credit Information

It is reasonable to believe that information on the creditworthiness of customers may be a joint product of various sales activities, particularly those involving market analysis and personal salesmanship. Also, sellers must perform at least minimal credit analysis before offering 10- or 15-day "transactions motive" trade credit. Consequently, sellers may be capable of producing certain kinds of credit information at a very low cost compared to the banks or specialized firms, such as Dun & Bradstreet.

In the absence of transaction costs, one would expect a market to arise for such information, and that its existence would eliminate this motive for trade credit. However, costs of information transmission between seller and credit analyst firms, difficulties of verifying the correctness of the information, and the "goodwill" value of protecting confidentiality concerning buyers' financial status may make it difficult to unbundle sales and credit analysis activities. This would leave sellers with a cost advantage in the retailing of credit.[8]

Speculation and Evidence on the Direction of Trade Credit Transfers

Each of the credit market imperfections considered suggests a net flow of trade credit from financially strong and/or large firms to weaker and/or smaller firms. The credit-rationing literature suggests that borrowers with low financial leverage (and, ceteris paribus, low financial risk) have their loan demands satisfied, whereas high leverage firms do not. Hence the latter will receive trade credit from the former; the implied interest rate will be high to compensate the trade creditor for his risk.

To the extent that usury laws limit interest rates on corporate loans in some states, high-risk firms will have unsatisfied loan demand that may be met by trade credit. More important, usury laws will cause trade credit flows from incorporated firms to the more risky among the unincorporated firms. Since risk is expected to be negatively related to firm size, it can also be expected that credit rationing and usury laws cause trade credit to flow primarily from large firms to small. Imperfect unbundling should cause a similar flow because relatively large oligopolistic firms engage in those sales activities that produce credit information as a joint product, while the smaller, more nearly perfectly competitive firms do not.

Table 11.1 provides evidence that corroborates these hypotheses. For manufacturing corporations, ratios of receivables-trade debt generally rise with the asset size category (although they fall somewhat for the two largest categories).[9] In addition, the ratio is higher for manufacturers of durables (where firms tend to be larger for technological reasons) than for nondurables and for manufacturers than for mining or wholesale trade. Similarly, the proportion of short-term funds represented by trade debt falls with the size of manufacturing firms, and is substantially less for manufacturing firms than for trade corporations (which are smaller on average).

Table 11.1 also reports equity-debt ratios for corporations by size and type. It can be seen that the leverage ratio is rather closely related to size and corporate type, which suggests that some of the observed relationship between size and trade credit flows may also be caused by the association among size, risk, and banks' willingness to extend credit.[10]

The relationship between corporate size and trade credit flows suggests that the transfers implicit in the grants economics of trade credit have an interesting implication for economic growth. As Schwartz [15] pointed out, trade credit is a means by which large firms can participate in financing the growth of their smaller customers; in so doing, they ease one of the major constraints on their own growth—the size of their markets.

Cyclical Variations in Trade Credit

The relationship between credit availability and the size and financial strength of firms implies that in times of tight monetary policy, trade credit would increasingly replace bank credit as a source of funds for small or financially weak firms. A. Meltzer [10] and F.

TABLE 11.1

Trade Credit and Risk Ratios for Corporations, by Size and Type, First Quarter 1976

	Receivables / Trade Debt	Trade Debt / Current Liabilities	Total Equity / Total Debt
Manufacturing corporations, by asset size (millions of dollars)			
All	2.01	0.338	2.40
Under 1	1.57	0.495	1.81
1-5	1.65	0.447	1.94
5-10	1.87	0.396	2.02
10-25	2.12	0.368	2.31
25-50	2.20	0.370	2.07
50-100	2.38	0.347	2.04
100-250	2.48	0.317	2.06
250-1,000	2.39	0.319	2.10
1,000 and over	1.91	0.299	2.79
Corporations, by type			
Durable manufacturers	2.14	0.297	2.36
Nondurable manufacturers	1.88	0.390	2.44
Mining	1.64	0.331	1.71
Wholesale trade	1.32	0.510	1.42
Retail trade	1.00*	0.420	1.47

*The numerator of this ratio is largely consumer credit, not trade credit.

Source: U.S. Federal Trade Commission, *Quarterly Financial Report for Manufacturing, Mining and Trade Corporations*, Second Quarter, 1976.

Brechling and R. Lipsey [2] report evidence that credit periods are lengthened in tight money periods. Jaffee's regressions show that increased credit rationing raises net trade credit of the largest manufacturing corporations and significantly reduces net trade credit of the smallest manufacturing corporations (with a lag in both cases) [5].

Jaffee, Laffer [7], and Schwartz [15] all infer from this evidence that this cyclical revision of trade credit flows reduces the dampening effect of monetary policy on real expenditures. Schwartz further notes that firms may charge for the increased trade credit by raising list prices, and hence that restrictive monetary policy may induce an inflation of list prices, even though at the same time generating a reduction in the present value of prices.

Trade credit revision may also serve to reduce the discriminatory impact on small firms of tight monetary policy. However, discrimination against small firms may be increased if (list) price controls are used. This is because price ceilings will not only inhibit an increased supply of trade credit (why give more credit if you cannot charge for it) but may also cause changes in relative prices that are detrimental to smaller firms (and labor), as the net suppliers of trade credit have an opportunity to increase their real prices in the face of list price controls simply by reducing the length of the credit period they offer their customers. Hence, as Schwartz concludes, "Failure to recognize that firms typically sell the monetary resource along with their unique product can . . . result in a misspecified formulation of aggregate economic policy" [15, p. 654].

GRANTS EFFECTS OF TRADE CREDIT IN PERFECT FINANCIAL BUT IMPERFECT PRODUCT MARKETS

Although it is believed that imperfections in credit markets do in fact induce large, financially strong firms to extend credit to weaker firms at a cost below that of bank credit (that is, $r_i^S < r_i^B$), it is interesting to consider whether or not imperfect product markets, ceteris paribus, can also account for trade credit. Separate consideration of the effect of product market imperfections will enable one to determine whether or not product and credit market imperfections cause the same direction of trade credit flows. Thus, in this section it is assumed that $r_i^S = r_i^B$, and the effects of oligopoly and discriminating monopoly are considered.

Trade Credit as Disguised Oligopolistic Price Competition

The economic theory of oligopoly, such as it is, suggests that successful collusion leads to similar or identical list prices that are higher than would exist in perfect competition. Rivalry among firms takes the form of attempts to increase sales by product differentiation or by disguised price cuts (such as under the table discounts, free services, and so on). Because an increase in any of the trade credit terms—d, D, or effective N—reduces the effective or present value price, P^E, for a given list price, it is clear that trade credit is a device for cutting price. Because a firm's actual credit terms commonly differ from its stated terms and are not readily observable by competitors, trade credit can be a good device for effecting disguised price cuts. When used for this purpose, the credit must flow from seller to buyer.

To illustrate the grants implications of this motive for trade credit, one of the most familiar oligopoly formulations will be used: the kinked demand curve model of price enforcement.[11] Let there be some list price, P*, which all firms agree to enforce by matching any list price decreases. However, assume that firms are free to adjust trade credit terms so as to set effective price at whatever level maximizes individual profit. If a firm believes the others will not offer trade credit and will keep effective price equal to P*, then it will consider its own effective price demand curve to be rather elastic; this is illustrated in Figure 11.1 by the dashed portion of the demand curve below P* labeled D^E.*

The firm will thus set effective price such that its marginal cost equals its effective marginal revenue (the dashed line, MR^E). It can now be seen that a firm with low marginal cost (for example, MC_1) will tend to set liberal trade credit terms because it gains from a lower effective price, while a firm with high marginal cost (MC_2) will set tight credit terms. To the extent that industries with larger firms behave as oligopolists, and to the extent that the smaller firms in an industry have higher marginal cost owing to unrealized scale economies, this model implies the same direction of trade credit flows as does the imperfect capital markets mode: The largest firms will be the major extenders of trade credit.[12]

When selling firms use trade credit to reduce effective prices, the buying firms that benefit the most are those with the highest alternative costs of credit. This is illustrated in Table 11.2. Starting from fairly typical base case terms of 2/10, net 60, a doubling of the net period (stated or de facto) to 120 days reduces effective price to a firm with an 8 percent cost of credit by only 0.42 percent, whereas it cuts P^E to a 24 percent cost of credit firm by 3.92 percent. Comparable increases in the discount percentage or the discount period do not reduce effective price as much, particularly for high cost of

---

Even if the firm believes the others will set effective prices below P, it will not expect retaliation to its own decisions; it will simply project its elastic effective price demand curve somewhat to the left of D^E.

FIGURE 11.1 The Kinked Demand Curve Model of Price Enforcement with Adjustable Trade Credit Terms

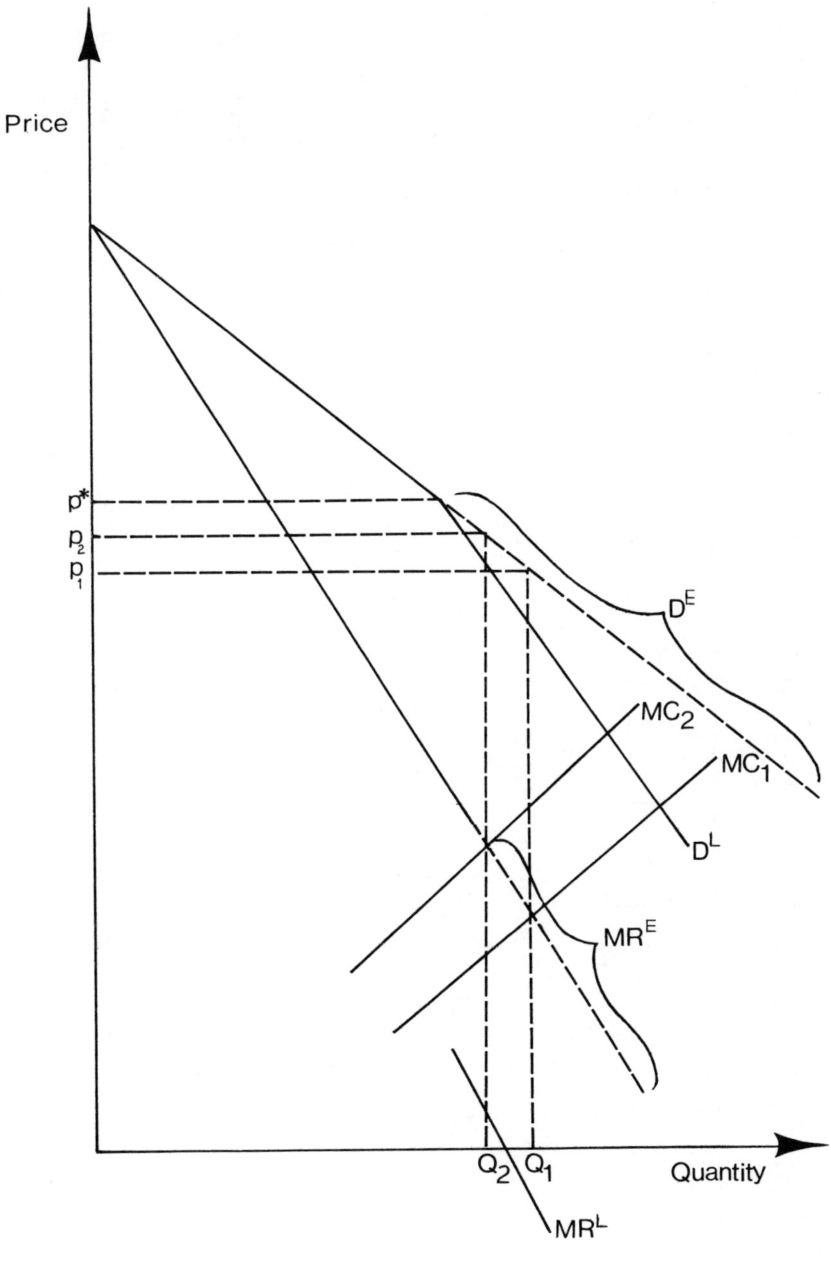

TABLE 11.2

Illustration of Price Effect of Changes in Trade Credit Terms

$$\frac{P^E}{P^L} \left[= \min \left\{ \frac{1}{(1 + r_i^B)^N} , \frac{(1 - d)}{(1 + r_i^B)^D} \right\} \right] \text{ and choice of period (D or N)}$$

Base case: d = 0.02, D = 10, N = 60

	$r_i^B = 0.08$ per Year			$r_i^B = 0.12$ per Year			$r_i^B = 0.18$ per Year			$r_i^B = 0.24$ per Year		
	P^E/P^L	D or N	Percent Cut in P^E	P^E/P^L	D or N	Percent Cut in P^E	P^E/P^L	D or N	Percent Cut in P^E	P^E/P^L	D or N	Percent Cut in P^E
Base case	0.9778	D	—	0.9767	D	—	0.9705	N	—	0.9608	N	—
N = 120	0.9737	N	0.42	0.9608	N	1.63	0.9418	N	2.96	0.9231	N	3.92
d = 0.04	0.9579	D	2.04	0.9568	D	2.03	0.9552	D	1.58	0.9536	D	0.75
D = 20	0.9757	D	0.21	0.9735	D	0.33	0.9702	D	0.03	0.9608	N	0.00

Source: Compiled by the authors.

capital firms. Hence, it is expected that across firms, the effective net period will be considerably more variable than the discount terms.

Trade Credit as a Means of Price Discrimination

Table 11.2 also suggests another motive for trade credit in monopolistic product markets. Scanning across the table for any of the trade credit terms shows that offering the same terms to all buyers results in a lower effective price to high cost of capital buyers. (The effect is strongest with lengthy net periods and weakest with large discounts or lengthy discount periods.) The price discrimination model suggests that if high costs of capital buyers also have higher (absolute value) demand elasticity, it is profitable to charge them a lower price. Trade credit may be an effective means of accomplishing this when overt discrimination is illegal or frowned upon.

Why might firms with a high cost of capital have more elastic demand for ingredient or capital inputs? One reason is that high cost of financial capital should lead a rational firm using standard discounted cash flow capital budgeting methods to reject physical capital investments that would be attractive to other firms and thus to be, ceteris paribus, relatively less capital-intensive. Such a firm might be stimulated to buy physical capital at lower effective prices.* Further, because it allocates more of its budget to ingredient inputs, it might have a greater demand elasticity for them.†

Another reason why firms with a high cost of capital may have greater demand elasticity is the associated high risk of failure. If a small difference in theprice of resources can make the difference between continued existence and failure, demand elasticity would necessarily be large.

The price discrimination motive for trade credit suggests that companies will be more likely to set long effective credit periods than large discounts or long discount periods, as the discriminatory effect of the former is the greatest.‡ The discrimination motive is

---

*It seems that this same reasoning may partially explain why so many capital investments are financed by leases (the long-term counterpart to trade credit) rather than by bonds or bank debt. Leasing at favorable terms is a powerful alternative means of offering a (discriminatory) lower price on capital items.

†While the availability of substitutes is the primary determinant of elasticity, it can be shown that, with this held constant, elasticity is positively related to the relative expenditure on an input.

‡The effect of, for example, N - 120 may be even greater than Table 11.2 suggests, because a firm with 8 percent cost of capital,

also consistent with the observed direction of trade credit flows, from large concentrated sectors to more competitive sectors and to firms with higher costs of capital. This motive also offers an explanation for the complex terms of trade credit, namely, all customers are made the same offer, 2/10, net 30, although it is known who will select the 2/10 price and who will choose the net 30 price. Alternatively stated, if all customers were identical, only a simple offer—net 15, for instance—would need to be stated.

Thus far, profit-motivated price discrimination has been discussed; philanthropic sentiments may be another possible motive for price discrimination through a complex trade credit offer. Direct corporate philanthropy, largely to nonprofit organizations, is considerable,[13] and there is reason to speculate that some firms may have both altruistic reasons for making gifts to other firms and incentives to disguise these gifts in the form of trade credit.

A long-standing, hard-working customer who is sole proprietor of his own firm may seem to his suppliers to be as deserving a subject of aid as the client of a social agency. Yet a direct gift or price reduction may be viewed as unfair competition or, even worse, as potentially illegal, by competitors. So a quiet lengthening of the credit period may provide the perfect conduit for aid. Whether this motive for trade credit is quantitatively important is not known, but it is consistent with the observed direction of trade credit flows. *

CONCLUSION

Quantitatively, trade credit is a major source of funding extended and received by U.S. firms. Conceptually, it is a complex form of credit transfer that has several implications for grants economics. In this chapter two major reasons for credit extension—financing and pricing motives—have been treated.

The chief implications derived from the financing motive concern (1) the propensity of larger firms to finance the growth of their smaller customers so as to ease the constraint of market size on their

---

for example, may be reluctant to take advantage of a long credit period for fear of lowering its current asset-current liabilities ratio and hurting its credit rating. Its choice of the discount period instead would raise its effective price to 0.9778.

*When reading this study, Kenneth Boulding observed: "I particularly appreciated the notion of charity-deserving customers, as my own father, I discovered when he died, had been insolvent for 20 years and had been sustained by his suppliers in his very small plumbing business."

own growth, and (2) the extent to which tight monetary policy can cause trade credit to be substituted for bank credit in a way that diminishes the efficacy of any given degree of aggregate monetary stringency but also mitigates the discriminatory effects that can follow from a tight money policy. The major implications derived from the pricing motive are that trade credit can be used to conceal a change in the general level of a firm's prices and to disguise the use of a discriminatory pricing policy.

One purpose of this chapter was to bring together and assess some of the evidence on the size and directions of flows of trade credit. The main conclusions that can be drawn from the data are (1) trade credit is the largest source of short-term credit to corporations, (2) corporations as a whole are net extenders of trade credit to unincorporated firms; (3) manufacturing corporations extend more and use less trade credit proportionately as their size increases, and vis-a-vis mining and trade corporations; and (4) in periods of tight money and increased credit rationing, large corporations extend more trade credit and small corporations reduce their net extension of trade credit.

The main purpose was to consider the economic motives for trade credit, and, in so doing, to explain the observed flows. The financial motive for trade credit arises out of credit market imperfections that enable large, or low-risk, firms to lend funds to small, or high-risk, firms at a marginal cost below their debtors' opportunity costs. The imperfections considered were credit rationing and usury laws (which limit bank loans to high-risk firms) and imperfect unbundling of sales activities and credit information (which gives imperfectly competitive sellers a cost advantage in retailing credit to buyers). Credit rationing and usury laws tend to explain the cyclical variations in trade credit flows.

A pricing motive arises from the fact that trade credit can be a means of disguised price competition or of price discrimination. Only imperfectly competitive or monopolistic sellers will offer trade credit for this purpose, and within an oligopolistic industry the most liberal trade credit terms will be offered by the firms with the lowest marginal cost. The firms for which trade credit represents the largest effective price cut (and which, therefore, will be most likely to switch their demand to the sellers offering trade credit) will be those with the highest cost of capital. Thus, the pricing motive also suggests a trade credit flow from large and efficient firms to small, financially risky firms. Further, disguised price competition through trade credit terms may serve to move effective prices closer to those that would prevail in perfectly competitive equilibrium, thus tending toward restoration of market efficiency.

Trade credit is only a special case of the larger subject of delayed payment, which also encompasses such diverse arrangements as consumer credit, leasing, and pension funds (delayed payment for labor services). Surprisingly, the economic motives for delayed payment have received scant attention in the literature, and their legal and policy implications have gone almost totally unrecognized. Perhaps this discussion of trade credit motives will be helpful in analyzing the broader set of delayed payment arrangements.

NOTES

1. The source of these figures is the aggregate balance sheets presented in the U.S. Federal Trade Commission [20, Table G-2, p. 56; and Table K-2, pp. 80-81]. The aggregate corporate liability figures, including retail trade, are trade debt, $133 billion; short-term bank credit, $58.8 billion; total short- and long-term liabilities to banks, $111.8 billion.

2. Lindsay and Sametz [8] and Jaffee [5] report evidence that suggests large, profitable firms are net extenders of trade credit. Schwartz [15] demonstrates that firms that can borrow at lower interest rates will be net extenders. Both Jaffee and Schwartz suggest that credit rationing causes small firms to substitute trade credit for bank credit. Meltzer [10], Brechling and Lipsey [2], and Laffer [7] demonstrate that tight monetary policy causes a substitution of trade credit for bank credit.

3. Schwartz [15] has shown how to determine optimal N when $r_i^S < r_i^B$ and both rates rise with the amount borrowed.

4. The conditions underlying this proposition and its proof may be found in, for example, Sharpe [17] and Rubenstein [12].

5. Merton [11] and Arzac, Schwartz, and Whitcomb [1] prove that interest rates must be positively related to the borrower's returns variance and financial leverage, respectively, in competitive credit market equilibrium.

6. None of these papers offers a particularly convincing rationale for a common interest rate, however; and Arzac, Schwartz, and Whitcomb [1] show that in the absence of institutional restrictions on interest rates, competitive equilibrium will generate a leverage structure of interest rates.

7. See Jaffee [5] for further development of this point.

8. Note that buyers would generally have no such advantage in retailing credit to sellers. This is because their purchasing activities generally concentrate more on the product than on the producer. An exception would be purchasers of products that do not have substi-

tutes and where failure of a particular producer would thus injure the buyer. It is for just such industries (construction, shipbuilding, aircraft) that Schwartz [15] reports that prepayment is common.

9. Jaffee [5, Table 6.1] presents earlier data of this sort as well as survey data indicating that small firms substitute trade credit for bank credit when the latter is rationed.

10. Because the size of a firm relative to the size of both its suppliers and customers seems at least partially to explain the direction of trade credit flows, it would be interesting to regress trade credit-trade debt ratios by industry on own industry concentration ratios, supplier industry concentration ratios and buyer industry concentration ratios. For methods of calculating buyer concentration ratios, see Lustgarten [9] and Guth, Schwartz, and Whitcomb [3; 4].

11. This model is not universally admired (see Stigler [19]). But it does offer a plausible explanation for some instances of oligopoly behavior if it is used as a model of price enforcement, as is done here, rather than of price determination.

12. It might also appear that large buyers may have substantial market power that they could use to exact disguised price concessions, in the form of favorable trade credit terms, from smaller suppliers. This is doubtful for two reasons: (1) Guth, Schwartz, and Whitcomb [4] report empirical evidence that concentration among buyers of a product is almost invariably substantially less than among sellers; (2) a highly concentrated buyer is likely to be financially strong with a low alternative cost of credit, making it more difficult to provide substantial price reductions to him via trade credit terms (see Table 11.2).

13. Schwartz [13] reports evidence on the size of corporate charitable expenditures, and evidence that a philanthropic motive might indeed underlie these transfers. See also Schwartz [14] for a theoretical analysis of the economic rationality of philanthropic behavior.

REFERENCES

[1] Arzac, E., R. Schwartz, and D. Whitcomb. "The Leverage Structure of Interest Rates." Working paper, January 1977.

[2] Brechling, F., and R. Lipsey. "Trade Credit and Monetary Policy." Economic Journal 73 (1963):619-41.

[3] Guth, L., R. Schwartz, and D. Whitcomb. "The Use of Buyer Concentration Ratios in Tests of Oligopoly Models." Review of Economics and Statistics 58 (1976):488-92.

[4] _____. "Buyer Concentration Ratios." Journal of Industrial Economics. Forthcoming 1977.

[5] Jaffee, D. Credit Rationing and the Commercial Loan Market. New York: Wiley, 1971.

[6] Jaffee, D., and F. Modigliani. "A Theory and Test of Credit Rationing." American Economic Review 59 (1969):850-72.

[7] Laffer, A. "Trade Credit and the Money Market." Journal of Political Economy 78 (1970):239-67.

[8] Lindsay, R., and A. Sametz. Financial Management, An Analytical Approach. Homewood, Ill.: Irwin, 1967.

[9] Lustgarten, S. "The Impact of Buyer Concentration in Manufacturing Industries." Review of Economics and Statistics 57 (1975):125-32.

[10] Meltzer, A. "Mercantile Credit, Monetary Policy, and Size of Firms." Review of Economics and Statistics 42 (1960):429-37.

[11] Merton, R. "On the Pricing of Corporate Debt: The Risk Structure of Interest Rates." Journal of Finance 29 (1974):449-70.

[12] Rubenstein, M. "A Mean-Variance Synthesis of Corporate Financial Theory." Journal of Finance 27 (1973):167-81.

[13] Schwartz, R. "Corporate Philanthropy." Journal of Finance 23 (1968):479-97.

[14] _____. "Personal Philanthropy." Journal of Political Economy 78 (1970):1264-91.

[15] _____. "An Economic Model of Trade Credit." Journal of Financial and Quantitative Analysis 8 (1974):643-57.

[16] Seiden, M. The Quality of Trade Credit. Occasional Paper 87, National Bureau of Economic Research, 1964.

[17] Sharpe, W. Portfolio Theory and Capital Markets. New York: McGraw-Hill, 1970.

[18] Smith, V. "A Theory and Test of Credit Rationing: Some Generalizations." American Economic Review 62 (1972):477-83.

[19] Stigler, G. "The Kinky Oligopoly Demand Curve and Rigid Prices." Journal of Political Economy 55 (1947):432-49.

[20] U.S. Federal Trade Commission. Quarterly Financial Report for Manufacturing, Mining and Trade Corporations. Second Quarter, 1976.

PART V

Subsidies in Federal Credit Programs

12

The Use of the Government's Credit Power

MURRAY L. WEIDENBAUM

The arsenal of government power over the economy is extensive, including the authority to tax, the ability to spend the proceeds of that taxation, and the capability of issuing rules and regulations determining or influencing private behavior. One of the lesser known components of that arsenal is the government's power to provide credit to various individuals and organizations in the economy.

As will be demonstrated, most of the credit activities do not appear in the federal budget. Many do not involve any direct federal expenditure at all. Hence, they seem to be a rather painless way of achieving national objectives. In the main, the federal government is "merely" guaranteeing private borrowing or sponsoring ostensibly private institutions.

Is this use of the government's credit power a variation of the proverbial "free lunch?" In this context, the costs as well as the benefits that may flow from this often overlooked aspect of government interaction with the private sector will be examined.

THE VARIETY OF GOVERNMENT CREDIT PROGRAMS

Over the years, substantial numbers of credit programs have made their way through the legislative process of the federal government. These programs emerged on an ad hoc basis, with each program directed toward providing assistance in overcoming a specific problem at hand. As a result of this gradual but very substantial accretion, federal credit program subsidies are now provided to a great many and variety of sectors of the U.S. economy—housing, agriculture, transportation, health, education, state and local governments, small business—as well as to foreigners.[1] The total amount of credit provided under federal auspices has risen substantially during the past decade.

TABLE 12.1

Major Federal Credit Programs, Fiscal Year 1975
(new commitments, millions of dollars)

Category and Agency	Direct Loans On Budget	Direct Loans Off Budget	Guaranteed Loans	Government-Sponsored Enterprises	Total
Aid to business					
Commerce	15	—	699	—	714
Interior	22	—	—	—	22
Transportation	37	—	177	—	214
Export-Import Bank	—	3,813	8,708	—	12,521
Federal Deposit Insurance Corporation	100	—	1,723	—	1,823
General Services Administration	—	—	72	—	72
Small Business Administration	520	—	1,365	—	1,885
U.S. Railway Association	—	34	—	—	34
Subtotal	694	3,847	12,744	—	17,285
Aid to farmers					
Agriculture	6,329	1,060	8,577	—	15,966
Farm credit agencies	—	—	—	20,910	20,910
Subtotal	6,329	1,060	8,577	20,910	36,876
Aid to local governments					
Housing and Urban Development	590	—	1,252	—	1,842
Justice	40	—	—	—	40
District of Columbia	232	—	—	—	232
Subtotal	862	—	1,252	—	2,114

Aid to individuals					
Health, Education and Welfare	543	—	1,388	—	1,931
Housing and Urban Development	11,779	—	4,791*	—	16,570
Veterans Administration	524	—	3,602*	—	4,126
Federal Home Loan Bank System	1,305	—	—	12,694	13,999
Federal National Mortgage Association	—	—	—	4,434	4,434
Student Loan Marketing Association	—	—	—	144	144
Subtotal	14,151	—	9,781	17,272	41,204
Aid to foreign governments					
Security assistance	437	—	616	—	1,053
Development assistance	478	—	26	—	504
Subtotal	915	—	642	—	1,557
Miscellaneous					
Federal Financing Bank*	—	—	—	—	—
All other	95	—	6	—	101
Subtotal	95	—	6	—	101
Grand total	23,046	4,907	33,002	38,182	99,137

*Duplicate transactions have been eliminated.

Source: From Special Analyses, Budget of the United States Government, Fiscal Year 1977 (Washington, D.C.: U.S. Government Printing Office, 1976).

There are three major uses of the federal government's credit power (see Table 12.1 for details).

Direct Loans by Federal Departments and Agencies

Direct loans extended by federal agencies, such as the 2 percent loans made by the Rural Electrification Administration, generally involve significant subsidies because the loans are made at interest rates below those available in the private sector. In many cases, the government also absorbs the administrative expenses and losses arising from loan defaults, thus further increasing the amount of the subsidy. Although not formally considered a federal credit program, the relatively generous progress payments made by the Department of Defense do represent interest-free provision of working capital to government contractors on a very large scale. Direct loans are still an important form of federal credit aid, accounting for almost $28 billion of the total of $99 billion of federal and federally assisted credit extended during the fiscal year 1975. However, in recent years, direct loans have been exceeded in size by the various guarantee programs and lending activities of government-sponsored but privately owned credit agencies.

Moreover, a rising share—almost one-fifth in fiscal year 1975—of these direct loans has been excluded from the budget totals. These are the lending activities of the so-called off-budget agencies of the federal government, such as the Rural Electrification Administration and the Export-Import Bank. These latter agencies are all part of the federal government, using federal funds and federal employees to carry on their activities. Their common characteristic is that in each case the Congress has passed a law stipulating that some or all of their financial transactions cannot be included in the budget.

The justification often given is that these programs ultimately will generate offsetting revenues and hence be no burden to the taxpayer. However, this rationale is of dubious value. First, those revenues may not always equal the off-budget outlays. And, second, many government programs that are included in the budget also generate offsetting receipts. Thus, the off-budget treatment is a sheer subterfuge for understating the size of the budget and diluting the effectiveness of the budgetary review process.

Loans Guaranteed by Federal Departments and Agencies

Loan guarantees now account for a major share of federal credit programs. The attractiveness of this mechanism to government policy makers stems largely from the fact that the loans themselves are made by private lenders and thus are excluded from the federal budget. Technically, all that the government does is to assume a contingent liability to pay the private lender if the private borrower defaults. Loans made under some housing subsidy programs have experienced very high default rates in spite of their being backed by the security of real property. Other new programs generate higher risks because there has been a tendency to move toward the guarantee of loans that require little or no collateral in connection with the guarantee.

During the last several years, however, an interesting but unexpected movement has occurred between this category and direct off-budget loans. This has resulted from the formation of the Federal Financing Bank. The basic reason for establishing that "bank" was to consolidate the market borrowings by the rising number of federal credit agencies. Such consolidation, it was reasoned should enable the various federal credit agencies to raise the funds they need at lower interest rates and also provide the Treasury Department with greater control over the timing and amount of borrowings by the various federal agencies. To a substantial extent, the bank has served that purpose. However, its charter also gives it the authority to purchase many of the private loans that carry a federal guarantee. As a result, some of the effort to reduce the pressure on the budget via extending guarantees is being offset by rising federal borrowings to finance the repurchase of these guarantees. This involuted procedure is hard to defend on any rational ground.

Loans by Federally Sponsored Agencies

Ostensibly private institutions such as the Federal National Mortgage Association, the Federal Home Loan Banks, and the farm credit agencies are not included in the total of federal spending, and they raise their funds primarily through borrowing in the nation's capital markets. However, these privately owned agencies possess various tax advantages and are able to borrow funds in the market at low interest rates because of the implicit government backing of their debentures and other issues. Loans made by these sponsored agencies have increased sharply over the past decade. They now comprise the largest single form of federal credit assistance to the private sector.

IMPACT ON TOTAL SAVING AND INVESTMENT

The conclusions of the empirical literature on the impacts of federal credit programs on the total flow of saving and investment in the U.S. economy are clear. These programs do little if anything to increase the total flow of saving or investment. They mainly change the share of investment funds going to a given industry or sector of the economy and, in the process of doing so, exert upward pressures on interest rates as investment funds are bid away from other sectors.

In commenting on existing programs of federally assisted credit to the private sector, Henry Kaufman, the distinguished economist with the investment house of Salomon Brothers, has written: "Federal agency financing does not do anything directly to enlarge the supply of savings. . . . In contrast, as agency financing bids for the limited supply of savings with other credit demanders, it helps to bid up the price of money."[2] In referring to borrowing by the federal government and its agencies, Albert Wojnilower has made a similar observation:

> Because these governmental borrowers need have few if any worries about creditworthiness or meeting interest payments, they can preempt as much of the credit markets as they choose. As a result, the Federal sector has become one of the most relentless sources of upward pressures on interest rates.[3]

In a comprehensive study of federal credit programs for the prestigious Commission on Money and Credit, Warren Law of Harvard University concluded that they have created inflationary pressures in every year since World War II.[4] Patricia Bowers has noted what she terms "costs" of federal credit programs. One cost arises from the fact that, given the availability of funds, an increase in credit for housing means lesser amounts for other borrowers. The two borrowing groups most adversely affected by tight credit are state and local governments and small businesses. A further cost is that the operations of the federal credit agencies tend to increase the level of interest rates above the level that would have prevailed if they had not entered the credit markets.[5]

This phenomenon occurs for a variety of reasons. The total supply of funds is broadly determined by household and business saving and the ability of banks to increase the money supply. This is the basic limit on the availability of funds referred to by Bowers. The normal response of financial markets to an increase in the demand for funds by a borrower, such as is represented by a federal credit program, is an increase in interest rates so as to balance out the demand for funds with the supply of saving. But the federal government's demand for funds is "interest inelastic" (the Treasury will generally raise the money that it requires regardless of the interest rate) and the interest elasticity of saving is relatively modest. Thus, weak and marginal borrowers will be rationed out of financial markets in the process, while the Treasury and other borrowers pay higher rates of interest.

Important insight into the effects of federal credit programs on capital markets has been provided by Bruce MacLaury, president of the Brookings Institution and a former deputy undersecretary of the Treasury:

> The more or less unfettered expansion of Federal credit programs and the accompanying deluge of agency direct and guaranteed securities to be financed in the credit markets has undoubtedly permitted Congress and the Administration to claim that wonder of wonders—something for nothing, or almost nothing. But as with all such sleight-of-hand feats, the truth is somewhat different.[6]

MacLaury goes on to point out that there are extra costs associated with introducing new government credit agencies to the capital markets. These costs involve selling issues that are smaller than some minimum efficiently tradable size and selling securities that only in varying degree approximate the characteristics of direct government debt in terms of perfection of guarantee, flexibility of timing and maturities, "cleanness" of instrument, and so on. As a result of such considerations, the market normally charges a premium over the interest cost on direct government debt of comparable maturity. That premium ranges from one-fourth of 1 percent on the well-known federally sponsored agencies, such as the Federal National Mortgage Association, to more than 0.5 percent on such exotics as New Community Bonds. In general, if cost of financing were the only consideration, it would be most efficient to have the Treasury itself provide the financing for direct loans by issuing government debt in the market.

Reduced efficiency occurs in the economy by providing a federal "umbrella" over many credit activities without distinguishing their relative credit risks. A basic function that credit markets are supposed to perform is that of distinguishing different credit risks and assigning appropriate risk premia. This is the essence of the ultimate resource-allocation function of credit markets. As an increasing proportion of issues coming to the credit markets bears the guarantee of the federal government, the ability of the market to differentiate credit risks inevitably diminishes. Theoretically, the federal agencies issuing or guaranteeing debt would perform this role, charging as costs of the programs differing rates of insurance premiums. In practice, all of the pressures are against such differential pricing of risks.[7] This is a hidden cost of federal credit programs.

IMPACT ON SECTORS OF THE ECONOMY

The very nature of federal credit assistance is to create advantages for some groups of borrowers and disadvantages for others. The literature provides clear answers on who will tend to be rationed out in the process. It is unlikely to be the large well-known corporations or the U.S. government. It is more likely to be state and local governments, medium-sized businesses, private mortgage borrowers not under the federal umbrella, and consumers, thereby contributing to additional economic and financial concentration in the United States.

The competition for funds by the rapidly expanding federal credit programs also increases the cost to the taxpayer by raising the interest rate at which the Treasury borrows its own funds. As shown in Table 12.2, there has been a massive expansion over the past decade in the public borrowings that have been undertaken to finance federal government credit programs. (These figures understate the overall expansion in federal credit activities, as they do not encompass the full extent of federally assisted credit.) In 1960, the federal share of funds raised in private capital markets, using the Federal Reserve System's flow of funds data, was about 12 percent. By 1970, the government's share had risen to 23 percent, and reached 36 percent in 1975. The figures for 1975 do, of course, reflect the enormity of the slack in the economy for that year.

Virtually every session of the Congress in recent years has enacted additional federal credit programs. Since 1960, the Federal National Mortgage Association (Fannie Mae) has been joined by the Government National Mortgage Association (Ginnie Mae), Student Loan Marketing Association (Sally Mae), and, most recently, the U.S. Railway Association (Fannie Rae).

SUBSIDIES IN CREDIT PROGRAMS

Substantial subsidy elements exist in most federal credit programs, which, of course, make these activities especially attractive to the recipients of the benefits. The subsidy element typically is fundamental, in that the basic purpose of the government's involvement in credit activities is to provide certain categories of borrowers with credit on terms that are more favorable than those available in private markets.[8]

As stated by the President's Commission on Budget Concepts:

> Most federal loan programs contain at least some element of subsidy. In fact, if this were not true, a serious question could be raised about the appropriateness of such ac-

TABLE 12.2

Impact of Federal Government on Credit Markets
(billions of dollars)

	Fiscal Year			
	1960	1965	1970	1975
A. Federal borrowing (budget financing)	2.2	4.0	3.8	50.9
B. Federally assisted borrowing (outside of budget)	3.3	6.8	12.6	13.9
C. Total (A + B)	5.5	10.8	16.4	64.8
D. Total funds advanced in credit markets	43.4	69.6	90.5	177.9
E. Federal portion (C ÷ D, percent)	12.7	15.5	18.1	36.4

Source: Computed from data supplied by the Federal Reserve System flow of funds accounts and the Treasury Department.

> tivities being conducted by the Federal Government rather than by private financial institutions. To the extent that Federal loans include a subsidy element by lending at more favorable interest rates than the cost of money to the Government (or the even higher cost of money obtained through private sources) they are at least in part grants or transfer payments rather than loans.[9]

To the extent that social goals are achieved regarding preferred expenditure flows and resource uses, subsidies can be regarded as beneficial. At the heart of a subsidy is a political decision to favor some at the expense of others. Because a credit subsidy involves a balancing of interests, it would be useful to have fairly well-developed notions regarding the incidence of benefits and costs of any specific program in question. In light of the variety of credit programs, it simply is not possible to make firm statements with broad applicability. We must rely on available data and specific analyses.

In an intriguing study of the home mortgage purchase program of the Government National Mortgage Association, George von Furstenberg has shown that the principal result of that government credit program has not been to increase the volume of resources going into housing. Rather, the credit programs have mainly provided arbitrary subsidies to many homeowners who otherwise would have had to pay more for their home mortgages. In addition, many of them could have obtained the private financing in the absence of the government subsidy.[10]

Most frequently the improved terms take the form of an interest rate that is lower than the rate charged to private borrowers. Also, the length of the loan and the loan-to-value ratio may be more favorable. In addition, subsidies may result from inadequate fees or premiums that do not cover administrative costs and losses on credit guarantees. At the heart of a subsidy is a political decision to favor some at the expense of others.

Credit program subsidies may be discussed in terms of (1) the benefit to the borrowers, (2) the "opportunity cost" to the government, or (3) the out-of-pocket or "cash cost" to the government. The benefit-to-borrower concept is perhaps the most attractive to the economist as a measure of the impact of federal credit aid on demand and on the allocation of resources. Yet the benefit concept poses the most formidable measurement problems. Some lenders may use the insurance and guarantee programs simply because they are there, making loans that they would have made in any case, though on somewhat more stringent terms. In contrast, guaranteed loans to submarginal borrowers, for example, may be in principle at least as income generating as government transfer payments. In practice, however, it is difficult to identify these benefits unequivocally.

There is no conclusive method of measuring the extent to which loans under some guarantee programs might have been made without the government guarantee. This is particularly true of guaranteed loans at market rates of interest, such as the regular mortgage insurance program of the Federal Housing Administration and the Export-Import Bank guarantees. It is not clear in such self-supporting programs whether there is a substantial benefit to the borrower or whether in many cases the borrower would have been able to obtain nonguaranteed credit on essentially similar terms.

On the other hand, many loans clearly would not have been made without the government guarantee. An extreme example is the loan guarantee program for public housing, where virtually all of the principal and interest payments are made by the federal government. That is, the rental income from public housing projects barely covers current operating and maintenance expenses, and in some projects not even those expenses are covered. Thus, the public housing bonds are ultimately retired almost entirely from annual debt service contributions by the federal government.

Consequently, the credit program subsidy for a $10 million bond-financed public housing project is approximately $10 million, and the benefit to the borrower is equivalent to a $10 million cash grant. It will not be attempted here to measure the "opportunity costs" to the government of using its resources for federal loan programs. That is, given limited resources, what would be the return to the government (or to the private sector) from investment in alternative projects?

Table 12.3 attempts to measure only the value of the interest rate subsidy that accrues to federally assisted borrowers. The subsidy is defined as the value of the difference between the interest rate that the borrower pays under government assistance and the rate that would have to be paid for a comparable private loan. These interest differentials arise in several ways. The interest rates used in the government credit program may be set by law below those prevailing in private markets. Alternatively, the interest rates may be set at the Treasury's borrowing costs, providing private borrowers credit at low rates otherwise available only to the federal government. In the case of the loan guarantees, the guarantee provides an implicit subsidy by eliminating the risk to the lender of loss through default. This ordinarily enables the borrower to obtain the lower interest rate that is usually associated with less risky investments.

As an estimate of the interest rates that would be available to private borrowers in the absence of federal credit programs, a 10 percent rate has been assumed here. That figure is considered to be a reasonable estimate of the average private sector cost of borrowing. Because interest subsidies occur throughout the life of a loan, the calculation of interest subsidies requires the conversion of a stream of payments into a single "present value." This capitalization is performed by discounting future subsidies by 10 percent a year before accumulating them into a single amount.

The results are shown in Table 12.3 for the major federal credit programs for which subsidy data are available. On the basis of the assumptions made here, federal credit extended in fiscal year 1975 will generate $6.4 billion of subsidies during the life of the loans made during that 12-month period. That amount is equal to about 7 percent of the total federal and federally assisted credit (excluding government-sponsored enterprises) provided during that year. The proportion of subsidy to total amount of the loan, however, varies substantially from program to program. Unlike subsidies in other federal spending programs, credit subsidies tend to be hidden. Hence, their magnitude remains generally unknown to either the public or to most government decision makers.

THE FORESEEABLE TREND

The upward trend in the size and number of federal credit programs shows no signs of slowing down. During the last few years, the Congress has approved a new loan guarantee program to assist industry in the commercial development of energy from geothermal re-

TABLE 12.3

Interest Subsidies in Federal Credit Programs, Fiscal Year 1975
(millions of dollars)

Agency and Program	Borrower Loan Terms		Annual Subsidy per $100 Million	Commitments	Cumulative Subsidy
	Percent	Years			
Direct loans					
Funds appropriated to the president					
International security assistance	6.0	10.0	2.5	437	69
International development assistance	4.0	40.0	5.2	478	243
Agriculture					
Price support	7.1	2.1	1.6	1,101	33
CCC: Public Law 480	2.3	33.0	6.1	747	436
Farmers Home Administration	5.2	33.7	4.1	4,481	1,758
Rural Electrification Administration	5.5	35.0	3.9	1,241	398
Health, Education and Welfare					
Education and health education	3.0	15.0	4.6	380	133
Medical facilities	6.7	25.0	2.7	30	7
Housing and Urban Development					
Urban renewal	6.8	0.7	1.8	493	6
Low-rent public housing	—	1.5	8.4	82	9
Federal Housing Administration	9.5	40.0	0.5	842	39
Government National Mortgage Association	8.5	27.0	1.2	11,779	1,371
Housing for elderly	9.8	40.0	0.2	—	—
Veterans Administration					
Insurance policy loans	5.0	15.0	3.4	152	40
Education loans	6.5	6.0	2.1	1	*
Housing	9.0	29.4	0.9	369	30
District of Columbia	8.0	30.0	1.7	232	38
Export-Import Bank	8.1	6.0	1.1	3,813	191

Federal Financing Bank purchases of unsubsidized loans	7.8	5.0	1.3	1,125	57
Federal Home Loan Bank Board	8.0	30.0	1.8	1,305	219
Small Business Administration					
Business and investment loans	6.9	8.7	1.9	279	31
Disaster loan fund	5.3	11.0	3.0	241	48
United States Railway Association	7.5	20.0	2.5	—	—
Total major subsidized direct loans					5,156
Selected guaranteed loans					
Health, Education and Welfare					
Health maintenance organizations	7.0	20.0	2.3	—	—
Medical facilities	6.7	25.0	2.7	89	22
Student loan insurance	4.4	13.0	3.7	1,299	345
Housing and Urban Development					
Urban renewal	4.6	0.7	6.5	493	21
Low-rent public housing	—	41.5	7.8	741	566
Mortgage insurance (subsidized)	5.0	40.0	4.4	476	206
Interior: Indian loans	8.0	20.0	1.5	—	—
Department of Transportation: WMATA guarantees	6.3	40.0	3.3	177	58
Total major subsidized guaranteed loans					1,217
Agency debt issues financed by Federal Financing Bank					
Tennessee Valley Authority	8.0	3.0	1.1	1,435	41
U.S. Postal Service	8.0	3.0	1.1	1,000	29
Total debt issue subsidies					70
Grand total					6,443

*Less than $0.5 million.

Source: From Special Analyses, Budget of the United States Government, Fiscal Year 1977 (Washington, D.C.: U.S. Government Printing Office, 1976).

sources (the Geothermal Energy Research, Development, and Demonstration Act of 1974), voted credit to the nation's largest city (the New York City Seasonal Financing Act), and authorized the Federal Energy Administration to guarantee loans for new underground coal mines (the Energy Policy and Conservation Act). In addition, several congressional committees have held hearings on proposed legislation to provide as much as $100 billion for credit assistance via an Energy Independence Authority. In November 1976, the governors of seven northeastern states called for the creation of a Regional Energy Development Corporation, which would use federally guaranteed bonds to finance coal development and other projects to foster regional growth.

In December 1975, the Farmers Home Administration (an agency of the U.S. Department of Agriculture) expanded its credit operations to provide up to a 90 percent guarantee on private loans that companies obtain for use on plants in rural areas. There have been little if any offsetting reductions during recent years in the scope of existing federal credit activities.

SUMMARY

Contrary to the popular view, government credit programs are not costless, either to the Treasury or to citizens in general. Three distinct costs of these government programs can be identified:

1. The economic cost. As they do little if anything to increase the total supply of investment funds in the economy, government credit programs take credit away from other potential borrowers. These unsubsidized borrowers might have contributed more to society than the recipients of the government-supported credit. This can be the situation where the presence of federal credit encourages individuals or organizations to incur expenditures that they would forego in the absence of the federal subsidy.

2. The initial fiscal cost. To the extent that government credit programs increase the total size of government-related credit, they cause an increase in the interest rates that are paid in order to channel these funds away from the private sector. Some increase, therefore, results in the interest rates paid on the public debt, which is a direct cost to the taxpayer.

3. The ultimate fiscal cost. When defaults occur on the part of the borrowers whose credit is guaranteed by the federal government, the Treasury winds up bearing the ultimate cost of the credit. In such cases, government credit programs become a form of backdoor spending, whereby federal expenditures are incurred in the absence of direct appropriations for the purpose.

Several ways have been suggested to deal with the various problems that arise from the expansion of federal credit programs. One general approach is to require that all proposals to create new federal credit programs or to broaden existing ones be accompanied by an appraisal of the relation among the interest rate charged in the program, the rate that would be charged by competitive and efficient private lenders, and the rate necessary to cover the government's costs.

A more detailed method is to establish controls over the total volume of federally assisted credit. Even though no immediate impact on the federal budget may be visible in most cases, the influence on the allocation of resources, and on the composition of income and employment, may be very considerable. At present, many of these federal credit programs tend to have virtually a blank check on the nation's credit resources. Under this second method, they would no longer be treated as a "free good."

One way of controlling federal credit programs is to impose a ceiling on the total borrowing of federal and federally sponsored credit agencies, both those "in" and those "out" of the budget. In addition, the Congress could enact a ceiling on the overall volume of debt created under federal loan guarantees. It would be important to establish procedures to permit review of commitments far enough in advance to permit evaluation of their likely impact when the commitments become actual loans.

A third method of controlling federal credit programs more effectively is to require these credit programs to be reviewed and coordinated along with other federal programs in the preparation of the government's annual budget and economic plans. At the present time, numerous federal credit programs—guaranteed and insured loans and loans by federally sponsored enterprises—escape regular budget and program review.

Perhaps the most fundamental proposal does not deal with federal credit programs at all, but with the underlying conditions of which they are symptoms. Hence, if an economic climate more conducive to private saving and investment can be created, that will reduce the need for private borrowers to seek federal credit assistance. The creation of that climate may require a tax system that tilts in favor of saving rather than consumption and a fiscal policy that avoids the large Treasury deficits whose financing competes with private borrowers. Until these fundamental changes are achieved, continued expansion of federal credit programs seems to be likely.

NOTES

1. Detailed information on individual credit programs is presented in Special Analysis E, Special Analyses, Budget of the United

States, Fiscal Year 1977 (Washington, D.C.: U.S. Government Printing Office, 1976), pp. 88-115.

2. Henry Kaufman, "Federal Debt Management: An Economist's View from the Marketplace," in *Issues in Federal Debt Management* (Boston: Federal Reserve Bank of Boston, 1973), p. 171.

3. Albert M. Wojnilower, "Can Capital-Market Controls Be Avoided in the 1970's?" in *Containing Inflation in the Environment of the 1970's*, ed. Michael E. Levy (New York: Conference Board, 1971), p. 42.

4. Warren A. Law, "The Aggregate Impact of Federal Credit Programs on the Economy," in *Federal Credit Programs*, ed. Commission on Money and Credit (Englewood Cliffs, N.J.: Prentice-Hall, 1963), p. 310.

5. Patricia F. Bowers, *Private Choice and Public Welfare* (Hinsdale, Ill.: Dryden Press, 1974), pp. 494-96. See also Alan Greenspan, "A General View of Inflation in the United States," in *Inflation in the United States* (New York: Conference Board, 1974), p. 4.

6. Bruce K. MacLaury, "Federal Credit Programs—The Issues They Raise," in *Issues in Federal Debt Management* (Boston: Federal Reserve Bank of Boston, 1973), p. 214.

7. Ibid., p. 217.

8. These issues are examined in depth in Murray L. Weidenbaum, *Subsidies in Federal Credit Programs* (Washington, D.C.: American Enterprise Institute for Public Policy Research, 1972).

9. *Report of the President's Commission on Budget Concepts* (Washington, D.C.: U.S. Government Printing Office, October 1967), p. 51.

10. George M. von Furstenberg, "Distribution Effects of GNMA Home Mortgage Purchases and Commitments under the Tandem Plans," *Journal of Money, Credit and Banking*, August 1976, pp. 373-89. Reprinted in this volume.

13

Grant Elements in the Operation of Federally Sponsored Credit Agencies in the Home Mortgage Market

PATRIC H. HENDERSHOTT
KEVIN E. VILLANI

The scope and composition of federal support of the home mortgage market has changed dramatically during the past decade. Total federal holdings of home mortgages, either direct or indirect via advances to savings and loan associations, have increased from less than \$10 billion to over \$70 billion. In 1965, federal support equaled about 4.5 percent of the total outstanding stock of household home mortgages. By 1975, this proportion had almost quadrupled to 16.5 percent. Put another way, the book value of the outstanding stock increased by \$239 billion during the past decade, while federal support increased by \$61 billion, or 26 percent of the increase in the stock. The form of the support has also changed markedly, shifting from direct purchases by the Federal National Mortgage Association during the 1966–70 period to private mortgage pools backed by the Government National Mortgage Association in recent years.

Much attention has been focused on the impact of home mortgage purchases of federally sponsored credit agencies (FSCAs) on total mortgage flows and residential construction activity. This focus is understandable as the mortgage-lending activities were designed to have an impact on these markets. A major finding of most investigators has been that, owing to the sensitivity of institutional investors to relative yield changes, the impact has been greater on the structure of interest rates than on total home mortgage credit flows. FSCA home mortgage purchases pushed home mortgage rates down, while FSCA issues of short-term securities to finance the purchases pushed short-term rates up.

This is a slightly revised version of a paper read at a joint session of the Annual Meetings of the Association for the Study of the Grants Economy and the American Economic Association, December 1975.

Earlier work has failed to push the analysis further. Obviously, these interest rate changes altered the interest income and/or expense of various economic units, and this alteration determines which economic units gain or lose from the policy. Shifting the distribution of income from rich households to poor households is likely one of the important goals underlying mortgage-support and other selective credit policies and thus would appear to be a minimum requirement of any such policy.[1] The primary goal of this chapter is to deduce the income-distribution impact of mortgage-support policies.

The nature of recent federal support of the home mortgage market is discussed first. Then an estimate of the impact of the increased mortgage purchases of FSCAs on financial markets is summarized and translated into changes in net interest income (earnings less expenses) of the various sectors of the economy. Next, the relationship between the activities of the FSCAs and deposit rate ceilings is established. In the final section all gains and losses of nonhousehold sectors are passed through to households as taxpayers and asset holders. A matrix containing estimates of the percentage of financial assets held and liabilities outstanding by households in income quintiles is then utilized to distribute the total gains or losses on each financial instrument among the different income groups. Summing the gains and losses within each quintile determines the net cost-benefit of the policy to the quintile.

SUPPORT OF THE HOME MORTGAGE MARKET DURING THE LAST DECADE

The federally sponsored credit agencies include the Federal National Mortgage Association (FNMA) and the Federal Home Loan Banks (FHLBs). These institutions were originally created and owned to varying extents by the federal government and were designed to support, directly or indirectly, the home mortgage market. They are currently privately owned, and thus are not included in the federal budget; they finance their lending activities largely through issues of securities. The FNMA purchases mortgages directly, while the activities of the FHLBs include the extension of advances to savings and loan associations (SLAs) to allow them to purchase residential mortgages as well as direct purchases in the secondary market by the subsidiary Federal Home Loan Mortgage Corporation (FHLMC). The mortgage holdings of FSCAs include, in addition to those of the FNMA and FHLMC, mortgage pools held by private institutions and financed by securities guaranteed by the Government National Mortgage Association (GNMA).

Direct and indirect support of the home mortgage market by FSCAs and by on-budget federal government agencies, such as the

TABLE 13.1

Net Federal Support for the Home Mortgage Market
(billions of dollars)

	1965	1966	1967	1968	1969	1970	1971	1972	1973	1974	1975
FSCAs	2.5	4.4	5.5	7.2	11.0	16.1	20.9	25.2	31.6	41.4	50.8
Advances (net)	4.9	5.9	3.0	3.9	8.3	8.3	6.1	6.5	13.4	19.4	14.4
Federal (net)	2.0	2.7	3.5	4.4	4.6	4.5	4.3	3.7	2.6	3.2	5.8
Total	9.4	13.0	12.0	15.5	24.9	28.9	31.3	35.4	47.6	64.0	71.0

Sources: Board of Governors of the Federal Reserve System, Federal Reserve Flow of Funds Accounts, 1946–1975 (Washington, D.C., 1976); and various issues of the Federal Reserve Bulletin.

GNMA, is indicated in Table 13.1. Advances are net of saving and loan deposits at FHLBs, and federal government holdings are net of small quantities of outstandings. The direct home mortgage holdings of FSCAs have risen from $2.5 billion at the end of 1965 to over $50 billion at the end of 1975. These holdings grew steadily between 1965 and 1971, doubling every two years. Although the rate of growth has slowed since then, the absolute magnitude of FSCA net home mortgage acquisitions has continued to grow, reaching a peak of nearly $10 billion in 1974 and 1975. The recent growth is attributable to the new forms of support, the GNMA-guaranteed mortgage pools and the secondary market purchases of the FHLMC. As Table 13.2 indicates, the pools and FHLMC purchases account for two-thirds of the increase in FSCA net mortgage acquisitions since 1970.

In addition to the direct acquisitions of the FSCAs, FHLBs have indirectly supported the market through their advances to SLAs (Table 13.1). This support is intended to cushion the impact of disintermediation and is therefore closely related to the interest rate cycle, as is indicated by the declines in 1967, 1971, and 1975 and the particularly sharp increases in 1969 and 1973-74. The support by agencies still in the federal budget increased gradually until 1969, when the GNMA pools and FHLMC activities were introduced, and then declined in early 1974. In late 1974 and 1975, the GNMA acquired mortgages for its own account in an attempt to stabilize residential construction. These acquisitions exceeded $2 billion in 1975.

TABLE 13.2

The Composition of FSCA Holdings
(billions of dollars)

	1970	1971	1972	1973	1974	1975
FNMA	15.2	16.7	17.7	20.4	23.8	25.8
FHLMC	0.4	0.9	1.8	2.4	4.2	4.6
GNMA pools	0.5	3.2	5.6	8.7	13.3	20.4
Total FSCAs	16.1	20.9	25.2	31.6	41.4	50.8

Sources: Board of Governors of the Federal Reserve System, Federal Reserve Flow of Funds Accounts, 1946-1975 (Washington, D.C., 1976); and various issues of the Federal Reserve Bulletin.

THE IMPACT OF FSCA PURCHASES ON SECTORAL INTEREST INCOME

The impact on financial markets and housing outlays of $18 billion of home mortgage purchases by FSCAs during the 1966-71 period has been analyzed in an earlier paper by P. H. Hendershott and K. E. Villani [5] and appears in Hendershott [4, Chapter 16]. The analysis consisted of simulation experiments of a multisector, multisecurity flow of funds model.[2] The impact of the increase in FSCA holdings on interest rates and the mortgage market—the difference between values in a control simulation and values when FSCA holdings were frozen at the end-1965 level—is summarized in Table 13.3. Continuing (and growing) mortgage purchases of FSCAs lowered the mortgage rate by 106 basis points. The increased short-term security issues of FSCAs to finance the purchases raised short-term interest rates by 67 basis points. The corporate bond rate fell by 19 basis points, an average of the changes in the other two rates. Thus, the activities of the agencies can be interpreted as lowering the spread between the mortgage and bond rates by 87 basis points (106 - 19). This is about two-thirds of the one and a third percentage point decline in the spread between these yields observed during the late 1960s and early 1970s.[3] The $18 billion increase in FSCA mortgage holdings raised the total stock of mortgages by only $3 billion (one-sixth of the increase in FSCA holdings) from the end of 1965 to the end of 1971.

This is an important result and is consistent with findings of others, for example, A. H. Meltzer [8]. Mortgage purchases by FSCAs will not increase mortgage issues dollar for dollar. When FSCAs increase their holdings, other sectors decrease theirs (see the following paragraph). Even beyond this, the increased mortgage issues that are forthcoming do not generate an equal increase in housing outlays. Loan-to-value ratios will rise as households substitute mortgage credit for other forms of debt in the financing of a wide range of financial and nonfinancial assets.

The decline in the mortgage rate relative to the bond rate resulted in many changes in the flows to the market for home mortgages. All but $3 billion of the $18 billion increase in FSCA holdings was offset by about equal decreases in the quantities of mortgages demanded by thrift institutions and by life insurance companies in response to the lower mortgage rate. Life insurance companies switched primarily into corporate bonds, although some of the funds were channeled into nonhome residential and commercial mortgages. Savings and loan associations increased their demand for nonhome residential mortgages by a minute amount. However, they did use nearly $3 billion of their funds to repay advances (or to increase advances less than otherwise) from the Federal Home Loan Banks rather than

TABLE 13.3

Cumulative Impact of Approximate Freeze in FSCA Mortgage Holdings at End-1965 Level

	Observed 1971.4	Policy Impact	Difference
Interest rates			
Prime commercial paper rate	5.03	0.67	4.36
Corporate bond rate	7.64	-0.19	7.83
Home mortgage rate	7.82	-1.06	8.88
Home mortgages			
Mortgage demand			
Agencies	20.9	17.9	3.0
Nonbank savings institutions	177.3	-7.8	185.1
Other finance	35.2	-7.0	42.0
Commercial banks	48.0	-0.1	48.1
Mortgage supply (households)	296.1	3.0	293.1

Sources: Board of Governors of the Federal Reserve System, Federal Reserve Flow of Funds Accounts, 1946-1975 (Washington, D.C., 1976); and various issues of the Federal Reserve Bulletin.

purchase home mortgages. A shift into bonds and nonhome mortgages by mutual savings banks accounted for almost two-thirds of the decrease in thrift demand for home mortgages. The shifts out of home mortgages allowed these financial institutions to avoid part of the costs of lower yields on home mortgages.

The change in relative interest rates and in portfolio holdings implies a redistribution of interest income/expense for all economic units that hold/issue financial instruments. Net interest income for a sector (INC) is defined as interest income less interest expense:

$$INC = \sum_i RA_i A_i - \sum_i RL_j L_j$$

where RA_i refers to the yield on the ith asset A_i and RL_j denotes the cost of the jth liability L_j. The interest-bearing financial instruments are bank savings accounts, thrift (nonbank) savings accounts, policy loans, consumer credit, short-term securities, long-term securities, and home mortgages.* Sectors that are net debtors tend to have negative net interest income, while net creditors tend to have positive income. Given that the net financial asset holdings of one sector are liabilities of others, net interest income summed across all sectors is zero.

The impact of the FSCA activities on net interest income of the various sectors is indicated in Table 13.4. The impact is measured as the difference between net interest income, calculated with the interest rates and quantities of financial instruments in the fourth quarter of 1971 generated by a control simulation, less net interest income, calculated with the rates and quantities in the same quarter produced by a simulation holding FSCA mortgage holdings at their end-1965 level.† The impacts are long-run effects insofar as the entire long-term asset holdings and liabilities outstanding are assumed to be rolled over at the changed interest rate yields and costs. The calculations are likely to understate the long-run changes in net interest income for two reasons. First, the calculations are based on end-1971 balance sheets, and portfolios have grown considerably since then. Second, the calculations assume that FSCAs are purchasing home mortgages at a rate of about $5 billion per year. During 1974 and 1975, purchases were nearly $10 billion per year.

As expected, thrift institutions (savings and loan associations and mutual savings banks) lose the most, $2 billion, because of their substantial holdings of home mortgages. Other mortgage holders—other finance (insurance companies, retirement funds, and mortgage bankers) and commercial banks—also lose, but part of their losses, especially those of commercial banks, are offset by the greater returns they earn on short-term securities. The U.S. Treasury also

---

*Shorts include bank loans, open-market paper, agency securities, Treasury bills and notes, large negotiable certificates of deposit, and Eurodollar deposits. Longs encompass corporate, foreign, state and local, and Treasury bonds, and commercial, multifamily, and farm mortgages.

†One percentage point has been subtracted from the home mortgage rate in the computations of interest income to make this rate roughly comparable to the corporate bond rate. This adjustment corrects for the greater servicing costs and risk and lower liquidity of home mortgages relative to Aa corporate bonds and is designed to prevent the relatively large shifts from mortgages to other long-term securities from giving misleading results. In any event, the adjustment does not alter the measured impact on the income of any sector other than FSCAs by as much as $100 million.

TABLE 13.4

Annual Net Interest Income Redistribution Effects of FSCA Activities
(billions of dollars)

Gainers		Losers	
Households	2.2	Thrifts	2.0
State and local governments	0.9	Other finance	0.7
Nonfinancial businesses	0.1	Treasury	0.5
FSCAs	0.1	Commercial banks	0.2
Rest of the world	0.1		
Total	3.4	Total	3.4

Source: Simulation results calculated by the authors.

loses owing to the higher interest rate it pays on its substantial short-term debt.

Households gain $2.9 billion in lower home mortgage interest expense, although $0.7 billion is lost on lower income from long-term security holdings. The other substantial gainer is state and local governments, which benefit from both the lower yield on their long-term debt and the higher yields on their short-term assets. Nonfinancial business is one of the sectors least affected by the FSCA policy. Because businesses issue well over twice as much long-term debt as short, their total interest cost does not rise sharply. Moreover, this rise is offset by greater interest earnings on their holdings of certificates of deposit (CDs) and Treasury bills.

Although households are by far the largest gainers, because of the lower mortgage rate, they ultimately bear the burden of the losses. Treasury losses must be financed by higher taxes (or lower expenditures). Also, the income lost by thrifts would eventually accrue to households in the form of interest paid out to thrift depositors (see the next section), and households would also suffer from the lower returns to insurance and pension fund reserves. Likewise, the gains of state and local governments would be expected to flow to taxpayers. The real issue, then, is the distributional impact on the income of various subgroups of households.

FSCA PURCHASES AND DEPOSIT RATE CEILINGS

An important assumption underlying the allocation of nonhousehold losses to households in the following section is that the rates on deposits at thrifts and commercial banks would have been higher during the 1967-71 period in the absence of FSCA purchases than the rates actually were. Establishing the relationship between the FSCA purchases and the deposit rate ceilings is the purpose of this brief section.

When rate ceilings became binding in late 1965, the Federal Reserve raised the rate ceiling on time deposits, as it had in similar situations in 1957, 1962, and 1964. Possibly in an effort to get the ceilings out of the way once and for all, the increase was the largest ever; the ceiling on deposits of maturity less than 90 days was increased from 4 to 5.5 percent and that on longer term deposits was raised from 4.5 to 5.5 percent. Apparently to the surprise of the Federal Reserve, large commercial banks rapidly took advantage of the increased ceilings to bid aggressively for deposits. This created two problems. First, smaller commercial banks, fearing reduced profits, lobbied intensively against the higher deposit rates.[4] Second, the higher bank deposit rates generated a flow of funds from thrifts to banks. Given the tendency of commercial banks to invest less heavily than thrifts in residential mortgages, such competition was detrimental to housing and thus anathema to the housing lobby. In response to these pressures, the Federal Reserve rolled back the ceiling on time deposits, other than large negotiable CDs, to 5 percent.

In spite of sharp increases in open-market interest rates during the 1966-69 period, the ceiling rates on bank and thrift accounts were unchanged. The failure of the authorities to raise the ceilings can be attributed at least partly to the mortgage purchases of the FSCAs. Because investments of savings and loan institutions, and mutual savings banks to a lesser extent, are limited by chartering provisions and minimum investment standards, the thrifts were unable to avoid most of the impact on their income of the lower mortgage rates induced by the FSCA purchases (and the higher advances rate attributable to the FSCA issues). As a result, thrifts could not afford higher deposit rates. (It is noteworthy that the increases in rate ceilings in 1970 and 1973 were preceded by significant increases in thrift income and were immediately followed by declines in income.) Had deposit rate ceilings on commercial bank deposits not existed, thrifts would have experienced a substantial loss of funds to commercial banks whose income was favorably influenced by the higher short-term rates. The thrift industry might not have survived; at a minimum, the desired relative reduction in mortgage rates and stimulation of housing would not have occurred. Thus, the ceiling rates were frozen and banks experienced significant increases in earnings.

THE IMPACT OF FSCA PURCHASES ON THE NET INTEREST INCOME OF HOUSEHOLD QUINTILES

How the income gains and losses of nonhousehold sectors are passed through to households is now considered. The largest loss is that of depositors. In the absence of the FSCA purchases, thrift mortgage interest income would have been substantially greater, and the regulators would have likely raised rate ceilings to allow this income to be paid to depositors. With higher deposit rates, however, deposit flows to thrifts and thrift mortgage purchases would have been greater. Moreover, these purchases would have lowered the home mortgage rate relative to what it otherwise would have been (the 8.88 percent in Table 13.3). In order to allow for all the interactions in the financial system, the thrift savings account rate has been endogenized in such a way that all hypothetical income gains of thrifts in the absence of FSCA mortgage purchases are passed through to depositors via higher deposit rates.* The commercial bank deposit rate is increased equally, the assumption being that the ceiling on bank rates would have been raised equally and commercial banks would have been willing to pay the higher rate. This simulation underlies the calculation of the ultimate income effects.

The computed sectoral gains and losses based on these assumptions regarding deposit rates are given in Table 13.5. The impact on households is partitioned into the gains and losses associated with the specific assets and liabilities they hold. The household sector is now a net loser because the deposit income it would have acquired had there been no increase in FSCA holdings is treated explicitly as a loss. Households still gain substantially on home mortgages, although the gain is less than before because higher deposit flows cushion the rise of the mortgage rate in the absence of FSCA purchases.† Commercial banks are viewed as large gainers because deposit rate ceil-

---

*That is,

$$Rsv^* = Rsv^c + \frac{INC_t^* - INC_t^c}{SVN^*}$$

where Rsv is the thrift savings account rate, INC is the interest income, SVN is the quantity of savings accounts at thrifts, asterisks denote values when FSCA mortgage holdings are frozen at the end-1965 value, the c superscript denotes control values, and Rsv^c is used in the calculation of both INC_t^* and INC_t^c. The thrift deposit rate rises by just over a half percentage point.

†The combination of the FSCA purchases and the accompanying low savings account rates reduces the mortgage rate by 82 basis points.

ings required by the FSCA policy held their interest expense below what they would have been willing to pay for funds. Other financial institutions and the Treasury are still losers and state and local governments are still gainers. The state and local gain is smaller, however, and nonfinancial businesses have become slight losers because of their loss of interest income on their deposits at commercial banks.

While the thrift loss has been passed through to households, the gains and losses of the other sectors must still be shifted. The first column of Table 13.6 reflects this shift. The loss of other finance and the gain on policy loans have been distributed to holders of insurance and pension reserves; the gains of commercial banks and FSCAs and loss of nonfinancial businesses have been aggregated and passed on to holders of primary securities; the loss of the Treasury and the gain of state and local governments have been shifted to taxpayers;* and the minor gain on consumer credit has been added to the gain on home mortgages.

The income quintile matrix (rows 1 through 5 and columns 2 through 6) indicate estimates of the percentages of the outstanding stocks of claims held by households in each of five income quintiles. The estimates are from data compiled by D. Projector and G. Weiss [9] from a survey based on end-1962 data. Not surprisingly, most financial claims are held and issued by the highest income quintile. This group earned 42 percent of household income in 1971 and undoubtedly held a higher proportion of household wealth. Also not surprising is the preference of the higher income (wealth) households for nonsavings account assets.

Rows 6 and 7 of the table contain estimates from a 1967 Tax Foundation study of 1965 data on the proportion of federal and state and local taxes paid by households in the different income quintiles [1]. They are consistent with the usual assumptions regarding the significant progressivity of the federal income taxes and slight regressivity of state and local taxes; the highest income quintile earned 40.5 percent of the income in 1965 and paid 52 and 37 percent, respectively, of federal and state and local taxes.

The "income to be distributed" in Table 13.6 is distributed among the five income groups in Table 13.7. The numbers in the first seven rows in Table 13.7 are obtained by multiplying the income to be distributed, column 1 in Table 13.6, by the relevant proportions

*The assumption that gains and losses in government interest are offset by changes in taxes is not crucial because the combined loss for all government units is small (less than $100 million). An assumption that the offset is in government expenditures would not markedly alter the results.

TABLE 13.5

Gains and Losses Assuming That Higher Thrift Income in the Absence of FSCA Purchases Would Have Been Passed through to Depositors via Higher Deposit Rates and Commercial Banks Would Have Raised Deposit Rates Equally

Sectors	Interest Gain Owing to FSCA Activities
Households :	-0.81
Bank savings accounts	-1.37
Thrift savings accounts	-1.83
Primary securities	0.06
Mortgage debt	2.18
Consumer credit	0.10
Policy loans	0.05
Other finance :	-0.42
Nonfinancial businesses	-0.29
Treasury	-0.61
State and local governments	0.52
Commercial banks	1.43
FSCAs	0.11
Rest of world	0.07
Total	0.00

Source: Compiled by the authors.

of the gain-loss accruing to that given quintile. Row 8 is the sum down each of the columns for the five quintiles. This row is the "bottom line," indicating the net annual interest income gained or lost by households in the different income groups.* The data suggest that the lowest quintile loses about $200 million, the second lowest over $100 million, the middle quintile gains nearly $100 million, the second from the highest gains over $200 million, and the highest quintile loses slightly.

*The sum across row 8 is slightly negative because domestic households lose, on net, to the rest of the world, which holds large quantities of short-term U.S. Treasury debt.

TABLE 13.6

Percentage Distribution of Household Asset Holdings, Liability Outstandings, and Tax Payments by Ascending Income Quintiles

	Income to Be Distributed	Matrix of Income Quintiles				
Savings accounts at commercial banks	-1.37	0.11	0.14	0.12	0.15	0.48
Savings accounts at thrifts	-1.83	0.09	0.10	0.12	0.18	0.50
Insurance and pension reserves	-1.37[a]	0.02	0.06	0.12	0.18	0.62
Primary securities	1.31[b]	0.04	0.10	0.08	0.17	0.61
Mortgage debt	2.28	0.02	0.06	0.17	0.27	0.48
Federal taxes	-0.61	0.03	0.10	0.15	0.20	0.52
State and local taxes	0.52	0.07	0.14	0.19	0.23	0.37

[a]Other finance plus policy loans.

[b]Nonfinancial businesses, commercial banks, FSCAs, and primary securities.

Source: Data on assets and liabilities are from D. Projector and G. Weiss, Survey of Financial Characteristics of Consumers, Board of Governors, Federal Reserve System, 1966.

The income shifts can be explained largely by the distribution of savings account holdings and home mortgage debt outstanding. The low, lower-middle, and highest income groups have low mortgage debt relative to savings account holdings. Low income and wealth households are unable to meet down payment requirements, while low-income, wealthier households, predominately retirees, tend to have paid off their mortgages. Moreover, low-income households find renting relatively cheaper; the after-tax mortgage rate, and thus the cost of homeownership, are inversely related to income. Those with very high incomes, on the other hand, tend to spend relatively less of their income on housing and to borrow a smaller proportion of the housing outlay. With relatively low mortgage debt, these quintiles benefit relatively little from low mortgage rates. The middle and upper-middle income households with relatively large mortgage debt are the gainers. Other influences also matter. The most impor-

TABLE 13.7

Gains or Losses Induced by the Increase in FSCA Mortgage Holdings, by Income Quintiles
(billions of dollars)

	Income Quintiles*				
Holders of					
Bank savings accounts	-0.15	-0.19	-0.16	-0.21	-0.66
Thrift savings accounts	-0.16	-0.18	-0.22	-0.33	-0.92
Insurance and pension reserves	-0.01	-0.02	-0.04	-0.07	-0.23
Primary securities	0.05	0.13	0.11	0.22	0.80
Mortgage debt	0.05	0.14	0.39	0.61	1.09
Payers of					
Federal taxes	-0.02	-0.06	-0.09	-0.12	-0.32
State and local taxes	0.04	0.07	0.10	0.12	0.19
Income shifts	-0.20	-0.11	0.09	0.22	-0.05

*The approximate divisions between the income quintiles for 1975 are, in thousands of current dollars, 7.5, 12, 16.5, and 24.

Source: Compiled by the authors.

tant of these are the high-income households' net gain on primary securities and insurance and pension reserves and net loss on taxes. But it is the distribution of deposit holdings and mortgages outstanding that dominates the outcome.

SUMMARY AND CONCLUSION

The starting point of this analysis is an estimate of the impact of FSCA mortgage purchases during the 1966–71 period on interest rates and sectoral balance sheets. The effect of the purchases on the net interest income (earnings less expenses) of households, nonfinancial businesses, commercial banks, thrifts, insurance companies and pension funds, state and local governments, and the Treasury is then calculated. Next, the gains or losses of the nonhousehold sectors are passed through to households as taxpayers and asset holders. Finally, the gains and losses of taxpayers, asset holders, and mortgagors are allocated among household income quintiles according to the distribution of total household assets, liabilities, and tax payments among the quintiles.

The purchases of home mortgages by the FSCAs are seen as generating a redistribution from those with low and lower-middle incomes to middle and upper-middle income households. This outcome is easily explained. The big gainers from the mortgage-support policies are mortgagors, who benefit from the lower mortgage rate, and the big losers are savings account depositors, who receive lower interest because thrift income is lower. And both low- and very high-income households tend to have low mortgage debt relative to savings deposits, while the reverse is true for middle and upper-middle income households.

The redistribution of income from those with low and very high incomes to those with middle and upper-middle incomes is probably not unique to this government policy. The federal tax structure is not nearly as progressive as the marginal tax rates presented in the tables would suggest, for example, as many of the remaining tax loopholes are what might be termed "middle-class deductions." Moreover, many of the expenditure programs initially conceived to help the poor have been expanded to include the middle class.[5] This result will not be surprising to students of the politics of allocation. An observation made by Aaron Director about 15 years ago, known as "Director's law," predicts this result: Public expenditures are made for the benefit of the middle classes and financed with taxes that are borne in considerable part by the poor and the rich.[6] We may expect a democratic government to make economic decisions that are perceived as being in the best interest of its constituents. People with middle and upper-middle incomes participate more fully in the electoral process, both as voters and party workers, and are represented by more effective lobbies (unions and trade associations) in state and national legislatures than people with lower incomes. These people should be expected to be the beneficiaries of laws passed by such bodies. The very rich, on the other hand, are, owing to their small numbers, the most vulnerable to redistributive policies.

The findings suggest an extension of Director's law. The federal government's economic power extends far beyond its taxing and expenditure policies to the regulation and protection of industry. The politics of allocation suggest that these policies will also be designed to benefit the middle class.

NOTES

1. For a volume devoted to developing a framework for analyzing selective credit policies, see Kaminow and O'Brien [6]. The

chapters by Kaminow and O'Brien, Kaminow and Rao, and Penner are particularly useful in laying out some of the broader issues.

2. The analysis was restricted to the pre-1972 period because 1971.4 was the last quarter of data used in the estimation of the model. The underlying flow-of-funds model and a wide range of simulation experiments are described in Hendershott [5].

3. Cook has investigated this episode, and concluded that the increase in mortgage acquisitions of the FSCAs was likely the most important cause.

4. Much of the interpretation in this paragraph is owed to Andrew Brimmer, who was a member of the Board of Governors during 1966. For a more detailed discussion of ceilings on deposit rates paid by both commercial banks and thrifts during the 1965-66 period, see Grabler and Doyel in Friend [3, pp. 1259-65].

5. For a discussion of the manipulation of federal taxes and expenditures to the benefit of the middle class, see Stockman [11].

6. An explanation of Director's law is presented in Stigler [10].

REFERENCES

[1] Allocating Tax Burdens and Government Benefits by Income Class. New York: Tax Foundation, 1967.

[2] Cook, T. Q. "The Residential Mortgage Market in Recent Years." Economic Review (Federal Reserve Bank of Richmond), September-October 1974.

[3] Friend, I. Study of the Savings and Loan Industry. Federal Home Loan Bank Board, 1969.

[4] Hendershott, P. H., and K. E. Villani. "The Federally Sponsored Credit Agencies: Their Behavior and Impact." Paper presented at the winter meetings of the Econometric Society, San Francisco, December 1974. Revised October 1975.

[5] Hendershott, P. H. A Flow of Funds Financial Model: Estimation and Application to Financial Policies and Reforms. Lexington, Mass.: Lexington Books, Heath, 1977.

[6] Kaminow, I., and J. B. O'Brien, eds. Studies in Selective Credit Policies. Philadelphia: Federal Reserve Bank of Philadelphia, 1975.

[7] Kane, E. J. "Short-Changing the Small Saver: Federal Government Discrimination against Small Savers during the Vietnam War." Journal of Money, Credit and Banking, November 1970.

[8] Meltzer, A. H. "Credit Availability and Economic Decisions. Some Evidence from the Mortgage and Housing Markets." Journal of Finance, June 1974.

[9] Projector, D., and G. Weiss. Survey of Financial Characteristics of Consumers. Board of Governors, Federal Reserve System, August 1966.

[10] Stigler, G. "Director's Law of Public Income Redistribution." Journal of Law and Economics, September 1970.

[11] Stockman, D. A. "The Social Pork Barrel." The Public Interest, Spring 1975.

14

Distribution Effects of GNMA Home Mortgage Purchases and Commitments under the Tandem Plans

GEORGE M. VON FURSTENBERG

Since January 1974, the Government National Mortgage Association (GNMA) has been authorized to purchase regular mortgages on new single-family homes at interest rates one or two percentage points below the market. In spite of the large volume of commitments and purchases that have since been made, housing starts reached an eight-year low at the end of 1974 and recovery has been slow thereafter. Although single-family starts were less depressed than multifamily starts, preliminary indications are that tandem programs have had little effect in raising starts [7]. They are, however, conveying large income transfers. This study seeks to estimate the interest savings to mortgagors and any possible benefits to mortgagees that are likely to be conferred by the programs described below.

Tandem, or piggyback, procedures were first introduced in 1968 partly to minimize the effect of federally assisted mortgage credit programs on the unified budget balance. Because the net lending of government agencies represents an outlay above the line, GNMA's acquisition of below-market interest rate mortgages increased the budget deficit by the full amount of the purchase price. Under tandem, these mortgages were resold to the private market at a price sufficiently below par to afford a normal return to investors. Thus, only the discount or the present value of the interest subsidy represented an outlay and the cycle could continue "in tandem" with further purchases.

Tandem activities were first limited to mortgages insured by the Federal Housing Administration (FHA), which involved either in-

---

Reprinted by permission. George M. von Furstenberg, "Distribution Effects of GNMA Home Mortgage Purchases and Commitments under the Tandem Plans," Journal of Money, Credit, and Banking 8, no. 3 (August 1976):373-89.

terest rates well below the market (3 percent under Section 221[d][3], Title II of the Housing and Urban Development Act) or steep interest reduction payments (down to interest costs of 1 percent under Sections 235 and 236 of the same act). However, in September 1971, this subsidy program was extended to FHA mortgages insured under unsubsidized programs and to mortgages guaranteed by the Veterans Administration (VA).* In contrast to the heavily regulated older subsidy programs, currently the only eligibility conditions for extended tandem are that the newly constructed homes must qualify for regular FHA/VA insurance and that the amount of the mortgage may not exceed $38,000, except in high-cost areas, such as Alaska and Hawaii.† In October 1974, a tandem program for conventional home mortgages was added by GNMA after a commitment and purchase program for interest-reduced conventional mortgages had first been pioneered by the Federal Home Loan Mortgage Corporation (FHLMC) in May. Even though FHLMC, unlike GNMA, may hold the mortgages it acquires for extended periods, the FHLMC program is referred to as tandem as well. A description of the programs added since the start of 1974 follows.

On January 21, 1974, GNMA was authorized to purchase FHA/VA mortgages on up to 200,000 new homes at an interest rate of 7 3/4 percent. GNMA's purchase price was first set at 96 percent of par. Alternatively, a price of 98 percent could be paid beginning December 1, 1974, provided the interest rate was moved to 8 1/4 percent. On May 10, 1974, GNMA was authorized to commit to purchase FHA/VA mortgages on another 100,000 units. This program was not used until commitment authority under the previous program had been exhausted toward the end of October. The first commitments under the May 10 program were made at an interest rate of 8 percent in October before the rate was raised to 8 1/4 percent in December. The bulk of the commitments came only after the rate was reduced again to 8 percent in March 1975, with the purchase price remaining at 98.

---

*The GNMA supertandem programs 22 and 21 were added for unassisted single-family and multifamily mortgages to the assisted programs 18 and 17.

†The value for FHA/VA mortgages was $33,000 prior to September 11, 1974. The limit was raised to $38,000 ($40,500 for a four-bedroom unit) in the Housing and Urban Development Act of 1974. The value limit on all commitments made under the Emergency Home Purchase Act of 1974 (EHPA), including the $1 billion FHA/VA authorization of January 1975 (program 24), is $42,000. The value limits have discouraged participation in high-cost areas, especially the Northeast.

On October 18, 1974, a conventional GNMA tandem program became law. A maximum of $7.75 billion in commitments was authorized under the Emergency Home Purchase Act (EHPA) of 1974 for the purchase of conventional mortgages. When the first $3 billion was released, the interest rate was set at 8 1/2 percent, but, because of provisions of the law tying the rate to changes in the yield on intermediate term governments, this rate was reduced to 8 1/4 percent for December and to 8 percent for January. After the first $3 billion had been used, an additional $3 billion was authorized on January 16, 1975 at an interest rate of 7 3/4 percent, including $1 billion FHA/VA mortgages. Because of the attractive terms, almost the entire amount was committed on a single day, January 22. The remaining $1.75 billion, grossed up to $2 billion to include some previous commitments that had been canceled, was made available in August 1975 at an interest rate of 7 1/2 percent.*

The dollar volume of FHA/VA commitments actually made since the start of 1974 under all the GNMA-extended tandem programs for new single-family homes had swelled to around $8 billion by the middle of 1975. Compared with this, only $0.8 billion of new home and $2.3 billion of existing home commitments were made from September 1971 through 1973. The $8 billion consisted of $4.5 billion under the January 21, 1974 program, $2.5 billion under the May 10 program, and $1 billion of FHA/VA commitments made available under the January 16, 1975 extension of the October 18 program, which was originally limited to conventionals. In addition, $3 billion of conventional home mortgage commitments at 8 3/4 percent interest, authorized under another part of the May 10 program, was issued by FHLMC in the late spring and early summer of 1974. Another $7 billion of commitments to purchase conventional home mortgages was issued by the Federal National Mortgage Association (FNMA) and FHLMC on behalf of GNMA after passage of the EHPA in October 1974. This total includes a small amount of existing home mortgages.† All the other programs are restricted to previously unoccupied homes de-

---

*This amount is included in the present estimates. The mortgage value limit is $42,000 under this program, but 75 percent of all mortgages are required to have a face amount of $36,000 or less.

†Existing home mortgages were administratively limited to 10 percent of the total. With new homes defined as homes started or completed after October 18, 1973, over 90 percent of the mortgages purchased by FNMA and FHLMC under program 30 were on new homes according to information available on a sample basis through 1975. FNMA and FHLMC act purely as agents for GNMA under this EHPA program for conventional mortgages and GNMA is the acquiring agency.

fined as new homes with the home mortgage limit set at $42,000 ($55,000 in Alaska and Hawaii) to qualify under the tandem program for conventional mortgages.

THE TANDEM PROGRAMS FOR FHA/VA HOME MORTGAGES

Table 14.1 shows the commitments made under each of the three different extended tandem programs for FHA/VA mortgages authorized since January 1974. Commitments to purchase home mortgages remain valid for one year, and one extension for no more than 3 months is allowed. Purchases start 1 to 4 months after the commitment date and end 12 to 15 months after that date with up to 85 percent of the commitments originally issued taken up during this period provided it remains profitable to do so.

FHA/VA commitments are issued mainly to mortgage bankers at a fee of 0.5 percent. Since the GNMA purchase price is 98 percent of par,* the holder of the commitment may charge up to two and a half points to recoup these costs. In addition, lenders charge one and a half to two points for originating the loan. Though points are paid by home sellers, the price of homes sold with subsidized financing is raised to shift this cost to the buyer so that the effective yield to the lender and interest costs to the borrower are identical. Hence, the effective interest rate to the mortgagor is taken to be equal to the stated rate under the tandem contract plus four and a half points (four points since July 1975)† amortized over a 12-year period on the assumption that, on the average, 30-year loans are prepaid at the end of that time. This rate can be compared with the effective commit-

---

*The price was 96 prior to December 1, 1974. Nevertheless, no more than four and a half points are assumed to be passed on to mortgagors closing prior to that time. The additional commitment fees for 3-month extensions beyond the initial 12-month commitment period, which are 1/8 percent for the FHA/VA and 1/4 percent for conventional single-family home mortgages, are also not assumed to be passed on for late deliveries.

†In negotiations with Congress prior to passage of the Emergency Housing Act of 1975 on July 2, GNMA agreed to limit the number of points that may be added to the purchase price of a home to no more than four. This act authorized $10 billion additional mortgage commitments at an interest rate of 7 1/2 percent, subject to appropriations. The first $3 billion released in January 1976 was restricted to multifamily mortgages (program 23).

TABLE 14.1

Interest Savings to Mortgagors under the FHA/VA Extended Tandem Programs, GNMA[a]
(millions of dollars)

	FHA/VA Commitment Rate Two Months before Month Shown (percent)	January 21, 1974 Program (7 3/4 percent)				May 10, 1974 Program (8 percent)				January 16, 1975 Program (7 3/4 percent)			
		Commitments	Purchases	Points Saved (percent)	Amount Saved	Commitments	Purchases	Points Saved (percent)	Amount Saved	Commitments	Purchases	Points Saved (percent)	Amount Saved
1974													
January	9.10	1	—	—	—	—	—	—	—	—	—	—	—
February	9.00	239	—	—	—	—	—	—	—	—	—	—	—
March	8.93	171	—	—	—	—	—	—	—	—	—	—	—
April	8.73	773	—	—	—	—	—	—	—	—	—	—	—
May	8.68	646	10	2.03	0	—	—	—	—	—	—	—	—
June	8.70	286	40	2.16	1	—	—	—	—	—	—	—	—
July	9.03	516	80	4.34	3	—	—	—	—	—	—	—	—
August	9.29	625	140	6.00	8	—	—	—	—	—	—	—	—
September	9.39	571	180	6.60	12	—	—	—	—	—	—	—	—
October	9.59	553	240	7.87	19	47	—	—	—	—	—	—	—
November	9.95	—	240	10.03	24	236	—	—	—	—	—	—	—
December	10.01	—	240	10.39	25	—	—	—	—	—	—	—	—
1975													
January	9.99	—	260	10.27	27	—	20	8.66	2	993	—	—	—
February	9.56	—	180	7.68	14	—	10	6.02	1	—	20	7.68	2

March	9.46	—	140	7.06	10	167	10	5.40	1	5	40	7.06	3
April	9.10	—	120	4.79	6	792	20	3.09	1	—	50	4.79	2
May	8.84	—	100	3.09	3	923	40	1.37	1	—	40	3.09	1
June	8.70	—	40	2.16	1	1	30	0.42	0	—	20	2.16	0
July	9.00	—	130	4.64	6	—	100	2.93	3	—	60	4.64	3
August	9.16	—	90	5.67	5	—	100	3.98	4	—	50	5.67	3
September	9.12	—	80	5.42	4	—	120	3.72	4	—	70	5.42	4
October	9.13	—	70	5.48	4	—	150	3.79	6	—	70	5.48	4
November	9.44	—	60	7.44	4	—	150	5.78	9	—	80	7.44	6
December	9.60	—	50	8.43	4	—	140	6.77	9	—	70	8.34	6
1976													
January	9.53	—	50	8.00	4	—	150	6.34	10	—	80	8.00	6
February	9.55	—	50	8.12	4	—	200	6.46	13	—	70	8.12	6
March	9.25[b]	—	—	—	—	—	200	4.56	9	—	60	6.24	4
April	9.25[b]	—	—	—	—	—	200	4.56	9	—	50	6.24	3
May	9.25[b]	—	—	—	—	—	100	4.56	5	—	20	6.24	1
June	9.25[b]	—	—	—	—	—	50	4.56	2	—	—	—	—
Total	—	4,381[a]	2,590[a]	—	188	2,166	1,790	—	89	998	850	—	54

[a]From September through November 1974, \$223 million of commitments was made to purchase FHA/VA 8 3/4 percent mortgages with face amounts of between \$33,000 and \$38,000 outside high-cost areas. In addition, \$466 million of commitments to purchase FHA/VA 8 1/4 percent mortgages was made from December 1974 through February 1975 under the May 10 program. As these commitments are not estimated to yield significant benefits to mortgagors, they are disregarded.

[b]Estimated.

Sources: U.S. Department of Housing and Urban Development; Government National Mortgage Association; and calculations by the author.

ment rate on FHA/VA home mortgages calculated by the Department of Housing and Urban Development (HUD) in the same fashion that prevailed two months before the mortgage is closed and delivered to GNMA.*

Most home buyers obtain mortgage commitments at fixed rates one or two months before the date of closing from mortgage lenders. As these lending institutions have accumulated GNMA commitments, the lag from commitment to closing is likely to be the same for the home buyer, whether or not GNMA is involved. Furthermore, primary lenders, particularly mortgage companies, typically deliver mortgages closed at below-market rates with a lag of only a few weeks to GNMA, and interim financing is obtained from commercial banks. In spite of the low mortgage interest rates, savings and loan associations (SLAs) may at times hold tandem mortgages somewhat longer, for instance, as an alternative to investment in Treasury bills, but such instances are believed to be rare. Hence, the effective rate on mortgages purchased by GNMA in any given month may be associated correctly with the commitment rate that prevailed on FHA/VA mortgages without GNMA assistance about two months earlier.† If the mortgagor would have secured unassisted FHA/VA mortgages in the absence of the tandem program, the difference between these rates indicates the size of the benefits to mortgagors.

The present value of the subsidy can be estimated by calculating the total discount at which the tandem mortgages would have to be loaned out to raise the effective rate to the level of the conventional rate. After subtracting four and a half (four) points from this total discount, the net discount saved by mortgagors is obtained, which is identified as "points saved," that is, the present value of the interest saving per $100 of face amount, in Table 14.1. Multiplying the amount of actual or prospective mortgage purchases by points saved in percent yields the estimated dollar volume of the potential subsidies involved. As part of the acquisitions occur only in 1976, the calculation is based on extrapolations of purchases and effective interest rates beyond December 1975, the last month for which data were

---

*The commitment rate on new home mortgages fluctuated between 8.57 and 8.93 percent from January 1974 to June 1975. Because this rate was frequently not competitive during this period, the volume of new FHA/VA mortgages was correspondingly low. To obtain a more representative rate, the total rate on all FHA/VA commitments was used that moves quite closely with the rate on conventional mortgage commitments reported later. The effect of using an alternative rate is shown in the footnote on p. 251.

†A four-month lag is used later for sensitivity testing.

available. While the estimates reported in Tables 14.1 and 14.2 are based on a single forecast rate of 9 1/4 percent, the sensitivity of the expected benefits to the future level of interest rates is examined later in this chapter.

With this proviso, only the January 21, 1974 program involving an interest rate of 7 3/4 percent is estimated to convey substantial interest savings to mortgagors whose present value, $188 million, approaches 7 percent of the roughly $2.6 billion commitments expected to be taken up.* The 8 1/4 percent commitments under the May 10, 1974 program are expected to yield little or no benefit to mortgagors. Partly because of their small size, even the 8 percent commitments and the 7 3/4 percent commitments authorized on January 16, 1975, are estimated to convey only comparatively minor interest savings. The savings under the two FHA/VA programs authorized after January 1974 are estimated to amount to only $143 million, bringing the total cash equivalent benefits to home mortgagors to $331 million.

THE TANDEM PROGRAMS FOR CONVENTIONAL HOME MORTGAGES

The 1 percent commitment fee used in the uninsured programs is supplemented by a loss reserve and marketing fee of 1 1/2 percent. The savings and loan associations and mortgage bankers who obtain most of the conventional mortgage commitments sell mortgages at par rather than at 98 percent as under FHA/VA, but again two and a half points are being charged by GNMA at the front end if the commitments are taken up. In addition, home buyers pay one and a half to two points to primary lenders to compensate them for the cost of mortgage origination. Hence, the interest savings on conventional mortgages purchased under the GNMA tandem program plus one extension shown in Table 14.2 can be calculated in exactly the same way as on FHA/VA mortgages, except that the FHLMC commitment rates on conventional mortgages two months prior to the date of GNMA purchases are now used as the referent against which the subsidies are measured.†

---

*If the yield on FHA-insured loans in the private secondary markets two months prior to the month shown in the Federal Reserve Bulletin is substituted for the HUD series used in Table 14.1, the present value of the interest saving would be $204 billion rather than $188 billion. The difference is slight because the series is close, although, in the former, prepayment after 15 years rather than 12 years is assumed to calculate the effective yield.

†Fees or points are shown separately from the "going rate" in the FHLMC market survey on mortgage commitment rates. Hence,

TABLE 14.2

Interest Savings to Mortgagors under the Conventional Extended Tandem Programs[a]
(millions of dollars)

	Conventional Commitment Rate Two Months before Month Shown (percent)	FHLMC May 10, 1974 Program (8 3/4 percent)				GNMA October 18, 1974 Program (8 1/4 percent/8 percent)				GNMA January 16, 1975 Extension (7 3/4 percent)			
		Commitments	Purchases	Points Saved (percent)	Amount Saved	Commitments	Purchases	Points Saved (percent)	Amount Saved	Commitments	Purchases	Points Saved (percent)	Amount Saved
1974													
May	8.76	1,379	–	–	–	–	–	–	–	–	–	–	–
June	8.90	582	–	–	–	–	–	–	–	–	–	–	–
July	9.29	1,039	–	–	–	–	–	–	–	–	–	–	–
August	9.45	–	20	2.28	0	–	–	–	–	–	–	–	–
September	9.63	–	90	3.45	3	–	–	–	–	–	–	–	–
October	9.90	–	190	5.18	10	–	–	–	–	–	–	–	–
November	10.32	–	190	7.78	15	–	–	–	–	–	–	–	–
December	10.39	–	210	8.21	17	1,445	–	–	–	–	–	–	–
1975													
January	10.15	–	170	6.74	11	/810	–	–	–	1,930	–	–	–
February	9.96	–	90	5.56	5	–	10	6.85	1	19	–	–	–
March	9.77	–	80	4.36	3	–	30/10	5.67/7.32	2/1	34	10	8.96	1

April	9.44	—	70	2.22	2	—	30/20	3.60/5.28	1/1	—	30	6.94	2
May	9.22	—	50	0.74	0	—	30/30	2.16/3.87	1/1	—	60	5.56	3
June	9.12	—	80	0.07	0	—	30/20	1.50/3.22	0/1	—	50	4.92	2
July	9.23	—	100	0.81	1	—	50/50	2.72/4.43	1/2	—	110	6.12	7
August	9.22	—	30	0.74	0	—	50/40	2.66/4.37	1/2	—	120	6.06	7
September	9.25	—	50	0.95	0	—	50/40	2.86/4.56	1/2	—	130	6.24	8
October	9.30	—	110	1.28	1	—	90/60	3.19/4.88	3/3	—	160	6.56	10
November	9.48	—	30	2.48	1	—	130/80	4.35/6.02	6/5	—	210	7.69	16
December	9.59	—	—	—	—	—	150/70	5.05/6.71	8/5	—	160	8.37	13
1976													
January	9.50	—	—	—	—	—	120/60	4.48/6.15	5/4	—	150	7.81	12
February	9.40[b]	—	—	—	—	—	80/50	3.84/5.52	3/3	—	100	7.19	7
March	9.25[b]	—	—	—	—	—	40/40	2.86/4.56	1/2	—	100	6.24	6
April	9.25[b]	—	—	—	—	—	/20	/4.56	/1	—	50	6.24	3
Total	—	3,000	1,560	—	69	1,445/810	890/590	—	34/33	1,983	1,440	—	97

[a]In October and November 1974, $698 million of commitments was made to purchase conventional 8 1/2 percent mortgages on new homes under the October 18 program. Because of the comparatively high rate involved, no significant benefits are expected to be derived by mortgagors, so these commitments are disregarded.

[b]Estimated.

Sources: U.S. Department of Housing and Urban Development; Government National Mortgage Association; Federal Home Loan Mortgage Corporation; and calculations by the author.

The only major difference that arises relates to the May 10, 1974 program of FHLMC, which is financed by the Federal Home Loan Bank Board borrowing from the Treasury at 7 7/8 percent interest. FHLMC purchased the 8 3/4 percent conventional mortgages at par with loss reserve, servicing, and administrative expenses provided for by the spread of seventh-eighths percentage points. Only the one-half percentage point commitment fee remains at the front end. Hence, points saved are calculated under this program by subtracting two and a half rather than four and a half or four (since July 1975) points from the total point discount that would raise the yield on 8 3/4 percent mortgages to the effective interest rate on conventional home mortgages. This rate is deduced from the rate on commitments made two months prior to the GNMA purchase with a four-month lag used later in this chapter for sensitivity testing. Deliveries have been made on little more than half of the commitments made in 1974, as those loan originators who found the 8 3/4 percent rates attractive and had ample liquidity preferred to utilize their own funds for current lending.

Table 14.2 shows that interest savings of almost $100 million can be expected from the 7 3/4 percent conventional GNMA tandem program as extended in January 1975. The $2 billion 7 1/2 percent commitments made in August 1975 after an additional allocation was authorized in June are now shown in Table 14.2, but the interest savings can readily be calculated. On the assumption that commitment rates average 9 1/4 percent in 1976 when 85 percent of the commitments are expected to be exercised, this saving is $135 million. Including this amount, the sum total of the cash equivalent benefits to mortgagors under the conventional tandem programs is expected to be $368 million. Hence, the total benefits to mortgagors under all of the tandem programs authorized from the start of 1974 through June 1975 are estimated to be $699 million.

If commitment rates from January 1976 on, which are related to expected GNMA purchases from March 1976 on, would average 9 percent rather than 9 1/4 percent, the total savings would be reduced to $657 million. On the other hand, if rates would be 9 1/2 percent, the total cash equivalent benefits to mortgators under the FHA/VA and conventional tandem programs combined would rise to $741 million. If commitment rates four months, rather than two months,

---

an effective rate was calculated for both 80 and 95 percent loan-value ratio mortgages on the assumption that these mortgages have 30-year maturities and are prepaid after 12 years. A simple average of the two effective rates was then taken to approximate rates applicable at average loan-value ratios of around 90 percent.

prior to the month of purchase were used to calculate points saved, the total savings would be $664 billion. The estimates are sensitive to the choice of interest rates, as varying the rate in the forecast by 25 basis points causes a 6 percent change in total benefits, even though less than one-quarter of the total expected purchases had not yet been made by the end of February 1976. The estimates are less sensitive to the precise length of lag assumed from the dates of commitment to purchase during the entire period, as interest rates have not changed consistently in one direction.

THE BENEFITS TO MORTGAGE ORIGINATORS

Obtaining extended tandem commitments and subsequently selling home mortgages to GNMA or FHLMC* may be of substantial benefit to mortgage lenders if it facilitates portfolio adjustments that may be necessary, for instance, because of greater than expected reductions in liquidity. Significant losses may be associated with the sale of illiquid mortgage instruments whose quality cannot readily be ascertained by the buyer. Similarly, if mortgagees have issued uncovered commitments in the past at effective rates that are lower than the secondary market yield on offers subsequently accepted by FNMA, losses would be incurred that can be avoided by using the tandem plans.†

In the 1974-75 housing slump, the yield on accepted offers in FNMA's auction of four-month commitments to purchase conventional home mortgages exceeded the effective rate on new home mortgages closed by more than 50 basis points from May through November 1974,

---

*Sales are made to FHLMC rather than GNMA only under the May 10, 1974 conventional tandem program. The mortgage value limit under this program is $45,000 if mortgages have loan-value ratios of 90 percent or less and $42,000 with 90 to 95 percent loan-value financing.

†These losses are owing to rising interest rates and merely realized through sale to FNMA. GNMA insulates mortgagees against rising rates and allows them to avoid these losses. However, if rates, instead of moving higher than expected, move lower, FNMA commitments allow lenders to realize capital gains on past commitments to their borrowers, because mortgagees can convert FNMA's 12-month standby commitments to the average yield on accepted offers in the most recent auction of fixed 4-month commitments at any time before the convertible 12-month standby commitments expire. GNMA commitments afford no such opportunity because of below-market interest rates and the fixed price paid by GNMA.

TABLE 14.3

Mortgage Interest Rates in Primary and Secondary Markets on Loans Closed, Rates on Advances and Commitments, January 1974 through June 1975

	Effective Rate on FHA/VA Loans Closed	FHA/VA Yield in Private Secondary Market[a]	Average Rate on New FHLB Advances[b]	Effective Conventional Rate on New Home Mortgages Closed[c]	Average Yield on Four-Month FHA/VA Mortgage Commitments Accepted by FNMA	Average Yield on Four-Month Conventional Mortgage Commitments Accepted by FNMA
1974						
January	8.99	8.58[d]	8.23	8.52	8.71	8.77
February	8.85	8.54	8.13	8.62	8.47	8.61
March	8.73	8.66	7.84	8.64	8.54	8.54
April	8.70	9.17	8.49	8.67	9.04	9.08
May	8.95	9.46	8.79	8.74	9.40	9.52
June	9.21	9.46	8.92	8.85	9.52	9.61
July	9.35	9.85	9.32	8.96	9.84	9.88
August	9.60	10.30	9.39	9.09	10.25	10.31
September	9.93	10.38	9.54	9.19	10.58	10.69
October	10.01	10.13	9.40	9.17	10.22	10.39
November	9.95	9.53[d]	8.78	9.27	9.88	10.04
December	9.67	9.51	8.40	9.37	9.53	9.71

1975						
January	9.52	8.99	7.92	9.33	9.23	9.46
February	9.26	8.84	7.49	9.11	8.92	9.12
March	8.99	8.69	7.20	9.06	8.84	8.98
April	8.85	9.14[d]	7.20	8.96	9.05	9.20
May	9.05	9.16	7.30	8.90	9.28	9.42
June	9.12	9.06	7.30	8.96	9.09	9.21
July	9.17	9.13	7.30	8.89	9.14	9.23
August	9.16	9.32	7.50	8.89	9.39	9.45
September	9.32	9.74	7.70	8.94	9.76	9.83
October	9.55	9.53	7.70	9.01	9.91	9.96
November	9.56	9.41	7.50	9.01	9.33	9.44
December	9.56	9.32	7.30	9.01	9.31	9.37

[a]Because discounts are amortized over 15 years rather than 12 years in the effective yield published, this series is not strictly comparable to the primary market HUD series in column 1. To achieve comparability, 0.1 was added to the rates shown before they were used in the calculations described in the text, assuming that a discount of around seven points prevailed during the summer of 1974.

[b]FHLB advances are made for a maximum of five years. Rates during the last half of 1974 were affected by a $4 billion program of internally subsidized advances authorized on May 10, 1974. For a description see FHLB Journal, June 1974, pp. 2-6.

[c]Because initial fees and charges are amortized over ten years in the FHLB series, this series is not strictly comparable to those in columns 1, 5, and 6. This series is also affected by a fixed sampling distribution that gives excessive weight to states with binding usury ceilings and low loan volume when rates are at a peak. Tandem mortgages also get into this series.

[d]Estimated.

Sources: Federal Home Loan Bank Board; U.S. Department of Housing and Urban Development; and Federal National Mortgage Association.

as shown in Table 14.3. The rate on new FHLB advances also exceeded the effective mortgage rate during most of this period and savings inflow was depressed until October 1974. The liquidity of the thrift institutions was low and loan commitments were curtailed.* All these signs point to a period necessitating portfolio adjustments through borrowing and secondary market operations that would be avoided at the prevailing rate differentials if money and credit market developments had been fully anticipated. Given the variety of adjustment strategies open to mortgagees, the precise gains conferred on them by the availability of tandem programs are uncertain. Nevertheless, the evidence clearly points to the period from April to October 1974 as the one during which most such benefits would be expected to occur.

The difference between the effective rate on FHA/VA loans closed during this period and the corresponding secondary market rate can be used to fix the likely order of magnitude. If mortgagees had to sell loans in the secondary market rather than to GNMA, what would they have lost? As can be seen from the first two columns of Table 14.3, the secondary market rate exceeded the primary market rate only during the seven months ending with October 1974 and then was well below the primary market rate until April 1975. Assuming the same amount of FHA/VA mortgages would have been sold in the secondary market, if there had been no tandem purchases, as the sum total of both conventional and FHA/VA mortgages actually sold to GNMA and FHLMC from April through October 1974 allows the benefits to mortgagees to be inferred from the losses on secondary market sales that could be avoided because of tandem.

Tables 14.1 and 14.2 show that $690 million FHA/VA mortgages and $300 million conventional home mortgages were purchased by GNMA and FHLMC during the credit crunch period. The excess of the secondary market yield of FHA/VA home mortgages over the effective rate on loans closed can be translated into an additional dis-

---

*The liquidity ratio of SLAs declined from a 1974 high of 8.93 in March to a low of 7.20 percent in September. Consequently, seasonally adjusted mortgage loan commitments outstanding at SLAs were reduced 25.5 percent from April to October 1974. Another sign of distress was the extremely large volume of mortgage offers received by FNMA in March and April 1974 and the small percentage of these offers accepted in both the FHA/VA and the conventional home mortgage auctions of four-month commitments. Actual and desired commitments outstanding with lenders may remain out of balance for a period of up to one year after an unexpected tightening in the money and credit markets, and implicit home mortgage commitments may arise from construction loans made to builders.

count on the FHA/VA 30-year loans closed at ceiling rates of 8.5 to 9.5 percent during the period from April to October 1974 and prepaid after 12 years. The benefits of sales to GNMA and FHLMC are then found to be $29 million, provided selling in the private secondary market was the costlier alternative avoided.

If, instead of taking this alternative, it is assumed that mortgagees would have obtained FNMA commitments in the credit crunch period, the estimated benefits would still be quite small. Most of the additional FNMA commitments ultimately would not have been exercised because the liquidity of mortgage lenders was rapidly restored after October 1974 and because mortgage rates then declined. Hence, the commitment fees paid to FNMA, equal to one-half of 1 percent of mortgage principal, would be lost, as the insurance cover obtained by lending institutions would turn out to have been unneeded in retrospect. The maximum amount of commitment fees that might have been saved on $7 billion* tandem commitments rather than FNMA commitments being issued during the credit crunch period would have been $35 million. Because GNMA would be most unlikely to accept such a large volume of additional commitments during a seven-month period,[1] there may have been some additional benefits of size. Nevertheless, it is difficult to see how a money value of more than $40 million could be put on the benefits conferred on primary mortgage lenders by the tandem programs during the credit crunch of 1974.

THE POSSIBLE EFFECT ON HOUSING STARTS

The income transfers that may be conveyed to mortgagors and mortgage lenders under the $8 billion FHA/VA and the $10 billion conventional tandem programs authorized from the start of 1974 through June 1975 probably amount to between $600 and $800 million. The cash equivalent benefits are only about 4 percent of the $18 billion total committed and 6 1/2 percent of the $11.5 billion GNMA and FHLMC purchases that are expected to result. All but about 5 percent of the total income transfers were estimated to go to mortgagors rather than to mortgagees, on the assumption that these mortgagors would have obtained mortgage commitments at market rates in the absence of the extended tandem programs.

This assumption may be incorrect if marginal borrowers were induced to buy homes at the tandem rates who would not have purchased

*The amount if $7.5 billion if the $0.5 billion of 8 3/4 and 8 1/2 percent commitments made in September and October 1974 are included. These commitments were not shown in Tables 14.1 and 14.2 because they are not expected to yield significant benefits to mortgagors.

homes at the higher conventional rates. However, apart from the limits on the mortgage amounts, there are no restrictions on the group of mortgagors eligible for tandem mortgages. The program is not focused on buyers who are more likely to be marginal.* Hence, it can be assumed that the beneficiaries are selected at random from among the roughly 50 percent of all new home buyers whose mortgages are below the value limit. Of course, if tandem commitments had been authorized in a volume sufficient to meet all demands, no rationing or nonmarket selection system would need to be specified to determine the effect of the rate reductions on starts. The $18 billion tandem commitments made from January 1974 through June 1975 would be sufficient to finance approximately 560,000 homes if all commitments were exercised. Even though only about $6 billion mortgages were delivered in 1975, the 200,000 moderately priced homes that could be financed at an average mortgage amount of around $30,000 would represent almost one-quarter of the approximately 850,000 single-family home completions registered in 1975. Hence, tandem mortgages were made available in 1975 to about half of all home buyers who qualified under the value limit in the lower-priced half of the market, and rationing is likely to have occurred in some areas.

The effective level of the tandem rate is estimated to have been about 86 basis points below market on the average.† With a market rate of around 9.5 percent, this represents a 9 percent reduction in interest rates. Preferred estimates of the interest elasticity of demand for single-family starts are -1.3 and -1.4. Less clearly identified estimates of the mortgage interest rate elasticity of starts reported in the literature range from -0.6 to -2.8.[2] The 9 percent reduction in interest rates on moderately priced homes, therefore, may

---

*Profiles for the GNMA conventional home mortgage program 30 conducted through FHLMC have been developed for $0.8 billion mortgages purchased under this program up to December 16, 1975. The average annual income of mortgagors was $21,516, with more than 40 percent reporting incomes above this amount. The average loan amount was $34,145, the average down payment was $8,347 (excluding invalid observations), and the average purchase price $42,720. The income and down payment data suggest that the program was not focused on marginal borrowers.

†The $699 million interest saving to mortgagors is divided by $11.5 billion mortgage deliveries to yield a subsidization percentage of 6.08 points on average. At interest rates of around 9.5 percent and with prepayment of mortgages after 12 years, a basis point reduction in the interest rate produces about a 0.071 point discount. Hence, a rate reduction of 86 basis points is equivalent to a discount of 6.08 percent.

raise the level of starts by from 6 to 30 percent, but with 13 to 14 percent, corresponding to an elasticity of about -1.35, considered most likely. Hence, only around 50,000 of the 380,000 moderately priced single-family homes expected to be financed under the tandem programs described in this chapter might not have been sold without tandem. For the other 86 or 87 percent of tandem-supported buyers, subsidies are intramarginal and benefits are estimated correctly by the present value of the interest savings and not by a somewhat smaller sum.*

Tandem authorizations may also raise starts from the supply side. They may, for instance, lower the concern of mortgagees about becoming overcommitted, because they can sell mortgages to GNMA if necessary. Thus, lenders may be less hesitant to extend new loan commitments when their liquidity is low. SLAs, however, chose to increase their liquid asset ratio to over 10 percent in the spring of 1975—the highest in two years and about four percentage points above required levels—in spite of the availability of tandem programs for conventional mortgages. Other mortgage lenders were equally cautious. Hence, there is no evidence that the tandem programs had any demonstrable effect in reducing the amount of excess liquidity desired.

Other supply effects are more probable. Mortgage purchases under the tandem program can raise the supply of funds in the mortgage market directly if government agencies borrow from nontraditional sources. If FHLMC borrows $1.6 billion from the Treasury to purchase all mortgages delivered under the May 10, 1974 program and if FNMA manages to borrow as much as $4.4 billion under EHPA from sources other than the thrifts and commercial banks, a maximum of $6 billion will have been raised from creditors who do not normally invest in mortgages. Even if this entire amount represented a net addition to funds in the mortgage market and had the same effect on starts as a $6 billion increase in the savings capital of the thrift institutions, only about 50,000 starts would be added on this score.[3] Since the increase in the quantity of mortgage credit demanded will be effective in the mortgage market as a whole only if there is a matching increase in the quantity supplied, a crude estimate of the total effect on annual starts from the tandem programs is 50,000 units, or about one additional start per $230,000 of tandem purchases, if the supply and demand assumptions used in this conjecture are correct.

In a dynamic context, the effect could for a while be greater, as there may be more buying of homes now rather than later if subsidized rates for the lower-priced segment of the mortgage market are ex-

---

*The gain in consumer surplus is less than the product of rate reduction and the amount of credit if mortgagors would not have demanded less credit at market rates.

pected to be temporary and market rates are not expected to fall. In addition, an unusually large proportion of any additional flow of funds into the mortgage market may be committed to new home mortgages if the demand for existing homes is not raised by the tandem programs. The additional starts induced by tandem could then be greater than estimated, but probably not much greater.[4]

SUMMARY AND QUALIFICATIONS

The principal benefit derived from tandem programs lies in the interest savings to mortgagors. Assuming that effective mortgage interest rates will stabilize at 9 1/4 percent in the first half of 1976, the present value of interest savings to mortgagors was estimated to amount to around $700 million in relation to the $11.5 billion tandem commitments expected to be taken up.

It was also estimated that 86 to 87 percent of the mortgagors involved in tandem would have demanded new home mortgages in the absence of the tandem programs at the prevailing market rate. However, if no new sources of mortgage funds were tapped in the course of financing the tandem purchases, some unsubsidized borrowers would have to be crowded out through a rise in the market rate to the extent subsidized borrowers who were previously below the margin now add to the total quantity of credit demanded. Conversely, if new funds were injected into the mortgage market through tandem in sufficient volume, the rate on unsubsidized mortgages might fall as more additional funds are supplied than are demanded by the previously submarginal borrowers whose demand for mortgage credit is made effective through subsidies. In the special case where the increased supply of new home mortgage credit just matched the increased demand at the market rate that would have prevailed without tandem, only about 50,000 new housing starts were estimated to result from the tandem programs authorized from January 1974 through June 1975.

Figure 14.1 helps explain how the estimates of both transfers and housing starts depend on the supply-demand assumptions that were made. Without tandem, the equilibrium level of the mortgage interest rate would be r and the amount of mortgage credit provided per period would be OC. Making D'D of tandem mortgages available and selecting beneficiaries at random from among all those demanding credit at the subsidized rate, r_s, means that the fraction $D'D/r_sD$ of all mortgagors demanding credit at any market rate of no less than r_s receive interest-subsidized tandem mortgages, with the remaining demand satisfied in the unassisted private market along D'd. However, D'd is not the demand schedule relevant for determining the market rate facing unassisted borrowers and private lenders, as the

FIGURE 14.1 Mortgage Credit Supply and Demand with Random Selection of Subsidy Recipients

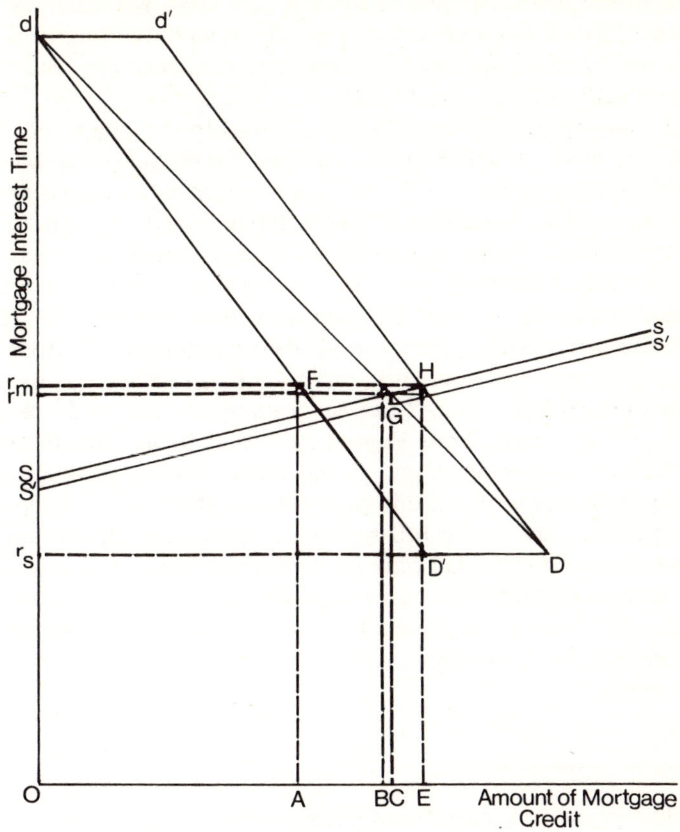

total demand for credit is obtained by adding in the quantity directed to the subsidized borrowers, d'D. Hence, assuming no new sources of funds are tapped by the tandem financing operations,* the intersec-

---

*If it is assumed that little or no financing of GNMA and FHLMC purchases is provided from outside the mortgage lending industry, mortgage originators exchange indirect for direct holdings of mortgages, as interests in GNMA pools, guaranteed mortgage certificates, and related participation devices tend to be sold back to the industry. Outside suppliers of funds, such as pension funds and life insurance companies, have taken large positions only sporadically when interest rate differentials favored investment in mortgage-backed securities.

tion of Dd' with the original supply schedule Ss determines the rate for the unsubsidized borrowers, who demand credit of OA out of a total of OE, where AE equals D'D. At the rate r_m, unsubsidized borrowers would have lost and lenders would have gained,* as indicated by the consumer and producer surplus areas extending to the right of $r_m r$ to the intersection with D'd and Ss, respectively, Subsidized borrowers would have gained FGDD'.

If the supply schedule is now shifted to the right, as assumed in the special case on which the numerical estimates were based,† and the shift to S's' happens to be such as to lead back to the original rate r, the welfare positions of both lenders and unsubsidized borrowers are the same as without tandem, and subsidized borrowers again obtain the gain indicated by FGDD'. In estimating the benefits to mortgagors for the special case examined in this chapter, the area FGDD' was approximated by the slightly larger area FHDD'.‡ The small percentage of previously submarginal borrowers among those who obtain tandem-assisted credit is shown by the ratio of GH to FH.

It is also clear from Figure 14.1 that if the supply schedule were shifted farther down and to the right, the distribution of benefits would again become more complex than in the special case assumed, as the market rate would fall below r. Both subsidized and unsubsidized borrowers would gain and private mortgage lenders would lose. Hence, the results reported here represent a first attempt to quantify the distribution of benefits conferred by the new tandem programs under highly simplified conditions.

---

*The gains to mortgagees discussed earlier are of an entirely different origin, as they would arise only in the transition from disequilibrium during which tandem programs may reduce the cost of portfolio adjustment; they are not derived in the static framework used here.

†If GNMA and FHLMC purchases of extended tandem mortgages are financed in part by selling securities to the Treasury, to the Federal Financing Bank, or to other nontraditional lenders, more funds will be channeled into the mortgage market. Although additional borrowing by the U.S. government or its sponsored credit agencies puts upward pressure on money market rates and draws some savings out of the thrift institutions at given Regulation Q ceiling rates, complete offset within the mortgage market is extremely implausible.

‡If GH is between 13 and 14 percent of FH, as previously estimated, FHDD' exceeds FGDD' by about 7 percent, reducing the cash equivalent benefit to mortgagors from about $700 million to $650 million.

NOTES

1. In all of 1974, FNMA accepted $3 billion of commitments to purchase FHA/VA and conventional home mortgages. For a discussion of the interplay between demand (offers received) and supply (offers accepted) factors in determining the FNMA commitment rates, see Kaufman [6].

2. With tandem funds rationed, the ratio of marginal to intramarginal borrowers would not change if borrowers are selected at random from among all those who demand credit at subsidized rates, even though the total amount of commitments is less than the demand. Hence, use of the interest rate elasticities remains justified to determine the percentage of tandem-supported borrowers likely to be marginal. See Kearl et al. [5] for an excellent review and critique of available estimates.

3. In previous work, a rise in savings flow to all operating savings and loan associations of $3 billion per half year was estimated to raise the annual rate of starts by approximately 3/PBO times 30,000 initially, where PBO is the Boeckh construction cost-price index for residences (1967 = 1). See von Furstenberg and Herr [3, pp. 138-40]. Since PBO is 1.8 in 1975, around 50,000 additional housing starts would be expected from a $6 billion inflow. For a discussion of how increased savings flow feeds through to housing starts, see Fair [1, p. 80], Jaffe [4, p. 176], and Fromm and Sinai [2].

4. Other researchers found that the demand for housing is raised by 30,000 units per billion dollars of older tandem commitments for the steeply subsidized Sections 235, 236, and 221(d)(3) mortgages, but by only 3,000 VA units per billion of unsubsidized commitments. Unsubsidized commitments did not measurably increase the demand for FHA starts. Moreover, negative housing supply responses reduced the effect of increased demand on starts in some cases. See Taylor [7].

REFERENCES

[1] Fair, Ray C. "Monthly Housing Starts." In National Housing Models. Edited by R. Bruce Ricks, pp. 69-84. Lexington, Mass.: Lexington Books, Heath, 1973.

[2] Fromm, Gary, and Allen Sinai. "A Policy Simulation Model of Deposit Flows, Mortgage Sector Activity, and Housing." Paper presented at the Econometric Society meetings, San Francisco, December 27-30, 1974.

[3] von Furstenberg, George M., and Eric B. Herr. "The Normal Demand for Housing Completions and the Stock Adjustment Pro-

cess in Housing Starts." Journal of Economics and Business 27 (Winter 1975):131-40.

[4] Jaffee, Dwight M. "An Econometric Model of the Mortgage Market." In Savings Deposits, Mortgages and Housing. Edited by Edward M. Gramlich and Dwight M. Jaffee, pp. 139-208. Lexington, Mass.: Lexington Books, Heath, 1972.

[5] Kearl, J. K. Rosen, and C. Swan. "Relationships between the Mortgage Instruments, the Demand for Housing and Mortgage Credit: A Review of Empirical Studies." In New Mortgage Designs for Stable Housing in an Inflationary Environment. Edited by F. Modigliani and D. R. Lessard, pp. 93-109. Federal Reserve Bank of Boston Conference Series no. 14. Boston: Federal Reserve Bank of Boston, 1975.

[6] Kaufman, Herbert M. "The Role of FNMA in the Mortgage Market." Paper presented at the Western Economic Association meetings, San Diego, Calif., June 25-28, 1975.

[7] Taylor, R. Frederick, and Ronald Utt. "A Study of the Impact of the Government National Mortgage Association's Tandem Plan on Housing Production." Prepared for the Office of Program Analysis and Evaluation, U.S. Department of Housing and Urban Development, Washington, D.C., August 1975.

15

Grant Elements Implied by Present and Proposed Tax Treatment of Income on State and Local Government Securities

PATRIC H. HENDERSHOTT
TIMOTHY W. KOCH

In 1913, Congress established a federal income tax that exempted interest on all government securities from the tax. Later legislation (1941) removed the exemption of interest earned on federal government securities but not on state and local government securities. No rationale was provided then as to why the exemption was retained for municipalities, and none has emerged since.[1]

The present tax exemption entails an implicit federal subsidy through the tax system. The magnitude of the subsidy or "tax expenditure" is the lost tax revenues to the U.S. Treasury resulting from investors receiving tax-exempt interest income. Some investors prefer tax-exempt income and are thus willing to accept lower before-tax yields on tax-exempt securities than on comparable taxable securities. Thus, the exemption lowers the borrowing costs of state and local governments (STLs) considerably below those of borrowers who issue fully taxable securities.* However, a significant portion of the total tax subsidy goes to high-income individuals and corporations. For example, it was estimated that in fiscal year 1976 the U.S. Treasury would lose $4.8 billion in tax revenues as a result of the exemption. Of this, $3.5 billion would go to STLs in the form of reduced interest payments and $1.3 billion would be retained by high-income investors [8]. Critics thus claim that the exemption is inefficient (only part of the subsidy goes to STLs) and inequitable (it reduces the progressivity of the federal income tax). Various structural changes have been proposed to increase the efficiency and equity of the subsidy. The proposals also have been stimulated by a desire of some to increase the size of the subsidy to STLs. The two most

---

*State and local governments include the various states, the District of Columbia, U.S. territories, and their political subdivisions. Tax-exempt securities are the debt instruments issued or guaranteed by these government units.

prominent proposals are a taxable bond option for STLs with a fraction of the interest cost paid by the federal government and the elimination of the tax exemption on income from various types of currently tax-exempt securities.

The present analysis attempts to identify and measure the subsidies both in the current tax treatment of the income on STL securities and implied by adoption of the alternative proposals. As a framework for this analysis, the behavior of the primary participants in, and the working of, the market for tax-exempt securities is discussed. Then the subsidy components and equity implications of the present tax treatment of STL securities are analyzed. Finally, the impact of proposed reforms within the tax-exempt market is examined, and a summary concludes the analysis.

THE MARKET FOR TAX-EXEMPT SECURITIES[2]

Tax-exempt debt consists of both short-term and long-term obligations issued by STLs. The short-term obligations, primarily tax warrants and housing authority and bond anticipation notes, have maturities within one year and are usually issued in anticipation of short-run revenues. As these revenues are collected, the notes are retired. (Prior to 1976, New York governments relied heavily upon short-term issues as a means of permanently financing current operating budget deficits, a practice that contributed to their eventual financial crisis.) Because most government units are legally prohibited from long-term borrowing to finance current expenditures (again New York appears to have been an exception), most long-term bonds are issued for new construction. These securities take the form of either general obligation debt secured by the "full faith, credit and taxing power" of the issuer or revenue debt secured by revenues from the facility being constructed. With general obligation bonds, issuers pledge to raise funds by whatever means necessary, including raising taxes, to meet payments on the debt. Normally, revenue bonds are not guaranteed, but typically a system of sinking funds or reserves is established to ensure investors that they will be paid.

The market for tax-exempt securities is only a small component of the private capital market where all borrowers bid for the investment dollars of various investor groups. Because of the interest exemption, yields on tax-exempt securities are lower than those on comparable taxable securities. This situation effectively limits the demand for tax-exempts to investors in relatively high tax brackets.*

*Investment income is typically exempt from state and local government taxes only on government issues in the state or locality of the investor.

Commercial banks (CBs) and property insurance companies (PINSs) subject to the full corporate income tax, as well as high-income individuals, absorb virtually all tax-exempt issues. Other investors are either tax-exempt, per se (state and local governments and pension funds), or subject to such low effective tax rates that the after-tax return on taxable securities exceeds that on tax-exempts (thrift institutions and life insurance companies).

Theimpact of tax rates on the demand for tax-exempts is best illustrated by an example. Suppose the pretax yields on tax-exempt and taxable securities of equivalent risk and maturity are 7 and 10 percent, respectively. (The ratio of yields on the highest quality 10-year STL and U.S. government bonds has averaged 0.7 over the last two decades and has varied between 0.64 and 0.78.) Firms or other investors having sufficient profits or income to be in the 50 percent tax bracket find tax-exempts yielding 2 percent more after taxes than comparable taxables, 7 to 5 percent. On the other hand, investors in the 20 percent bracket would find taxables yielding 1 percent more after taxes, 8 to 7 percent. In general, investors in marginal tax brackets less (greater) than 30 percent would find taxable (tax-exempt) securities more attractive.

Profit-maximizing CBs and PINSs should purchase taxable securities until the earned income is sufficient to cover all expected expenses and generate profits of $50,000, the earnings level at which their tax rate jumps to 48 percent, because the after-tax yield on taxable securities exceeds that on tax-exempts up to this point. All remaining funds should be invested in tax-exempts.* Thus, the demands for tax-exempts by CBs and PINSs are largely dependent on the level of their profits and vary little with changes in relative interest rates.

Because household investors are subject to a wide range of tax rates, the demand for tax-exempts by households is highly interest-sensitive. Households are indifferent between taxable and tax-exempt securities that provide equivalent after-tax returns. For example, investors with marginal tax rate t' are indifferent between taxable securities yielding $\overline{Rtx}$ and comparable tax-exempt securities yielding Rex' such that

---

*In addition to tax-exempt securities, CBs and PINSs make other tax-sheltered investments, such as purchases of equipment for leasing and the establishment of foreign operations, to take advantage of accelerated depreciation allowances and various tax credits. Households also utilize alternative tax shelters such as equities with their partially taxed capital gains and real estate with accelerated depreciation allowances. Use of these alternative tax shields reduces the demand for tax-exempts.

$$Rex' = (1 - t')\overline{Rtx}$$

Given Rex' and $\overline{Rtx}$, households in marginal tax brackets greater (lower) than t' find tax-exempts (taxables) offering a higher after-tax return. As the tax-exempt rate rises relative to the taxable rate, the demand for tax-exempts by households rises as investors in successively lower tax brackets find tax-exempts yielding more than taxables. When CBs and PINSs invest little because of low profits, STLs attract funds from households by offering higher tax-exempt rates that appeal to a greater number of individual investors.

Participation in the tax-exempt market during the last five years can be reasonably divided into three intervals. Table 15.1 presents relevant data for the years 1972-73, 1974-75, and 1976. The profits of CBs and PINSs were substantial in 1972 and 1973. As a result, they absorbed over two-thirds of the net issues, while households purchased less than one-third. The 1973-75 recession altered the situation drastically. Increases in loan losses and property insurance claims cut profits of both CBs and PINSs and they bought only 30 percent of net issues. Tax-exempt rates rose relative to taxable rates, inducing households to absorb over 50 percent of net issues. Net purchases by other investors exceeded $5 billion in 1975 and in 1976. This appears to be almost entirely owing to investment by public and private institutions in New York issues as part of the "solution" to the New York financial crisis. During 1976, CB profits continued to be adversely affected by large loan losses, while PINS profits increased substantially owing to smaller claims and higher policy premiums. As a result, CB tax-exempt purchases as a proportion of net issues dropped further to 13 percent and PINS purchases rose to 21 percent. The net increase in purchases of these sectors and "other investors" lowered tax-exempt interest rates relative to taxable rates, discouraging household purchases.

The behavior of investors within the tax-exempt market can be best characterized through a diagrammatic analysis. Figure 15.1 represents the market for homogeneous tax-exempt securities. For simplicity, it is assumed that the supply of tax-exempt securities (S) is independent of the tax-exempt rate (Rex) and that the comparable taxable rate ($\overline{Rtx}$) is fixed. The demand for tax-exempt securities rises as tax-exempt rates rise relative to taxable rates because investors in successively lower tax brackets find tax-exempts attractive. In equilibrium, the after-tax returns on tax-exempts and taxables are equal for the marginal investors, so that

$$Rex^* = (1 - t^*)\overline{Rtx}$$

TABLE 15.1

Flow of Funds within the Market for Tax-Exempt Securities
(billions of dollars)

	1972-73	Proportion	1974-75	Proportion	1976[a]	Proportion
Commercial banks	12.9	0.41	7.2	0.19	2.4	0.13
Property insurance companies	8.4	0.26	4.3	0.12	3.8	0.21
Households	9.4	0.30	19.9	0.54	7.2	0.40
Other investors	1.0	0.03	5.5	0.15	4.8	0.26
Total	31.7	1.00	36.9	1.00	18.2	1.00
(Rex/Rtx)[b]	—	0.66	—	0.72	—	0.64

[a]First three quarters of 1976, at seasonally adjusted annual rate.

[b]Yields on ten-year maturity low-risk bonds.

Sources: Quantity data from the Federal Reserve Flow of Funds Accounts; yield data from Solomon Brothers and Hutzler.

where Rex* is the present tax-exempt rate and t* is the marginal tax rate of investors who are indifferent between taxable and tax-exempt bonds.

The shape of the demand curve depends on the effective tax rates of purchasers of tax-exempts. At the end of 1975, commercial banks and property insurance companies held almost 60 percent of the tax-exempts outstanding and the noninterest-sensitive other investors held 8 percent. Table 15.2 provides data pertaining to the tax brackets of households that held the remaining issues.[3] As one would expect, household tax-exempt holdings are concentrated among those investors subject to the highest marginal tax rates. Almost 70 percent are held by individuals in tax brackets higher than 50 percent. The demand curve in Figure 15.1 is representative of these data. Segment I refers to the demand from individuals in marginal income tax brackets greater than 48 percent. The initial vertical portion indicates the demand of investors in the maximum 70 percent tax bracket; these investors are indifferent between taxables and tax-

FIGURE 15.1 The Market for Tax-Exempt Securities

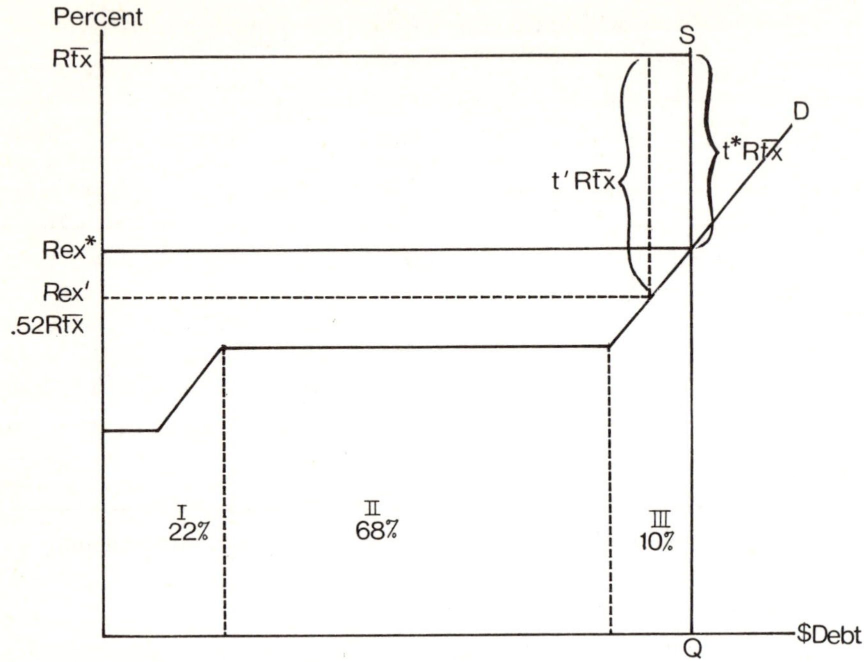

exempts when Rex = 0.3 Rtx. Segment II represents the major portion of tax-exempt demand, that by fully taxed firms and other investors. When Rex = 0.52 Rtx, these investors are indifferent. Finally, households with effective tax rates lower than 48 percent are included in Segment III.* The percentage of the outstanding stock demanded by the different classes of investors is given beneath each segment.

---

*The fact that households in tax brackets below 0.30 hold as much as $10 billion in tax-exempts has been interpreted by some as implying "irrational" behavior. There are four alternative explanations. First, the tax-exempts may have been purchased when tax-exempt yields were high relative to taxables (at some times it has been profitable for households in the 0.23 bracket to purchase exempts). Second, state and local units exempt the interest of their own issues from their own taxes. New York residents in the 0.20 bracket occasionally have found tax-exempts earning an after-tax yield exceeding that on taxables. Third, the household may have had temporarily low income when the survey was taken. Over the life of the tax-exempt they may have an average tax rate well over 0.30. Fourth, households may have overestimated their future income when they purchased the tax-exempt.

TABLE 15.2

Distribution of Household Tax-Exempt Purchases by Marginal Federal Income Tax Rate

Tax Bracket (percent)	Percentage of Interest Received	Relative Proportion of Total Issues
14-20	4.7	1.50
21-30	10.5	3.36
31-40	9.1	2.91
41-50	6.3	2.02
51-60	31.8	10.18
61-70	37.6	12.03
Total	100.0	32.00

Source: Compiled by the author.

In order to illustrate the operation of the tax-exempt market, consider what happens to the tax-exempt rate if CB or PINS profits increase or if personal income tax rates are lowered uniformly. A rise in profits increases the need for tax-sheltered income, thereby raising the demand for tax-exempts. Diagrammatically, Segment II of the demand curve in Figure 15.1 lengthens, effectively shifting the interest elastic portion of the demand curve (Segment III) out and lowering the tax-exempt yield. A reduction in all marginal tax rates moves some households from tax brackets above 48 percent (Segment I) to below 48 percent (Segment III). This is tantamount to a shift of the entire demand curve to the left, and it raises tax-exempt yields.

GRANTS IN THE PRESENT TREATMENT

The tax exemption of STL interest payments contains two elements of federal subsidy through the loss of tax revenues to the U.S. Treasury. First, the cost of borrowing is lower for issuers of tax-exempt securities, because tax-exempt interest rates are lower than rates on comparable taxable securities. Second, high-tax-bracket investors receive a partial windfall return from purchasing tax-exempts because the after-tax yield on tax-exempts exceeds the yield at which they are indifferent between comparable fully taxed and tax-exempt securities. The source of each subsidy component is revealed in Figure 15.2.[4] The market-clearing tax-exempt rate and quantity are Rex* and Q, respectively. Because STL borrowing costs are

FIGURE 15.2 The Subsidy Components in the Present Treatment of Tax-Exempt Securities

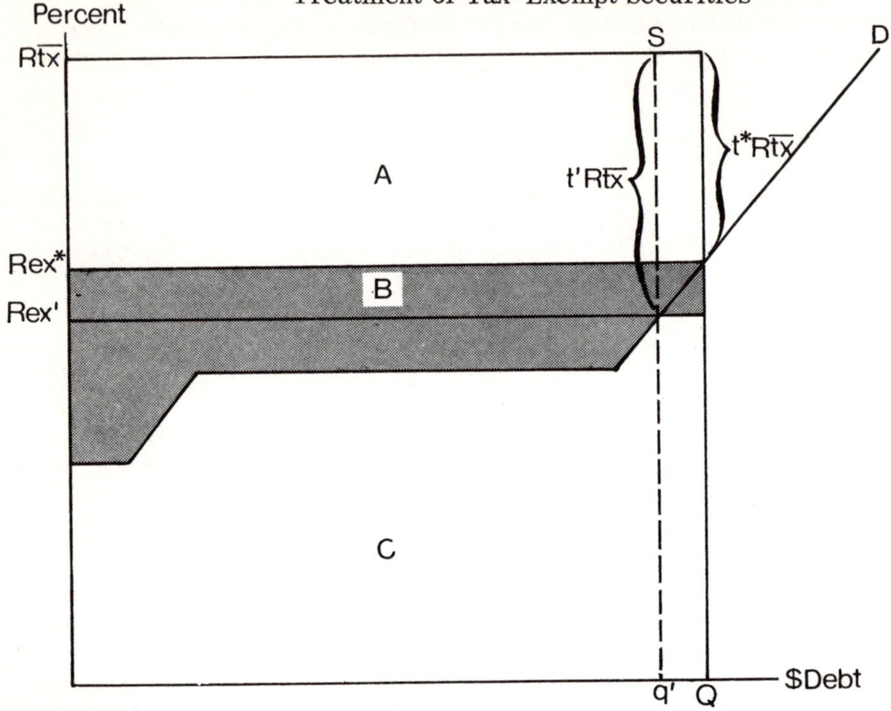

t*$R\overline{tx}$ lower than those of issuers of taxable securities, the shaded area A represents the aggregate interest savings to STLs resulting from the tax exemption and the sum of areas B and C represents aggregate STL interest payments. Investors in tax brackets higher than t* receive windfall gains from purchasing tax-exempts because the market-determined tax-exempt yield is greater than that needed to induce them into the market. An investor with tax rate t' (t' > t*), for example, receives a windfall return on each dollar invested equal to Rex* - Rex'.

Aggregating across all marginal tax rates greater than t*, one finds that area B represents the total windfall return to high marginal tax bracket investors and the sum of areas A and B represents the loss of tax revenues to the U.S. Treasury. Two implications are clear. The higher the market-clearing tax-exempt rate is relative to the comparable taxable rate (the lower t* is), the lower the interest savings to STLs is and the greater the windfall return for all investors. That is, the efficiency of the tax exemption declines with increases in the interest rate ratio. Similarly, the higher an investor's marginal tax rate is, the great his windfall return is.

The subsidy to high-income investors is clearly inequitable. It is incorrect, however, to argue that high-income investors use tax-exempt securities to avoid all tax. To the extent that tax-exempt interest rates are lower than taxable rates on comparable securities, investors pay an implicit tax, the benefits of which accrue directly to the issuer in the form of lower interest costs. The implicit tax rate for all investors is t*, the marginal investor's tax rate, because this is the percentage by which Rex falls short of Rtx. Returning to the example where the risk equivalent tax-exempt and taxable yields equal 7 and 10 percent, respectively, an institution in a 50 percent marginal tax bracket will earn a windfall of 2 percent (7 percent less the 5 percent after-tax yield on taxable securities). The windfall is not 5 percent, the return on taxable securities he avoided paying in taxes, because he accepted a 3 percent reduction in his rate of return by purchasing the tax-exempt security. The issuer of the security is the beneficiary of this 3 percent, or the difference between the 5 percent the investor avoided and his 2 percent windfall.

The exact magnitude and proportionate distribution of the subsidy to various investor groups is not known. Among other things, it depends upon the availability and distribution of alternative tax shelters among investors (see footnote on page 269). The more that present holders of tax-exempts would shift to alternative sources of tax-sheltered investment income, the less would removal of the exemption increase tax revenues of the Treasury. The impact of the subsidy also depends on how taxable interest rates would respond to removal of the interest exemption. To the extent that current investors utilize other tax shields, the demand for taxable securities will rise proportionately less than the supply, forcing taxable interest rates and Treasury revenues higher. On the other hand, to the extent that STL construction outlays financed by debt issues are sensitive to interest costs, removal of the exemption would, by raising these costs, reduce STL issues, and the demand for taxable securities would rise more than the supply, lowering taxable rates and Treasury revenues.

The direction of change in the taxable rate is thus uncertain. In the calculations of a distribution of the windfall income to commercial banks, property insurance companies, and households, investors are assumed to have no alternative sources of tax-sheltered income and taxable interest rates are assumed to be the same in the absence of the exemption as in its presence. These assumptions allow utilization of the average marginal tax rates of current holders of tax-exempts and reported taxable yields in the calculations. Because some investors will, in fact, shift to other tax shelters, the estimates will be biased upward.

One possible distribution of the 1975 windfall income to different investors is presented in Table 15.3. In terms of the notation in Figure 15.2, the windfall income to investors with marginal tax rate t' is

$$(t' - t^*)Rtx^{p}q'$$

TABLE 15.3

A Possible Distribution of Windfalls Owing to the Interest Exemption (billions of dollars)

	t'	t^*	Rtx^p	q'	Windfall $(t' - t^*)Rtx^pq'$	Efficiency t^*/t'
Commercial banks	0.48	0.36[a]	0.056	102.8	0.69	0.75
Property insurance companies	0.48	0.34	0.067	34.3	0.32	0.71
Households						
Medium incomes ($t'<0.34$)	0.24[b]	0.34	0.07	14.5	-0.10	1.42
Medium high incomes ($0.34 \leq t' \leq 0.5$)	0.42[c]	0.34	0.07	8.0	0.04	0.81
Very high incomes ($t'>0.5$)	0.60[d]	0.34	0.07	51.3	0.93	0.57
Nonfinancial corporations	0.48	0.34	0.07	4.5	0.04	0.71
Other	0.10[e]	0.34	0.07	15.1	-0.25	3.40
Total				230.5	1.67	0.75[f]

[a]Weighted average of 0.34, t^* for longs, and 0.42, t^* for shorts (see footnote on page 275 for further explanation), where the weight attached to 0.42 is the ratio at the end of 1975 of the quantity of shorts outstanding to the holdings of CBs.

[b]Average of 0.14 and 0.34.

[c]Average of 0.34 and 0.50.

[d]Average of 0.50 and 0.70.

[e]Average of 0.00 and 0.20.

[f]Average efficiency ratio calculated as $\sum_i (t^*q'Rtx^p)_i / \sum_i (t'q'Rtx^p)_i$.

<u>Source:</u> Compiled by the authors.

where t* is the implicit tax rate paid in 1975 by holders of tax-exempts,* q' is the holdings at the end of 1975, and Rtx^p is the average taxable rate earned on the portfolio of taxables held by the sector.† Values of these variables are given in Table 15.3. The final column is a measure of the efficiency of the exemption, t*/t'. The closer this ratio is to unity, the less is the windfall per dollar of interest earned and the more efficient is the exemption.

The data in Table 15.3 are revealing. One might expect that commercial banks, which hold fully half of the tax-exempts of high-income investors (all sectors except medium income households and others), would receive most of the windfall gains. Instead, very high income households, with only a quarter of the securities, receive nearly half the windfall. These differences reflect the different efficiency ratios of the two sectors; tax-exempt income is worth more per dollar to these households than banks because the former are in higher tax brackets (t' = 0.60 versus 0.48) and pay a lower effective tax rate (t* = 0.34 versus 0.36). The overall efficiency ratio, a weighted average of the sector efficiency ratios, is 0.75, and the total estimated windfall is $1.66 billion.‡

THE TAXABLE BOND OPTION

In December 1975, Senator Theodore Kennedy and Representative Henry Reuss presented a bill authorizing a federal subsidy for

---

The ratio of tax-exempt to taxable interest rates rises, and thus t declines, the longer the term to maturity of the securities. The calculations in the table incorporate two values for t*, one for securities with maturity less than or equal to one year (0.42) and another for securities with maturity greater than one year (0.34). The 0.34 is an average of 0.42 and 0.30, the average ratio of long-term yields, where weights of one-third and two-thirds were applied. Because the relatively low yields on short-term tax-exempts are purportedly owing to the preferences of commercial banks, banks are assumed to hold the short terms.

†The yields for commercial banks and property insurance companies are from published sources; those for the other sectors are estimated.

‡This efficiency rate is slightly above the 0.73 implied by the data given in the Congressional Record [5] and cited earlier ($3.5 billion in STL reduced interest payments divided by $4.8 billion in lost Treasury tax revenues). The difference in estimates of the windfall, our $1.66 billion versus their $1.3 billion, is apparently owing to different assumptions regarding the level of interest payments.

STLs issuing taxable bonds equal to 40 percent of the interest costs of borrowing. Such an option supposedly would reduce the inequities of the federal income tax treatment of STL interest payments, divert most of investors' windfall gains toward lower borrowing costs for STLs, and stabilize STL borrowing rates by making them proportional to taxable rates. Earlier, the U.S. Treasury Department had proposed a similar option but with a 30 percent subsidy rate. In the following paragraphs the diagrammatic analysis is employed to demonstrate the working of a subsidized taxable bond option, and then the question of the appropriate subsidy rate is considered.

The impact of a taxable bond option on the tax-exempt market depends on the size of the subsidy rate. Let the Treasury subsidize a percentage ρ of taxable STL interest charges. Given an option, STLs will issue the type of debt that minimizes their costs. With reference to Figure 15.1, only tax-exempts will be issued if $\rho < t^*$, because the postsubsidy cost of taxable debt will be greater than that of current tax-exempt obligations. For example, suppose that the yield on taxable bonds equals 10 percent, t^* equals 0.3 and a subsidy rate of 20 percent (or 0.2) is introduced. Because the marginal investor in tax-exempts has a tax rate of 30 percent, STLs are able to place all of their debt as tax-exempts at rates equal to 70 percent of the taxable rate. If STLs issued their debt as taxable securities, the net borrowing cost would increase to 80 percent of the taxable rate or one percentage point higher per dollar of debt issued.* Tax-exempt borrowing rates would be lower than the after-subsidy taxable rates for all subsidy rates less than 30 percent. Likewise, only taxable debt will be issued if $\rho > t^m$, where t^m equals the maximum marginal tax rate of individual investors, because investors in all tax brackets will find taxable securities offering a higher after-tax return than tax-exempts. The postsubsidy cost of issuing taxable debt must be lower because the subsidy rate would exceed any possible market-determined value of t^*.

STLs will issue both types of securities if the subsidy rate is somewhere between these extremes, that is, if $t^* < \rho < t^m$. Historically, t^* has averaged near 0.3 for longer term bonds and t^m currently equals 0.7. In this case, STLs will issue the amount of tax-exempts that will equate the postsubsidy tax-exempt rate Rex^s to the cost of taxable debt to STLs:

$$Rex^s = (1 - \rho^s)\overline{Rtx}$$

*This assumes that taxable rates will not change with the introduction of a taxable bond option, a possibility examined below.

where ρ^s is the actual subsidy rate employed. To issue more tax-exempt debt would require offering a tax-exempt rate above the cost of taxable debt; to issue less tax-exempt debt would entail foregoing the opportunity of substituting less expensive tax-exempt debt for taxable debt. The actual quantity of tax-exempts issued is determined by the shape of the demand curve, that is, by the investment of those investors who still find tax-exempts attractive at the rate Rex^s.

Figure 15.3 is useful for indicating the impact of a subsidy in the range $t^* < \rho^s < t^m$ on STLs, the Treasury, and investors. S now refers to the STL supply of both tax-exempt and taxable bonds; D still denotes the demand for tax-exempt securities only. The introduction of the taxable bond option lowers the cost of borrowing for STLs from Rex* to Rex^s. At this interest rate, Q_1 of STL debt will be issued as tax-exempts and $Q - Q_1$ as subsidized taxables. Investors with marginal tax rates less than ρ^s will find taxable STL bonds offering a higher after-tax return. Only investors with tax rates greater than ρ^s will purchase tax-exempts. Both the size and proportionate distribution of the total federal subsidy (tax revenue foregone plus explicit interest payments to holders of STL taxable debt) are changed.

Before the option, the lost tax revenues to the Treasury were represented by A + B, of which STLs received A and high-income investors received B. With the option, the net Treasury costs will increase by an amount represented by C_2, the difference between the cost of the interest payments $[\rho^s \overline{Rtx}\,(Q - Q_1)]$, which equals area $A_2 + B_2 + C_2$, and the increased tax revenues, area $A_2 + B_2$, on new taxable debt. Because investors who drop out of the tax-exempt market are in tax brackets less than or equal to that of the new marginal investor in tax-exempts, the average tax rate of investors in new taxable STL bonds is less than the subsidy rate and thus increased tax receipts will be insufficient to cover the new direct subsidy costs. In addition to receiving this increase in federal costs, C_2, STLs also capture $B_1 + B_2$ of the windfall interest income that previously accrued to high-tax investors. Previous tax-exempt investors in tax brackets less than ρ^s would shift out of tax-exempts, losing any windfall they had, and the windfall interest income of higher tax bracket investors would fall by $\rho^s - t^*$ per dollar invested.

The higher the subsidy rate, the greater is the increase in federal costs (area C_2) and the lower are STL borrowing costs (Rex^s) and the windfall to high-tax-bracket investors (area B_3). The use of a high (0.4 to 0.5) versus a low (0.3 to 0.35) subsidy rate would thus appear to be simply a question of trading off the cost to the Treasury (federal taxpayers) against the gain in efficiency and equity, the shift of $B_1 + B_2$ from investors in high-tax brackets to STL governments (taxpayers). Given the size of C_2 vis-a-vis $B_1 + B_2$, the cost would

FIGURE 15.3 Market for STL Debt with Subsidized Taxable Bonds

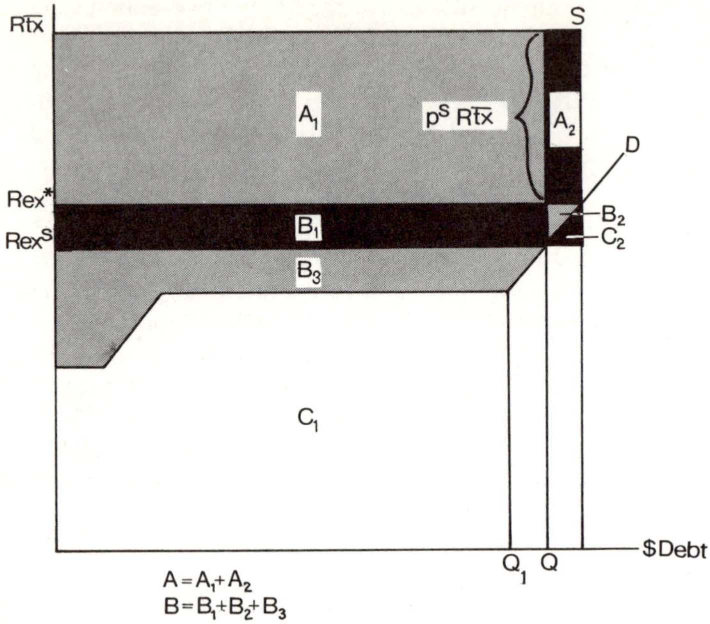

appear to be well worth it. Moreover, because the gain to STLs, $B_1 + B_2 + C_3$, far exceeds the cost to the federal government, C_2, STLs ought to be willing to compensate the federal government. This could be achieved by cutting back slightly on revenue sharing.* Regrettably, the matter is not so simple. First, the above analysis probably understates the costs to the Treasury by a significant amount. Second, undesirable allocative effects will likely result from a high subsidy rate. That is, efficiency in a federal subsidy will be gained at the expense of a loss in overall economic efficiency.

The understatement of federal costs follows from two above-noted assumptions underlying the diagrammatic presentation. Tax shelters other than STL tax-exempt debt do exist and will be at least partially utilized by investors. Thus, the Treasury will collect something less than $A_2 + B_2$ in added tax revenues, raising its net cost.

---

*This method of financing, while not causing a shift of resources from federal taxpayers to STLs (and their citizenry), would entail a shift among STLs. Those with high debt relative to revenue-sharing funds would gain at the expense of those with relatively low debt.

Moreover, the reduction in the borrowing costs of STLs will likely raise the supply of STL debt (the supply curve in Figure 15.3 would be downward sloping, rather than vertical, to the extent that the STL construction outlays financed by debt issues are sensitive to interest costs). The increased debt, all of which will be taxable, will raise the Treasury's direct subsidy outlays. Moreover, this increase in debt implies an increase in the total supply of securities in the economy. Given an unchanged demand, interest rates in general will rise. This will increase federal direct subsidy costs (recall that the subsidy is proportional to the yield on taxable securities); it will also increase the interest cost on existing Treasury debt.

This brings us to the allocative effects. A high subsidy option lowers STL borrowing costs and, to the extent that STL debt issues are interest-sensitive, raises the borrowing costs of other sectors, including households and businesses. This implies a shift in the structure of the capital stock of the economy away from housing and business plant and equipment toward state and local capital. Given that the rationale for the current subsidy of STL capital outlays via the tax exemption of the interest on their debt is questionable, further subsidization would almost certainly lead to a less efficient distribution of the capital stock.

The present tax-exempt subsidy is both inefficient and inequitable. A high subsidy rate taxable bond option would increase the efficiency and equity of the exemption, but possibly at a significant cost to the Treasury (taxpayers) and to the efficiency of the economy. A low subsidy rate option would still prevent STL borrowing costs from rising relative to those of other sectors (and STL costs historically have done so during credit crunches) and would thus probably be desirable. But such an option would have a negligible impact on the efficiency and equity of the present exemption.

The optimal solution would seem to be a combination of removal of the tax-exempt status on STL debt and a low ($\rho = 0.3$ to 0.35) subsidy rate. This would not affect STL borrowing costs, and it would eliminate the windfall income (transfer it to the Treasury) of investors in tax exempts.* A major drawback with mandatory subsidized taxable debt from the STLs' viewpoint is that it would then be a relatively simple matter for the federal government either to make the subsidy contingent on particular behavior of STLs or to reduce the subsidy rate.

---

*To the extent that investors purchase alternative tax-sheltered assets, something less than all of the windfall income would be transferred to the Treasury.

ELIMINATION OF THE EXEMPTION FOR POLLUTION CONTROL BONDS

Since 1936, tax-exempt securities known as industrial revenue bonds have been used to finance investment by nonfinancial corporations. Initially, these securities were issued solely as an inducement for firms to locate within the issuing government's jurisdiction. States would use the proceeds of an issue to build facilities designed according to a corporation's specifications and make payments on the debt out of lease-rental revenues obtained from the firm. Because of rising tax-exempt interest rates and a concern over lost tax revenues to the U.S. Treasury resulting from large-scale use of industrial revenue bonds in the late 1960s, Congress removed the tax exemption on most of these issues in 1968. Exceptions included industrial revenue bonds issued for investment in public sports facilities, docks and wharves, pollution control facilities, and other such "socially desirable" goods.

Because Congress subsequently mandated pollution control outlays for firms, the bulk of the recent upsurge in tax-exempt borrowing for nongovernment purposes has involved pollution control bonds.* Under existing regulations, these bonds are issued by state and local government agencies with the debt service costs secured by revenues obtained from the private user of the facilities financed. Thus, they effectively represent debt of private corporations. Since 1973, reported issues for pollution control by nonfinancial corporations have accounted for between 10 and 15 percent of total net tax-exempt issues. Equivalent amounts have been reputedly issued (privately placed) but not recorded [7].

The question as to whether corporate investment in federally mandated facilities should be subsidized is somewhat complicated. The granting of a subsidy to firms (indirectly to consumers who purchase the goods produced by the firms) for not polluting the environment lowers the cost of production below the true economic cost and thus leads to an inefficient allocation of resources. As such, any subsidy is inappropriate. On the other hand, there is a tradition in the United States founded on equity considerations that new or revised federal tax regulations should not impose costs on taxpayers retroactively. On these grounds corporate investment in pollution control facilities for plants already in operation should be subsidized.

---

*During the early 1970s, Congress passed the Federal Water Pollution Control Act and Clean Air Act, which required firms either to utilize the best pollution control technology available or to cease operation.

The use of tax exemption to lower borrowing costs as the subsidy vehicle is another question. The increased supply of tax-exempt securities resulting from borrowing for pollution control purposes raises borrowing costs for all tax-exempt issuers and enables high-income investors to receive ever larger windfall returns from holding tax-exempts.[5] The optimal solution here appears to be to remove the exemption on all pollution control (industrial revenue) bonds and to use direct transfers to subsidize corporate expenses attributable to pollution control requirements on existing facilities.

Figure 15.3 is useful for indicating the impact of the removal of the exemption on pollution control bonds. Suppose that Rex* represents the initial equilibrium tax-exempt yield and Rex^s the equilibrium yield after the exemption is eliminated. The stock of pollution control bonds was $Q - Q_1$, so that removing the exemption on them reduces the stock of tax-exempts to Q_1. As was the case with the taxable bond option, the efficiency and equity of the subsidy via the tax exemption of interest are improved. STLs gain B_1 and the federal government gains B_2 from high-tax investors. It also gains A_2 from other investors. Because A_2 equals the savings nonfinancial corporations previously gained from the exemption, the Treasury's gain is more than enough to finance a direct transfer to nonfinancial corporations of magnitude equal to the former indirect subsidy.

SUMMARY

The exemption of interest payments on STL securities from the federal income tax has long been recognized as a major federal subsidy with part of the benefits accruing to STLs in the form of lower borrowing costs and the remainder going to high-tax-bracket investors as windfall income. In this analysis, the subsidy components are derived and an approximate distribution of current tax-exempt windfall income among commercial banks, property insurance companies, and high-income households is calculated. Assuming these investors have no alternative tax-sheltered investments, individuals with marginal tax rates greater than 50 percent receive over half the total windfall, even though they hold less than 25 percent of all tax-exempt securities.

A subsidized taxable bond option, whereby STLs would issue taxable bonds and the federal government would pay a proportion of the interest, is being considered as a means of increasing the efficiency and equity of the tax exemption. The option would indeed achieve this goal, and the higher the subsidy, the greater would be the efficiency and equity. However, the greater the subsidy, the greater the cost to the Treasury and the lower the borrowing costs of

STLs relative to households and businesses. Given that the rationale for STLs currently borrowing at only 70 percent of the market rate of interest is unclear, further reductions in STL borrowing rates would almost certainly lead to a less efficient (productive) distribution of the capital stock. The optimal economic solution would appear to be mandatory subsidized STL debt with a subsidy rate of 30 percent. This would not lower STL borrowing costs further at the expense of households and firms, and it would eliminate the windfall income of current investors in tax-exempts (transfer it to the Treasury, thereby lowering net Treasury costs). If this is not politically feasible, then a one-third subsidy is advocated. This would ensure that all investors in tax-exempts pay at least a 33 percent implicit tax, and it would prevent STL borrowing costs from rising relative to those of other sectors both over the long term and over the interest rate cycle.

Tax exemption has been used to lower the borrowing costs of firms investing in pollution control equipment, as well as of STLs. This seems inappropriate on two grounds. First, the prices of all goods and services should fully reflect all costs, including those to prevent pollution of the environment. No subsidy should be made, except to firms required to modify existing plant and equipment. Second, a subsidy via tax exemption is both inefficient and inequitable. The cost of this subsidy (lost Treasury tax revenue) exceeds the cost of a direct outlay of equivalent value to firms. Moreover, forcing the financing of pollution control investments through the tax-exempt market raises the borrowing costs of STLs. The optimal solution would be to eliminate the current exemption of interest income on pollution control bonds and replace this indirect subsidy with a direct outlay from the U.S. Treasury to qualifying corporations.

NOTES

1. There does not appear to be any constitutional prohibition against taxing interest on state and local debt; the Sixteenth Amendment allows for a federal tax on income from whatever source derived. Huefner [4] provides a complete discussion of the constitutional and historical background of the exemption.

2. A detailed analysis of this market is provided in Hendershott and Koch [2].

3. Galper and Peterson [1] provide these estimates based on the distribution of tax-exempt holdings by income class derived from a 1963 survey updated by Pechman and Okner [5].

4. This analysis follows Huefner [3].

5. An estimate of the increased borrowing cost is provided by Peterson and Galper [6].

REFERENCES

[1] Galper, H., and G. Peterson. "The Equity Effects of a Taxable Municipal Bond Subsidy." National Tax Journal, December 1973.

[2] Hendershott, P. H., and T. W. Koch. An Empirical Analysis for the Study of Financial Institutions. Monograph Series in Economics and Finance, Center for the Study of Financial Institutions, New York University, 1977-78.

[3] Huefner, Robert. "Municipal Bonds: The Costs and Benefits of an Alternative." National Tax Journal, December 1970.

[4] _____. Taxable Alternatives to Municipal Bonds. Boston: Federal Reserve Bank of Boston, 1972.

[5] Pechman, J., and B. Okner. "Individual Income Tax Erosion by Income Classes." The Economics of Federal Subsidy Programs. U.S., Congress, Joint Economic Committee, 92d Cong., 2d sess., 1972.

[6] Peterson, G., and Galper, H. "Tax Exempt Financing of Private Industry's Pollution Control Investment." Public Policy, Winter 1975.

[7] Simon, W. Statement on Tax Reform and Capital Formation. U.S., Congress, House, Ways and Means Committee, July 8, 1975.

[8] U.S., Congress. "Municipal Bond Market: Why It Needs Help." Congressional Record, December 17, 1975.

PART VI

Conclusion

16

Grants Economics in the Future of the Financial System

THOMAS FREDERICK WILSON
KENNETH E. BOULDING

The journey through this volume has given some overall impressions that serve as a basis for projecting the future course of grants economics in the financial system. In reflecting on the work in this volume, three accomplishments have been observed: (1) A solid foundation has been built for policy recommendations and further research; (2) obstacles line the route, but the measurement of implicit grants is by no means an utterly frustrating experience; (3) the financial system serves very poorly as an instrument for the achievement of redistributive objectives.

The nature of grants in the financial system and the distributional implications of public policies and private practices are now much clearer. The Schwartz-Whitcomb study of trade credit is extraordinarily rich in testable hypotheses; it could stimulate considerable research activity. Dunkelberg's work on consumer credit is also highly suggestive, and along with the map sketched by Scherer, could provide the framework for identifying and measuring the redistributive effects of much of the consumer protection legislation in this area. The policy debate engaging Ruebling and Havrilesky is likely to continue far into the future, but they allude to a host of inflation-induced transfers that deserve empirical inquiry. The Hendershott-Villani model and von Furstenberg's analytic procedure might be applied to assess implicit grants in the operation of other federal credit programs, and the econometric approaches conducted by Pyle and Phaup can be used to measure the effect of other regulations. These and other analytic techniques might be employed to address some of the issues discussed in the Preface and the Introduction, as well as those cited in the individual chapters. A comparative systems approach to this subject would be most fascinating. A number of policy recommendations are presented in this volume. The proposals advanced by Wilson, Cohn, Weidenbaum, and Hendershott and Koch are firmly based on their analyses.

This collection of papers appraises optimistically the measurability of implicit grants. The dollar values of such transfers are estimated in nine of the fifteen chapters; this includes those by Johnson, Wilson, Pyle, Phaup (even though the institutional grants are zero), Dunkelberg, Weidenbaum, Hendershott and Villani, von Furstenberg, and Hendershott and Koch. In some cases, however, these are partial estimates, and some of them are a little shakier than others. Moreover, the ultimate distributional impact by income classes is not always clear. Nonetheless, they do stand as concrete evidence that the estimation of implicit grants is not the futile exercise that is sometimes supposed.

The government's manipulation of the financial system to attain distributional objectives may be far less successful than is usually suspected, and it might even turn out to prove the ubiquitous presence of the principle of "implicit irony." The costs in terms of economic efficiency, moreover, may be very high. These observations are supported by most of the studies. Havrilesky and Weidenbaum are harsh critics of the government's use of the financial system as a vehicle for redistribution. Unfortunately, the political calculus still unambiguously favors the utilization of these devices.

Studies launched by students of the grants economy do eventually influence policies. The accumulation of knowledge will further strengthen the capacity for judging the wisdom of prospective changes in the structure of the financial system, as well as verifying retrospectively the distributional consequences of prevailing policies. If the grants economy expands along the growth track projected, the call for "distributional impact statements" will become increasingly urgent and the machinery for producing them will become increasingly efficient.

INDEX

adaptive expectations, 79
Alaska, 245, 247
American Bank and Trust Company v. Federal Reserve Bank of Atlanta, 44
American Finance Association, 153
Arkansas, 164, 166, 178
Articles of Confederation, 43, 44
Arzac, E., 195
automatic teller machines, 121

bad debt losses, 175, 184
Bank of England, 7-8
Bank of Japan, 13
Bank of the United States, 43
bankruptcy, 160, 174
banks (see, commercial banks)
barter, 39
bills of credit, 42, 43, 44
Boeckh construction cost price index (PBO), 264
Boulding, Kenneth E., 87, 114, 170, 204
Bowers, Patricia F., 216
branching (see, commercial banks)
brassage, 39
Brechling, F., 197-98
Briscoe v. Bank of Kentucky, 43, 44
Brookings Institution, 217
Burns, Arthur F., 72

California, 160, 166, 169, 176
Canada, 32
Canadian banks, 27
central bank, 13, 26-27, 38, 60, 72, 81, 116
certificates of deposit (CDs), 53, 88, 90, 99, 233, 235
check clearing, 119
Chicago, University of, 32
Civil War, 43
Clean Air Act, 282
Cleveland (Fourth Federal Reserve) District, 121-23, 125, 130, 131, 132, 138
Cochrane-Orcutt method, 92
commercial banks (CBs): branching, 114-15, 120-23, 126; business loan rationing, 195; consumer credit, 156, 157, 161-62, 163-64; demand deposits and credit extension, 80; deposit rate ceilings, 80, 87-100, 106-07, 235-36; discrimination by sex, 150, 153; and federal credit programs, 216-17; fractional reserves, 4-5, 41, 47; and FSCAs, 233-40; international operations, 26-27; loans, 233; mortgage lending, 80, 258-61; 100 percent reserves, 4-5, 47-48; profitability, 47-49, 120, 123, 128, 136, 139; reserve requirements, 114-20, 122-39; seigniorage, 3-4, 15-17, 27, 38-54, 60-61; tax-exempt securities, 268-69, 283
commercial paper, 53, 104, 130
Commission on Money and Credit, 216
competition in laxity, 120
Comptroller of the Currency, 118
Conference on International Monetary Problems, 40
Constitution (see, U.S. Constitution)
Constitutional Convention, 43, 44
consumer credit, 155-88, 232
corporate bonds, 104, 231-32, 233-34
correspondent banks, 119

cost-benefit analysis, 154
credit cards: consumer credit, 156, 163-66, 169, 176, 178-79, 182-87; sex discrimination by issuers, 150; technology, 74
credit crunch, 76, 281
credit rationing, 79-80, 166, 173-74, 178, 184, 195, 198, 205
credit unions, 121, 157, 161
crowding out, 75
customer-bank communications terminals (CBCTs), 121

deadbeat, 160
defaults, 160
demand deposits, 39, 45, 50, 60, 80, 119, 122, 125, 134
department stores, 150
Director, Aaron, 241
Director's law, 241
discount window (facility), 51, 119, 139
disintermediation, 88, 105
dollar diplomacy, 20
dollar imperialism, 20
Dun & Bradstreet, 196
Dunkelberg, William, 174
Durbin, J., 91
Durbin's test, 91

electronic funds transfer systems, 74
Emergency Home Purchase Act of 1974 (EHPA), 245-46
Emergency Housing Act of 1975, 247
Energy Independence Authority, 224
Energy Policy and Conservation Act, 224
England, 7
Equal Credit Opportunity (ECO) Act of 1975, 149-54, 183
Eurocurrency, 27
Eurodollar, 4, 13, 27, 233
European banks, 27
Export-Import Bank, 214, 220

Fair Credit Billing Act, 183
Farmers Home Administration, 224
Federal Deposit Insurance Corporation (FDIC), 6, 142
Federal Energy Administration, 224
Federal Financing Bank, 215, 264
federal funds, 48, 130
federal government (see, U.S. government)
Federal Home Loan Bank Board, 254
Federal Home Loan Banks (FHLBs), 109, 215, 228, 230, 231
Federal Home Loan Mortgage Corporation (FHLMC), 228, 230, 245-46, 251, 254, 255, 258-59
Federal Housing Administration (FHA), 220, 244-59
Federal National Mortgage Association (FNMA), 215, 218, 227, 228, 246, 255, 259, 261
Federal Open Market Committee, 60
Federal Reserve: discount rate, 51; earnings, 46-53, 60-61, 116; Federal Reserve Banks, 39-54, 115, 138-39; Federal Reserve Board, 13, 44-54, 153; Federal Reserve notes, 46, 61, 116; Federal Reserve System, 17, 39-54, 72, 118, 150, 218; float 50; interest rate ceiling, 50, 234-35 (see also, Regulation Q and Interest Rate Adjustment Act); monetary policy, 70-81; reserve requirements, 114-20, 122-39; reserves and monetary control, 48-52, 120, 136; seigniorage, 6, 26, 39-54, 60-61
Federal Reserve Bank of Cleveland, 121
Federal Trade Commission, 150

Federal Water Pollution Act, 282
federally sponsored credit agencies (FSCAs), 215-16, 225, 227-41
fiduciary money, 3, 5-10
finance companies, 150, 153, 156-57, 170, 183
fiscal policy, 225 (see also, U.S. government)
Fisher, Irving, 45, 52-53
floating of exchange rates, 21, 32
foreign bonds, 233
Franklin National Bank, 51
free coinage, 39
free riders, 178-79
Friedman, Milton, 52
functional cost analysis, 119
Furstenberg,George M. von, 219

General Motors (GM), 16-17
Geothermal Energy Research, Development, and Demonstration Act of 1974, 224
Germany, 4
Gold Exchange Act of 1934, 43
gold standard, 20
Government National Mortgage Association (GNMA), 218, 219, 227, 228, 230, 244-65
grant, 3-5, 16-17, 38-40, 48-54, 76, 97, 98, 99, 120, 121, 138, 165, 173
grants economics, 87, 192
Great Britain, 20
Great Depression, 104
Grubel, Herbert, 10, 40, 45

hard money, 42
Harvard University, 216
Hawaii, 245, 247
Hendershott, Patric H., 231
high-powered money, 4, 12, 39, 45, 48
housing, 79-80, 87, 97, 151-52, 211, 244-65
Housing and Urban Development (HUD): Act, 245; Department of, 245, 250
housing starts, 259-62

Illinois, 142
implicit grants, 87, 149-50
indexation, 62
inflation: anticipated, 28-29, 64, 66-68, 74-75, 77-78, 105-06; and government policies, 59-68, 70-81; and thrift institutions, 105-06, 111; unanticipated, 5, 28-29, 31-32, 37, 62-64, 68, 71, 74-76, 107; welfare cost, 66, 68
inflation tax, 21, 24, 28, 29-30, 31-32, 37, 74
insurance companies, 240 (see also, life insurance companies and property insurance companies)
Interest Rate Adjustment Act of 1966, 87, 89, 96-97, 99, 102
interest rate ceilings: and consumer credit, 156, 158-63, 165-66, 169, 183; on deposits (see, commercial banks, Interest Rate Adjustment Act, mutual savings banks, Regulation Q, savings and loan associations); and FSCAs, 234-35; on loans (see, usury laws); on mortgages, 80
interest rates (see, commercial banks, consumer credit, corporate bonds, credit rationing, crowding out, disintermediation, Federal Reserve, federally sponsored credit agencies, Government National Mortgage Association, inflation, inflation tax, Interest Rate Adjustment Act, interest rate ceilings, monetary policy, mortgages, mutual savings banks, savings and loan associations, seigniorage, tax-exempt securities, trade

credit, U.S. government, usury laws, yield curve)
International Monetary Fund (IMF), 11-12, 20, 29
international monetary system, 3-5, 9-14, 20-37
international reserve currency, 5, 12, 20-21, 25-28, 31-32, 37
Interstate Commerce Commission, 150

Jacksonians, 43
Jacoby, Neil, 49
Jaffee, D., 195-96, 198, 199
Japan, 13, 32
Japanese banks, 27
Johnson administration, 72
Johnson, Harry, 9-10, 14-15, 40, 46
Juilliard v. Greenman, 43

Kane, E. J., 108
Kaufman, G. G., 108
Kaufman, Henry, 216
Kennedy, Senator Edward, 277
Kentucky, 122-23, 125, 128, 130, 134
Keynesian, 62, 70, 79
Klein, Benjamin, 41-42

Laffer, A., 199
laissez faire, 44
Law, Warren A., 216
lawful money, 42
legal tender, 17, 42
Legal Tender Cases, 43
life insurance companies, 111, 231, 269
Lipsey, R., 198
Lorenzetti v. American Trust Company, 44

McCullock v. Maryland, 43
Machlup, Fritz, 10
MacLaury, Bruce K., 217
Maine, 170
Maisel, Sherman, 49
Martin, William McChesney, 72
Marxian tradition, 20
Meek, Paul, 43
Meltzer, A. H., 197, 231
Minnesota, 164, 166
Modigliani, F., 195-96
monetarist, 62
monetary policy, 38, 48-52, 70-81, 197-99, 232-40
monetize, 81
money: seigniorage, 3-17, 21-27, 38-54, 60-61; supply, 14, 71, 75-78, 216
mortgages: federal credit programs, 218; Government National Mortgage Association, 244-65; mortgage lenders, 102-12, 259; mortgage market and rates, 79-80, 227-41; price level adjusted, 111; pools, 228; rationing, 80
Mote, Larry R., 145
mutual funds, 103
mutual savings banks: deposit rate ceilings, 80, 87-99, 102-11, 235; and FSCAs, 233, 236, 240; as mortgage lenders, 80, 102-11, 231-32, 259-61; savings accounts, 232-34

Nardinelli, Clark, 32
Nathan v. Louisiana, 44
national banks, 118, 119, 142
National Commission on Consumer Credit, 151
National Commission on Consumer Finance, 158
neoclassical theory, 71
New Community Bonds, 217
New York, 51, 166, 169, 176, 178, 180, 183-84, 268, 270
New York City, 4, 166
New York City Seasonal Financing Act, 224
Nixon administration, 72
Norman v. Baltimore and Ohio, 43

Ohio, 121-22, 123, 128, 130, 134
Ohio River, 121
oligopoly, 199-200, 205

Pennsylvania, 121-23, 128, 130, 134
pension funds, 111, 240, 269
philanthropy: corporate, 204
Phillips curve, 76
pollution control bonds, 281-84
President's Commission on Budget Concepts, 218
price controls, 199
price discrimination, 203-04, 205
price expectations effect, 76
price level adjusted mortgages (PLAM), 111
Projector, D., 237
property insurance companies (PINSs): investment in tax-exempt securities, 269-77, 283
Proxmire, Senator William, 159
Pyle, David H., 50, 107

rational expectation, 79
Regional Energy Development Corporation, 224
Regulation B, 150-51, 153
Regulation Q, 50, 89, 99, 264
remote facilities, 121
reserve requirements: commercial banks, 114-20, 122-39; Federal Reserve, 115-16, 118-20, 138-39; fractional reserves, 4-5, 41, 47; 100 percent, 4-5, 47-48; seigniorage, 26, 39-54, 60-61; states, 119-20, 122-23, 138
Reuss, Representative Henry, 277
Roman legislators, 158
Rome, 160
Ruebling, Charlotte, 41
Rural Electrification Administration, 214

Salomon Brothers, 216
saving, 78, 215-16, 225
savings and loan associations (SLAs): and bank branching, 121; deposit rate ceilings, 79-80, 87-99; and FSCAs, 228-30, 231-40; as mortgage lenders, 79-80, 102-12, 250-51, 258, 259-61; savings accounts, 233-34
savings and time deposits: deposit rate ceilings (see, interest rate ceilings); reserve requirements, 119, 122-23, 134
savings banks (see, mutual savings banks)
savings institutions (see, commercial banks, mutual savings banks, and savings and loan associations)
Schwartz, Robert A., 193, 195, 197, 199
Seiden, M., 192
seigniorage: domestic, 3-9, 14-17, 21-25, 38-54, 60-61; international, 9-14, 21-27, 30, 32
Smith, James F., 153
Smith, V., 195
South Africa, 9
special drawing rights (SDR), 10-12, 27-28, 46
state banks, 120
state and local governments (STLs): and federal credit programs, 211, 216, 218; and FSCAs, 234-40; implicit grants, 149; tax-exempt securities, 130, 267-84
Stephenson, J., 174
sterling, 20
Student Loan Marketing Association, 218

tandem plans, 244-64
tax-exempt securities, 267-84
tax expenditure, 150, 267
Tax Foundation, 237
term structure of interest rates, 78, 79-80

Texas, 166
thrift deposits (see, savings and time deposits)
thrift institutions (see, mutual savings banks and savings and loan associations)
trade credit, 18, 74, 191-206
traveler's checks, 44
Truth in Lending, 156, 183

unemployment, 64-67, 76
Uniform Commercial Code, 183
unit banking, 121-22, 128, 138
U.S. Congress: credit programs, 214; deposit rate ceilings, 87; Equal Credit Opportunity Act, 150-51; money, 42-44; tax-exempt securities, 282
U.S. Constitution: commerce clause, 44; Fifth Amendment, 43; monetary provisions, 41-45, 53-54; Sixteenth Amendment, 284; Tenth Amendment, 43
U.S. Department of Agriculture, 224
U.S. Department of Defense, 214
U.S. dollar standard, 21
U.S. (federal) government: bonds, 90, 269; budget deficit, 75-78; credit allocation, 79; credit programs, 211-25; debt, 27, 63, 108; implicit grants, 149-50; inflation, 59; inflation tax, 32, 36-37; international finance, 26-27, 32-37; note, 63; seigniorage, 3-17, 38-54; spending, 73-75; tax on interest income, 267 (see also, U.S. Congress and U.S. Treasury)
U.S. Railway Association, 218
U.S. Supreme Court, 43-45
U.S. Treasury: bills, 26, 233; bonds, 233; Comptroller of the Currency, 118; credit programs, implications of, 215-17, 220, 224; Federal Home Loan Bank Board borrowing, 254; and FSCAs, 233-34; interest cost, 60; interest on Federal Reserve notes, 46, 61, 116; notes, 60, 233; regulation, 118; securities, 4, 16, 128, 130; tax and loan accounts, 4, 50; tax-exempt securities, implications of, 267, 274-82, 284
usury laws, 80, 119, 166, 196, 198, 205

vault cash, 15, 115, 123
Veazie Bank v. Fenno, 43-44
Veterans Administration (VA), 245-59, 265
Vietnam, 32
Villani, Kevin E., 231

Washington (state), 166, 169, 178, 183
Washington, D.C., 13
Weiss, G., 237
welfare economics, 149
West Virginia, 122-23, 125, 128, 130, 134, 136
Whitcomb, David K., 195
Wilson, Thomas F., 5, 16
window dressing, 122
Wojnilower, Albert M., 216
World War II, 7, 11, 49

Yeager, Leland B., 10, 11
yen, 13
yield curve, 78-80

ABOUT THE EDITORS AND CONTRIBUTORS

KENNETH E. BOULDING is professor of economics at the University of Colorado, Boulder, and director of the Program of Research on General Social and Economic Dynamics in the university's Institute of Behavioral Science. Professor Boulding has published widely in the area of grants economics, including his book on The Economy of Love and Fear: A Preface to Grants Economics. He has been the president of the Association for the Study of the Grants Economy since 1970. Professor Boulding holds a B.A. and an M.A. from Oxford, and is the recipient of numerous honorary degrees.

THOMAS F. WILSON is associate professor of economics at Butler University, Indianapolis. From 1968 to 1970, he was an economist with the Federal Reserve Bank of New York. Dr. Wilson has published several papers in grants economics and in monetary economics. He was a coeditor of Browsing in Political Economy. Dr. Wilson holds a B.A. from the American University, Washington, D.C., and a Ph.D. from Columbia University.

RICHARD A. COHN is assistant professor of finance at the Alfred P. Sloan School of Management, Massachusetts Institute of Technology. In 1975-76, he was also assistant professor of finance at the University of British Columbia. Professor Cohn, who received his A.B. from Harvard University in 1969 and an M.B.A. from Stanford in 1972, has published extensively in the area of financial intermediation. His articles have appeared in the Journal of Business, Journal of Finance, and other publications.

WILLIAM C. DUNKELBERG is currently associate professor of economics and associate director of the Credit Research Center at Purdue University. Professor Dunkelberg received his Ph.D. in economics in 1969 from the University of Michigan, where he was also a study director at the Survey Research Center. From 1969 to 1974, he was a member of the faculty at Stanford University. In addition to his teaching and research activities, Professor Dunkelberg has served as a consultant to the Federal Reserve Board, the Federal Trade Commission, the Department of Labor, the National Commission on Electronic Funds Transfers, and the National Commission on Consumer Finance. He has also testified before Congress on various consumer credit issues. Professor Dunkelberg has written numerous articles and books on consumer behavior and research methodology, including publications in the American Economic Review, Review of Economics and Statistics, Journal of Money, Credit and Banking, and Journal of Marketing Research.

GEORGE M. VON FURSTENBERG is professor of economics at Indiana University, Bloomington. Prior to his return to Indiana, he served for several years as senior staff economist with the President's Council of Economic Advisers. His publications have focused on public finance, capital formation, and housing finance, and he has recently been appointed director of a major research project on capital investment and saving sponsored by the American Council of Life Insurance. As a member of the 1977 Brookings Panel on Economic Activity, he is currently engaged in research on investment determinants. His Ph.D. is from Princeton University.

THOMAS HAVRILESKY is associate professor of economics at Duke University and visiting professor of economics at Erasmus University, Rotterdam. He has held visiting professorships at Monash University, Melbourne; Rice University, Houston; and Simon Frazer University, Vancouver. He was an assistant professor of economics at the University of Maryland and a research fellow at the Federal Reserve Bank of Chicago. Professor Havrilesky has published numerous articles in the theory and practice of monetary policy. His work has appeared in the Journal of Finance, Journal of Money, Credit and Banking, Southern Economic Journal, and Journal of Political Economy. He is an author or coauthor of five currently available textbooks and books of readings in monetary theory and policy and money and banking. Professor Havrilesky holds B.S. and M.A. degrees from Pennsylvania State University and a Ph.D. from the University of Illinois.

PATRIC H. HENDERSHOTT is professor of economics and finance at Purdue University. He has previously taught at Florida, New York, and Northwestern Universities and has served as a research economist for the Federal Reserve Board. He has been an associate editor of the Journal of Finance and a member of the board of directors of the American Finance Association. He has done studies for a number of federal agencies and is currently working on a contract for the Department of Housing and Urban Development. He has published widely in the areas of monetary economics and macrofinance, including books titled The Neutralized Money Stock: An Unbiased Measure of Federal Reserve Policy Actions and A Flow of Funds Financial Model (Volume 1 of Understanding Capital Markets). Dr. Hendershott received his Ph.D. from Purdue University.

HARRY G. JOHNSON was Charles F. Grey Distinguished Service Professor of Economics at the University of Chicago from 1966 until his death in 1977. He was also professor of economics at the Graduate Institute of International Studies, Geneva. From 1959 to 1974, he was professor of economics at the London School of Economics. Dr. Johnson was a truly exceptional economist, whose contributions to the literature spanned the entire field. He concentrated on monetary and international economics. Dr. Johnson's books include Money, Trade, and Economic Growth and Essays in Monetary Economics. Dr. Johnson held degrees from the University of Toronto, Cambridge University, the University of Manchester, and Harvard University. His Ph.D. was from Harvard University.

BENJAMIN KLEIN is associate professor of economics at the University of California, Los Angeles, and a research associate at the National Bureau of Economic Research. During 1975-76, he was a law and economics fellow at the University of Chicago Law School. Dr. Klein has published widely in the area of monetary theory and inflation. His articles have appeared in the American Economic Review, Journal of Political Economy, Journal of Money, Credit and Banking, and Economic Inquiry. Dr. Klein holds a B.A. from Brooklyn College, City University of New York, and an M.A. and Ph.D. from the University of Chicago.

TIMOTHY W. KOCH is an assistant professor of economics and finance at Baylor University. He holds a B.A. from Wartburg College and a Ph.D. from Purdue University.

MARVIN PHAUP, JR., is a principal analyst at the Congressional Budget Office, Washington, D.C. Until 1976, he was a senior economist at the Federal Reserve Bank of Cleveland. Some of Dr. Phaup's work in banking and monetary economics has been published in the Journal of Political Economy, Review of Economics and Statistics, and Journal of Economics and Business. He holds a B.A. from Roanoke College and a M.A. and Ph.D. from the University of Virginia.

DAVID H. PYLE is professor of business administration, University of California, Berkeley, and consulting regional economist to the Fourteenth Region of the Office of the Comptroller of the Currency. He is currently the president of the Western Finance Association. Dr. Pyle has published on various topics concerning financial intermediaries. This work has appeared in the Bell Journal of Economics, Journal of Finance, and Journal of Financial and Quantitative Analysis. Dr. Pyle holds a B.S. from the University of Akron, an M.B.A. from the University of Chicago, and a Ph.D. from the Massachusetts Institute of Technology.

CHARLOTTE E. RUEBLING is a venture analyst with Ralston Purina Company. Prior to joining that company in 1976, she was an economist at the Federal Reserve Bank of St. Louis for several years. A number of her articles concerning monetary and public finance topics have appeared in that bank's Review. Dr. Ruebling holds a B.A. degree from Colorado College and M.S. and Ph.D. degrees from Iowa State University.

JOSEPH SCHERER is an economist with the Federal Reserve Bank of New York, where he heads the government finance section. He is also an adjunct professor of economics in the graduate school, Pace University, and previously taught in the graduate division of the City University of New York and at Bowdoin College. Articles by Dr. Scherer have been published in the Journal of Finance, National Tax Journal, and other journals. Dr. Scherer holds a Ph.D. in economics from the University of Chicago.

ROBERT A. SCHWARTZ is professor of economics at the Graduate School of Business Administration of New York University. Some of the subjects on which Dr. Schwartz has published include philanthropy, trade credit, market concentration, the organization of securities markets, and correlation patterns in security returns. His articles have appeared in the Journal of Finance, Journal of Political Economy, Review of Economics and Statistics, Journal of Financial and Quantitative Analysis, Journal of Industrial Economics, and Journal of Banking and Finance. Dr. Schwartz holds a B.A. from New York University, an M.B.A. from the Graduate School of Business Administration of Columbia University, and a Ph.D. from Columbia University.

KEVIN E. VILLANI is an economist with the Office of Economic Affairs, Department of Housing and Urban Development. He is the coauthor of a book on housing finance reform and several papers on the behavior of federally sponsored credit agencies and mortgage investors. He received a Ph.D. degree in 1974 from Purdue University and has served as an economist with the Federal Reserve Bank of Cleveland.

MURRAY L. WEIDENBAUM is professor of economics at Washington University, St. Louis, and director of the Center for the Study of American Business. From 1969 to 1971, he was assistant secretary of the Treasury. Dr. Weidenbaum has published extensively in the areas of federal budgeting and government presence in business decision making. His books include Government-Mandated Price Increases, Government Credit Subsidies for Energy Development, and Business, Government, and the Public. Dr. Weidenbaum holds a B.B.A. from the City College of New York, an M.A. from Columbia University, and a Ph.D. from Princeton University.

DAVID K. WHITCOMB is associate professor of finance at the Graduate School of Business Administration, Rutgers University. He was previously associated with Bernard M. Baruch College (CUNY), New York University, and the RAND Corporation. Dr. Whitcomb has worked in the areas of externalities, industrial organization, the structure of securities markets, and correlation patterns in security returns. His articles have appeared in the Journal of Finance, Journal of Political Economy, Review of Economics and Statistics, Journal of Financial and Quantitative Analysis, Journal of Industrial Economics, and Journal of Banking and Finance. He is also author of Externalities and Welfare. Dr. Whitcomb holds a B.S.B.A. from Babson College and a Ph.D. from Columbia University.

RELATED TITLES

Published by PRAEGER SPECIAL STUDIES

HOUSING FINANCE AGENCIES: A Comparison between States and HUD
Nathan S. Betnun

THE FUTURE OF COMMERCIAL BANKING
edited by
Wray O. Candilis

FEDERAL GRANTS-IN-AID: Maximizing Benefits to the States
Anita S. Harbert

INFLATION: Long-Term Problems
edited by
Lowell C. Harriss

*COST-BENEFIT ANALYSIS: New and Expanded Edition
E. J. Mishan

MANAGING COMMERCIAL BANK FUNDS
Emmanuel N. Roussakis

*Also available in paperback.